"Bristol's own"

12th Battalion Gloucestershire Regiment

1914-1918

Dean Marks

First Published in Great Britain by Dolman Scott Ltd

Copyright © Dean Marks 2011

Cover Design by Dean Marks and Peter Beech, Vanity Graphics

All rights reserved. No part of this publication may be reproduced, stored in a retrieval system or transmitted in any form or by any means, electronic, mechanical, photocopying, recording or otherwise, without the prior permission of the copyright holder

ISBN 978-1-905553-83-9

Author contact: 12gloucesters@gmail.com

www.dolmanscott.co.uk

This book is dedicated to all those men who saw fit, at the outbreak of the Great War, to give up all they knew and held dear to serve their country and enlist into the ranks of 'Bristol's Own'

Contents

The Parable of the Old Man and the Young	v
Foreword	vi
Preface	vii
Introduction	viii
Chapter I 1914 - The Lamps are going out	1
Chapter II 1914 – Alert Appreciation of Orders	7
Chapter III 1914 – Tweed to khaki	33
Chapter IV 1915 – Army Ways	58
Chapter V 1915 – Goodbye to Bristol	84
Chapter VI 1915 – France	98
Chapter VII 1916 – Anybody's Own	109
Chapter VIII 1917 - Soldier on	155
Chapter IX 1918 – Year of movement	178
Chapter X Old Comrades Association	197
Chapter XI Consecration of the Colours	201
Chapter XII Gloucester Cross	204
Chapter XIII Vignettes	211
Appendix I Officers Roll	220
Appendix II Roll of Honour – Officers	229
Appendix III June 1915 Nominal Roll	231
Appendix IV Roll of Honour – Other Ranks	263
Appendix V Awards	294
Appendix VI Battalion Battle Honours	299
Appendix VII Glossary and Acronyms	300
Acknowledgements	304

The Parable of the Old Man and the Young

So Abram rose, and clave the wood, and went,
And took the fire with him, and a knife.
And as they sojourned both of them together,
Isaac the first-born spake and said, My Father,
Behold the preparations, fire and iron,
But where the lamb, for this burnt-offering?

Then Abram bound the youth with belts and straps,
And builded parapets and trenches there,
And stretchèd forth the knife to slay his son.
When lo! an Angel called him out of heaven,
Saying, Lay not thy hand upon the lad,
Neither do anything to him, thy son.

Behold! Caught in a thicket by its horns,
A Ram. Offer the Ram of Pride instead.

But the old man would not so, but slew his son,
And half the seed of Europe, one by one.

Wilfred Owen

Foreword

by
Major General Robin Grist CB OBE
Colonel, The Gloucestershire Regiment 1991-94

To describe a book as 'unique' is to risk a wave of correspondence to prove one wrong. I believe, however, that to find such a comprehensive history of any Service Battalion in the First World War is rare. To find one that combines contemporary material, including press reports and letters with recollections of those who took part set against the framework of the war is even rarer.

It has taken Dean Marks over 30 years to collect all the material for this record and without his passion, which can probably be described as an obsession, this would never have happened. This is therefore an important book as it will be of great value to social historians, particularly those with an interest in Bristol, amateur and professional historians researching the 1st World War and, perhaps most of all, to the descendants of "Bristol's Own", 12th Battalion, The Gloucestershire Regiment.

Bristol's connection to The Gloucestershire Regiment began in 1782, when it was decided to link numbered infantry regiments with specific parts of the country for recruiting purposes. The 61st Foot therefore became the 61st (South Gloucestershire) Regiment. As the City of Bristol was part of Gloucestershire the link between the 61st and the City was a strong one. In 1881 the Cardwell Reforms led to the 28th (North Gloucestershire) Regiment and the 61st (South Gloucestershire) Regiment becoming the 1st and 2nd Battalions, The Gloucestershire Regiment. At the same time the 1st (City of Bristol) Gloucestershire Rifle Volunteers became the 1st (City of Bristol) Volunteer Battalion, The Gloucestershire Regiment and the new regiment's headquarters and depot was established at Horfield Barracks in the City, where it remained until 1940.

There were three sorts of infantry battalion in the 1st World War, Regular, Territorial and Service. The Regular Battalions contained, as their name implies regular soldiers, whose full time job was soldiering, often somewhere in the Empire. Territorial Battalions were composed of volunteers, who met once a week in a local drill hall and gave up a weekend once a month for military training; some had previously been regular soldiers and some had volunteered for 'Home Service Only'. The Service Battalions were an initiative proposed by Lord Kitchener to boost the size of the Army quickly and were for 'General Service'. Initially they were composed entirely of volunteers although later in the war conscription had to be introduced to provide reinforcements.

To put the 12th Battalion in context The Gloucestershire Regiment consisted of 24 battalions in the 1st World War of which 16 actually took part in the fighting, the remainder were training reinforcements or in reserve. Of the 16 only two, the 1st Battalion and the 8th Battalion, another Service Battalion, won more Battle Honours than the 22 won by the 12th.

It is often said that the Gloucestershire Regiment 'raised' 24 battalions but as this book makes clear the raising of a Service Battalion was almost entirely done by the local community. Dean Marks has captured the enthusiasm with which this happened in Bristol and the difficulties that had to be overcome, vividly. Once the battalion moved to France it found itself tested in some desperate battles and it was not found wanting despite the casualties. Through his interviews with survivors he has depicted life in and out of the trenches, the courage and the horror of a war that seems impossible to conceive today, in a way which evokes admiration and pride but also helps one to understand the motivation, which kept such battalions giving of their very best.

Without this book the 12th Battalion, The Gloucestershire Regiment would be little more than a few paragraphs in the Regiment's 300 year history, which is full of major battles that affected the history of the nation. It deserved to be much more than this; to be recognised as adding lustre to the Gloucestershire Regiment reputation, which it undoubtedly did, and the Regiment owes Dean Marks huge thanks for what he has done. More than this, however, this book is a wonderful tribute to the men of "Bristol's Own' and to Bristolians in general.

Preface

In 1977 whilst feverishly fiddling with my tiny transistor radio searching for Radio Luxembourg one evening, I accidentally found a channel being transmitted very clearly. It wasn't music, it was a discussion. More to the point it was veterans of World War One talking of their experiences. I listened to those men and I was mesmerised by what I was hearing. That radio broadcast was the catalyst for what has interested me for the last thirty plus years. I became increasingly fascinated with the stories of World War One and the men that fought it. I visited the battlefields and read as many books on the subject that I could find and began, as a pastime, collecting postcard photographs of WW1 soldiers and groups of soldiers that practically every junk shop had several shoeboxes full of. I collected all sorts, but was particularly interested in any with soldiers wearing the Gloucestershire Regiment cap badge. I would eagerly snap them for the princely sum of 2p each!

Before long my collection grew to large proportions. I then tried to identify which battalions they belonged to. The 'Imperial Service' badge meant a Territorial battalion, either 4th or 6th from Bristol or maybe the 5th from Cheltenham and Gloucester and slouched hats were worn by 6th battalion. But, among them, were many that were marked 'Bristol's Own' or 'New Bristol Battalion' or simply 'BB'. I had no idea what unit this was, so I took myself off to meet Andy Stevens of 'Past Times' the local Gloucestershire Regiment expert. He informed me I was looking at men of the 12th Battalion Gloucestershire Regiment, affectionately known locally as 'Bristol's Own'. The battalion was a Service battalion of the regular army specially formed in Bristol at the outset of World War One in answer to Lord Kitchener's call for men.

Well, that sounded interesting. A special Bristol battalion indeed. I immediately got myself off to the library to read all about this battalion. But I was disappointed. There was nothing, or at least very little available to read. No battalion history had been written and books covering the Gloucestershire Regiment in general would only dedicate a paragraph or two to this particular battalion. The staff at the Bristol Council Records Office, at the time, when asked for any material relating to the 12th Battalion Gloucestershire Regiment or 'Bristol's Own', gave the reply: "who"? It was clear, these men had been forgotten.

That was the start of a crusade to learn as much as possible about the battalion. In subsequent years, I studied the battalion War Diary, collected old magazine cuttings, read the wartime newspapers, dug out long forgotten memoirs, narratives, diaries, scrapbooks and audiotapes, and studied maps. I even tracked down sons and daughters of men that served, but of most interest was meeting and interviewing original battalion veterans, which I regarded as a pleasure and a privilege. Alas, those wonderful old characters are no longer with us, but I still cherish the memories of meeting and speaking with such a modest group of gentlemen.

For some years I had harboured the thought of gathering all the information I had collected and presenting it as a battalion history. However, I always convinced myself that I was not an author and had no idea where to start. That was, before I received constructive advice from several people, when I re-thought the process. Now the book is written and the result is what you are about to read.

This book is written from the heart. In the spirit of the battalion and in the memory of all the men that served with the battalion so many years ago, many of whom, I am sure, would have wanted their story told. Ninety seven years have passed since the jingoistic days of September 1914 when a group of men, many young and some not so young, took the decision to leave all they knew and held dear and set out on a once in a life time adventure into the unknown. This is the story of that adventure.

Dean Marks

Introduction

Boulogne – November 1915, the dock area rang out to the sound of a military band's rendering of 'Sambre at Meuse'. A year of war, of khaki clad comings and goings had made the population of Boulogne indifferent to such events. It is on record that, like the people of Boulogne, the rendering on that day of the marshal air, that had been on the lips of the red trousered attacking French army ten months previously, was also 'indifferent'.

In the previous fourteen months the 'professional' young men of Bristol and its environs had flocked to join one of the many service battalions answering the call of King, Country and Kitchener. 'Bristol's Own', the 12th Battalion Gloucestershire Regiment had arrived in France.

Once rid of the cobbled streets of Boulogne and the bustle of Gare Central, they were borne by train to the outskirts of Amien from where a day's march would deliver them to the Somme River marshes of Suzanne and Maricourt, and the first shocks of death and maiming. Four years later, decimated on many a battle front and bolstered by replacements, many of whom would have had difficulty in even locating the city of Bristol on the map, 'Bristol's Own' was to be cynically renamed 'Anybody's Own'.

Why, over ninety years later, recall those years of suffering, pride and anguish? Wars big and small have continued to interrupt the lives of ordinary men and women. Young men, some as volunteers, some as pressed men, have continued to slog their way to conflicts for causes questionable. The boredom, the fear of combat, the afterglow of initial excitement that disclaims glorification has been experienced by so many.

Can anyone but an infantryman of that period, from whatever nation or background, begin to understand the filth and squalor, the nine-tenths boredom and fatigue interspersed with one-tenth of exhilaration at overcoming personal fear? Place names such as 'Maricourt', 'Delville Wood', 'Longueval' 'Guillemont', the 'Brick Stacks', 'Fresnoy', 'Gheluvelt', 'Passchendaele', 'Nieppe' and 'Cornet Perdu' mean little or nothing in modern parlance, but those place names were never forgotten by the men who were there.

Television and library books will inform those who wish to know, of wars through the ages in all theatres of operation. This collection of memorabilia is from a war, but then not really about a war. In fact it is in contrast to patriotic rhetoric; rather it is about the men who have peered out over the years from sepia tinted photographs and their human experiences. Men who are no longer with us, but who have given us their thoughts and recollections and who now are unable to comment on a city that appears to have forgotten them.

Albert Fairchild

Chapter I

1914 - The lamps are going out.....

In the early years of the twentieth century it was generally considered that a European war was never far away. How it might start, for what reasons, and at what time were the only real questions. After the Victorian and Edwardian eras the British Empire was at its zenith, with the Royal Navy the most powerful in the world. No one doubted Britain's ability to deal with any would be aggressor.

By 1914, many factors – industrialisation, nationalism, military and naval rivalry together with colonialism – combined to prepare the nations of Europe, and some further a field, for war. The inter-relationships of these factors were complex and uncertain.

It is popularly accepted, that the First World War began as a direct result of the assassination, in Sarajevo on 28th June 1914 of the Austrian Archduke Franz Ferdinand. This event was certainly the catalyst for the appalling war that took place between 1914 and 1918. But did the unfortunate events that unfolded during July and early August 1914 provide Imperial Germany with the excuse it had been looking for to take Europe to war?

Kaiser Wilhelm II

Wilhelm II, King of Prussia, became Kaiser of Germany in 1888. He dismissed Chancellor Bismarck in 1890 and dismantled the complex alliance system Bismarck had set up, which had helped to maintain peace in Europe. He also encouraged an aggressive foreign policy, which did little to stabilise Europe.

He was described as a disturbed, cruel and sometimes even dangerous man. He was mentally unstable, and was unfit to rule, being obsessed with military matters and an over-reliance on military advisers. Even some of his contemporaries doubted his sanity and in 1891 Lord Salisbury, the British Prime Minister,

1914 – The lamps are going out.....

wondered whether Wilhelm was 'all there'. Nonetheless, it was the Kaiser's wish to make Germany the most powerful nation by striving for a position of hegemony in Europe and ultimately worldwide. He was happiest when surrounded by his military and naval entourage whom he valued above everyone else - he had only contempt for civilians.

On the 8th December 1912 the Kaiser called an *ad hoc* War Council meeting to which no civilians were invited. The exclusion of civilian decision-makers from this meeting may have suggested its relevance. Only those advisers whom he considered important were invited. 'Mere' civilians, even the Imperial Chancellor, Theobald von Bethmann Hollweg, were not invited. They would simply be informed of the outcome of the meeting and confronted with the decisions made.

The meeting was conducted against the international background of the Balkans War, which broke out between the Balkan League and Turkey on 8th October 1912. Initially, the Kaiser had decided to stay out of the conflict. By December, however, the crisis had escalated and a European war appeared increasingly likely. The Kaiser with outrage met the news from London of Britain's resolve not to stay neutral in a possible conflict on the Continent, but to come to France's aid in case of hostilities between Germany and France. Any doubts he may have had regarding Britain's alleged friendly attitude were now dispersed and it was time to act. His military and naval advisers agreed. Helmuth von Moltke, the Chief of the General Staff, explained that he considered a war unavoidable and advocated it 'the sooner the better', arguing that the current diplomatic situation was as favourable as it had ever been. From a military point of view, Germany would in time lose the slight advantage she currently possessed over her future enemies, and war would soon cease to be a feasible option for Germany's decision-makers.

In the event, the State Secretary of the Navy, Admiral von Tirpitz, objected to these immediate plans, requesting that hostilities be postponed for approximately 18 months until the navy was more fully prepared for such a conflict. The participants of the meeting reluctantly agreed to such a delay. The proposed delay would take untill to the middle of 1914.

The meeting appeared a clear indication of Germany's intentions. Above all else, it revealed that the deranged Kaiser was not alone among the highest levels of the German military elite in being willing to contemplate aggressive war.

Assassination Sunday June 28th 1914
In faraway Bosnia Archduke Franz Ferdinand, nephew of Emperor Franz Joseph of Austria, heir to the monarchy of the Hapsburgs, and his wife Sophie, were visiting the town of Sarajevo to inspect Austrian troops there. Bosnia, and its sister province Herzegovina, had been former Turkish possessions, which had been annexed by Austria-Hungary in 1908. Many Serb inhabitants were bitterly resentful at not being allowed to join Serbia, their native state. One of them, a grammar school student named Gavrilo Princip, shot the Archduke and his wife dead as they drove through the streets in an open car.

On the news breaking in Europe the German Chancellor was immediately given the Kaiser's order to arrange, via the press, that the public be informed of Germany's interests that would be at stake as a result of any Austro-Serbian conflict.

Nearer home, few people had even heard of Bosnia, nor Serbia. Fewer still considered the ripples, caused by the tragedy that had taken place that day, would or even could eventually reach them. After all, Serbia must be a very small country and so far away? How could it possibly affect their way of life?

On the 28th June Bristolians were enjoying yet another glorious summer Sunday. Among the middle classes straw boaters and parasols were in abundance as some visited the County Ground to witness J. S. Fry and Son beat Downend by 101 runs. Families strolled on the Downs and still more took advantage of the many attractions of the Bristol International Exhibition. The Exhibition, which had opened on 28th May, had been a huge success. Situated at Ashton Meadows, Bower Ashton, it featured large concert and dance halls, exhibition buildings, replicas of Bristol's Norman Castle and Shakespeare's England, band stands, pleasant gardens and walkways, refreshments, souvenirs and many exhibits and amusements.

1914 – The lamps are going out.....

Archduke Franz Ferdinand

Great Britain was languishing in an Edwardian ideal of security and innocence that existed before 1914. Events in Europe would change this. The world would never be quite the same, ever again. As a future way of life unfolded on a daily basis, the Bristol Times & Mirror newspaper kept its readers informed:

Monday June 29th
*'**Archduke disregards warnings**' It is understood that the Serbian Minister in Vienna in the name of his Government officially warned the Austrian Government that the police had knowledge of plots against the life of the Archduke. The latter refused to pay any heed.*

*'**Consternation in Berlin**' The utmost horror and consternation has been aroused by the crime, which is a terrible blow to the dual monarchy. No one has yet dared to gauge its possible affect upon the stability of Europe.*

Tuesday June 30th
*'**The Sarajevo Crime and its Consequences**' The shock of Sunday's double crime is still reverberating in the capitals of Europe, will there be an accession of fresh hate and suspicion between the Southern Slavs and the Germans and elements of the dual Monarchy?*

Thursday 2nd July
*'**Sarajevo Crime – Impossible for Archduke to Leave Alive**' Persons connected to the suite of the Archduke, who have just returned from Sarajevo, say that the plot against the Archduke was so widely extended that it was impossible for him to leave Bosnia alive.*

Thursday 23rd July
*'**Austria's Courteous Note to Serbia**' In well informed quarters it is believed that the Austro-Hungarian note to Serbia will not be presented until the end of this week. It is understood that no demands will be made upon Serbia to which she will not be able to accede without loss of dignity. The Austro-Hungarian note will be "courteous" and will place no time limit upon the Serbian answer.*

Saturday 25th July
*'**Austria's Demands from Serbia**' A very grave situation has arisen. Austria has presented an ultimatum to Serbia demanding that she suppress all anti–Austrian activities and allows Austro-Hungarian police access to Serbia in order to conduct an enquiry into the assassination.*

The Austrian Premier, in the Lower House yesterday, stated that nothing was demanded but which Serbia must conceive her natural and neighbourly duty. They had gone up to the utmost limit of patience, and the step now taken was necessary in the vital interests of the Monarchy.

1914 – The lamps are going out…..

An important meeting of the Russian Cabinet was called to consider the situation. It is stated that Russia will intervene in order to induce Austria to extend the period of grace in order that the Powers may exercise diplomatic action. The seriousness of the situation is added to by the attitude taken up by Germany, who, it is stated, will allow no interference of a third party in the quarrel. The Kaiser himself assured Austria of Germany's support in whatever measures she took against Serbia, the so-called "Blank Cheque."

Monday 27th July
'The Serbs agreed to all of the Austrian demands bar one'. *The Austrians were so surprised by the humility of the Serbian reply that the foreign minister hid it for 2 days from the Germans. The Kaiser himself commented that the reply was "a great moral victory for Vienna, and with it, every reason for war disappears!"*

But – News was received in London yesterday that Austria, after receiving Serbia's reply to her ultimatum, declared war… Serbia had mobilised its troops, constitutional laws have been suspended, and the whole of Austria Hungary has been placed under martial law. France informs Russia of her complete readiness to fulfil her alliance obligations to her, in the event of a dispute with Germany. France stops all army leave and recalls her troops from Algeria and Morocco.

'A Needless Calamity' *Statesmanship may yet avert the needless calamity of a European war. Serbia agreed to most of Austria's demands, yet Austria had made other demands no state could accept and with these Serbia was unable to comply.*

'England and the Crisis' *Should there arise a desire to test our adhesion to the principles that form our friendship and that guarantee the balance of power in Europe we shall be found no less ready and determined to vindicate them with the whole strength of the Empire than we have been found in the past. That we conceive interest and duty and honour all demand of us, England will not hesitate to answer to their call.*

Thursday 30th July
'Situation of "Extreme Gravity"' *Up to last evening no further light on the European situation was obtainable in reliable quarters beyond that convened in the Prime Minister's brief statement in the House of Commons that the situation is very grave and attempts are in progress to prevent any wide extension of the conflict between Austria and Serbia.*

'Russia Mobilises' *Committed to the defence of the Slav nations, Russia finally decides on general mobilisation. Austria announces general mobilisation. Germany insists Russia halts her mobilisation and demands to know if France will remain neutral if Germany goes to war with Russia.*

Sunday 2nd August
Germany issues a note to Belgium demanding free passage of troops through Belgian territory for the attack on France. Britain assured France that the British Fleet would protect the French coast and shipping from German attack.

Monday 3rd August
'German invasion of France' *St. Petersburg message states that Germany has declared war on Russia. France mobilises its forces. Germany, it is stated, has invaded France?? Without any formal declaration of war, Germany invades Luxemburg.*

'Army Manoeuvres Cancelled' *The War Office announces that all training arrangements of the regular troops, including the Army Manoeuvres are cancelled.*

'The Army Mobilisation – Proclamation Today' *The War Office last night issued the following statement:*

"With reference to this afternoon's announcement of the Government decision to mobilise, it is officially stated that the proclamation will be signed tomorrow, and the necessary orders for the Reservists to return to the colours and the Territorials to be embodied, will then be issued"

1914 – The lamps are going out.....

'Germany declares war on France' Belgium refuses German demands, and the king of the Belgians appeals for the preservation of Belgian neutrality. The Germans know that Britain has promised to defend Belgium under the Treaty of London of 1839, and wants the British Government to ignore this treaty in order to allow the German Army to pass through Belgium and so keep Britain out of the war.

Tuesday 4th August
'Flagrant Violation of the Laws of Nations' In the House of Commons that evening, Mr Asquith announced the despatch by Britain of an ultimatum to Germany. The Premier said a telegram had been sent by Sir Edward Grey to the British Ambassador in Berlin informing him of the appeal made by the King of the Belgians for diplomatic intervention. Belgium had categorically refused to sanction a flagrant violation of the law of nations. The German Government had been asked to give a satisfactory reply by midnight on the question of Belgian neutrality. The British Government had requested an assurance that the neutrality of Belgium would be respected by Germany, and asked for an immediate reply. The German Ministry had notified Belgium that as the latter had declined their well-intentioned offer, they regretted it would have to be necessary to carry it out by force of arms.

PREMIER'S MOMENTOUS SPEECH.

GERMANY GIVEN UNTIL MIDNIGHT TO REPLY.

"FLAGRANT VIOLATION OF THE LAWS OF NATIONS."

Germany entered Belgium. The British Cabinet considered that the violation of Belgian territory would oblige Britain to intervene. An ultimatum was served on Germany, set to expire at 11 p.m., calling on her to withdraw from Belgian territory. The ultimatum was not satisfactorily answered. Germany declared war on Belgium. After midnight, mobilisation was ordered as Britain went to war with Germany.

BRITISH ASSURANCE TO BELGIUM.

Serbia was indeed a small country, however, during the summer of 1914, seven European nations went to war. The conflict was to be so gigantic, so terrible it would be known thereafter simply as:

'The Great War'

1914 – The lamps are going out.....

Sir Edward Grey, the Foreign Secretary, was deeply disturbed by the fact his policies had failed to prevent war. He found words to express a tragic sense of civilisation overtaken by doom. Watching from a Foreign Office window in Whitehall on the evening of 4th August, a lamplighter at work in St. James's park, he remarked to a colleague; *"The lamps are going out all over Europe. We shall not see them lit again in our lifetime"*

Sir Edward Grey

Chapter II

1914 - Alert Appreciation of Orders.....

Who stands if freedom fall?

All day on the 4th August the inevitable approach of war had been the topic of conversation everywhere. The next morning the newspapers carrying the latest news sold out as quickly as the newsboys could carry them onto the streets. Everywhere the news was read with excitement and anxiety, and though for the most part men were glad to receive definite news – news that put an end to the strain and tension of the previous few days – women did not take the news so calmly. Groups of people stood at street corners, and discussed the situation excitedly, and at Bristol's Tramway Centre there was much cheering and singing of the National Anthem.

Bristol Times & Mirror Tuesday 4th August - 'Will Lord Kitchener Become War Secretary?'
"The public has confidence in Lord Kitchener and, in a war, opinion counts for a great deal. We therefore, desire very earnestly upon the Prime Minister that he should endeavour to enlist Lord Kitchener's service at least for the term of the war. Our military correspondent suggests that Lord Kitchener, who is at present at home, would make an admirable Secretary of State for War, and this suggestion appeals to us very strongly. Lord Kitchener is a capable administrator, and a first rate organiser."

The Prime Minister, Mr. Asquith announced that the German Government had been asked to give a satisfactory reply, by midnight on the 4th, on the question of Belgian neutrality. Germany replied before 11 p.m. but the reply received was unsatisfactory and so; War was declared. The declaration, it was officially stated, was made by England upon Germany.

France, Germany and Britain were bound by a treaty guaranteeing the neutrality of Belgium. A treaty, the German Chancellor is reported to have called, "A scrap of paper." Britain though, had more historic reasons for wishing to safeguard Belgium – its channel ports. These real reasons were however brushed over by political rhetoric.

The Prime Minister, Mr. Asquith:
"It was only when we were confronted with the choice between keeping and breaking solemn obligations – between the discharge of a binding trust and of shameless subservience to naked force, that we threw away the scabbard. The issue was one which no great and self respecting nation, certainly none bred and nurtured like ourselves, in this ancient home of liberty, could, without undying shame, have declined. We are with them heart and soul, because by their side and in their Company we are defending at the same time two great causes – the independence of small states and the sanctity of international covenants."

The current state of affairs in Europe constituted a great emergency and His Majesty the King deemed it proper to provide sufficient means for military service and ordered the General Mobilisation of the Army, the Army Reserve to be called out for permanent service and also the embodiment of the Territorial Force. Local businesses immediately did what they could to help in any way. In line with the King's order, the Imperial Tobacco Company was very patriotic in announcing that any of its employees who may be called upon to rejoin the Navy or Army or any of the national services would receive from the Company such an amount of salary or wages as was required to make up their service pay to the same level as their peacetime pay, and in every case situations would be kept open. In the midst of such patriotism a sizeable number of men committed to join up intent on doing their bit, Bristol Tramways losing 200 of its men on the first day of war.

The effect on the small recruitment office, in Old Market Bristol, was chaotic. Run by a Major assisted by four Sergeants, it was ably suited to deal with the trickle of peacetime enquiries, but found to be totally unprepared and woefully inadequate when faced with such a deluge of would-be recruits.

1914 – Alert Appreciation of Orders

Overnight Bristol took on a war footing. The various Territorial Force units and reservists, including the 4th and the 6th Gloucesters were under orders to move at short notice and the army took over Avonmouth docks and railway station. An invaluable embarkation point, the six-year-old Royal Edward Dock would become of crucial importance to the country's war effort. By 8th August convoy after convoy of men and equipment made their way through the Bristol streets, up Whiteladies Road and across the Durdham Down on their way to Avonmouth, which soon became jam packed. The Army quickly mobilised and equipped several thousand men on the dockside in preparation for disembarkation to France. From local stables 1,000 horses were requisitioned for war work and the crew of a German sailing ship, the *Elfrieda,* moored in the City Docks were picked up by Bristol police and the small ship seized as a prize of war.

On the 6th August Bristol's Lord Mayor, Alderman John Swaish, published a message to the citizens of Bristol:

"*In the very serious position in which the nation is now placed, it becomes us all to possess our souls in patience and to be temperate in all things. I am confident that Bristol will maintain its high position for loyalty and patriotism.*

"*Whatever the demands of our beloved country may be, as far as our resources permit we shall readily respond, and all classes will vie with each other to do their most and their best.*

"*The selfishness and wastefulness that might produce inconvenience, want, and panic we must carefully avoid. The news of the war that will reach us day by day, almost hour by hour, may have startling variation, at one time news of victory, at another, news of defeat. Let us accept both with all the calmness and all the courage we possess, or else the elation of triumph may be sadly qualified by the deep depression of defeat.*

"*May we not haggard long to wait for the end of this terrifying war, and then may we take good opportunity to sing our Te Deum!*"

Lord Mayor of Bristol
Alderman John Swaish

Immediately war was declared Lord Kitchener was indeed appointed Secretary of State for War. His appointment was opportune as it was his belief, contrary to popular opinion, that not only would the forthcoming conflict not be over by Christmas, it would in fact be a prolonged struggle.

If he were right in his belief, the Regular and Territorial Armies, once committed on the battlefield, would soon need to be reinforced by large numbers of men. With characteristic decision making which marked him as a great man, he declared Britain must have a second army. In no time at all, parliament passed a bill authorising the raising of a 'New Army' which was to comprise of eighteen divisions. On August 9th Kitchener made the gargantuan appeal for 100,000 volunteers to form this 'New Army' or 'Kitcheners Army' as it was soon to become popularly known.

1914 – Alert Appreciation of Orders

Lord Horatio Kitchener

In a meeting of the Bristol Chamber of Commerce, held on the 12th August and chaired by Bristol's Lord Mayor, it was announced that the objective was to enlist recruits for the King's Army and the country's service. In all parts of the country the matter had been taken up by local authorities with enthusiasm and men had shown their loyalty and patriotism by offering their services.

Bristol, up until that time, had made no special attempt, whereas Birmingham had enlisted five times the number of Bristol's response. It was identified that if the expected numbers of men were to be properly enlisted, the current method of recruiting in the city would have to be changed and a more organised approach be established.

Before the meeting had closed The Bristol Citizen's Recruiting Committee was formed, with Sir Herbert Ashman Bart., being elected as Chairman. A Bristol appeal for men was made and the proprietors of the Colston Hall came forward and offered the facility to the Committee, it being opened as a special recruitment centre from 10 a.m. Friday 14th August.

Lt. Col. W.E.P. Burges O.B.E. was made recruitment officer. His appointment was a worthy decision. He had previously joined the South Gloucestershire Militia in 1880 gaining proficiency in military affairs and passing on to the 3rd Battalion Gloucestershire Regiment which he later commanded for five years until his retirement in 1913. Among his military distinctions were the passing of the tactical course for field officers and the field artillery course for infantry officers, as well as winning the Distinguished Certificate, Hythe Military Course. He was also a local man residing at 'The Ridge', Chipping Sodbury, and the son of Mr. Edward Burges, of Yate, and cousin of the late Mr. D. T. Burges (ex Town Clerk of Bristol).

By the 20th August 323 men had enlisted at the Colston Hall and the rate of enlistments grew rapidly with, by the 2nd September 2274 men having 'joined up', 440 of whom enlisted on the 1st September. It soon became apparent that many men were expressing a wish to join a special Bristol battalion. The same idea had previously been discussed by the Bristol Citizens Recruiting Committee at its formation and was supported wholeheartedly by its Chairman, Sir Herbert Ashman, who immediately approached the War Office on the 27th August with the idea. On the 3rd September Sir Herbert received the following telegram:

"Lord Kitchener thanks you for valuable help offered by Bristol. He sanctions your scheme of enrolment of names and formation of a battalion. In communication with the General Commanding the Southern Command."

Sir Herbert Ashman,
Bart.

Bristol thus had its chance of standing in line with London and other large commercial centres and, with those words to encourage them, Bristol would have no difficulty in enrolling a thousand young men necessary for a battalion. The conditions of service for this special battalion were published on the 4th September. A proper regimental number was not immediately issued and so, the full title of this formation was to be: New Bristol Battalion Gloucestershire Regiment. From the very beginning the battalion was known affectionately by the apt sobriquet 'Bristol's Own'.

The Recruiting Committee had decided that as Bristol was proud of its commercial history, it was up to the young professional and business men to prove themselves worthy of that past by applying for places in the new battalion. In their opinion, there were hundreds of professional and commercial men in the city who had been waiting for the opportunity to show their determination to do their duty as soldiers. The Committee was determined to attract the right kind of recruit and made it clear that applications to join the new battalion would only be received on the proper printed forms available at the Colston Hall, the Commercial Rooms, the Liberal, Constitutional and Clifton Clubs and various banks and insurance offices.

Applications were to state the man's surname, Christian name in full, age, present employment (if any) and previous military service, or special qualifications.

The idea of the battalion caught on immediately among the classes for whom it was intended. Something that was not at all surprising as, in the air of 1914 there was a feverish romanticism, fuelled by many elements of Edwardian life and culture. Overall there was an invincible belief in the superiority of all things British; and an innocently misguided vision of war as a great and gallant adventure.

After a day or two the applications began to arrive, and those accepted were informed they would, in due course, receive notification of when and where they were to attend for medical examination. A telegram was received by the recruiting office from an anxious candidate from Ilminster, Somerset enquiring if the Bristol battalion was full yet and, if it was, was there any use in coming. Such was the popularity of the battalion, however, that among the applications, to the consternation of the Recruiting Committee were men that did not meet the requirements. The Committee felt very strongly about this and a message was published in the Bristol Times & Mirror, on the 5th September:

"It cannot be too strongly emphasised that the battalion is for mercantile and professional men only, and it will save the committee a lot if those not qualified will refrain from filling up the forms."

BRITONS

"YOUR COUNTRY NEEDS YOU"

JOIN YOUR COUNTRY'S ARMY!
GOD SAVE THE KING

THE NEW BRISTOL BATTALION GLOUCESTERSHIRE REGIMENT

To the Mercantile and Professional Men of the City of Bristol and Neighbourhood.

Lord Kitchener has sanctioned the enrolment of Single and Married Men of the City of Bristol and Neighbourhood between the ages of 19 and 35, who are willing to join the Colours for the duration of the War. The Battalion is to be a Battalion of Mercantile and Professional young men, under Officers of the Regular Army.

CONDITIONS:—

Married men are eligible and get separation allowance.

You must be between the ages of 19 and 35.
You agree to serve for the period the war lasts.
You agree to serve at Home or Abroad as may be required.
Clothing and Equipment will be supplied free by the Government.
Full Army pay.
The Battalion is to be an Infantry one, and will constitute a unit of the Regular Army.
Seven days' notice of calling up will be given.

If you wish to serve your Country in this time of stress, obtain the necessary application form at the New Battalion Offices, Colston Hall, Bristol, or any of the Bristol Banks, fill same in and send to

THE CHAIRMAN,
Bristol Citizens' Recruiting Committee,
New Battalion,
Colston Hall, BRISTOL.

1914 – Alert Appreciation of Orders

There are, usually underlying and sometimes hidden reasons to most decisions. The Citizens Recruiting Committee's commitment to offer places in the battalion to men from a commercial background, though well considered, may not have been purely for the reasons stated. It was actually based on a directive from above. Kitchener recognised that the army would require significant support and those workers in such industries as agriculture, manufacturing, mining, engineering and transport were less easily spared for the army than those in 'white collar' occupations. Men that filled positions such as clerk or shop assistant would, therefore, be initially targeted. The Committee's description 'Mercantile and Professional' seems to fall therefore, rather conveniently, and exactly into this line of thinking. The ranks of the city's insurance offices,

banks, commercial travellers, tobacconists, confectioners and myriad other such establishments paid a heavy price as their men applied to join the battalion.

By Monday 7th September 4,000 Bristol men had rallied and enlisted in various units and corps. In the first weeks it was a novelty to see so many men crowding the Colston Hall to join up and many people gathered outside to cheer on those patriotic young men. However, one elderly gentleman complained to one of Bristol's newspapers:

"It is extremely irritating to see so many young men loafing around the Recruitment Centre."

The general consensus of opinion was that all available men of military age should be placing their services at the disposal of their country in its hour of need. The local press did its bit in persuading, or shaming, men into joining up, with comments such as:

"The country is answering so splendidly to the call that no one who can volunteer wants to be left out. And 'Bristol's Own' forms the ideal corps in which you can stay with your friends, train with your friends, fight (if the opportunity comes) with your friends, and when it's all over, fight the whole thing over again with your friends in the years to come."

First medical examinations took place at the Colston Hall on the 7th September. The doctors commenced their work at 5 p.m. and were much impressed by the physique of many of the candidates. By the

1914 – Alert Appreciation of Orders

THE GOVERNMENT APPEALS FOR ANOTHER 500,000 MEN.

MEN OF BRISTOL THINK!

Do You Realise What Defeat Means?

Every man who comes forward now helps to assure our success. DON'T WAIT
If YOU do others will, and then you may all be too late.

**EVERY YOUNG MAN SHOULD FEEL IT HIS DUTY
TO COME FORWARD AND HELP HIS COUNTRY.**

YOU ARE WANTED.

THE NEW BRISTOL BATTALION
OF THE
GLOUCESTERSHIRE REGIMENT

is filling up, but we not only want One Battalion of 1,000 men. Let Bristol show a
good example, and enlist TWO BATTALIONS!!!

PROFESSIONAL & MERCANTILE MEN COME TO THE COLSTON HALL
AND FILL UP APPLICATION FORMS.

All information will be given you at the OFFICES OF THE NEW BATTALION,
COLSTON HALL, BRISTOL, or Application Forms can be had at the Banks, Insurance
Offices, etc., etc.

BRISTOL CITIZENS' RECRUITING COMMITTEE.

GOD SAVE THE KING.

RECRUITING AT COLSTON HALL.
Doctors' examination—measuring, eye testing, etc.

1914 – Alert Appreciation of Orders

11th September one hundred men had been medically examined and attested and the very first man to join the new battalion was Mr. Dan Anstey of Bishopston. Recruits continued to come forward including Arthur Beacham who had suspected that war would begin and returned to his native city from Australia and Henry Barber who gave up his job as commercial traveller in West Africa to join the special Bristol battalion.

Mr. Dan Anstey of Bishopston was the first man enlisted into the battalion

Within a week one complete Company had been medically examined, attested and enrolled. In less than a fortnight, 500 recruits – practically half the battalion – had been enlisted. However, some men were turned down on account of the raising of the height requirement of an infantryman by no less than three inches. This War Office regulation meant no candidate under 5ft 6ins could be accepted. This disappointed many men that were intent on joining the battalion. Men that, apart from their height, would have proven to be excellent soldiers – just what the country was asking for. The War Office's objectivity was, therefore, difficult to understand.

NOTICE TO RECRUITS.

HEIGHT STANDARD RAISED.

The Press Bureau this evening issued the following communique. It is requested that the following notice may be prominently announced and given wide publicity:—It has been decided that, until further orders, the minimum height for all men, other than ex-soldiers, who enlist in the infantry of the line will be raised to 5ft. 6in. and the minimum chest measurement to 35¼in.

14596 Pte. William Ayres

"When I was eighteen, I had gone away to work in Leamington Spa, but my time there was short, for the year was 1914, and war broke out in August.

"I soon became restless as I saw the crowds pouring into the recruiting centres, and when I heard that a city battalion was being raised in Bristol, I came home and enlisted on the 22nd September."

16612 Pte. Sam Bollom

"I picked up a form from the Commercial Rooms and quickly completed it, hurrying along to The Colston Hall to hand it in. Having undergone my medical examination I was told I had a heart defect. I protested and told them I ran regularly but I was rejected and told: 'Take it easy and you may reach eighty'."

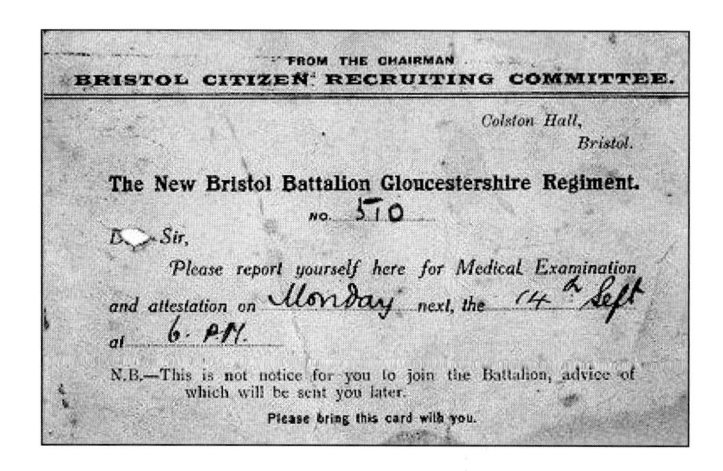

```
              FROM THE CHAIRMAN
      BRISTOL CITIZEN' RECRUITING COMMITTEE.
                                    Colston Hall,
                                          Bristol.

      The New Bristol Battalion Gloucestershire Regiment.
                         No. 510
      Dr Sir,
           Please report yourself here for Medical Examination
      and attestation on  Monday   next, the  14th Sept
      at  6. P.M.
           N.B.—This is not notice for you to join the Battalion, advice of
                    which will be sent you later.
                       Please bring this card with you.
```

14019 Pte. Leslie Cheston.

"I had decided soon after the war broke out to join up. I wrote to my parents explaining my intentions and received a letter from my father:

"My Dearest Leslie, We were not altogether surprised to receive your letter this morning and to hear that you had made up your mind to serve your King and Country. We are proud of you that you see your duty in a clear light and are prepared to do it like a man. Do so by all means and may God bless you and keep you safe while you are away."

On the 11th September Leslie Cheston joined the ranks of 'Bristol's Own'

14780 Pte. Ralph Ivor Smith

As Bristol had decided to form a battalion from people around the area and outskirts, I thought there would be more chance of meeting someone I knew. I went along to the Colston Hall on the 18th September 1914. As I was not of age I had to put my age on. On entering, the recruiting Sergeant's first words to me were "Taking bits of bloody boys in the Army now are we"? Fortunately he did not ask for an age certificate. I was passed A1, took the oath and was duly attested. Taking the King's shilling, I immediately ran home and gave it to my mother, having to explain to her what and why. Didn't dare stay too long to see the effect on her and went back to work.

The backgrounds of the recruits were very diversified. There were many well known local sportsmen, including rugger players in the form of the Captain of Bristol Saracens, Norman Spafford, and James Friend, one of Bristol Rugby Club's best forwards; Cricketers Risdon Kemp-Welch and J. Barnett; and Mr. A. Avent, English Amateur Lightweight Boxing champion. There were grammar school masters and pupils, medical students, artists, musicians and concert singers, managers and staff of insurance offices, grooms and warehousemen to name just a few.

1914 – Alert Appreciation of Orders

> **BRISTOL'S OWN.**
>
> THE FIRST HUNDRED RECRUITS.

On Thursday 10th September, Bristol Times & Mirror published the following thought provoking verse sent in by the occupier of Providence Cottage, Fishponds:

"The Call"

Do you see men in bowlers,
 Without collars wearing wraps?
Do you see them mix with others,
 Lawyers, clerks, and country chaps?
They are lads who heard the summons,
 Leaving kinsmen, country, all;
They are going to "face the music"
 They have heard the trumpet call.

Do you stand aside and cheer them,
 As they swing along the street?
Do you say, "They're plucky fellows!"
 While they go the foe to meet:
Will you cheer them when all is over,
 When the battle din shall cease,
When at home our boys are marching,
 Having fought the fight of peace?

When you see the medal flashing
 O'er the hearts that beat so true,
Will there come a twinge of conscience,
 Will you shout as now you do?
Will you stand around some corner,
 Feeling very sick at heart,
Knowing when your country called you
 That you failed to play your part?

Yet there's time to do your duty,
 Even now they're calling you:
Even now your place is vacant
 Neath the old red white and blue!
You can yet turn out a hero
 On the field across the waves;
So arise and teach the foeman
 "Britons never shall be slaves"

Whether such persuasion was necessary is hard to tell. The feeling, at the time, was that the war would be over by Christmas. This, combined with the high state of patriotic fervour prevalent, ensured a continual flow of would be soldiers.

Many good men up and down the country had been rejected due to the new minimum height regulation. The War Council soon came to its senses and realised that a good number of men were being turned away effectively hindering its efforts to raise its New Army. As a result, the order was rescinded by an announcement on the 14th September. The committee lost no time in sending out telegrams that very morning to the 74 disappointed candidates informing them of the change in the conditions.

> **FORMER HEIGHT STANDARD ALLOWED.**

1914 – Alert Appreciation of Orders

14406 Pte. Ernest Shanks
"I lived at 2 Hughenden Road, Horfield and was one of the first men to offer my services to the new Bristol Battalion. But I was rejected as being too short. I was very disappointed. However, a few days later I received a telegram from the Chairman of the Recruiting committee informing me of new regulations regarding height measurements.

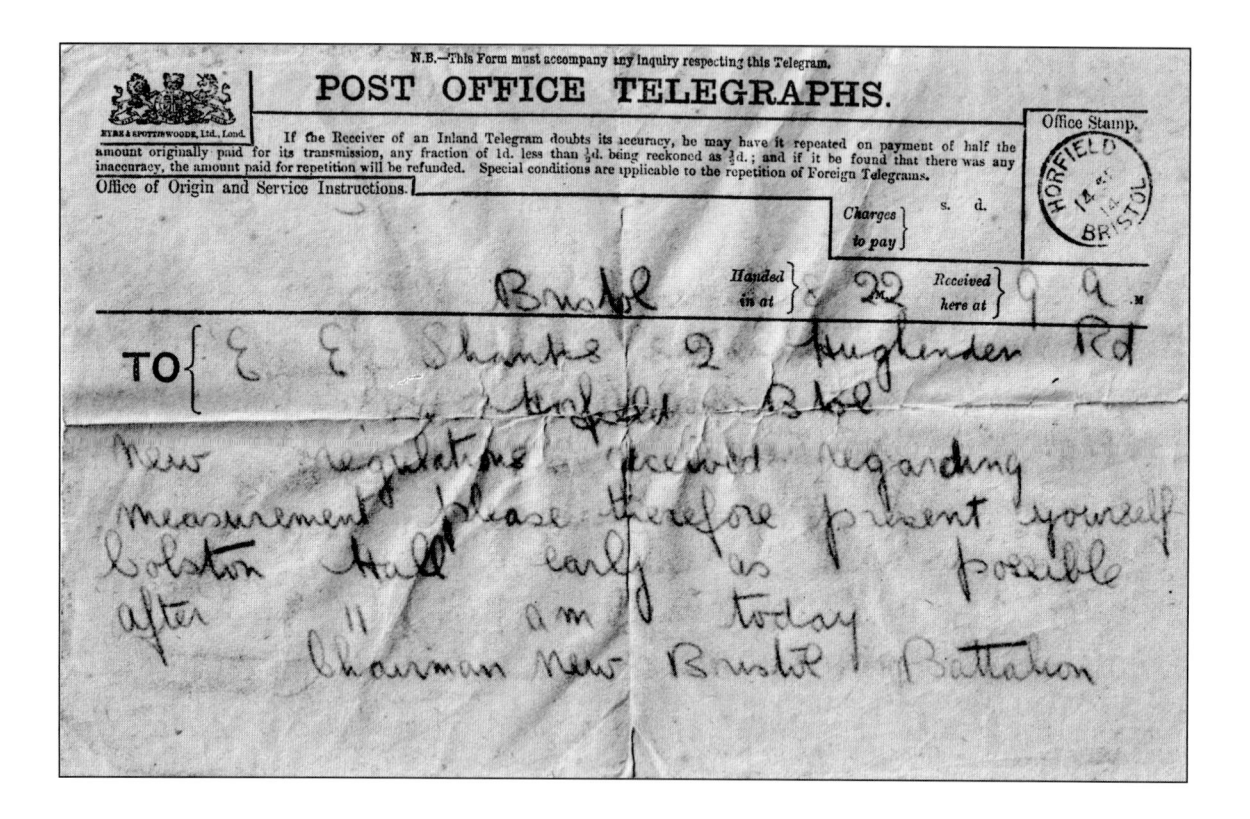

> POST OFFICE TELEGRAPHS.
>
> TO: E. E. Shanks, 2 Hughenden Rd, Horfield, Bristol
>
> New regulations received regarding measurements please therefore present yourself Colston Hall early as possible after 11 am today
>
> Chairman New Bristol Battalion

The ranks of the battalion were filling rapidly. However, no commander had been appointed up until mid September. The role was to be somewhat unique in as much as it was not simply a matter of taking over a battalion, but building one from scratch. This was very much in the minds of the Committee. Not an easy decision but, one that had to be made. One name came up immediately as a man that not only had the skills but most importantly had the character to form the special Bristol battalion. Soon after the middle of the month it was announced by the War Office that they had appointed, to everyone's delight, Lt. Col. W. E. P. Burges, as commander of the New Bristol Battalion.

Lt. Col. Burges had been doing excellent work in connection with the Bristol Recruiting Campaign and his appointment was well received, it being felt that he would be a capable and popular commander. Simultaneously with the appointment of Lieutenant-Lt. Col. Burges, a number of other appointments were announced, though some were of a provisional and temporary nature:-

1914 – Alert Appreciation of Orders

Lt. Col. W.E.P. Burges

Lieutenant-Lt. Col. and Honorary Lt. Col.: William Edward Parry Burges
Late Commanding Officer 3rd Batt'n. Glos. Regiment (S.R.) Retired October 1913

Major and Second In Command: Captain William Arthur Russrum Blennerhassett
Late Derbyshire Regiment. Seven years, ten months in Regular Army. Retired as Lieutenant. Matabele War, 1896, medal. Lieutenant MM Police. Boer War, 1898-1903. Natal N. Rifles to Kitchener's F. Scouts. Captain and Adjutant. Transval Vol. on Staff as Adjutant until 1903. Two medals, eight clasps, including Seige of Ladysmith, Elands Laagte and Langs Nek. Fifteen years service.

Majors
William Beauchamp Stansfield – Late Major West Indian Regiment. Retired 1903. Commanding troops St. Lucia at retirement. Karina Expedition, 1898, medal and clasp; Ashanti Expedition, 1900, medal. Since retirement, up to August last has been coaching officers for the Military Competitive Promotion and Staff College Examinations.
Chandos Brydges Lee-Warner - Late Captain 3rd Batt. Glos. Regiment.
Frank Wilson Fox – Late Captain S.A.L. Horse.
Captain and Adjutant: Russell James Kerr - Late Adjutant (1900-1903) to the 3rd Batt. Glos. Regiment

Captains
Arthur William Clifford
Late 1st Batt. Glos. Regiment
William Henry Bourchier Saville
Late Captain R.G.A.V.
Henry Archer Colt
Late Lieutenant R.N.
Henry Pile-Leschallas
Three years in 5th Batt. N. Rifle Brigade; three years 17th Lancers; passed for Lieutenant.
Charles Frederick King
late Paymaster Dept. R.N.

1914 – Alert Appreciation of Orders

Lieutenants
John Longhurst Likeman
Served in South Africa as a Private; afterwards Lieutenant and Inspector, Brit E.A. Police.
Thomas McGregor Allison
1896-1904, S.M.R.E.
Ernest Harry Burris – O.T.C.
Thomas Balston – Eton and Oxford O.T.C.
Roy Ebdon Machon – O.T.C. Oxford cert. "A" & "B"

Second-Lieutenants
Charles Donald Fowler – O.T.C. Bedford College, three years
Brian Fitzgibbons – Rugby and Oxford O.T.C.
Kenneth Ford – Late Marlborough School O.T.C. cert. "A"
George Eric Rowe Gedye
Arthur Vernn Shewell – Late Sherborne O.T.C.

Quartermaster: Sergeant Major Arthur Hooper
Late Sergeant Major Depot Gloucester Regiment.

Battalion officers just prior to leaving Bristol in June 1915

1914 – Alert Appreciation of Orders

Coincidental with the attestation of the first hundred recruits, the Recruitment Committee received, from Mr. Fred E. Weatherly, a practicing barrister and song writer, a patriotic song written especially for Bristol's Own and entitled 'Bravo, Bristol'.

Frederick Weatherly was born and brought up in Portishead, Somerset before moving to Bath. After schooling at Hereford Cathedral School he graduated from Oxford University with a degree in Classics in 1871.

After leaving the university, Weatherly remained in Oxford, briefly working as a schoolmaster and then as a private tutor. He continued in that capacity until 1887 when he qualified as a barrister, practising first in London and then in the west of England. He remained active in the legal profession until the end of his life. *The Times* wrote of his dual career, "His fertility was extraordinary, and though it is easy to be contemptuous of his drawing-room lyrics, sentimental, humorous and patriotic, which are said to number about 3,000 altogether, it is certain that no practising barrister has ever before provided so much innocent pleasure.

Later, his ballad "Roses of Picardy", written in 1916 and set to music by Haydn Wood, was one of the most famous songs from World War I.

'Bravo, Bristol' was set to music by the well-known composer Ivor Novello. The celebrated writer, in writing to the Committee, described the music as: *"tuneful and easy, and yet not commonplace"*:

Bravo, Bristol

When the stalwart Merchant Venturers set out in days of old.
They sailed, with a Bristol blessing, to find a land of gold;
And now there's a grimmer journey, there's a sterner task today,
But the men of Bristol answer in the good old Bristol way:

It's a rough long road we're going,
It's a tough long job to do.
But as sure as the wind is blowing,
We mean to see it through!
And what though your ranks are thinning?

You fight on just the same
You fight for the sake of England,
And the honour of Bristol's name!

O the men and boys of Bristol ye swarm from far and wide,
The rich man and the poor man–thank God–are side by side!
March on! Our hearts go with you! We know what you will do;
The spirit of your fathers is alive today in you!

It's a rough long road we're going,
It's a tough long job to do.
But as sure as the wind is blowing,
We mean to see it through!
Who cares how the guns may thunder?
Who recks of the sword and flame?
We fight for the sake of England,
And the honour of Bristol's name!

And when the seas are free again, and the bloody fields are won.
We'll tell our Bristol children what Bristol men have done;
And their deeds shall ring forever from the Avon to the sea.
And the song of the march of the Bristol men-the songs of their sons shall be:

It's a rough long road we're going,
It's a tough long job to do.
But as sure as the tide is flowing,
We mean to see it through!
Who cares for what the victory cost us?
We must win it just the same:
You fight for the sake of England,
And the honour of Bristol's name!

When published by Messrs. Boosey both author and composer stated that all proceeds would be donated to the Regimental Fund of the Bristol Battalion. The song was immediately adopted by the battalion.

The Colston Hall now doubled as Bristol's Recruiting Centre and also as H.Q. to the new battalion. Space was, understandably, at a premium. On Wednesday 16th September, with 500 recruits enlisted, medically examined and attested, and under very careful planning, the first parades got under way being carried out by squad, the timings being 9.45 a.m., 10.45 a.m., 2.45 p.m. and 3.45 p.m.

As they proudly paraded in their civilian dress, the recruits were marked for their smartness and noted by the drill instructors for 'their quickness and of their alert appreciation of orders'. Lt. Col Burges, as Recruiting Officer, had had the opportunity of selecting experienced N.C.Os from among applicants passing through his office. Some of whom had served with him before and many of whom had Boer War experience. These men were to form the backbone of the new battalion and supply the training and experience necessary to mould it into a skilled fighting force. Of these men the following took the first parade: ex-Supt Turner, Sergeant Major Bealing, Colour Sergeant A. Casling, Colour Sergeant Townsend and Sergeant Lloyd.

So now this large group of civilian volunteers were classed as soldiers but dressed in their tweeds, bowler hats and straw boaters they did not look like soldiers. Nor did they live as soldiers. Authorities throughout Britain found themselves unprepared for the mass of men that had answered Kitchener's call. Where were they to be housed? Throughout the country there was nothing or at least very little, in the way of accommodation for these men and Bristol, at that time, was no exception. As a temporary arrangement, the War Council passed the 'New Army Order' stating, until such time as satisfactory accommodation could be made available, the men would feed themselves and live at home. For their 'inconvenience' and out of pocket expenses each man received a daily allowance of 3 shillings. Now a guinea a week in 1914, on top of the princely sum of a shilling a day pay, was most welcome and entirely acceptable to many a young man of limited means.

> **NEW ARMY ORDER.**
>
> **ONE GUINEA per WEEK**
> FOR
> **RECRUITS**
> FROM DAY OF ENLISTMENT UNTIL PROVIDED BY WAR OFFICE WITH QUARTERS AND FOOD.
>
> **MEN OF BRISTOL.**
> YOUR COUNTRY WANTS YOU.
> ENLIST NOW
> IN
> **BRISTOL'S NEW BATTALION.**
>
> By special permission of the War Office, and in consideration of Battalion being started under former standard of measurement, ENLISTMENT MAY CONTINUE ON OLD CONDITIONS. Will those rejected on account of measurement please re-apply?
>
> COMPANIES 1 and 2 complete, and will commence drilling immediately.
> Full particulars COLSTON HALL.

    Whilst the new recruit provided his own 'billet' he was treated with a respect which, considering he was in the army, was a very marked feature. Parades were attended on receipt of a post card addressed to "so and so esquire" asking him in the most polite and courteous manner to find it convenient to be present. And, in order that he should stand out from the crowd as having offered his services to his country and as a 'new recruit' he was presented with a lapel badge proclaiming his membership of the battalion. These badges became a proud and coveted possession of every man.

'Bristol's Own' lapel badge indicated an
enlisted man

THE BRISTOL BATTALION GLOUCESTER REGIMENT.

THE RIGHT HONOURABLE THE LORD MAYOR OF BRISTOL WILL ADDRESS THE BATTALION AT THE

COLSTON HALL, at 11 a.m., TO-DAY (MONDAY), 21st Sept.

The Grand Tier and Gallery will be Open to the Public.
(TRENCHARD STREET ENTRANCE ONLY.   DOORS OPEN AT 10.30.)

YOUNG MEN ARE SPECIALLY INVITED, and those willing to join the Battalion will be given full particulars at the Offices of the Battalion at the Hall.

MEN, YOUR COUNTRY NEED YOU!

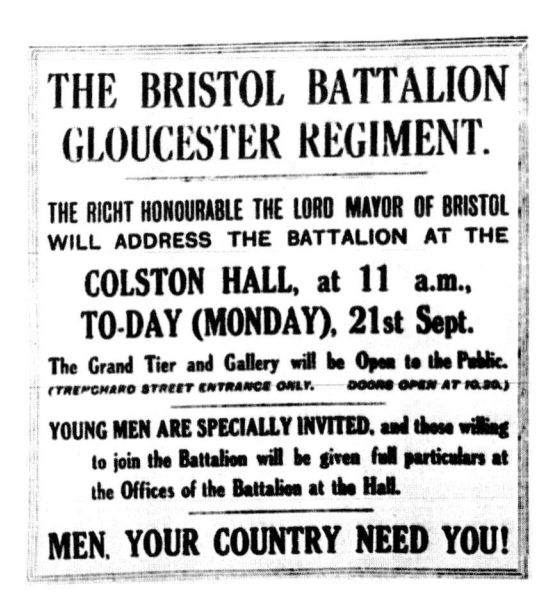

The first public showing of the new battalion occurred on Monday 21st September. The day started at the Colston Hall where the battalion paraded in front of the Lord Mayor, the Citizen's Recruiting Committee, a large group of well known and representative citizens and a large audience in the public gallery. The Lord Mayor's speech was most appropriate:

".....in the Bristol Battalion are men drawn from the professional and commercial classes, men of education and varied ability, whose services in this great cause will be invaluable. This is the type of man called for by the exacting demands of modern War – men with personality and resource. When battle lines now range over a front of 100 or 200 miles, or even more, it is no longer possible for the supreme commander to exercise direct or immediate control over the swaying fortunes of battle in any particular area. That must be left more and more to individual officers, and individual men, such as I see marshalled before me this morning. And I am quite sure you will do your part, and when you come back we will have another meeting in the Colston Hall to welcome you"

After his speech the Lord Mayor, escorted by Lt. Col Burges, inspected the men and was impressed by their physique and smartness. The inspection was followed by a march through the principal streets of the city, with the band of the 25th Company of the Boy's Brigade at the head, followed by the Lord Mayor's carriage, followed by the battalion, 700 strong, in column of fours. From the Tramways Centre the route taken was Baldwin Street, Bridge Street, Union Street, Lower Maudlin Street, Park Row, Queen's Road, to the Victoria Rooms and the return to the Colston Hall was by way of Park Street and all along was lined by enthusiastic people curious to see the battalion of civilians dressed not in khaki but in a mixture of tweed suits and flannels, heads adorned by flat caps, bowlers and straw boaters. At the corner of College Green, about thirty of the old Crimea and Indian Mutiny veterans were assembled with their standard bearer who held aloft the Union Flag and alongside it a broad banner bearing the words: *"We have done our duty; come and do yours."* As the battalion marched down Park Street, the banner caught their eye in the distance, and when they reached it they saluted the small group of old grey warriors, who returned their salute, to the great delight of the spectators.

The battalion was very much in the public eye and this was followed up the very next day with another stage in its development. The 22nd September saw the first battalion strength parade take place on the

1914 – Alert Appreciation of Orders

Artillery Ground situated on White Ladies Road. All men were invited by post card to attend this auspicious event. Almost 900 men had arrived at the Artillery Ground by 8.30am. Due to the restrictions of the Colston Hall in terms of space, this was the first time the battalion had actually paraded in full strength. Until then, parades and marches had been necessarily smaller affairs.

As the number of rifles available to the battalion fell far short of a battalion's worth it was decide that if every man was unable to carry one then none would. So the parade was not only presented in 'mufti', but also without arms, though this had no effect, as every man was proud enough to turn out in his best attire regarding the day as a very special one indeed.

Once the men had formed fours and were properly paraded, Col Burges carried out a full inspection. This took some time as he made an effort to speak to every man there.

14314 Pte. Harold Hayward
"The first parade in battalion strength, Lt. Col. Burges commanding, was on the Artillery Ground (Territorial) on White ladies Road, late in September. We were still in mufti (civies) and I would think that every enlisted man would have made an effort to be there on that first parade – enthusiasm was unbounded"

All including the Citizen's Recruiting Committee were surprised and pleased that well within a month, nearing the end Of September, since receipt of the first applications arrived, the battalion was nearing full strength. On the 24th September, around 100 places remained to be filled.

First battalion strength parade at the Artillery grounds, White Ladies Road on 22nd September

The make-up of an infantry battalion was 4 Companies: A, B, C and D of around 250 men in each. A Company comprised 4 platoons and each platoon comprised 4 sections. This formed the main fighting strength of a battalion. In addition were elements that comprised signallers, grooms or officers servants, orderlies, shoe makers, tailors, hairdressers, cooks, an ambulance section, pioneers and a machine gun section. Each Company would, however, provide the men to fill these roles but all men trained as infantrymen, no matter what role he intended to perform as the rule was: infantryman first, tradesman second. And so, in order to allow for this, an extra one hundred positions were to be made available, bringing the total battalion strength up to 1,100 men.

1914 – Alert Appreciation of Orders

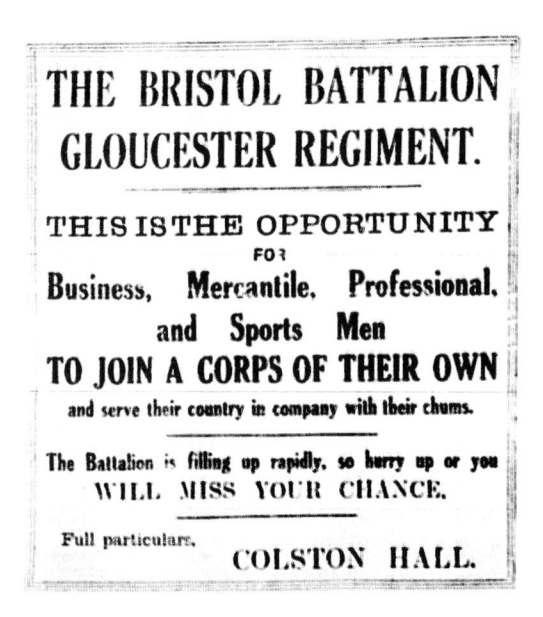

> **THE BRISTOL BATTALION GLOUCESTER REGIMENT.**
>
> **THIS IS THE OPPORTUNITY**
>
> FOR
>
> **Business, Mercantile, Professional, and Sports Men**
>
> **TO JOIN A CORPS OF THEIR OWN**
>
> and serve their country in company with their chums.
>
> The Battalion is filling up rapidly, so hurry up or you WILL MISS YOUR CHANCE.
>
> Full particulars, COLSTON HALL.

The question of housing the battalion had been raised at its conception. As grand as the Colston Hall was, it was proving extremely limited in terms of size and facilities and, as such, would prove an increasing hindrance in terms of training a battalion of infantrymen. There was, however, an alternative which, if available, would offer excellent opportunities.

The Bristol International Exhibition, had opened on the 28th May 1914. Two thousand workmen had turned 25 acres of uneven land between Ashton Avenue and Clifton Bridge Station into a grand series of picturesque buildings many of which were filled with thousands of unique and attractive artefacts and displays. There was space for concerts and other functions together with numerous sideshows and refreshments stands. The entrance was from Ashton Avenue and lead by bridge over the railway to the International Pavilion. Both sides of the entrance lobby were covered with coloured canvases representing farms, gardens and other scenes in the colonies. The greatest structure in the grounds was indeed the magnificent International Pavilion, an ornate building of plaster and timber, 150 feet high and 200 feet square. Also imposing was the Egyptian Hall that would take up to 1500 people. The Exhibition consisted of various mocked-up buildings, both factual and fictional. There being in one corner "Shakespeare's England" and in another "Old Plymouth" complete with Drake's flagship 'Revenge'. There were houses and shops of the 13th, 16th and 17th centuries, a replica of Bristol's Norman Castle, complete with museum of historical exhibits; Australia House; Bostocks Jungle with live lions and tigers; and a scenic railway. Special cheap rail excursions were available and throughout the summer of 1914 many people flocked to visit what amounted to be an Edwardian theme park. Entertainment included brass bands and dancing in a huge dance hall. By night, the Exhibition took on a new image when illuminated by thousands of electric light bulbs.

With the outbreak of war, the cheap rail excursions ended and the Exhibition fell into disuse. It was, by September, abandoned. But Col. Burges could see real potential and suggested to the Committee that the buildings, with some expenditure, could be made suitable. The Recruiting Committee, through its energetic chairman, approached the War Council. The buildings were surveyed by the Army Service Corps and reported as useless. However, the Committee did an excellent job in persuading the War Council to allow them to be bought at 5% over the highest tender and they were thus secured.

> **BUILDINGS BOUGHT BY THE WAR OFFICE.**
>
> **"BRISTOL'S OWN" BARRACKS**

It was announced on 21st September that, at last, talks had been brought to a successful conclusion. The buildings had been purchased by the War Office at a cost of £7500. The deal also secured the option of leasing the site. Bristol's new battalion would now have more space than it needed and would move into its new quarters immediately the necessary work was completed. Immediately men of the Royal Engineers and the Army Service Corps, assisted by private contractors, began work to bring the buildings up to standard. Many hundreds of pounds worth of timber, plant, electrical equipment and other unnecessary items were removed and parts of the Exhibition buildings that would serve no military purpose were disposed of with the exception of Bostocks Menagerie which contained several ferocious wild animals that had formed the basis of the popular Bostocks Jungle Display. It took longer than a month to find a suitable home for them. The new H.Q. offered what would become excellent Officer's quarters in the old Black and White houses of "Shakespeare's England" whereas the men would occupy huge barrack rooms such as those offered by the "Bristol Castle" replica. The former dance hall would provide a dining hall for the entire battalion with room to spare. The interior of the once splendid International Pavilion was to be converted into a huge gymnasium. The extensive grounds offered plenty of space for musketry training, bayonet fighting, trench digging and everything else that the battalion needed, whilst the adjacent Greville Smyth Park provided for an excellent open air drill ground. On a clear day the Exhibition buildings, being white, were visible from miles away. As a result it became popularly known as the "White City."

The Exhibition facilities, suitably arranged, provided 'Bristol's Own' with probably the finest quarters of any New Army battalion anywhere in the country. It was felt this factor was directly responsible for the ease at which such a high standard of training was achieved by the battalion during its eight month stay there. The first guard was mounted at its new H.Q. on 26th September with a Sergeant and 30 men. Among the men was Pte. William Ayres who, at the tender age of 18, was shocked at the course language used by his fellow guards, something his Baptist upbringing had not prepared him for, but to which he became accustomed over the coming months.

Bristol International Exhibition Centre
'White City'

View from Bedminster Down

Australia House

1914 – Alert Appreciation of Orders

Bristol Castle replica

International Pavilion

1914 – Alert Appreciation of Orders

View from a Bonded Warehouse

Shakespeare's England

1914 – Alert Appreciation of Orders

View from the Clifton Suspension Bridge

Main entrance from Ashton Avenue

Meanwhile, recruitment for the battalion continued unabated. The nearby town of Weston-Super-Mare had on its own account enlisted around 80 men known as the Weston Comrades Company. Under the training and watchful eyes of Sgt. Major H. Baker R.F.A., most of these men had been associated with various local athletic bodies and it was originally intended that they be offered to a Kitchener battalion of the Somerset Light Infantry. However, the congestion at Taunton had been so great that the delay necessary had proved irritating to the Westonians who then transferred their affections to the Bristol Battalion. Lt. Col. Burges and the battalion Second in Command, Major Blennerhassett attended the Town Hall in Weston where the Company of men was attested and issued with 3 shillings each. Lt. Col. Burges agreed to their wish that they would all be posted to one Company in order to stay together. He also stated that the men would continue to be trained by Sgt Major Baker and live at home, until such time as the work on the Exhibition buildings was complete and the new H.Q. operational.

Weston Comrades Company

Chapter III

1914 – Tweed to Khaki

During peace time the nation's industry, with regard to the rate at which it supplied arms, equipment and uniforms to the services, worked at a relatively sedate pace. As such, it was unprepared for the demands made upon it with the formation of the New Army. As a result, New Army units throughout the country, paraded in civilian dress, without any form of military arms, belts or knap sack equipment. These would eventually be provided by the War Council, whereas it was the responsibility of the respective recruiting authority, when provided with the sum of £8 10 shillings per man, to arrange for clothing and other equipment.

As far as clothing was concerned, there was a problem. There was an acute shortage of khaki material used in the manufacture of the standard Army Service Dress uniform. An alternative Melton blue material was, however, available. This was being used to provide a stop-gap uniform of a much simpler design. The textile industry of the North of England was well placed to tender for and provide this type of uniform and many battalions being formed in that part of the country were fitted out in this way by the end of September. In fact the 10th battalion Gloucestershire Regiment of Cheltenham were clothed this way. This type of dress uniform was considered for 'Bristol's Own' but the decision was made that the battalion would remain in civilian dress until such time as the correct issue khaki became available.

The end of the month of September brought with it sad news. Almost, at the very moment the battalion reached full strength, its driving force, Sir Herbert Ashman passed away. He died on Saturday the 26th after suffering an appendix problem for around a week. The one man, to whom the battalion owed so much, never saw the full fruits of his labours. He had been instrumental in launching the battalion and had worked diligently to facilitate the progress of recruiting for it. His death was a sad loss to 'Bristol's Own' and a still more grievous loss to the city, for his work as Chairman of the Recruiting Committee had been invaluable.

Beginning on 29th September parades took place adjacent to the Exhibition ground in Greville Smyth Park, which had been placed at the disposal of the battalion for drill. The men still lived at home but were under instructions to report at 7 a.m. each morning. Parades ran from 9 a.m. until 12.30 p.m. Re-assembling at 2 p.m. for a further three hours. Whilst the previous parades on the expansive Artillery Grounds were impressive, with the new parades there was a significant difference. The men paraded with rifles. The C.O. had acquired 400 old, obsolete Enfield rifles. Whereas these would have proved useless or worse in live firing, they proved of massive benefit in musketry training, were of tremendous benefit to drill and to the men's feeling of being. Their parading, under arms, always attracted large numbers of interested spectators. With parades came also the first guard duties at H.Q. and its surrounding area.

14138 Pte. Norman Pegg
"One of the features of life at Ashton in the early days was the guard. It was turned out in civilian dress, with unloaded rifles which the sentries had not yet then learned to manipulate. Marching in groups of ten men, the guard carried enough baggage for a large family proceeding on holiday. Such morsels as pickled herrings, salmon, boiled tongue and sandwiches were packed. What a figure we used to cut I cannot imagine, but we were constantly on the receiving end of the activities of the local 'playful' juvenile population who would honour us with missiles of all sorts. It was not easy trying to look dignified and being treated as a target for your pains."

Other activities were carried out, but around one third of all time in the early days at H.Q. was always devoted to drill. It was not entirely appreciated.

14509 Pte. Ewart Hale
Rifle drill was tedious. We sloped, trailed, presented, ordered, reversed, wheeled and piled. We did it for hours until we were totally exhausted. Then we did some more. We all wondered how it would help us when we faced the Germans.

14780 Pte. Ralph Ivor Smith
We used to drill in Greville Smyth Park. Skirmishing, rifle drill, guard duty, etc. Night marches took place some nights, chiefly the seven mile march around the boundary of Lady Smyth's. We were not allowed to speak, only in a whisper as everything had to be as quiet as possible."

At the same time, the battalion made limited use of its new H.Q. though work was not complete. The buildings and facilities were still being worked on and progress was proceeding with all speed. Meanwhile, at the Colston Hall the Bristol Citizens Recruiting Committee, being in charge of the battalion until officially taken over by the War Council, was busy dealing with all matters relating to equipment for the new H.Q.

Men at drill in Greville Smyth Park. The amusements of the Exhibition still evident in the back ground

Now that the members of the battalion were engaging in drills in and around their new H.Q. there was always a daily stream of men flowing towards Bower Ashton from all parts of the city. Every morning tram cars on the Hotwell Road and the Bedminster and Ashton routes were crowded inside and out with young fellows proudly wearing their 'Bristol's Own' lapel badge.

Early in October the battalion was visited and inspected by Col. Hacket-Thompson, of the Southern Command. It was intended that 'Bristol's Own', when officially accepted by the War Council, would be brigaded with battalions of the Birmingham 'Pals' of the Warwickshire Regiment. Lt. Col. Hackett-Thompson, from Warwick, was interested in seeing how the Bristol battalion compared to the progress of the Birmingham battalions. The parade was held in nearby Greville Smyth Park and the Lt. Col. expressed himself as being very pleased with the appearance and drill of the men.

Within a month of recruitment starting, on 5th October, full battalion strength was secured, but applications continued to be received and accepted. A fair number of recruits to the battalion would be transferred, due to special skills, to other units and corps. A full thirty five percent of the total number men enlisted into the battalion were lost due to commissions granted by the War Office. The additional applications were used to fill these spaces.

Men at drill in Geville Smyth Park, displaying their lapel badges

The Western Daily Press reported that the New Battalion had reached a thousand strong:
"*Rather less than a month ago the announcement was made that a Bristol Battalion of the Gloucestershire Regiment was to be formed, which was to be restricted to professional men and those engaged in mercantile pursuit. There were many that feared that after the magnificent response made for recruits for Lord Kitchener's Army and the great demands made upon the young men of Bristol by the various Territorial units, that some difficulty would be experienced in raising this new battalion. Fact that the confidence of the Bristol Recruiting Committee in the patriotism of the business and professional young men was not misplaced, however, is proved by the fact that over a thousand men have been enlisted, and are now preparing themselves for the business of soldiers in real earnest. It is well that the citizens should realise the significance of this particular response to the colours. All honour to them; long after the war is over their sacrifice will be remembered and spoken of with pride. The appeal for men for the new battalion had been made some time after the initial glamour of the battle cry when men were flocking to the recruitment office at a rate of 500 a day. To young men who were settled in regular employment, and who had had time to realise what enlistment for the period of the war meant, that a thousand men have come forward in less than a month under such circumstances is something of which Bristol might be proud, and it may be taken for granted that when this battalion is put to the supreme test of battle it will not be found wanting. Some, we believe, have an idea that this unit is not to be taken seriously as far as being ordered to the front is concerned, but every man has joined with the clear idea he will be called upon to fight, and there is just as much chance of the Bristol Battalion being, as the Lord Mayor said, at Berlin for the final reckoning, as any part of the British Army.*"

The question of obtaining officers and N.C.O.s with military experience for the battalion was dealt with by Lt. Col. Burges while acting as Recruiting Officer. He had the opportunity of selecting N.C.O.s from among applicants that came before him, many of whom had served with him previously. He was very fortunate in his selection of senior N.C.O.s but had to depend on suitable candidates to fulfil the junior N.C.O.s roles from the ranks. This worked well. In due course men were selected, based on their identified organisational and leadership qualities and passed through a Regimental N.C.O.s school and passed out by examination by the Adjutant and third in command, Captain R.J. Kerr. Lt. Col. Burges had kept open a number of vacancies in the list of Junior Officers for the express purpose of being able to take suitable men from the ranks to fill these

Potato peeling at H.Q.

vacancies. Therefore, from the lists of N.C.O.s men were selected to fill the Junior Officer ranks. Potential candidates would, in turn, sit further examinations before being recommended for commissions. His judgement was well founded. Almost without exception these men justified their promotion, many working up to high rank and in some instances commanding battalions of their own towards the end of the war. Among these men were: Capt. W.W. Parr, Lt. R. J. Fitzgerald, Lt E.A. Robinson, Lt. J. H. Allen and Lt. R. Hosegood.

All officers and N.C.O.s were, in due course, passed through various schools of instruction, physical training, bayonet fighting and signalling. As a result, on their return to the battalion they proved invaluable as instructors in all the latest methods and vogues.

The drilling of the various Companies proceeded very satisfactorily. In fact, the rate at which progress was being made considerably surprised the older and experienced men who were charged with their instruction. Lt. Col. Burges took a personal and very keen interest in this progress, watching the men on a daily basis becoming more fit and appreciative of the service they had entered.

In order to prepare the men and, more to the point, their feet for the countless miles they would be expected to cover when on active duty, much opportunity was taken for many and long route marches along Somerset country lanes to the delight of the locals but to the discomfort of the would-be soldiers. These challenges, however, were in stark contrast to the local guards that were mounted around the Cumberland Basin. Armed guards would be drawn from the ranks for daily and nightly duty, and these gave a foretaste of military law. Well at least, that was the plan.

The battalion was fully billeted at its new H.Q. before the middle of November. 'Bristol and the War' covered the event:
"Surely no other "Pals" battalion in the country (and there are now nearly a hundred of them) has been so lucky about accommodation. If some of the other similar units could see the headquarters of the "Bristols" with the fine drill halls, canteen and sleeping quarters and, last, but not least, the magnificent pageant ground for parading and drill, they would surely be green with envy."

1914–Tweed to Khaki

Route march, Somerset

Moving into H.Q.

Fatigue party of 'B' Company

Fatigue party

The offices nearest the entrance to H.Q. from Ashton Avenue were put to use as the Adjutants Room and the Orderly Room. The Sergeant in charge of the latter being H. C. Barber, assisted by privates A. D. Slocombe and S. W. Leonard. Sgt Barber was immediately inundated with work as a very important inspection followed close after the move to H.Q.

Saturday 14th November saw Major-General E. Dickson visit the battalion. In his role of Inspector of Infantry it would be his ultimate decision whether the battalion was suitable for the New Army. The inspection understandably, was extremely thorough. Lt. Col. Burges received a long interview, when he was questioned on the difficulties faced, solutions used, methods of selecting officers and N.C.O.s, men's attitudes, disciplinary issues and compliance with War Council directives.

The actual battalion inspection took place on the pageant ground at H.Q., the battalion turning out one thousand men strong. After the general salute had been given Major-General Dickson spoke with the second in command, Major Blennerhassett and then proceeded around the ranks inspecting every line and then conversing with the officers asking of their backgrounds and enquiring as to their previous military experience, if any. The N.C.O.s were similarly inspected and questioned by the General. This was followed by a complete tour and inspection of the whole of H.Q. and Greville Smyth Park, where the battalion did most of its drill. He announced he was very pleased with all facilities which he described as excellent for training. He afterwards expressed himself as very well pleased with the excellent progress which had been made with the training of the men and the quarters they had obtained, and said Bristol had a battalion of which it might well be proud.

In preparation for the battalion taking up full residence at H.Q. it was decided to employ the services of a civilian contractor to provide catering services. This was the case for the first two months as the appropriate men were not in place and so it was impossible for the battalion to feed itself. The War office allowance was 1/9d per day per man.

However, after some months sufficient cooks had been enlisted into the battalion and issued with 'cook's whites'. It was then felt that the battalion should carry out its own catering. The C.O. and the battalion's Quartermaster Sergeant studied the situation very closely and eventually came to the conclusion that the money allowed per man could be better spent or more to the point a saving could be made.

From then on the battalion bought it's food wholesale and even though small luxuries and variations of food were purchased very comfortable profits were made. Under this splendid organisation the meals were all that could be desired. For breakfast it was usual to begin with porridge and milk, followed by a popular breakfast dish such as bacon and eggs, ham, brawn, liver, sausages or kippers, with bread and butter and tea *ad lib*. At dinner the battalion's cooks provided such splendid and substantial fare as roast pork, beef, mutton, Irish stew, curry, along with plenty of vegetables such as cabbage, peas and haricot beans. There were liberal changes of puddings such as bread, rice, treacle and plum puddings, sweets such as apple pie; also plenty of stewed fruit and fresh fruit, oranges, bananas, and apples. At tea-time there was a liberal supply of bread and butter with jam and cake. When night operations were under way, hot soup was generally served out and for early morning parade coffee and biscuits were provided.

It was considered that no other battalion was as well or better messed during the war. The success of this led to a War Council enquiry when Officers visited the battalion. The result was that the messing allowance for the entire army was reduced to 1/4d per day per man and a huge sum saved by the country. The battalion received no thanks for its work. On the contrary, it was ordered to refund to the War Office the savings made which ran into several thousands of pounds. However, even with the variety of food provided, careful planning and management, the cost to the battalion of feeding was even lower at 1/1d per day per man allowing continued savings which were not, in this case reported to the War Council!

To everyone's delight, the War Council now indicated the correct style and regimental number of the battalion, and henceforward 'Bristol's Own' became known officially as the 12th (Service) Battalion Gloucestershire Regiment. It was natural that the men felt pride in the fact that they had been given "a habitation and a name."

Initially work was undertaken to continue preparing the grounds for military training. A replica of Drake's flagship 'Revenge' was dismantled, signs of a fairground nature were removed and replaced with those of a more military bearing and the many roads within H.Q. that were rapidly turning into seas of mud were repaired with cart loads of clinker from the local gas works.

With the official transfer of the battalion into its headquarters there began soldiering with a vengeance: training began in earnest with all men, by then, accommodated at H.Q. Then began hard working days and nights. 8 a.m. until 6 p.m. or 9 p.m. with an hour off for meals and longer hours during fine weather. There were also night exercises on 2 or 3 nights each week for battalion or Company work.

14596 Pte. William Ayres
"We signallers would find a quiet corner somewhere. We would use buzzers, flags, morse, semaphore and, on occasions, the Heliograph."

14398 Pte. Stan Streets
"My main memories of training at Ashton were of lots of drill, lots of trench digging and lots of route marches. All very tiring for an office chap like me. During the winter the accommodation was very cold and draughty."

13986 Pte. Robert Anstey
"The beds were very uncomfortable. The palliasses were unsafe, because they had the habit of collapsing, particularly when helped by some mischievous individual."

It is a fact that when a group of young men are constantly together, mischief is never too far away. In today's army it is very much disapproved of to have groups of men 'un-occupied' during training periods. The answer is what is known as 'concurrent activity' where alternative training or use of time is arranged. 1914 was no different. But there were times when men were, due to circumstances, left to their own devices. Such times were after lights out in the various dormitories or living quarters. Various groups of men would form to play practical jokes on there rival companies.
Palliases were rigged to collapse at the most unsuspecting times. Buckests of stinking water from the nearby cut would be emptied over dozing companions and particularly unpopular individuals would have a certain part of their anatomy liberally covered in boot polish.
Such activities were accepted to a certain degree and perpetrators would invariably, sooner or later, have their efforts repaid – with interest.

An aspect of training that was to all the men's liking was musketry. Special attention was taken with musketry training. Fortunately Lt. Col. Burges had been through a course at Hythe only two years before the war and in his day had been one of the best shots in the country. In the early days, he conducted the instruction himself. This was something not enjoyed by many other similar battalions. It is a fact that the 12th battalion eventually became very proficient in its shooting skills and it was said that the remarkable shooting record that the battalion later attained in both rifle and Lewis Gun was indeed down to the effort taken by its C.O.

Rifles initially issued to the battalion were purely drill purpose. They were of the old obsolescent 'Long Lee Enfield' type most of which were of Boer War vintage. They had received a long and busy life and, as such, were worn out and useless for actual use. They were of no use when it came to shooting. However, the men set to with them and stripped them and cleaned them and made them look very impressive indeed. Once they had finished with them they certainly took on a business like appearance. This was the intention. they made the men feel like soldiers when they carried them, despite the fact they wore flannels and flat caps. They were also of much use in providing for rifle instruction training. Much 'dry' training was provided which prepared the men for the real thing when it eventually occured.

14 Platoon 'D' Company

'B' Company men working near Drake's ship 'Revenge

The 'Knuts' at work near Australia House

As holder of the Distinguished Certificate, Hythe Military Course and a very able shot, the subject of musketry was very close to The C.O.s heart. So much so that he was intent on doing everything in his power to afford the battalion the best training it would be possible to give.

Much time would be spent in 'dry' training. That of weapon familiarisation, cleaning and then the application with sighting, aiming, judging distance and marksmanship principles. When resources permitted, these skills would be put into practise gaining the men actual shooting experience. The efforts were to be proven to have been well worth it.

The terminology of the day used by the military for it's current issue rifle, introduced in 1903, was "Rifle, Short, Magazine, Lee-Enfield or SMLE." The Lee Enfield enjoyed a good reputation with those who were issued with it. It had a ten-bullet magazine and its rate of fire in the hands of well-trained men was high. At the Battle of Mons, the advancing Germans believed that they were under fire from British machine guns. In fact, it was the well drilled infantry of the BEF using their standard issue Lee Enfield. A good infantryman would expect to shoot off about twelve well-aimed bullets in a minute.

This rifle, however, was in serious short supply in 1914. As such it was quite surprising that Col. Burges was able through his many useful contacts and good offices to acquire a total of 20 latest pattern SMLE rifles – from Col. C. Burges, Commanding 3rd Battalion at Maidstone. Admitably they were old and well used but serviceable and useful. These rifles gave the men their first taste of service rifle use and remained with the battalion, being used by each Company in turn, until it left Bristol.

In addition, the recruiting committee kindly provided an excellent under cover miniature range at H.Q. featuring every class of target, including landscape targets and simulated long range targets. Much time was spent here with the result that every man fired, a simulated, 200 to 300 yards on this range. In addition, the Committee secured the use of the nearby Clifton Rocks range (Hotwells) and 80,000 rounds of 0.303" ball ammunition. As such, every man fired a course before leaving Bristol.

New recruits parade with rifles in Greville Smyth Park. The crossed rifles in front being of the current issue pattern – the S.M.L.E.

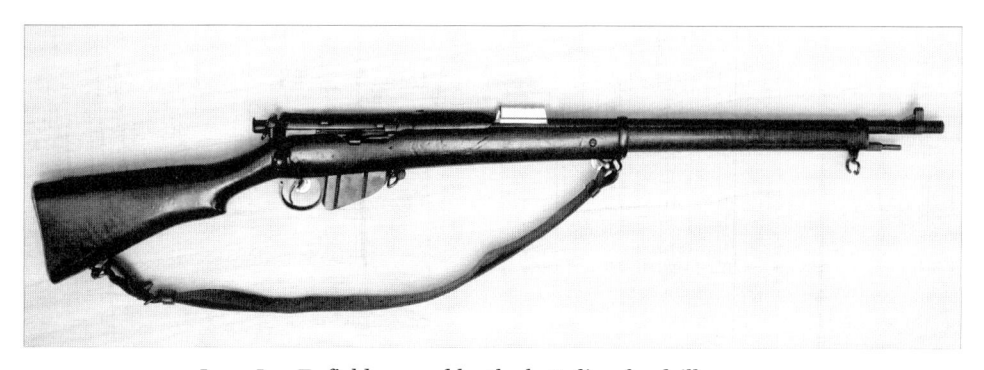

Long Lee Enfield as used by the battalion for drill purpose

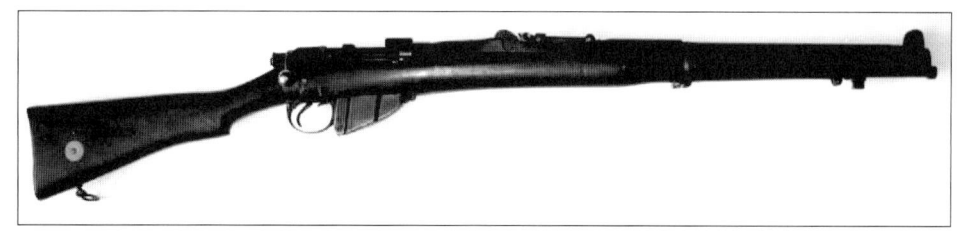

Short, Magazine, Lee Enfiled (S.M.L.E.) the current British Army issue rifle

Rifle instruction at Head Quarters. The Ashton Swing Bridge cabin is visible in the back ground

Returning from rifle drill

1914 – Tweed to Khaki

The final time the battalion paraded in civilian dress

Soon after the battalion was accommodated at H.Q. the men were delighted to hear that the issue of their uniforms and equipment was imminent. Industry had geared up relatively quickly to the manufacture of vast quantities of khaki material and manufacture of uniforms. The Citizens Recruiting Committee had been working very hard with local manufacturers to procure enough sets of uniforms to outfit the entire battalion. Various Bristol firms vied with each other in providing all that was needed. When the time came there were no shortages. Boots cost 14/6d a pair and were of excellent quality, all being soaked in castor oil before issue.

14596 Pte. William Ayres
"We were pleased to receive our uniforms in December. Making our way, in groups of thirty or forty, firstly to the tailors for measuring and issue and then to the boot makers for fitting of boots. Finally we were issued with our badges. One at the front and a small back-badge at the rear. The only regiment in the British Army to have a back badge. Some of us obtained extra back badges and had them made into brooches for sweet hearts, sisters and mothers."

14796 Pte. Frederick Taylor
"We got our uniforms around December 1914 and were very proud to wear them. I do remember that to start with the fitting of puttees was a bit of a job."

14365 Pte. Thomas Nelmes
"When we finally received our uniforms it was a really proud day for all of us. It felt so good to stand proudly in our uniforms after spending so much time as soldiers in civilian clothes. Unfortunately there was a shortage of 'Gloster' shoulder titles. We didn't get these for quite some time as I remember."

With the issuing of uniforms orders were given as to order of dress:
All Parades (except Church Parade and early morning parade) – tunic, trousers, puttees, belt with frog and cap. Greatcoats as ordered. For "Drill Order" 2 pouches to be worn in addition.
Church Parade – tunic, trousers, puttees, belt (stripped) – N.C.O.s above rank of corporal to wear side arms, caps and gloves. Great coats as ordered.
Early Morning Parade – As ordered by officer commanding Company.

Walking-Out Dress – Tunic, Trousers, puttees, belt (stripped), swagger stick if required – N.C.O.s above rank of corporal to wear side arms, caps, gloves, and canes. Greatcoats if required.

Opportunities were taken when circumstances permitted when men would return home to 'show off' their new business like appearances to families and friends and indeed, 'walking out' took on an entirely new meaning.

A weekly highlight was the arrival of Mr. E. C. Stevens from Arley Hill, Bristol. He was a photographer who visited on Saturdays. Mr. Stevens was permitted to visit H.Q. in order to take photographs. He would photograph men at work and play, in formal and informal groups. Men and officers were photographed included the C.O. and the other high ranking officers. The following week he would bring lots of photographs to sell to the men and then take more photographs. This continued throughout the battalion's stay at H.Q., resulting in a superb photographic history of the battalion albeit dispersed among all the men and the men's families.

Arthur of 'A' Company, photographed by Mr. E. C. Stevens,
proudly posses in his new uniform

There were enthusiastic scenes along the route in Weston-Super-Mare from the George Street Drill Hall, via Baker Street, Meadow Street and Regent Street to the G.W.R. Station, on Monday 9th November when the eighty Westonians – the Weston Comrades – who had enlisted in 'Bristol's Own', departed by the 11.05 a.m. train for final training at Head Quarters. The men were headed by Mogg's Military Band and marched through the heartily cheering crowds. Sgt. Major Baker R.F.A. took the opportunity to thank them for the keen attention and the support they had given him. He then formally handed over the 'Weston Comrades' to the command of Lt. Balston of "Bristol's Own." Cigaretes and packets of tobacco were presented to the men before they boarded the train taking them to Temple Meads of Bristol. The Weston Comrades, once installed at H.Q, were granted their wish - that of being kept together. All men were posted immediately to 'D'Company.

Arrival at Temple meads of the Weston-Super mare contingent

14596 Pte. William Ayres
"During November, I think, the group of men from Weston-Super-Mare that had been trained separately, arrived with us. They were all placed in my company -'D' Company. Among them were three brothers, the Amesbury brothers. I soon became a very close friend of Richard 'Dick' Amesbury."

    Despite the death of Sir Herbert Ashman, Lady Ashman continued to show a keen interest in the battalion which her husband had worked so hard to create. In November, her Ladyship presented a complete set of instruments for the formation of a band. Immediately, recruits were sought and many men volunteered, with the view that it might represent a slightly easier life with maybe some special concessions. In fact it didn't, but the battalion possessed some very able musicians among the volunteers. Also, many men who had never played a musical instrument before came forward. Eventually, a suitable group of musicians was recruited and the band, under the directorship of band master 'Drummie' Greenwood, turned into a real battalion asset both at home and abroad.
    But being a member of the band required a certain attitude and acceptance of responsibilities. The new musicians were expected to do their best to perfect themselves in the use of their instruments. This was achieved only by the most careful attention to the advice and attention of the bandmaster, whose orders they were always most implicitly to obey. They were expected to take great care of their instruments and any damage done by carelessness or neglect would be charged against the man in possession of the damaged instrument.

    New band members would practise during their normal off duty time. Flutists had little problem and even drummers were tolerated. Problems did, however, exist for the budding buglers. Due to the very nature of the sound levels produced when practising, it was necessary to find some isolated corner, somewhere distant from the goings on at H.Q. or at best stuff the 'loud' end with a stout sock in order not to incur the displeasure of surrounding comrades. But the band eventually became a proud part of the battalion both around the streets of Bristol during the various parades and marches, and eventually overseas where it became a real asset, not only to the battalion but also the brigade. Importantly, it became an inspirer of men's moral.

Battalion band. 'Drummie' Greenwood extreme left front row

14618 Pte. William Burnell
"My musical abilities were somewhat limited but I had played the flute as a boy. I volunteered and after a brief trial was accepted. It was a proud feeling to be part of the band, marching out in front of the whole battalion."

But more war-like training involved the men's daily routines. Among which was bayonet training exercises. The issue rifle was equipped with nothing less than a 17" bayonet. But for practise, much time was spent bayoneting bags of straw and each other, with spring loaded dummy bayonets whilst wearing body protection and face shields.

Bayonet fighting was given very high emphasis. It's actual intention though was more of a physcological one. To develop in a soldier aggressiveness and courage. The aim being to come to close quarters with the enemy and to use the bayonet. This was in fact an outmoded method of warfare but still taught with vigour, the bayonet charge being regarded as a measure of a unit's morale and cohesion. The tactic was to demonstrate to the enemy that a man, or a unit simply would not break. The bayonet itself was not regarded as important as much as the individual's will to fight to the last.

The bayonet was supposed to have been the greatest glory of the old British army. The capacity to fight at close quarters which it implied was supposed to distinguish the British with their professional traditions from the 'amateur' Germans. In actual fact, the war would prove, due to the machine gun and the high explosive shell that close quarter bayonet fighting would become the least common mode of fighting. Indeed too, it would very quickly be realised that the Germans were far from 'amateur.'

But, it was not so much the 'bayonet' as much as the 'discipline' required by bayonet work that was thought of as an end in itself. No other weapon required to such an extent the subduing of individual fear and robot-like obedience to orders. Practical knowledge such as map reading, trench survival, what to do to avoid machine gun fire or deal with an enemy strong point were considered secondary to this. As long as the 'professional and mercantile' soldier could be guaranteed to obey all orders, he could be considered as trained.

Bayonet fighting practise indoors

Practical knowledge of subjects that would be of real value were not taught for the very simple reason that they had not yet been learnt. Most of what was taught was probably obsolete by the time of the Boer War. As William Ayres stated, the signallers practised with flags and Heliograph. Tools which could never be used in the coming fighting.

The real skills were, unfortunately, as alien to the British Expeditionary Force, at that time fighting desperately in France, as they were to the time-served instructors following out of date manuals. The training was geared, however, to achieve one thing if nothing else: to ensure a soldier obeyed orders. This, of course, was helped by the constant barking of orders and inevitable humiliation and indecent suggestions spat out by senior N.C.O.s with years of service behind them.

Due to the calibre of the men that joined the battalion, its strength was being gradually eroded with men being posted and commissioned. In order to avoid the gaps in the ranks the Citizens Recruiting Committee approached the War office asking permission to form a fifth, reserve, company of a further 250 men.

Permission was received on 30th November. The advantages were soon pointed out of enlistment in such a corps, not the least of which being that the training was being carried out in Bristol, at the Exhibition ground, Ashton. The Headquarters, according to Major General Dickson, who had recently inspected the battalion, were unsurpassed. It was considered that obtaining that number of new recruits would be easily achieved.

On 2nd December the Western Daily Press reported:
"The great majority of enlistments at the Recruiting Office, now at the Guildhall, in Broad Street yesterday were for the new Company now being formed for the Bristol Battalion of the Gloucestershire Regiment, and

Bayonet fighting practise outdoors

BRISTOL'S OWN
Fifth Company (250 MEN) NOW BEING FORMED.
As there is likely to be a big rush to join this favourite local Battalion, applications should be made at once.
GUILDHALL, Broad, Street Bristol.

the expectations of the Citizens Recruiting Committee that the 250 men will be forthcoming in the course of a week or so seem likely to be realised. In discussing the matter yesterday, Major Carr, the chief recruiting officer, stated that he was more than pleased with the class of recruits coming forward. The majority of them are men of excellent physique and come from the commercial departments from Bristol business houses. When recruiting for the battalion was first opened many more applicants for enlistment were received than could be dealt with, and no doubt this will happen again, therefore an early intimation of a desire to join should be made at the Guildhall."

Immediately men came forward to enlist. One of the first men to join the new 'E' Company was Sam Bollom. He had attempted to enlist back in September but was rejected due to a heart defect. He had joined the Athletes Volunteer Corps from which he was seconded into 'Bristol's Own' with no difficulty in December.

In order to encourage men to join the new Company being formed, on Saturday 5th December a detachment of 180 men under Captain Colt and Lt. Burris with 2nd/Lt's. Sants, Clare-Smith and Bunnington and Regimental Sergeant Major Lane marched, for the first time in full uniform, on a recruiting parade around Bristol. The route selected for the march was through Clare Street, Corn Street, Wine Street, Dolphin Street,

'B' Company men at lunch

Castle Street, Old Market Street and Stapleton Road to the Rovers Football Ground, then returning via Robertson Road, Victoria Road, Lawrence Hill, Old Market Street, Bedminster Bridge, East Street, North Street and back to Headquarters at Ashton. It was commented that:
"The men were well drilled and smartly uniformed and have a most soldierly appearance."

Most Bristol newspapers and publications made no excuses for praising 'Bristol's Own' at every opportunity. After all, it was Bristol's pet battalion and it represented Bristol's war efforts. The poor Territorial Force battalions, the 4th and the 6th, who had been training for six years already, were somewhat in the shadow of the 12th. But generally speaking, the men of the 12th tended to show a suitable level of respect for their Territorial Force brethren.

In the world of the military there had always been great rivalry. Whatever the corps or regiment might be, was an irrelevance. To the men who comprised it, 'they' were the best, without doubt. The feeling of professional rivalry between Bristol's Territorial Force battalions and the 12th (Service) Battalion of the Gloucesters, otherwise known as 'Bristol's Own', was rather acute.

A certain amount of sympathy was felt for the opinion which existed between the 4th and the 6th Gloucesters to the effect that 'Bristol's Own' received more than its fair share of limelight despite the fact that most of the civilian population of Bristol was unable to conceal a certain amount of pride in its pet battalion.

And so, in order to settle the issue, for certain die-hards from both sides of the divide, on 10th December at 2.45 p.m. the rugby football stalwarts of the 4th and the 12th Gloucesters met at the County Ground. It was a competition on a level playing field, as it were, despite the fact 'Bristol's Own' had among its ranks some very respected players. Of course, each side had its supporters and critics and some, inclined to favour the Territorial side, were convinced that the Bristol Battalion would be beaten fare and square and that a certain poetic justice would be apt.

The game was fast and furious, with 'Bristol's Own' finally winning. Comments were immediately made to the effect that the result would go a long way towards a further swelling of the chests of 'Bristol's

Battalion Rugby team

Own'. And why not, they deserved it. The fact of the matter was, they won. As much as it might have been worthy to flatter the 4th, it could not be concealed that, they lost.

The pages of Bristol and The War reported on 19th December some rather unsportsmanlike comments: *"Perhaps the 4th Gloucesters are not satisfied and mean to make another bid for supremacy? If 'Bristol's Own' is allowed to win again, we will really begin to think they deserve it. If any man of the team thinks we imply that the luck of 10th December was not well deserved, we are not going to contradict him. From the friends who are jealous of the good name of the Bristol Battalion, we might hear they might have played a more scientific game, and that in certain combinations the 4th Gloucester boys could show them points. Of course, we expect to get into fearful disgrace for publishing such a criticism, and the Lord Mayor may even see fit to reprimand us for our presumption. But if any man of the Bristol Battalion desires to argue the matter with us, we must respectfully refer him to our fighting editor. The latter is past the military age but he stands over six feet, has prodigious calves and biceps, and is renowned in sporting circles for his persuasive manner with refractory strangers. He keeps appointments at any time, anywhere, with anybody; and nobody ever wants to argue with him twice"*

It is perhaps, not necessary to say that by this account the battalion was unpopular in some circles but, more to the point, that a definite jealousy over its popularity and success reined in certain quarters. Further more, quarters that one would have expected to have remained very much unbiased. But these comments were ignored and nothing is on record to suggest that the, afore mentioned 'fighting' editor was respectfully introduced to any of 'Bristol's Own' very able boxers. What may be said, however, is that the writer, not surprisingly, omitted to add his name to article.

Saturday 12th December saw another march through the city. This followed an inspection of the buildings and facilities at Head Quarters by the Lord Mayor; Alderman J. Swaish accompanied by the Sherriff, Mr. J. S. Stroud, and the members of the Bristol Citizens Recruiting Committee and various other dignitaries.

Lt. Col. Burges received the visitors at the main entrance. Under the guidance of Lieutenant and Quartermaster Hooper, the party made a thorough inspection of the barracks. Many were the evidences of military occupation, while the erstwhile splendour of the Bristol International Exhibition, with its huge buildings and costly exhibits, had given place to a grim scene of reality. The sunken bandstands had been turned into a platform for guns of the old type and the large pavilions now served as sleeping accommodation, with row upon row of neat mattresses placed on raised boards. The party carefully inspected all the arrangements. The canteen, coffee bar and Sergeants mess, all of which were seen to be suitably fitted up and conveniently furnished, were viewed and the sleeping quarters were noted as light, dry, spacious and airy. The messes and kitchens were also inspected and the general impression of the arrangements provided for housing the battalion was a very favourable one. Satisfaction was generally expressed.

The full battalion, under drill, was then inspected in Greville Smyth Park. Their smart and soldierly appearance drew forth many complimentary remarks. The battalion marched past in echelon from the right and then advanced in line of platoons and were finally drawn up ready for their march through the city.

The events of the day proved to be a very proud and moving moment for Lt. Col. Burges when his men were finally marshalled for the admiring eyes of Bristol, albeit initially in the form of the Lord Mayor, Sheriff, Chairman of the Recruiting Committee and other distinguished citizens and officials. The men stepped out proudly and smartly in their new uniforms and full marching equipment when they were greeted by cheer after cheer as they marched through Bristol after the review. Headed by the Lord Mayor's coach, which was preceded by mounted police and followed by the battalion band, the procession started at 3 o'clock.

The day was of some significance for the battalion. It marked what was referred as the end of the "infant" days of Bristol's "very own" battalion. The events of the day were the culmination of many weeks of patient work and waiting. The men were considered to have finally crossed the chasm from raw recruit to full blown soldiers, and the battalion's first formal march past was witnessed by all dignitaries.

Western Daily Press:
"There is one aspect of the military outlook locally which can be regarded with unqualified satisfaction: that is the splendid battalion Bristol has raised and equipped from amongst the professional and commercial classes. The inspection of the headquarters at Ashton and the march through the city furnished an opportunity which has long been anticipated for judging the probable capabilities of 'Bristol's Own' and military officers of long experience expressed the opinion on Saturday that for physique, intelligence and soldierly bearing it would be hard to find a better body of men in training for war. The party then crossed to the Greville Smyth Park where the inspection took place. Crowds of people were gathered for the spectacle. The battalion was in Company formation and presented an extremely smart appearance. On arrival of the Lord Mayor, the battalion presented arms, and his Lordship inspected each line. Prompt to time, the Lord Mayor, with an escort of mounted police, headed the route march through the city."

The route taken was Ashton Gate, North Street, East Street, Bedminster Bridge, Redcliff Street, Victoria Street, Bristol Bridge, Baldwin Street, Tramway Centre, Colston Street, Maudlin Street, Lower Maudlin Street, Union Street, Wine Street, Corn Street, Clare Street, St. Augustine's Parade, Hotwell Road and Ashton Road. Crowds of people lined the thoroughfares along which the battalion passed, many of whom taking up their position some time before hand. In the city centre and in the neighbourhood of St. Augustine's the crowds were very dense. Comments on its appearance were naturally made and generally the opinion was expressed that the battalion was the pride of its city.

Life in barracks was by no means monotonous and before Christmas there were few phases of soldiering with which the battalion was not, by then, intimately acquainted, from washing-up greasy dinner dishes and pots, to impaling Germans on a bayonet. The latter operation, owing to the scarcity of genuine Germans in the Bristol neighbourhood, was carried out upon Germans made of sacks and straw. Very interesting and exciting too were the sham fights conducted in Greville Smyth Park and spots further afield, both by day and by night.

The physical improvement effected among the men by all the rough, open air work and regular exercise, coupled with good, plain, wholesome food, soon manifested itself. By mid winter the whole appearance of the men was completely changed and, considering the men's usual sedentary occupations, this

Lord Mayor's Review 12th December 1914

Men awaiting inspection

The inevitable scrubbing of pans escaped few men

was a marked feature. The pale complexions and somewhat drawn features of many of the young fellows who had enlisted into the battalion straight from banks, office desks and counting houses, had given place to ruddy, rounded faces of perfect fitness; the round shoulders and slouching city walk had been replaced by a firm swinging step and upright carriage.

Beyond fatigues and physical exertion, leisure facilities were provided for the men to relax when not on duty or at work. Provided by the Church of England Men's Society (CEMS) was a fine reading and snooker room. A further library of books was added through the efforts of Mr. E. T. Morgan who had always shown a deep interest in the battalion, aided by a generous grant from the Bristol Libraries Committee and gifts from friends. Mr. Morgan had been able to put around 400 volumes at the services of the battalion. As the Commanding Officer, in his letter of thanks said: *"Such presents are greatly appreciated by the men as they afford both recreation and amusement during the long evening hours"*

Of course the evenings were always long but the commanding officer was rarely at a loss to usually find some form of exhausting training for the men such as the ever popular night marches and trench digging or the less active but in its way mundane guard duties. But there were, it should be said, rest breaks during which it was important to allow the men suitable leisure activities.

On the evening of Friday 18th December the Sergeants mess held a social evening and dance. In the Sergeants mess room at H.Q. the duties of Master of Ceremonies were carried out by Company Sergeant Major Shelper of 'B' Company. The room had been very well laid out for the event and an excellent string band was provided which was made up of battalion members under the able conductorship of Bandmaster 'Drummie' Greenwood. Lt. Col. Burges, Major Blennerhassett, Second in Command and Capt. Kerr, Adjutant and third in command along with many of the battalion officers attended. Dancing commenced early and was kept up until a late hour and during the evening songs and recitations were rendered by Second Lieutenant Lewis, Regimental QMS Cotterell and Sergeant Young. The Regimental Sergeant Major welcomed the guests and accompanied by his wife bade them farewell at the close of the evening.

Over the Christmas period a large number of officers and men were granted just over one week's leave. This was to prove to be the last Christmas at home for a long time for many of the men. They realised it and took full advantage. There were, however, some men who did not get leave or were unable to return home for various reasons. Because of this, arrangements were made to make their time at H.Q. something to be remembered. In the matter of gifts, not a single member of the battalion was empty handed. A profusion of good things of all kinds were showered on them. For Christmas dinner there was an ample supply of turkeys, ham, vegetables and, of course, the usual heaps of fruit, cake, plum puddings and other delicacies. The cooking arrangements in field ovens were highly praised by Lt. Col. Burges and other officers present. The tables were set by Private R. A. Woodman who, in a neat speech, proposed the health of the popular Commanding Officer who subsequently thanked the men and wished them all a happy time.

One last event was to mark the heady days of 1914. Though it involved various planned attacks and successful withdrawals it had no place in the instruction manual. New Year's night at Ashton was remembered by many. Snow was on the ground and the opportunity was taken by many adventurous young men to rush their 'enemies' quarters and snowball them out of bed. This led to the inevitable reprisals and the battle was carried on in all sorts of attire, with pillows intermingling freely with snowballs and lightly clad men intermingling freely with the snow.

And, at the conclusion of the festivities of the Sergeants mess ball, full advantage, and very possibly a certain amount of revenge was taken, when the unsuspecting men were 'bombed' as they stepped into the night air. As it turned out, many were in such an intoxicated state that it was a matter of sublime indifference to them as to whether it was raining snowballs or cats and dogs.

Christmas Dinner 1914 for the few that remained at H.Q.

Chapter IV

1915 - Army ways

"Discipline is the living force which turns a crowd of men into an army. It is absolutely necessary for the efficiency, safety and comfort of all ranks. The essence of discipline is instant and cheerful obedience, not only to commands given by word of mouth, but to all rules and regulations duly issued by proper authority. Soldiers were held personally responsible that they make themselves acquainted with such orders and in details of duty as were posted in quarters. Every soldier was instructed to comply with any order given by a superior without hesitation. His duty was to simply obey."

The men that constituted the battalion were shaping up. Now with their new uniforms they took on a more business like appearance. Practically ninety percent of the men had never soldiered before and consequently their ideas of discipline and military etiquette were, at first somewhat slack, if not amusing, but as every man was intent on doing his best it was surprising how quickly they shook down and got into 'Army ways'.

Men of 'A' Company pose with the Clifton Suspension bridge in the back ground

There was practically no serious crime and only one or two 'reported' cases of drunkenness – the principle crime was over-stopping leave. Good advice was never far away:

"It is the duty of every soldier to salute all commissioned officers who they know to be such, whether being dressed in uniform or mufti. The salute will be made with the hand furthest away from the person saluted. When passing an officer commence the salute three paces before arriving and lower the hand three paces after passing. Always remove pipe or cigarette."

If any man was under any illusion of what lay ahead of him, it was made clear to him:

"The object to be aimed at in the training of a soldier is to make him, in mind and body, a better man than his adversary on the field of battle. Fitness for war is the only thing that counts and every soldier

Battalion pets

Machine Gun section under instruction

should school himself to keep this constantly in mind. His first duty is to acquire a soldierly spirit. This will help him to bear fatigue, privation and danger cheerfully, will give him confidence in himself, his officers and his comrades and will produce such a high degree of courage and disregard of self that, in the day of battle, he will use his brains and his weapons coolly and to the best advantage. The soldier must learn to be proud of his profession and particularly so of his own regiment."

> **"BRISTOL'S OWN" FILMED.**
>
> Mr Sumpter, of the Bedminster Hippodrome Cinema, secured a fine film of "Bristol's Own" on the Downs this morning. It will be shown at the hall to-night. All the men and officers are recognisable.

The first announcement for the New Year arrived in the Bristol Times & Mirror on Friday 1st January:
"The following will represent the 12th (Service) Battalion Gloucestershire Regiment against the 8th (Service) Battalion, at Weston-Super-Mare tomorrow:- Pte. N. Hardy, Pte. W.C. Hicks, 2nd/Lt. J.P. Webb, Pte. F.G. Hore and Pte. E.J. Nyhan; Pte. J. Baker and Pte. J. Thould; Lt. R.E. Machon (capt.), 2nd/Lt. G.S. Lewis, Cpl. J.F. Bowerman, L/Cpl. C. Stradling, L/Cpl. G. Percy, Pte. J.E. Friend, Pte B.G.E. Machon and Pte. N.R. Spafford. Linesman, Sgt. W. Salvage."

An account of this game was, surprisingly, not published.

> **BRISTOL'S OWN**
> The Fifth Company will soon be complete.
> DON'T BE TOO LATE.
> COME TO THE GUILDHALL AT ONCE!
> GOD SAVE THE KING!

The 5th company, or to give it its official title – 'E' Company was now complete. For reasons which are now unclear, 150 men of the new company were immediately transferred to the four main companies and some men from the four main companies temporarily transferred to 'E' company presumably to help with training.

As the year of 1915 got under way the health and spirits of the men in their romantic barracks at Bower Ashton were infectious. In spite of draughty buildings and huge ramshackle structures, there was a remarkable absence of serious illness. While their barracks, intended only for the summer season, were showing signs of premature decay, the men themselves were standing up well. But the cold, damp winter weather ensured that the line of men reporting sick each morning was a steady constant. The usual place of work for the great majority of men was, of course, the bank, office and shop counter which offered dry and relatively warm comforts. However, the life of the soldier was altogether different and the vagaries of the English weather were something that had to be endured. The life and the conditions took some getting used to.

1915 – Army Ways

Some of the men of the fifth or 'E' Company

'E' Company men at Dinner

Luckily, most of the men were young, strong and fit and though inevitable complaints of colds, tonsillitis and influenza were troublesome, the battalion enjoyed a high average of health. Furthermore, the change effected in the appearance of some of the young men was miraculous.

But not all men were quite so young and fit. However, such was the prevalent feeling of being seen to be doing one's bit and offering one's services and to display a sense of loyal duty, that some men, whose ages were approaching the upper age limit and whose constitutions may possibly have not been as strong as those of their younger comrades, felt duty bound to enlist. One such man was 16511 Pte. Thomas Bowen who proudly enlisted during December into 'E' Company. He was aged 42 and had been feeling 'under the weather' for a few days but refused, despite advice from his pals, to report sick. He continued, considering his poorly feelings would pass. Unfortunately for Pte. Bowen things did not get better and he collapsed during training on the 18th February. He was conveyed immediately to the 2nd Southern General Hospital (Bristol Royal Infirmary) where he was diagnosed with pneumonia. His company comrades visited him regularly over the next few days taking fruit and magazines. But they watched as his condition worsened until he succumbed to his illness and died on the 21st.

Pte. Bowen's coffin leaving the Bristol Royal Infirmary

Pte. Bowen's funeral was conducted with full military honours on 24th February. Floral tributes were received from Pte. Bowen's friends and family, The Red Cross Society, the Officers, N.C.O.s and men of 'E' Company and the Citizen's Recruiting Committee. After a service in the Infirmary chapel, Captains Colt and Bingham Hall, with Lieutenants Lewis and Cooper, led men of 'E' Company through the city streets. Members of Pte. Bowens family joined the procession, the cortége proceeding to Arno's Vale Cemetery via the Tramways Center, Baldwin Street, Bristol Bridge, Victoria Street and the Bath Road. The coffin, borne upon a gun carriage was pulled by his comrades, the battalion band following behind. The deceased was laid to rest in 'Soldier's Corner' while the Rev. J. F. L. Southam, chaplain to the battalion, read the committal. Volleys were fired over the grave and the last post sounded.

1915 – Army Ways

Pte. Bowen approaches Arno's Vale Cemetery.
The gun carriage pulled by his 'E' Company comrades

The loss of Pte. Bowen came as a major blow to the battalion and particularly to the men of 'E' Company. He was the first of the battalion's casualties and though his death was not the result of an act of war, his loss was keenly felt.

16744 Pte. Joseph Brown
"Few of us were used to death, particularly of someone close. To us youngsters, Bowen was seen as something of a father figure and received respect, probably because of his age alone. Yes, he was older, but not really considered as being old, so it was a real shock when he died. It made us respect more fully nature's signals of impending illness."

On 20th February *Bristol and the War* published another very apt verse sent in by a patriotic citizen. Simply reported as F.D.B. of Bedminster:

*Bristol, acknowledged the "Pride of the West,"
A name that has ever commanded renown
Has leapt to the call with infinite zest,
A zest that will ripen but never lie down.*

*Her brave sons, regardless of culture or caste,
In one common cause have joined the fray;
They aye will be ready, like those in past,
To lay down their lives at dawn of the day.*

*To free trammelled countries from mad Kaiser's grip,
The blood of our soldiers is fast being shed;
But the day will arrive when from Kaiser we strip
The mail from his fist and the crown from his head.*

In that little enterprise, "Bristol's" we trust,
Will revel in glory, and frolic, and fun,
To see "Looting Bill" from his throne thrust
This thieving, most brutal and uncultured Hun!

Tho' sacrifices great they're called on to make,
In stout hearts and strong arms is victory sown:
They're "comrades in arms" for their country's sake,
So three cheers for the brave boys of 'Bristol's Own'

'A' Company 'pioneers'

Early in the spring of 1915 it was announced that the 12th Battalion Gloucestershire Regiment would become part of the 95th Brigade of the 32nd Division under General Ryecroft. The other units that would form the brigade were:

14th Battalion Royal Warwickshire Regiment (1st Birmingham City)
15th Battalion Royal Warwickshire Regiment (2nd Birmingham City)
16th Battalion Royal Warwickshire Regiment (3rd Birmingham City)

Lt. Col. Burges was instructed to produce a report on suitable camp sites that might suit brigade training. These sites were at Wells and Malvern. Though the report stated that the Malvern site was ill suited for training purposes, the War Council selected it. Arrangements for hiring the ground were practically complete when the decision was cancelled in favour of a site at Wensleydale in Yorkshire. As a result rumours were widespread within the battalion of an imminent departure.

Such thoughts of any impending departure were, for the time, put to one side on Saturday 12th March when another rugby football match, held at the County Ground, took place between the 12th and the 10th Gloucesters.

1915 – Army Ways

The Bristol Times & Mirror reported:

"*After a good game the 12th Gloucesters ('Bristol's Own') defeated the 10th Gloucesters, who came from Cheltenham, by 22 points to nil. The game was fought out keenly, and it was evident that the training the men are receiving as soldiers keeps them in the best condition, for the play was fast for 70 minutes and lasted well. 'Bristol's Own' were clearly the stronger and merited their win, though the visitors from Cheltenham deserve every praise for the plucky way they kept at it, despite the heavy score that was registered against them. Once the 12th had settled down, they put the issue beyond doubt, but so keen was the tackling that the 10th only had their lines crossed twice in the first half, Pte. Nyham and L/Cpl. Hicks scored tries and Pte. Hardy kicked a penalty goal. The winners were well served by Pte. Baker and L/Cpl. Thould at half, the last named making some good openings for his three-quarters. The strong running of Pte. Nyham was one of the features of the match and Pte. Esbester showed promise. L/Cpl. Hicks took his passes well but Pte. Hore was inclined to hold on too much. Forward the winners held the advantage and Lt. Machon was an efficient leader of the pack. On the other side the full back was plucky and it was evident that 2nd/Lt. Riddle, on the wing, with more opportunities, would have been dangerous. Pte. Nicholas was smart as scrum worker and Major Pritchard led a keen pack, but one which lacked cohesion.*"

The evening of Wednesday 17th March saw the arrangement of what turned out to be a very successful concert held at H.Q. for the officers and men by Miss Katherine Horsey (triple prize winner) by the kind permission of Lt. Col. Burges. Songs were rendered by Miss Florence Hopkins, Miss Lyla Williams, Miss Dorothy Hall, Miss Katherine Horsey, Mr. Herbert Manley, 2nd/Lt. Lewis and Miss Ruth Uncles. Also pianoforte solos were performed by Miss Katherine Horsey and Miss Eileen Lovell. The evening was enjoyed very much by the men as a pleasant break from 'things military'. Bouquets were presented to Miss Katherine Horsey and Miss Lyla Williams in grateful thanks.

Studies had been made of how well, or otherwise, regular units were faring in terms of medical aid to their men. This was certainly a new consideration as wounded men had always been regarded, due to their sudden incapacity as being of secondary importance exasperated also by the need to spare able men in order to attend to their needs. As far as the New Armies were concerned this very subject would receive some attention. Of course, it was not laid down as obligatory and so was up to each unit to decide and to define.

Usually, in time of war, band members became stretcher bearers. The battalion, however, decided that it would train a group of men to provide more a service than just that of carrying a wounded man from the battlefield. They would be trained also in rudimentary medical skills or battlefield medicine. They would treat and move wounded men. So, early in 1915 volunteers were sought to form such a group. Men of the correct temperament and ability were eventually taken from all Companies to make up the section. These men, alongside their normal infantry training, received special medical training relevant to their purpose. Dr. Eskell from the nearby General Hospital took these men and trained them at Headquarters and at the hospital. One day each week being allowed for visits to the hospital where the men were lectured under class room conditions.

The decision was a worthy one. In France the Ambulance section became a valuable battalion asset doing very good and brave work during the fighting that was to come. During the Battle of the Somme in 1916 no less than three Military Medals were awarded to section members.

16704 Pte. Jack Rutherford
"*I was one of 21 men that volunteered for the Ambulance section. I remained with it during my time with the battalion. We were well trained by Dr. Eskell and while at the Front were afforded special privileges, but the work was hard and dangerous. During the Somme battles many of us became casualties, but I was lucky.*"

14851 Pte. Frances Ballinger
"*Whilst under training, work with the ambulance section was always very interesting and it wasn't without it's benefits. We received our training from Dr. Eskell both at H.Q. and the local hospital. It was always enlightening and not for the squeamish! Early on, most work involved treating of men's blisters due*

Ambulance Section

to many miles marched regularly. Blisters were always a problem. When we went to France and the battles started quite a few of us became casualties with some dying. But we kept going and were very much appreciated, which made it all the more worth it I suppose."

14316 Pte. George Hawker
"I was proud to be a member of the ambulance section. They were a great group of pals and we worked together well. During the Somme battle my faith was put to the test. I was badly wounded and lost a hand. My war was then over, but I was awarded a Military Medal. If I'm honest though, I would have been happy to have been able to trade it for my hand at any time."

14796 Pt. Frederick Taylor
"Once we were in the thick of it I sometimes wondered if volunteering for the ambulance section was such a good idea. But we were a great team and worked well together. Because we shared such close comradeship, the fear of danger didn't last long once you got to work. And the work was busy. At times it was upsetting to see so many friends dead and wounded. Though there was little time to grieve. It was simply a case of getting on with things. It may sound callous, but it had to be. There were plenty of men that desperately needed our help.

"The training we received in Bristol was exceptional. Although we didn't realise it at the time, when put into practise it saved a lot of suffering and saved lives too. It was hard, dangerous work. But very satisfying knowing you were doing good and helping people – your friends.

1915 – Army Ways

Ambulance section in less formal mood

Ambulance section at work

1915 – Army Ways

Section of 'A' Company

Battalion marching along Ashton Avenue adjacent to H.Q.

Chipping Sodbury

Through the Lt. Col Burges' influential contacts in the Sodbury area he was able to secure parts of nearby Hawkesbury common for battalion field work. When fully arranged the battalion proceeded one Company at a time. Each Company took all available arms and marched the 18 miles from H.Q. One week's hard work was conducted there involving setting up camp, building of fortifications, section competitions, night exercises and, of course, the ubiquitous trench digging. The gentle art of erecting barbed wire and of removing the enemy's barbed wire also received much study. The local population of both Chipping Sodbury and nearby Yate were extremely supportive in offering their homes as billets for the men who enjoyed the change of scenery and air immensely.

'B' Company was the first and went out in the last week of March. It was the only Company to go out twice. The final visit being the last week of April. Though it was tough, the men enjoyed the break from H.Q. and practically every section had its photograph taken standing around the famous fountain and horse trough in Chipping Sodbury's Broad Street.

14780 Pte. Ralph Ivor Smith
After some training at Ashton with long route marches, each Company had a week's training at Chipping Sodbury. 'B' Company the first week, 'A' Company the second week and so on. We were billeted with local families for the week and trained on the Duke of Beaufort's land. We marched from Ashton to Sodbury and back, always marching with full equipment."

14596 Pte. William Ayres
"The Companies went to Chipping Sodbury separately. We were billeted around the town in people's homes. Two of us, myself and Pte. Bonnet, were lodged in a house in Horse Street. The owner was an official in the town, I think town clerk. A most comfortable lodging."

'D' Company leaving H.Q. on its way to Chipping Sodbury

1915 – Army Ways

Men of 'A' Company around the pump in Broad Street Chipping Sodbury

2 Platoon of 'A Company take a rest during trench digging activities

1915 – Army Ways

It had been decided, due to the success of forming a fifth company, and the fact that men were continually being lost to the battalion that a further sixth company would be raised. At around the end of April recruitment began. Still, feelings ran high and men came forward to join the special Bristol battalion.

Sports Day

Competition was always something very much encouraged within the military and the 12th Gloucesters were no exception. There was a large and enthusiastic attendance, which included a sizeable section of the civilian public, at Greville Smyth Park for the 'Bristol's Own' Easter Monday Sports Meeting. For in the 12th Gloucesters were to be found many prominent athletes. Hence the occasion formed a great attraction. The different events were keenly contested. The tug-of-war was considered the most challenging struggle when, after a long pull, 'E' Company were declared the victors over 'D' Company. The 100 yards officer's race aroused much interest and was won by 2nd/Lt. Lewis, again of 'E' Company which were victorious further when Sergeant Young won the Sergeants race over the same distance. Other events followed:

100 yards – Private Darlington, 'D' Company
440 yards – Private R. A. Amesbury, 'D' Company
Relay race – 'D' Company
Potato race - Private Leonard, 'B' Company
Wheelbarrow race – Privates Harding and Taylor, 'D' Company
Belt and Tunic race - Private Fear, 'D' Company

100 yards Sergeants race. 12th Glos.

Final 3 leg. race, 12th Glos.

New Neighbours - The Bantams

The 14th Battalion Gloucestershire Regiment (Bantams) had began using Headquarters for training from Spring 1915. Although, like the 12th battalion, the 14th were formed and trained in Bristol, it was not made up entirely of Bristol men. Rather it was of Gloucestershire men that were under the statutory height limit. Its level of training was clearly less advanced as that of the 12th battalion, so it was decided to offer promotion to men of the 12th that were willing to transfer into it. Any man applying for and being accepted would be immediately promoted Sergeant. One man who did transfer was 14489 Pte. A. E. Davis of 'C' Company. He was C.Q.M.S. by December 1915 and was commissioned in May 1917.

14780 Pte. Ralph Ivor Smith

"I was asked by my Company commander, Capt. Allison if I would like to transfer to the 'Bantams'. If so I would be transferred as a Sergeant. I turned it down as I wanted to stay with my pals."

Boxing Competitions

Among the many sportsmen in the battalion there were several gifted boxers. On the evening of 12th May the final bouts of a boxing competition between the residence of H.Q. in the form of the 12th Gloucesters, the 14th Gloucesters (Bantoms) and the 129th heavy battery Royal artillery were held. In front of a large crowd Major Blennerhassett presented the medals to the winners. Results were:

Middle weight – finals: Private Cleaves beat Private Dando (both 12th Gloucesters).
Welterweights - semi finals: Gunner Gingel (Heavy Battery) beat Private Collins (12th Gloucesters); Gunner Streeter (Heavy Battery) beat Gunner Howard (Heavy Battery); Final Streeter beat Gingel on points.
Lightweight – semi final: Private Oliver (12th Gloucesters) beat Private Green (12th Gloucesters); Private Edwards (12th Gloucesters) a bye. Final: Edwards beat Oliver who was handicapped by an injured thumb.

'B' Company boxers

Feather weight – semi final: Private Close (12th Gloucesters) beat Private F. Clark (12th Gloucesters); Private H. Clark (12th Gloucesters) beat Private Hawkins (12th Gloucesters). Final: Close beat H. Clark in the first round.
Bantam weight – semi final: Private Carsons (Bantoms) beat Private Marshall (Bantoms); Private Gove (12th Gloucesters) beat Private Lewis (12th Gloucesters). Final Gove beat Carson, winning on points

24h May – Empire Day

The image of a motherly Queen Victoria, Empress of India, as its paramount ruler was shared by an Empire spanning almost a quarter of the entire globe. However, it was not until after Queen Victoria died on 22nd January 1901, that Empire Day was first celebrated. The first 'Empire Day' took place on 24th May 1902, Queen Victoria's birthday. In Britain an Empire Movement was formed with its goal, in the words of its Irish founder, Lord Meath: "to promote the systematic training of children in all virtues which conduce to the creation of good citizens." Those virtues were also clearly spelled out by the watchwords of the Empire Movement: "Responsibility, Sympathy, Duty and Self-sacrifice."

1915 – Army Ways

The intention was to *"...remind children that they formed part of the British Empire and that they might think with others in lands across the sea, what it meant to be sons and daughters of such a glorious Empire"*, and that *"the strength of the Empire depended upon them and they must never forget it."*

Empire Day 1915 was remembered as the first occasion during the war when local loyalty and good feeling took an organised and military form. There had been smaller demonstrations and events of a military kind since the outbreak of war, but nothing to compare with the events of Monday 24th May 1915. It was particularly significant in that for the first time it was completely representative of Bristol's intense patriotism and warlike spirit. Every aspect of local military involvement was represented. The following was the order-of-march of the procession:

Mounted Escort
The Right Hon. Lord Mayor and Lieut.-General Pitcairn Campbell
The Sheriff and party
Sir J. Weston-Stevens and party
Band the Depot of the Gloucestershire Regiment
The Veterans
Cavalry from Southern Depot (Horfield) dismounted
127th (Heavy) Battery Royal Garrison Artillery
Detachment of the 1st South Midland Brigade Royal Field Artillery (Territorials)
Detachment of South Midland Royal Engineers (Territorials)
Bristol Citizen's Military Recruiting Band
12th (Service) Battalion Gloucestershire Regiment 'Bristol's Own'
14th (Service) Battalion Gloucestershire Regiment 'Bantoms'
Detachment 3/4th Battalion Gloucestershire Regiment (Territorials)
Detachment 3/6th Battalion Gloucestershire Regiment (Territorials)
Detachment 3rd South Midland Field Ambulance (3rd Line Territorials)
The St. John Ambulance Brigade and British Red Cross Society
Clifton College Officer's Training Corps
Bristol Volunteer Regiment, comprising Bristol University Volunteers .T.C.R., Coliseum Volunteer Corps, and Athletes Volunteer Force
City and Marine Ambulance Corps
1st Cadet Battalion Church Lads Brigade
Cadet Companies of 6th Battalion Gloucestershire Regiment
Fairfield Road Secondary School Cadet Companies
Merchant Venturers Cadet Corps
Bristol Boy Scouts
Bristol Battalion Boys Brigade

The route of the procession started in Queen's Square, through the Tramways Centre, College Green, Park Street, Whiteladies Road and on to Durdham Downs. All units involved quite rightly received tremendous acclaim and ovations from the thousands of spectators and well wishers on the procession route. It proved to be the battalion's last public appearance before their departure.

'A' Company at Swedish Drill

Leaving H.Q. for another route march

1915 – Army Ways

Thoughts of the battalion's impending departure had been on men's minds for some time. When the war began it was believed it would be a quick war and, even that it might be over by Christmas. Well, Christmas 1914 had come and gone. Newspapers were read with vigour to pick up every bit of news of the war's progress. Although, in 1915, things were not going at all well for the British, the newspapers told a different story. But whatever the final analysis, one thing was clear – there was a lot of fighting going on and soon, they would be part of it. Also there were the sights of the wounded soldiers in the various hospitals around Bristol. The experience of seeing some of these sorry men tended to focused the mind and cause the inevitable thoughts of 'what if'?

The Anstey brothers of 'A' Company: Dan, Joseph and Robert

How each individual felt about that is not easy to say. They seldom expressed their feelings that way. But there was probably a feeling of dread mixed with that of excitement and anxiety. They were becoming real soldiers but, at the same time, they realised they were untried and untested soldiers. How would they perform and how would they adapt to trench warfare and all it's unpleasant sides? Of course, no one knew. But each was determined. Determined, when the time came, to do his job to the best of his ability.

Each man was proud to be a member of 'Bristol's Own', proud to be serving his King and Country and indeed, proud to be in one of the finest regiment's in the British Army. Most had fathers and grand fathers that had served in the past. And so there were many family reputations to uphold and come what may those reputations would be upheld. They were now a true band of brothers and their camaraderie was strong. Every man knew he could rely on the man next to him and that that man could rely on him. It was a feeling that some months before would have been alien to all of them. Only servicemen, particularly infantryman could understand such a bond, an emotion clearly, not understood by the civilians.

But the men had other things on their mind as, before the time of departure for foreign shores came, there would be more preparation training, this time away from their beloved home city and it would certainly be growing in intensity. They would be meeting other similar soldiers from different parts of the country and working with them. That thought in itself, brought with it a feeling of excitement. The chance to pit themselves against other service battalions in friendly rivalry to see how well they compared.

BRISTOL'S OWN SOAP

Made in Bristol by Bristol labour and enterprise.

PURITAN SOAP

has won its way by reason of its outstanding purity and excellence.

It is made to suit the local water and for this reason alone is far more economical than any other soap. It saves its cost week by week in the clothes it saves.

It saves the clothes because it

CONTAINS OLIVE OIL

Puritan Soap in these difficult times represents the truest economy — most work done for least money spent.

Sold everywhere. A size for every need.
Christr. Thomas & Bros., Ltd., Bristol.

Farewell Gathering

Rumours abounded regarding the departure of the battalion and where it was headed once leaving Bristol. Even the newspapers printed their own interpretations. Despite a request by the General Officer Commanding (Southern Command) *'to refrain from publishing unqualified dates and times of the departure of the troops'*, the Western Daily Press announced on 18th May; *"The 12th Gloucesters are leaving for their camp at Malvern next week"*

Not surprisingly, the announcement was wrong on both counts. However, in the absence of any other official 'news' the excitable Recruiting Committee decided to take no chances and, considering that the battalion's departure was imminent, decided to act. In the very short space in time of one week it made all the arrangements for a grand send off at the Colston Hall on 25th May. Maybe a brash decision based on the questionable accuracy of the information but probably a worthy one. And, of course, the choice of the Colston Hall being the place of enlistment of nine out of every ten men in the battalion, and in playing such a vital role in the early days of the battalion was as apt as it was obvious.

On the night of the celebration, the Hall was filled to bursting. The floor was fully occupied by khaki clad men. Not only was the full battalion present, but they were joined by men of the neighbouring units at

No. 4 section of 1 Platoon 'A' Company at H.Q. By the end of the Somme battles five of these men were dead. Five others were granted commissions.

H.Q. in the form of the 127th and 129th Heavy Batteries of the Royal Artillery and the 14th Gloucesters. In all there were 1500 men in attendance. The grand tier and the balconies were also filled with privileged guests and family members.

Many local and many not so local musicians and artists provided the evening's entertainment while opportunities were taken between renditions to pay credit to all those of the Recruiting Committee who had played their part in the creation of the battalion. The Lord Mayor praised the battalion and said they were a 'pet' of the city of Bristol, a city that was proud of the standard the battalion of professional men had reached and how the hopes and expectations of the city would go with them when they departed.

At the close, the Lord Mayor read a telegram from Sir Joseph Weston-Stevens (acting Chairman to the Bristol Recruiting Committee) apologising for his absence and expressing his best wishes for the future of "Bristol's Own." The Lord Mayor also delivered a message from the wounded at Southmead Hospital, who wished 'Bristol's Own' the best of luck. He went on to say that this was not the first time he had had the pleasure of speaking to the battalion, for he had addressed them in that very hall in October last. He thought then that they were a splendid lot of fellows and he thought so still, only more so. He had had the pleasure and honour of inspecting them and he had been in the Company of Generals who had seen them march past and they all said, as had General Pitcairn-Cambell the previous day: "They are really a splendid body of men." He did not tell them that to make them conceited, but he wanted them to understand the reputation that they had to live up to. They were held in high affection by the people of the city of Bristol – the very name they bore was evidence of that. They were indebted for their creation as a battalion to the Bristol Citizens Recruiting Committee.

The Lord Mayor continued that it had been a great pleasure for both him and the Committee to have been brought into contact with Lt. Col. Burges, the Commanding Officer of the Bristol Battalion.

The name of Lt. Col. Burges was received with deafening cheers and the whole audience, rising, accorded the Commanding Officer musical honours. Lt. Col. Burges was praised for his steadfast approach in training the men and was told that the battalion's high standard was entirely due to his good work. There were loud cheers and the singing of *'for he's a jolly good fellow'* when the Lt. Col. Burges stood to give a short speech. He stated that he had no idea he was so popular, particularly when remembering the looks on men's faces at 07.30 each morning in the orderly room!

FOR KING AND COUNTRY.

COLSTON HALL, BRISTOL.
Tuesday, May 25th, 1915.

FAREWELL CONCERT

TO

12th (Service) Batt. Glos. Regt.
(THE "BRISTOL" BATTALION).

Chairman:
The Right Hon. THE LORD MAYOR
(Alderman J. SWAISH).

Grand Organ - - Mr. GEORGE RISELEY.

He first made reference to the excellent work done by the Recruiting Committee and then expressed his gratitude and that of the battalion for the admirable entertainment which had been given them that evening, and said that as the battalion had been so closely associated with the Colston Hall it was particularly fitting that the farewell should take place in that building. When the Recruiting Committee thought fit to nominate him for the position of commanding officer, he little realised the responsibility and the work that had to be done to bring the battalion to its present state of efficiency. The long and arduous training had been cheerfully borne. They were to be brigaded with the Birmingham battalions and he was sure that in a spirit of friendly rivalry, they would do their best to beat their Birmingham comrades.

He said, finally, they had a hard task before them and they had been handed the responsibility of the honour of their country and the honour of the Gloucestershire Regiment, a regiment second to none.

As it turned out, the send off was just a little premature, but that did not matter. In early June, the official announcement was made that the actual date of departure for four main Companies of the battalion was to be Wednesday 23rd June and its destination was to be Wensleydale in Yorkshire. Even at that time enlistments into the second of the two reserve Companies – 'F' Company - continued. Newspaper advertisements stated that a special platoon was to be formed that would be exclusively open to Police Constables.

> **THE BRISTOL BATTALION**
> (12th GLO'STERS)
> Will soon be going into camp for Final Training.
> ☞ **JOIN NOW**
> so that
> **THE SIXTH COMPANY**
> which includes a platoon for Police Constables, may
> be complete before they march away.

Planning began in preparation to move the battalion. Time was short and so not a moment was lost in the vast amount of work that had to be done, from stock checks, equipment checks and repairs, inventory audits, movement of men who were leaving the battalion for officer commissions and general postings, completion of final battalion roll, arrangements for the moving of thirty tons of battalion baggage and equipment to name but a few of the myriad of details that had to be addressed and dealt with before the 23rd. Much assistance in completing this work was again, gratefully received from the Recruiting Committee.

Much work was needed in order to pack all the battalion's equipment in preparation for its departure

1915 – Army Ways

The following correspondence passed between Lt. Col. Burges, 12th Gloucesters, and the Lord Mayor in relation to the departure of the battalion from Bristol:

"My dear Lord Mayor,
I have just heard that the time of our departure tomorrow is fixed at 9.45 a.m. and 11.15 a.m. for the respective trains. As we now appear to be finally off, I want to express, on behalf of myself, my officers and the battalion generally, our most grateful thanks to you personally and to the committee for all the ceaseless trouble and work you have done in connection with the battalion. I hope and believe the battalion will be a credit to its birthplace and to its raisers."
Yours sincerely,
P. Burges.

"Dear Lt. Col. Burges,
Au revoir to you and the officers and men of the 12th Gloucesters. The citizens will follow with deepest interest your progress in the national service.
Raised in our own city, the battalion has for us an unusual interest. We have the greatest confidence in your courage; we know that your men have education, good character, and great determination. Yours may be a hard task, but your fortitude will suffice, and, as in the days of old, the British won for this nation imperishable renown, so now you, in connection with his Majesty's forces generally, will do what you can to continue the fame of England upon a great and glorious eminence.
You go to fight for hearth and home; to make it possible for us to pursue our duties, and to live our English life. These are reasons why we much value the services which you now give to King and Country.
May we have the pleasure at no distant date of giving you a joyous return on your welcome home.
Yours faithfully,
John Swaish. Lord Mayor."

Departure

Though it was known where the battalion was going, it was not known how long this next stage in their training would last. Whether it might be a few weeks or months was unclear. What was clear was that the time of their embarkation to France, or to wherever, was drawing near. Men were excited and anxious.

Up until June 1915 there had been disastrous battles in 1914 and 1915, but the numbers of casualties had not been on the scale they would become in successive years. Also most of the units involved had been regular and the men involved had come from all over the country. The newspapers tended to play down defeats in its headlines, describing them more as set-backs. It was what might be described as misinformation and was designed to deny the people of Bristol and the country in general from knowing the truth. It worked extremely well. The people were not even vaguely aware of the real war situation and the casualties reported in Bristol newspapers had been a trickle, so the feeling of patriotism remained high.

When its 'pet' battalion was leaving the city on the first stage of its journey to the front, many citizens took the opportunity to show their support. Thousands turned out to cheer the men on. As Bristolians gathered along the route taken by the battalion during its last march through the city, from H.Q. in Ashton to Temple Meads Station, it was a very proud moment for them, but also one of reflection. But pride was uppermost. The battalion was cheered by huge crowds of citizens as they were lead by their own band and that of the recruiting committee.

The route taken included: Hotwells Road, St. Augustine's Bridge and Victoria Street. Due to excessive crowds threatening to block the way, sections of troops from the 14th Gloucesters, the Heavy Batteries of the Royal Artillery and the two reserve Companies of the 12th Gloucesters formed barriers particularly at the Tramways Centre, Bristol Bridge and the approach to the station. The crowd which had gathered at St. Augustine's Bridge was immense. Such was the strength of feeling that, though it was practically unknown for ladies to be unescorted, large groups of women were present, pushing bunches of flowers into the soldiers arms and also kissing them.

People who could get close enough patted them and shook their hands. Baldwin Street and Victoria Street were transformed into crowded avenues of people who cheered at the departing troops with tremendous enthusiasm. Tramcars and cabs were loaded with spectators fighting with each other to get the best view. People shouted *'Hoorah!'* hats were thrown into the air, handkerchiefs were waved, steamers in the docks sounded their hooters. The send off was a spectacle greater than anything that had ever been seen in the city thus far and something that would never be equalled.

The battalion eventually entered the station from a side entrance and proceeded to Midland Platform where their train awaited. It was not possible to allow the public into the station but tickets were handed out to families and friends. While waiting to board the train, the band played 'Tipperary' and the men took up the chorus, marking the time by tapping their rifle butts on the platform. At last, punctual to the minute, the men were all aboard and at 09.45 p.m. the train finally began moving out of the station as the recruiting band played *'Auld Lang Syne'*. Hands were waved frantically and faces thrust out of the carriage windows for a last look at friends and family on the platform. Hurried farewells were exchanged. The train receded into the distance and upon a thousand Bristol homes fell a sudden and poignant blank.

14780 L/Cpl Ralph Smith

"Mid June we marched to Temple Meads. The platform was sealed off so that no one could see us off. To everyone's surprise two girls came along asking for 'D' Company. They started asking for me. Both girls lived close to the house I lived in. A brother of one of them worked at Temple Meads and smuggled them in. Both of them kissed me goodbye."

14596 Pte. William Ayres

"There were masses of people pressing out onto the road, barely leaving enough room for our four abreast column to move along. The station incline was packed and orderly marching was not possible. It was all heart warming to be greeted so boisterously and to be given such a friendly send off."

14087 Pte. Arthur Jones

"As we marched through the city streets to Temple Meads station, I had packets of sweets and cigarettes, magazines and papers pushed into my hands, and several times was kissed by complete strangers."

Edward Bond. Ten year old nephew to 14002 Pte. Francis Bond

"My father and I wanted to see my uncle off at Temple Meads. I was so proud to belong to him. Before he set off, he gave me his 'swagger stick' with the Gloucesters crest at the top. That was the last time we saw him. He was killed in action on the 21st of July 1916 on the Somme."

Jim

All of the men in the battalion were, of course, volunteers. Also accompanying them on their journey North was another whose name did not appear on the nominal roll. Amongst them, as they paraded through the city streets on their way to foreign fields was another tenacious addition, in the form of the battalion mascot, a collie dog who was enlisted early in 1915.

No one knew from where he had come. He was clearly a stray and, but for his desire to 'do his bit' and the opportunity of taking up home with the battalion, would probably have met his maker, care of the dogs home.

When he initially showed up at Headquarters he was immediately shown the door. However, he was not to be put off and returned time after time. He pleaded so hard with such eloquent eyes and soft whimpers that he was eventually allowed to stay and unofficially put on strength. He became a proud member of the battalion and insisted on being part of and was allowed to accompany it on route marches. However, it was 1915 and life had its problems. Just when things seemed fine for the battalion's canine friend, another collie dog decided to challenge the coveted and privileged role. He was bigger, stronger and more masterful, and soon set upon the smaller and humbler dog whom though he fought valiantly, was overpowered. He then 'disappeared' giving up the 'mascotship' of the battalion to the newcomer. No one knew where he went or what sorrow he felt.

The 'new' dog started off well, but soon was in disgrace when he began snapping at the men. He received several reprimands, but after a particularly nasty attack on one of the band members he was duly court-martialled and removed under police escort to the, aforementioned, dogs home.

To everyone's surprise, and by some mysterious power of canine telepathic means, the former dog returned a few days later. With delight in his eyes and a spring in his step, he knew no bounds and remained with the battalion. On Wednesday 23rd June, Jim marched alongside the men decked out with red, white and blue ribbons. As the battalion pet and mascot, he was destined to follow them to the front and remain with them, on and off, throughout the war.

Depot Companies

The Depot, or reserve Companies, 'E' and 'F' were formed in order to maintain full battalion strength after the large numbers of men identified as special skills and officer material left the ranks. 'E' Company, as has been discussed already, began enlisting in December 1914 and completed on 19th February 1915 and 'F' Company began enlisting in April 1915. The latter Company only completed its enlistments just after the battalion received its orders to depart Bristol. The level of training in the two Companies, particularly in 'F' Company, fell far behind that of the four main Companies: 'A', 'B', 'C', and 'D'. As a result, it was decided they would continue their training, for the next several months, separate to the main battalion. They would join other Birmingham battalions of the Royal Warwickshire Regiment at Sutton Coldfield where they would receive training more appropriate to their current experience. Leaving three days after the main battalion on Saturday 26th June with Captain Colt leading their send off, though lacking the magnitude of three days earlier, remained a very hearty occasion. On Midland Platform *'Tipperary'* was again played by the recruiting band, only this time a couple of soldiers began to dance the 'bunny hug'. Their example was infectious with the result that soon over one hundred men were in full swing. Though the officers did not join in, it was clear from their smiles, they were amused by the men's antics. It was an excellent start for some men who had only been in uniform for a very short time.

Chapter V

1915 - Goodbye to Bristol

Wensleydale

The journey North went very well, due in part to the generous gift by the Cavalry Depot (Horfield) of providing each compartment with a bundle of eight different newspapers for the men to read. This forethought was very much appreciated. Arrival at their new quarters was around mid-day on the 24th when all were involved in removing the huge amount and weight of battalion kit and equipment. At the first opportunity the men wrote postcards for home. The poor postman struggled off with a very large sack.

The scenery was that of a typical Yorkshire Dale and the exhilarating effects of the keen moor-land air was not wasted on the men. The camp formed part of a huge canvas city within Lord Bolton's Park. To a great many members of the battalion, this was their first journey so far North of Bristol and the entire novelty of the experience was a delight to them.

The camp was between 600 and 800 feet above sea level and housed in bell tents which took twelve Private soldiers or one Lt. Col., or three Officers, or four Warrant officers, or four Sergeants. Other larger tents were provided for messing arrangements. This was a drastic change from those arrangements enjoyed at Headquarters in Bristol but were readily accepted as part of the great adventure that practically every man now felt. There were many other troops in the general area including several battalions of Highland Regiments.

14780 L/Cpl Ralph Smith
"The following day, after arrival, I was ordered to parade for the C. O.'s orders. About 25 had been told to parade, so many from each Company. Some were made up to Lance Corporal some Corporal and some Sergeant. Lt. Col. Burges then came along the line and congratulated each man. I still remember his words to me, 'Smith, you are devilish small but with the reports I have, I'm sure you'll be alright to lead a section'. I was pleased, but unsure of commanding men much older than me."

14596 Pte. William Ayres
"On the slopes across the valley, opposite our camp, was a Scottish Regiment, and to hear their bagpipes playing first thing in the morning and last thing at night, was a real joy".

Also gathered at Wensleydale were all the other battalions and units of the 95th Infantry Brigade of the 32nd Division, of which the 12th Gloucesters formed part. Nearest neighbours were the 15th Royal Warwicks. This was to be the first time the battalion had been presented with the opportunity of training alongside other Brigade units, bringing them closer to the realities of overseas service life.

14087 Pte. Arthur Jones
"Most of the men in this battalion were accustomed to a large city and plenty of people. The consequence was that the quiet of the Yorkshire moors came as quite a comparison. However, the few comparative disadvantages which the district possessed were more than compensated for by the advantages of the beautiful hilly countryside. Our camp, which was well situated in a valley, was on a portion of the grounds belonging to Lord Bolton, and only a few hundred yards away was the river Ure. Wensleydale, the valley of this river had, about half way up one of its slopes a rather long, rather low hill and on this 'island' the camp was situated among those of other battalions of our brigade."

14596 Pte. William Ayres
"Wensleydale was beautiful country and, though marching or even moving over the gorse-clad moors was very tiring, the villages and countryside were lovely."

1915 – Goodbye to Bristol

Lt. Col. Burges received the following letter from the Chairman of the Bristol Recruiting Committee dated 28th June 1915:

"*Dear Sir,*

At a meeting of my executive committee on Saturday the view was expressed that the departure of the Bristol Battalion from this city was a suitable opportunity to convey the appreciation of all the work you have under taken and the assistance you have rendered to this committee from its foundation.

"*They realise the enormous amount of work, energy and organisation entailed upon you personally during the early part of the recruiting campaign in Bristol. They also are fully cognizant of the assistance you rendered them in the formation of the 12th (Service) Battalion Gloucestershire Regiment and the endless details in connection with the training, housing, and equipping of this battalion. They feel that by your personality you have succeeded in gathering around you an excellent staff of officers and altogether have completed a battalion of which the City of Bristol and this committee may be justly proud.*"

By the end of the first week at Wensleydale the transport horses and mules arrived under command of Lt. Wilmot. Much good work was done fitting harnesses and breaking in animals. The 12th battalion's transport eventually became the best in the Division. At about the same time, the camp was badly damaged by a terrific storm which started one night and did much damage. Many of the bell tents were blown down and some of the larger mess tents. It took a full two days to put right the damage caused.

Lt. Wilmot Battalion Transport officer

14596 Pte. William Ayres
"One night the wind came up and many of our tents were blown down. What a scramble, twelve men struggling to get out of a fallen tent? When they were put up again we made sure they were well pegged!"

Some of the battalion officers at Wensleydale, during a lighter moment

At this time, the organisation of the battalion became the responsibility of the Army Council. The Lord Mayor, Alderman John Swaish, on behalf of the Bristol Recruiting Committee was gratified by the receipt of the following letter from the Army Council dated 18th July 1915:

"Sir,
I am commanded by the Army Council to offer you and those associated with you their sincere thanks for having raised the 12th (Service) Battalion Gloucestershire Regiment (Bristol), of which the administration has now been taken over by the military authorities.

"The Council much appreciate the spirit which promoted your offer of assistance and they are gratified at the successful results of the time and labour devoted to this object, which has added to the armed forces of the Crown the services of a fine body of men.

"The Council will watch the future career of the battalion with interest and they feel assured that when sent to the front it will maintain the high reputation of the distinguished regiment of which it forms part.

I am, Sir, your obedient servant,
B.B. Cubitt."

Intensive Company training by day and by night was now the order, occasionally varied by Brigade and Divisional days. Long route marches were practised frequently and, as the battalion had done a lot of marching in and around Bristol, they did well, consequently sustaining fewer 'march casualties' than any other battalion of the Brigade.

1915 – Goodbye to Bristol

There were two particularly memorable marches, the first being a night march of around sixteen miles timed to arrive at dawn to attack a Division from Richmond.

Capt H. A. Colt
"The staff work on this and other occasions was poor, and these days were inaugurated to improve it. We arrived half an hour late and deployed in a hurry and had to attack through shoulder high bracken which was very wet. After it was over we had an hour's rest and ate our haversack rations and then, forming the rear guard began our march back. After going two miles we were ordered back to pick up the waste left by the rest of the Brigade! A bit hard on us, as we were the only battalion which had cleaned up our ground. There was some grumbling but it had to be done. We consequently arrived in camp two hours after the rest of the Brigade. Everyman man marched in. A fine performance.

The other memorable march was not so long, but it was hard. The Division marched out some twelve miles before it was ordered to dig itself in as rapidly as possible. As a first attempt it was a good performance – the battalion's section of trenches being well and quickly done.

14585 Pte. Robert Barnes
"Rain was the outstanding feature on the Yorkshire moors for the first week or so after we arrived. On several occasions we had a thorough drenching. Operations were carried out on a fairly large scale over hill and moorland advancing through gorse and bogs and through chin high ferns. Training in Bristol was hard, but this was much harder. It was usual to work all day then be called out around midnight for a three hour march and an attack after climbing fences of all sizes. Finally, we would get back to camp around 5 a.m. for something to eat and rest."

14046 Pte Charles Dunkin (Letter to former schoolmaster)
"I thought you would like to hear from one of the 'old boys'. We really do not get much time for letter writing but, now and again, when we are on mess or tent orderly, we get a few minutes, so I have settled down to give you some idea of the work we have done since leaving Bristol. As you know, we had a right royal send off from the old city and we lads went away feeling the little we are doing is appreciated by the citizens.

"After a long journey, we arrived at a little station called Wensley at about 08.30 in the morning. The march to the camp was a matter of ten minutes or so, for which we were more than pleased. The camp was situated on a hill of about 600 feet above sea level; the exact spot was facing Penn Hill, one of the highest points on the Pennine Range. It did not take them long before they put us to some real work. It is grand country for army training, but it wanted some sticking, for with a full pack and rifle, well, had it not been for the will power which the boys of our battalion have, well, we should have fallen out in dozens."

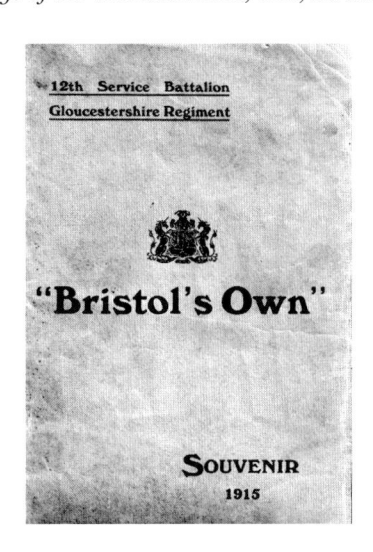

"The Yorkshire moors are, as I expect you know, covered in Heather, and are very hard to cover quickly on the ground. We had to carry out the attack and retirement: these two things are the points they play on. Well, we carried on with night attacks and marches until we were thoroughly fed up with the sameness of it. A night march with an attack at dawn was one of the things that tried the stability of the men.

" It was a case of falling in about eight o'clock in the evening with full pack, marching about ten or twelve miles, with a ten minute halt every hour, then take up a position, or attack one. All this is done on one army biscuit and a piece of cheese about one inch square, so you see we had to go for it, meaning to stick on until we dropped, which I am pleased to say very few did.

"Our camp at Wensleydale was about two and a half to three miles from any village of size, so we did not have much chance to waste our money in riotous living."

Whitburn

Just over one busy, fast moving, but generally enjoyable month was spent at Wensleydale. Camp was struck late July and the battalion and Brigade moved to Whitburn to complete its full musketry course. The two weeks spent there were in stark contrast to Wensleydale. The camp was unpleasant, untidy and very over crowded. Consequently the course was very hurried. With the exception of the C.O. no one had received any experience, except on paper of a full, modern musketry course. There were only forty rifles available, and these were in a poor state of repair and most inaccurate. The C. O. himself tested every one of the rifles and rejected eighteen of them as useless. He almost lost an eye when the bolt of one blew back.

While at Whitburn there was little time for leisure, but a few men managed to get away from time to time.

14596 Pte. William Ayres
"Whitburn was an awful place. Well, the camp was. I managed to get away for an afternoon while we were there. I went to Sunderland and visited a theatre. It was my first time. I don't remember the name of the play, but I do remember a local shop keeper being puzzled by my brass shoulder title that said; 'GLOSTER'. He commented: "Surely that isn't the correct way to spell Gloucester is it?"

14046 Pte Charles Dunkin
"It was really a fishing village, with about 500 houses in all. The butts were along the coast, and the camp situated right behind them, so we got the sea air blowing in the tent, while we slept. But the weather was very unsettled up there, but we got used to the damp. Before our musketry course started we were all instructed:

'Fire discipline means strict attention to the signals and orders of the commander – wild, unsteady fire is worse than useless. Each man should satisfy himself that every time he pulls the trigger he will hit the object aimed at. Rapid fire may be used when occasion demands, but must never become reckless expenditure of ammunition at the fastest possible rate'.

Although there was discomfort at Whitburn, the battalion did extremely well in its musketry and came out top of the 32nd Division with Sgt. Arthur Bailey of 'A' Company scoring the highest number of points of any man in the 32nd Division. The shooting consisted of practises ranging from 100 yards to 600 yards and details of grouping, snap shooting and rapid, in the prone, kneeling and standing positions. Sgt. Bailey was, before enlisting, a member of the Knowle Constitutional Rifle club and was on the clerical staff of the Bristol Tramways Company before enlisting in the battalion immediately on its formation.

Sadly, it was discovered on preparing to leave for Codford that 'Jim' the battalion mascot was missing. Nothing could be done and the battalion proceeded on without him.

1915 – Goodbye to Bristol

Sgt. Arthur Bailey – highest scorer of the 32nd Division

Codford

As the Brigade's time at Whitburn was nearing its end, orders were received to entrain for Codford on Salisbury Plain for divisional training. The battalion set off on 19th August, the journey South being long and slow arriving eventually at Wylie station which was around two miles distant from the camp. It took a full day to move all baggage from station to camp.

On the very southern edge of Salisbury plain lie two adjacent villages: Codford St. Peter and Codford St. Mary, both taking their names from their respective village churches. Near Codford St. Mary was built early in the war a large camp of wooden huts. The battalion occupied parts of camps 3 and 4 of the main Codford camp. The hutted accommodation offered greater shelter than the flimsy tents of Wensleydale, providing relatively comfortable quarters. The intention of training at Codford was to practise the battalion at working as part of the division whereas Wensleydale provided mainly brigade level training. With every step up the army organisation came more intense training. It involved harder work and longer hours.

The Command of Bristol's Own (27th July)

At the time Lt. Col. Burges was selected as Commander of the battalion, he had already been retired from the army for some years. He was aware that due to his seniority and the policy of the War Office of sending only comparatively young officers to the front, it meant that he would not be taking the battalion to war. He was the oldest C.O. in the 32nd Division. So the announcement made in late July, that his successor had been named, came with a certain degree of regret, but not surprise. It was considered among the whole battalion a pity that a man of such ability and one so popular with his fellow officers and men should, solely on account of his years, have to relinquish his command.

It was, however, gratifying that command of the battalion was passed to an officer with Bristol connections. Lt. Col Archer-Shee D.S.O. was, at one time, agent for the Bank of England in Bristol. He had commenced his service in the Royal Navy as a Midshipman on board HMS Cleopatra. He then left the Naval Service and joined the 18th Hussars and served in the South African Campaign throughout the Siege of Ladysmith, where he was awarded the Distinguished Service Order for distinguished conduct in the field.

Command was handed over to Lt. Col. Archer-Shee on the 16th August.

Lt. Col. Martin Archer-Shee DSO

Lt. Col. Burges commented on the battalion at the time of his handing over to Lt. Col. Archer-Shee:
"I am impressed with the earnest yet cheerful demeanour of the men and their excellent behaviour during my time with the battalion. They had all joined up to do a job. And in their determination to get on with that job, they were prepared to shed their civilian habits and attitudes which might interfere with their preparation for that task. As such, they may now be classed as soldiers."

Lt. E.H. Burris in a letter to Lt. Col. Burges
"Dear Col. Burges,
I feel that I should like to write you, especially as it was my misfortune to be away when you bid us farewell, to say how exceedingly sorry I am that you are no longer with us. After being with you and under your command for practically a year it does not seem the same here and I only hope that when the great heat does come off we shall do justice to all your labours for the welfare of the 12th. Trusting soon to hear that the country is still to have the benefit of your service."

I am, Yours sincerely
Lt. E.H. Burris."

The nature of the battalion's involvement in the war and, how it would fare in the front line once committed was at this time, unknown. For this reason, recruitment for the battalion continued. Indeed, some of the men that enlisted at this time and up until the end of 1915 would, find themselves posted to the battalion as drafts, during 1916.

The battalion was now entering its final phase of training before proceeding overseas. Consequently life at Codford was marked by very hard work, day and night operations being carried out on a large scale, frequently and in all weathers. Work was very hard and seen on a much larger scale than anything the men had done before. It became the norm to sleep out under the stars and during the cold autumnal nights much discomfort was suffered. It was a painful process to begin with, and never it got better, though its value in preparing the men for active service was appreciated. At the very least, it was a case of learning what 'extra' clothing would be needed in order to be as comfortable as possible. Men learnt quickly.

Usual procedure involved a march out in the afternoon, reaching the rendezvous early in the evening. Rendezvous being a field or piece of open ground. Here the men would make themselves as 'comfortable' as circumstances and the cold and the rain would permit. At around midnight it would be time to move again.

The men would start a long tramp over fields, roads, ditches and woods in Indian file, and eventually come to, an hour before dawn. A shivering wait, for an hour or more during which time most men would become part and parcel of the frozen soil. A rapid thawing took place during the ensuing dashing, running and crawling around until such time as the operation ended.

14780 L/Cpl Ralph Smith
"I went on a 'bombing' course. At that time the bombs or hand grenades that were available were very primitive. A bomb consisted of a tin filled with explosive which we filled through a small hole in the top, then cut a length of fuse 5 inches long and inserted it to a certain depth allowing a 5 seconds explosion. Off then to some trenches to test. Someone would light the fuse while we held the bombs at arms length. We then had to count to 3 before throwing it. Was pleased a few days later to hear I had passed and was entitled to wear a grenade on my sleeve."

14596 Pte. William Ayres
"We signallers were taken up on a hill for drill before breakfast – which was not very popular. We practised across the slopes with morse, semaphore, and even heliograph. We spent our first all night manoeuvre out on the plain – and wasn't it cold!"

1st and 2nd line practise trenches Salisbury Plain

The Royal Engineers had been busy on the plain. A full scale first and second line trench system had been dug with interconnecting communications trenches. The system went on for around a mile and could hold many hundreds of men. It was intended as acclimatisation in preparation for the real thing in France. Much time was spent in it during the day and at night. Dummy charges would be let off from time to time to simulate artillery and mortars. Snipers were set up out in front and would take pot shots if anyone exposed themselves. Umpires were on hand and had to determine casualties. As preparation for the men, it was regarded by all as immensely valuable.

1915 – Goodbye to Bristol

14803 Pte Robert Trott
"The simulated trench system that had been dug on the plain seemed very realistic to us at the time. It was very valuable in preparing us for the real thing. When we finally got to the real thing we reflected on how accurate it actually had been, but of course, the real thing was wetter and damaged by shell fire."

14916 Pte. Albert Pope
"The practise trench was good. Spending a night in it you really got the feel of what to expect. By that I mean not only how to conduct yourself in a trench but also how to try to stay dry and warm, and I mean dry and warm in relative terms."

2nd in Command Major Blennerhassett and Captain Clifford. *'The establishment does not provide a horse for the second in command'*

1915 – Goodbye to Bristol

BRISTOL'S OWN
12th (S) Batt. Glo'ster Regt.
ONE of the very finest in the country
WANT MEN.
Recruiting Office, Guildhall, Broad Street.

Lt. Col. Archer-Shee at Codford, soon after taking over command of the battalion

1915 – Goodbye to Bristol

Battalion officers in informal mood at Codford

2nd/Lt.'s Fitzgerald, Fitzmaurice, Parr and Gurney at Codford

1915 – Goodbye to Bristol

During August the main body of the battalion was joined by the two depot or reserve Companies, 'E' and 'F'. It was always intended to take full battalion strength of around one thousand men overseas and the two reserve Companies were formed with the view of maintaining that. As it was, however, battalion strength at that time was far in excess of full battalion strength numbers. At the time of the June 1915 nominal roll creation, the battalion had at its disposal 1,555 men. And so, a full review was carried out, resulting in many men being posted away from the battalion: men who had particular skills that would be of use to other units, men whose ages were considered near or even above the upper age limit were transferred to the 15th Gloucesters a unit formed as a reserve unit in order to train replacements for the battalion; some men were discharged on medical grounds; and still more granted commissions. 'E' and 'F' Companies were then disbanded and the men fed into the four main Companies. As a result, battalion strength at the time it sailed for France, apart from the officers, was 990 men. This is very odd as at this time Bristol newspapers were still placing advertisements for men to join the battalion. Why? Simple. Battle casualty replacements. Though this was clearly not pubilcised.

20089 Pte. William James
"I joined 'Bristol's Own' in May 1915 and was placed in 'E' Company. When the main battalion left for Yorkshire in June, 'E' and 'F' Companies went to Sutton Coldfield until we were reunited with the battalion at Codford in August. 'E' and 'F' were then split amongst 'A', 'B', 'C' and 'D' Companies, myself going to 'A' Company under command of Captain Colt."

The departure for France took place early on Sunday morning, 21st November 1915. The preceding day, was busy and the evening involved keen celebrations to mark the end of training in England. These celebrations were quite necessarily of an uproarious kind, but apparently there were no broken heads but very many fat ones the following morning. Any poorly feelings though were very quickly driven out early next morning by sheer exertion and exhaustion as the three mile march to the station was accompanied by a load which would have exasperated a pack mule.

The parade for departure took place in rather impressive surroundings in the early hours with the moonlight shining through a light mist. In these surroundings and with many men shivering, the chaplain, the Reverend J. F. L. Southam said a short prayer after which the journey for entrainment began.

14585 Pte. Robert Barnes
"We paraded in 'full marching order' at around 1 a.m. Sunday morning for the march to Wylie station for embarkation. And 'full marching order' meant heavier packs than ever before. We also wore our great coats and in our packs were our ground sheet, a spare pair of boots, a blanket, spare shirts, washing and shaving kit, writing material and numerous gadgets that our families and friends at home thought would surely be useful!"

14780 L/Cpl Ralph Smith
"Soon afterwards, everyone was confined to camp and guards placed around the camp so that no one could leave. Next night we paraded but did not know our destination. We were marched to Wylie station a few miles from the camp where a train was waiting to take us to Folkestone. That was 21st November."

Capt H.A. Colt
"At midnight that night we fell in. It was a bright moonlit night, but cold. With each man carrying one or more blankets, we marched from our camp at Codford to Wylie station where we entrained to the dismal tune of 'Keep the home fires burning'. At no time previously had I been fond of this piece of music; since that time I have positively loathed it.

"So we started on the 'great adventure' for which we had been so carefully trained. Some of us never to return, others to come home wounded (a good many to do this latter more than once), while a few were destined to remain out with the battalion till the end.

"None of us had any correct notion as to what exactly things would be like at the Front but we had several things in our favour, to wit:- our men were volunteers and of splendid physique and morale; we had been in training for thirteen months and during that time had come out on top of the Division in shooting; we knew that we could rely on each other to the death, and last but not least we knew that those at home would be looked after by the Comforts Committee."

Most of the battalion were glad to be finally off. The men had joined up to fight the Germans and they were now anxious to get on with it, remembering all the while that they were fresh troops and had not, as yet, tasted the very bitter and disheartening experiences of the battlefield.

14596 Pte. William Ayres
"The general talk on the way and in the train was: 'Where are we going?'. The most likely destination was France but there was always the possibility that it might be somewhere else."

The time on the train passed by and at about 11 a.m. it arrived at Folkestone harbour. The train was promptly vacated and the battalion proceeded aboard the ship 'Stranraer', struggling to fit into their life jackets. Including the battalion transport and baggage which had sailed on the 20th from Southampton to Le Havre, under command of Major Blennerhassett, the total battalion strength was 31 officers and 990 other ranks.

The disposition of the battalion at this time was as follows:

Commander: Lt. Col. M. Archer-Shee D.S.O. M.P.
2nd I/C: Major W.A.R. Blennerhassett
Adjutant: Captain J.K. Likemen
Captain T. Balston
M/C Gun Officer: Lt. A. V. Shewell
Quatermaster: Lt A. H. Lane
M.O. Lt. A. Johns
Transport: Lt T. A. Wilmot
Lt. H. E. V. Sants

'A' Company
Captain H.A. Colt
Captain C. D. Fowler
Lt. W.W. Parr
Lt. F. E. Gurney
Lt. J. H. Allen
Lt. R. Hosegood

'B' Company
Major Lee-Warner
Captain E.A. Robinson
Lt. Gedye
Lt. Fitzmaurice
Lt. R.J. Fitzgerald
Lt. G.R.A. Beckett

'C' Company
Lt. N. F. Ryder
Lt. S. Lloyd
Lt. C. Barrington
Lt.T. A. Wilmot

'D' Company
Captain T.M. Allison
Captain H.E.V. Sants
Lt. H. D. Cooper
Lt.H. E. Lambert
Lt. J. P. Webb
Lt. H. Taylor

1915 – Goodbye to Bristol

"GOTT STRAFE Glo'ster!"

DOUBLE GLOSTER

The Gloster Regiment "The Slashers"

Chapter VI

1915 - France

Before departure each man was issued with a card containing a message from Lord Kitchener to men of the Expeditionary Force:

"Be invariably courteous, considerate, and kind. Never do anything likely to injure or destroy property, and always look upon looting as a disgraceful act. You are sure to meet with a welcome and to be trusted; your conduct must justify that welcome and that trust.

"Your duty cannot be done unless your health is sound. So keep constantly on your guard against any excess. In this new experience you may find temptations both in wine and women. You must entirely resist both temptations, and, while treating all women with perfect courtesy, you should avoid any intimacy.
Do your duty bravely.
Fear God,
Honour the King."

20089 Pte. William James
"After reading Lord Kitchener's message, we all wondered what was in store for us. And it has to be said that some men were quite looking forward to it!"

The crossing to Boulogne was uneventful though a bit choppy. To most of the men it was yet another new experience.

14596 Pte. William Ayres
"I was sea sick on the crossing, but in the few moments when I was not being sick, I remember seeing the Royal Navy destroyers sweeping around and around our ship."

On arrival at Boulogne the battalion disembarked and, to the rather dissonant strains of "Le Sambre et la Meuse" somewhat indifferently performed by the band, marched to Ostrahove rest camp at the top of the hill overlooking the Channel.

14314 Pte. Harold Hayward
"As we passed through the town and proceeded up a very steep hill towards our camp I noticed women leaning from their windows, counting our numbers. I have often wondered why they did this."

The men marched into camp and immediately cast off their heavy packs. After having washed and fed, they were led by the C.O., on horse back, on a march through the town.

16612 Pte. Sam Bollom
"We marched past a V.A.D. hospital in town with bayonets fixed and arms swinging. We were full of beans as we hadn't seen any action. Then we heard a voice from a top window in the hospital shouting "Are you downhearted?" and we all yelled back "No!" when the voice answered "Well, you bloody well soon will be"

That night a group of officers, intent on making the most of what would probably be their last night of freedom for some time, set off into Boulogne for dinner. Apparently, one or two of these officers were so impressed with the cuisine that they went through the Table d' Hote a second time. Whilst the officers were enjoying themselves, the men were attempting to keep warm in their tents in the sub zero temperature.

16612 Pte. Sam Bollom
"The camp was not very clean. During the very first night there, the lice started getting at us. I

foolishly threw away my under clothes as I thought that would get rid of them. I then had to go through the winter without underclothes. I'll never forget it."

Next morning, 22nd November, Joseph Storch, battalion interpreter joined and the battalion entrained at Boulogne's Gare Central station.

Capt H.A. Colt
"We detrained and for the first time experienced the pleasure that we were so often to have, that of marching back alongside the railway line for two or three miles. This was not, however, the end of our journey as we had another five or six miles before we arrived at our destination. It was abominable going, and it had been freezing, while the snow was piled up by the side f the road."

20089 Pte. William James
"As I remember it we were going over high ground and the road was covered with ice. With our hob nailed boots, everyone had at least one tumble, but I don't remember anyone with broken bones."

It was usual practise throughout the army when on long marches to spend 50 minutes at the march followed by 10 minutes, after the tricky ritual of piling arms, at rest. The added weight of 'full marching order' became an uncomfortable nuisance.

14780 L/Cpl Ralph Smith
"On one march we saw the first taste of one of the army's punishments known as crucifixion. It was the sight of a soldier from some regiment in the centre of a village tied hand and foot to the wheel of a gun carriage. It was shocking to see and we later learnt he would have been taken down for meals, and sleep at night and then returned to his punishment."

14596 Pte. William Ayres
"When we left Boulogne our first marches were long ones and the weight heavy. Quite soon things began to be 'dumped'. Many pairs of boots were 'lost' and while we dare not lose our ground sheets or blankets, many of those extra 'might be useful' things were left behind. I remember watching one man who carefully went right through his pack, shaking his head at one thing and another, until he came to a jar of Vaseline. He threw the Vaseline jar as far as he could. Then everything remaining went back into his pack."

Capt H.A. Colt
"At about 11 a.m. we reached Buigny l'Abbe, a small village not far from Abbeville, where Major Blennerhassett and the transport and baggage had arrived the day before. Here we spent a few days quietly and uneventfully. However, lack of familiarity with local conditions was responsible for breaking of the village pump and for the mules being allowed to 'ring' the trees. One subaltern, it is true, did cause a certain amount of excitement, when, after two days in the village, he suddenly went to the Maire's at about 10.30 p.m. and demanded straw for his 'poor men'. Buigny l' Abbe was about as miserable a village as any we were billeted in."

Sunday 28th November the battalion moved off, eventually arriving at Bertangles, after a 16 mile march, where it remained a couple of days. It was here that certain officers used their initiatives to good effect. Finding themselves placed in a miserable billet, around which hung an unpleasant smell, it occurred to them to see the sort of billet occupied by the interpreter and the R.S.M. Within half an hour these officers had a new billet with a clean and comfortable mess room and excellent beds in an out building, while the interpreter – who did the billeting-declared that he would sooner sleep in an empty stable than the billet he had received in exchange from the officers.

14138 Cpl. Norman Pegg (in a letter to a friend)
"I think we can look upon our first few days in France with satisfaction. We have not seen any fighting yet but have accomplished three marches that would have tried the most tested pedestrian. All events which have taken place at and since our departure from Salisbury Plain produce a kaleidoscopiceffect

on the mind. First of all before marching from the camp, in the very early hours of one morning, the Lord's Prayer was repeated amid surroundings which I describe only as sombre. Then a short march, a long train ride, a trans-channel trip, and we were in France. We made a stay of a day or two at a place you have undoubtedly seen on the map but which had better remain nameless. Another fairly long train journey and a very hard march was the work of another day and then followed a sojourn of several days duration at a small village. Here we were billeted in barns, or anything which afforded cover from the inclement conditions. During all this time the weather was fair, without being fine, but when we next made a move, it became colder.

"Our second long march was to a large village, or small town, and the next day we accomplished the longest march we have done since we have been this side of the channel. We covered the long distance in good time. From the spot where we settled down for dinner we could see, in the far distance, a famous French town which I suppose, everyone knows, not geographically but historically. We are now in another village and I, at any rate, am comfortably situated in another barn, which contains plenty of straw and a rare variety of draughty holes and windy nooks. Of course, on active service nobody expects home-like conditions, but I will say that, in spite of the heavy marching we have done so far, it has been anything but dispiriting, and all of us are as cheerful as ever we have been. It is a fact that everyone I have met has certainly not given me the appearance of being down in the dumps. You may be interested to know that among some battalions out here we have already earned the soubriquet of 'pack mules' because we carry our loads on the tramp with apparently more ease than others we have met."

The next stop was Sailly Laurette. It was very overcrowded as the remainder of the Brigade were there also. This was 2nd December and the battalion was now only two days away from the front line. Excitement grew and, with the front line very close at hand, orders were received next day for the battalion to move less 2 Companies, 2 machine gun sections and half the ambulance section: in all 17 officers and 486 other ranks. The route took them via Bray-sur-Somme to Suzanne, a village a short distance from the front line trenches at Maricourt. Suzanne possessed a handsome chateau, the property of a well known French nobleman. The chateau, although not much more than a mile from the trenches was, even as late as 1916, unscathed. The village itself was not greatly damaged but the German snipers had the nasty habit of firing into the streets.

4th December was a landmark day for the battalion. It began its period of trench instruction under the watchful eyes of experienced regular troops. It consisted of 48 hours in the line, followed by 48 hours rest back at Suzanne.

14780 L/Cpl Ralph Smith

"Four of us out of each Company were told we had to parade on the evening as we had to have one night and one day of experience in the front line with regular troops of the 1st East Surreys. A guide came to us at night to take us to the long communication trench leading to the front line. Our first taste of real mud and also a dead soldier on a stretcher. I'm sure every one of us had a sense of shock and realisation but were afraid to show it. At Maricourt – 'A' Company were under instruction of the 2nd Battalion East Surreys and 'B' Company under instruction of the 2nd Battalion Inniskilling Fusiliers".

Capt H.A. Colt

"The next day 'A' and 'B' Companies marched to Suzanne, 'C' and 'D' Companies remaining at Sailly Lorette. On the way we had to cross the crest of a hill in artillery formation, as we were in view of the enemy. In Suzanne we were very crowded, as we were in addition to the normal garrison and there were quite a lot of civilians in the village. The following day the officers and Companies went into the line at Maricourt. The trenches occupied by us fell into three groups:

1. Nos. 10, 11, & 12 trenches
2. Nos. 13, 14, & 15 trenches
3. Nos. 16, 17, & 18 trenches

"No. 10 trench ran down an arm of the river. In the rear of it was an old water mill – beyond it was a rather nasty detached post. This was used as 'A' Company headquarters and also as a pigeon station. It is *superfluous to add that the undisciplined habits of the two pigeon fanciers soon got thoroughly on the nerves of the O.C. 'A' Company i.e. me!*

"No. 11 trench was principally remarkable for having an isolated post - 'The Crows Nest' – the reverse side of a steep cliff known as the Chaperu Gendarme.

"No. 13 trench was the only trench free from mud. It was on a bit of a hill. In the dead ground in the rear, from hear the Company cooks performed – and got shelled if they made too much smoke.

"No. 15 trench resembled a hand with outstretched fingers – it was really a glorified 'sap'.

"Nos. 12, 14, 16, 17, and 18 trenches were not remarkable for anything much, bar that the last named touched the Maricourt–Perronne road. Battalion H.Q. was in a dip about a mile in the rear."

Men of 1 Platoon 'A' Company in billets, Suzanne

From the billets in Suzanne the ingoing Companies had to proceed 'up the line' along a stretch of communication trench. Ordinarily this would have presented few problems, aside from the odd shell or sniper's bullet. But it was winter, and it was wet. Life in the trenches was a continual struggle against the mud. Although men worked hard with pumps, mud scoops and shovels, it was like trying to empty a bath with a teaspoon.

14780 L/Cpl Ralph Smith
"Our Company 'D', found the mud much worse than had been imagined. Instead of being quiet, there was so much swearing and shouting in the dark that the Germans thought an attack was in progress. They immediately sent up red flares and then the shelling started. Fortunately we suffered no casualties, only a shock to our dignity and a lesson well learned."

13986 L/Cpl. Robert Anstey
"Not a propitious time for breaking in a New Army battalion, the winter, probably the worst of the war, was marked by constant rain and some snow. Fortunately for us, we were associated with regular soldiers, who had a happy go lucky way of treating all things including the weather. So to them the miseries

of the mud were not very much at all. Here, the battalion held its first trench sector, on the high ground overlooking the Somme marshes."

Sentry duty was an important and critical skill the men had to learn. Clear Instructions were duly issued:

"Sentries are look out men posted to give timely notice of the movements or approach of the enemy. The first duty of a sentry is to see without being seen. He must not move about, nor should he lie down unless ordered to do so. Anything approaching drowsiness must be resisted with the greatest determination. A sentry who sleeps at his post commits a capital military crime, which is punishable on active service by death and at other times by imprisonment."

14314 Pte. Harold Hayward
"We proceeded up the communications trench for instruction under the Inniskilling Fusiliears. Rough lads but generous. No. 10 fire trench slopped down to the Somme marshes where we watched petrol engined boats mounted with machine guns patrolling the river manned by men of the Scottish Rifles. We were constantly baling the trench with our dixies but getting nowhere. The mud was so glutinous that it sucked at our gum boots so that all we could do was cut the straps and step out of them and continue in our stockinged feet. Strangely enough, the mud kept our feet warm but the wind was so cold."

14780 L/Cpl Ralph Smith
"My section was posted at an outpost called 'The Bluff'. It was an extended trench leading out from the front line, a kind of observation post. I had already noticed blood on the sand bags and discovered it was due to a raid carried out by the Germans creeping down at night and bombing it. I posted two sentries instead of the usual one throughout the night and also took turns myself. The men did 2 hours on and 4 hours off, while a Section Leader only had 2 hours off, having to post new guards every two hours, but I generally made up for my sleep in the morning.

"The trenches had been churned into mud, mud that was often waist deep! Before entering the trenches, every man took from a pile, two thigh length gum boots similar to waders. These were already wet and heavy with mud from constant use and, so equipped, we started on the slow journey to the front line.

"Later in the week 14639 Pte J. Clark was on guard in the trench when dawn broke. He was curious to see if there was any activity across no-man's land, started moving the periscope around and was promptly shot by a German sniper. He had to wait until nightfall on the stretcher before being taken away."

14596 Pte. William Ayres
"The mud was thick and slimy and in places the clay gave it an even thicker, sucking consistency that gripped and held the gum boot so that it could not be pulled out, in which case the unfortunate wearer could only lift his leg out of the boot and go on bare footed. The communication trench was not particularly long but, due to the conditions, it would take the whole of a long winter night to complete the relief with the outgoing battalion.

"Conditions were such that troops could not be left in the front line for more than 48 hours, so the tedious routine of relief had to be carried out every other night. The only shelter while in the line was the holes in the side of the trench, or in the crude dugouts, where the mud was often as deep as in the trench outside.

"We signallers used an early, simple type of field telephone that was connected between the Companies and battalion headquarters with thin wire – so thin and so easily breakable and when it was broken, usually by shell fire, out two of us would go to find the break and repair it."

14780 L/Cpl Ralph Smith
"We endured the going into the line because we had to. But when it was time for our relief, in the dark, of course, my pals and I used to climb over the back of the firing line and grope our way to the road. There was a risk of machine guns or spasmodic rifle fire or Very lights which lit up the whole ground."

13986 L/Cpl. Robert Anstey
"The trenches of course were full of that precious liquid, mud, and a great deal of the time was spent in pumping out the water. This would have been a fairly profitable and easy task but for a small defect in the

pumping machines. The idea at the back of the designer's mind was, no doubt, excellent but the pumps displayed a perversity which could hardly be foreseen. By using the handle, the water should have passed peaceably through the attached pipe and out of the trench altogether, but it persisted in spurting all over the energetic fellow who was manipulating the affair, dampening his energies and himself to an appalling degree."

Men of 1 Platoon 'A' Company in the trenches at Maricourt

Capt H.A. Colt
"The trenches at Maricourt were the worst we ever encountered in the way of mud. It appeared that, with the best of intentions, the floor of the trenches had been so tidied up that all hurdle revetment had been undercut. In fine weather this did not matter much. Just before we went in, however, there had been a week or two of hard frost, followed by a thaw and, simultaneously the trenches had begun to fall in. On top of this came the rain – the result being thick, sticky, Somme mud, which meant that to go into the trenches one had to plough through 2 ½ miles of a gluey composition that reached well over the knees.

1915 – France

"Nor would any description of Maricourt be complete that did not mention the rats. Those beastly rodents simply swarmed! In a very short time all the packs and haversacks had holes chewed into them. One man, determined to safeguard his breakfast, concealed it on his person when he lay down to rest. In about half an hour he was awakened by a struggle in progress on his chest. Two rats had made their way through his greatcoat and tunic and were wrestling for his loaf of bread!"

Conditions in the trenches had, so far been a rude awakening to the men, though they were accepted and tolerated. It was also accepted that of all the experiences that made up their lot, being cold and damp, or even wet, represented the biggest factor in reducing morale. Wet feet rapidly became cold feet. Whale oil was available and religiously applied, under orders, to men's feet. This was intended to ward off possible trench foot and its most unpleasant effects. It did not, however, remove the discomfort. The battalion began to suffer trench foot casualties.

Cold, for the men was another and possibly the greatest enemy. A man might wear long johns, thick socks, wool vest, a thick army shirt and knitted cardigan, but still the cold would get to him. He might double his vests, add newspapers and oiled waistcoats, it made little difference. All this, in addition to the hazards of war and of the duties of a sentry, standing to, signal communications, feeding and the normal process of just keeping alive.

14803 Pte Robert Trott
"The cold crept under our clothing, our fingers were numb and our joints ached. Fires were not possible so it was simply a matter of jumping up and down and swinging our arms around. Puttees did not stop mud from getting into your boots. And the gum boots made your skin wrinkled in preparation for trench foot. It was weeks before I regained any feelings in my toes."

Lice were a common menace and a constant problem to all men and entirely inescapable. They looked like tiny lobsters and fed twelve times a day by holding onto clothing fibres with their six feet as they drank blood. They bred in dirty clothing and laid five eggs daily. Scratching in the filthy conditions of trench life risked impetigo, boils or ulcers. Few counter measures were possible. Thumb nails were used to crack visible lice eggs followed by a candle run up the seams of clothing: the art was to destroy the lice without burning a hole in the clothing. Powder was issued to smear over the body to combat the lice. The men, however, swore it only fed them. They were known as 'chats'. 'Chatting' was a highly sociable activity of two pals delousing each other and talking at the same time. The term remains in our social vocabulary today.

Concerned people from home sent out various remedies to the problem of lice. *Harrison's Pomade* went under the slogan 'Kill that insect Tommy'. So the advertising said, 'It kills every insect in hair and body' and could be had from all chemists at 4 1/2d per tin. The front line lice were only marginally deterred by it. *Keating's Powder* was another favourite. But in the end the only real check was the army laundry service and this only for a time if all clothes were treated. But there would be eggs that would escape the treatment in the seams of the clothes.

Lice caused Trench Fever, a particularly painful disease that began suddenly with severe pain followed by high fever. Recovery - away from the trenches - took up to twelve weeks. In addition to the lice were the inescapable 'nits' which infested hair. Many men chose to shave their heads and pubic hair entirely to avoid this prevalent scourge.

Next on the list of loathsome creatures were the rats. Rats were a constant companion in the trenches in their millions they were everywhere, gorging themselves on human remains they could grow to the size of a cat. With an absence of cats in the front line, surplus food dropped and corpses lying around rats multiplied with amazing fertility. Men armed themselves when possible with shovels and killed them in their dozens, but they were fighting a losing battle as only 1 pair of rats could produce 900 offspring in a year.

Though they were a constant and numerous pests in the trenches, the rats generally preferred parapet sand bags to trenches and would burrow in the dead rather than risk the retribution of the living. Often the only relief men could get from them was to pull a great coat right over the head, and try to ignore what was scampering about over and around. But again, thanks to the example set them by the regular soldiers there, the men remained cheery, regardless. But the men's displeasure didn't end with lice and rats. In the trenches and shell holes were multitudes of frogs. Huge slugs and horned beetles crowded the sides of the trenches.

Lt. Gedye from a letter sent to the Bristol Times & Mirror dated 19th December:
"We are getting used to the life now, although the mud is awful, which is right up to the waist in places. We have had some casualties, of course, but considering the amount of shells that come over and the constant sniping, it is surprising there have not been more. We shall be in the trenches on Christmas Day but expect to be merry and bright. The fellows keep up their spirits surprisingly well, and some of the battalions that have been here since the beginning of the war are simply wonderful. One fellow fell into a great shell hole at five o'clock one night up to his waist, and was dug out at eight the next morning. It froze around him, when he came up into the fire trench he was whistling!"

Pte. Fred Hore of 1 Platoon 'A' Company in a trench at Maricourt

1915 – France

14314 Pte. Harold Hayward
"Maricourt was a quiet sector compared with what we were to experience later. Apart from the threat of snipers, the shelling consisted of two or three 'whizz-bangs' coming over each night. I remember on one occasion a Bosche aeroplane dropped 15" long steel darts onto us. No one was injured but they became the source of great interest as everyone wanted to inspect them."

Within a few days 'C' and 'D' Companies had received their initiation under the 1st East Surreys and the 1st D.C.L.I. respectively. All four Companies had now experienced front line duties while their operational abilities were assessed. They all showed up well compared to other 95th Brigade battalions in their initial effort and were by 9th December adjudged fit for active service.

Of the many aspects of trench life the 12th Gloucesters learnt at Maricourt, profound respect for the German snipers probably topped the list.

13986 L/Cpl. Robert Anstey
"Besides being a remarkable rifleman, he had patience and would lie in wait for a victim for hours. There were, of course, British snipers and with a view to stimulating the sharp shooter of one of the companies to increased exertions, an officer offered a monetary reward for every German who was bowled over in this way. This, no doubt, had its effect on added earnings on the part of our marksmen".

As Christmas approached, it was Christmas 1914 that was on the minds of many. The fine food, the cosy billets, the merriment and the family atmosphere. It was hard to imagine a greater contrast as they left their parcels from home with the transport and proceeded 'up the line' on Christmas Eve, where they were to remain until Boxing Day. On Christmas Day however, the German snipers seemed to possess a little more good will than usual. They remained quiet all day.

14780 L/Cpl Ralph Smith
"We spent Christmas Day 1915 in the front line, amongst all that bloody mud with a cup of cold stew for our Christmas dinner. That stew had to be brought through all that mud so I really think we all thought of the difficulties of getting it to us. For washing and shaving we saved a little of our mug of tea and wetted our face and neck with the shaving brush then shaved the best we could. If there was snow then we used to melt that."

14314 Pte. Harold Hayward
"The Germans, not 300 yards in front of us were celebrating, evident by the amount of smoke rising from numerous fires. Things were not as good for us for our hot rations failed to turn up."

On the 26th December came a major re-organisation. The 95th Brigade transferred to the 5th Regular Division. The Birmingham city battalions of the Royal Warwickshire Regiment were moved to other brigades of the 5th Division. The 12th Battalion Gloucestershire Regiment remained and were joined by three regular battalions:

1st Battalion Duke of Cornwall's Light Infantry
1st East Surrey Regiment
1st Devonshire Regiment

Billets in Suzanne improved after the Brigade adjustment. However, even then a certain company commander was heard on one occasion to upbraid his Company Quartermaster Sergeant at the poverty of the accommodation allotted to him in exchange for his comparatively comfortable trench!

In general, army issue clothing was not designed for the cold and wet conditions experienced in the trenches. Socks, for example, were constantly wet and not enough pairs were issued to allow the wearing of a dry pair whilst the wet ones dried. Men would write home asking for extra socks and additional warm clothing.

With so many of the officers and men drawn from Bristol families it was not surprising that those at home were anxious to see to it that comforts be sent to the men on active service and, to that end, a committee was formed of officer's wives and mothers with Mrs. Robinson of Lawrence Weston as honourable Treasurer and Mrs. Holman of Grey House, Downs Park East as honourable Secretary . The idea of a Ladies Comforts Committee originated with the wife of the C.O. Mrs. Archer-Shee, who, with the wife of the Second-in-Command, Mrs. Blennerhassett, took the initial steps in the movement which resulted in £100 being raised but, satisfactory as that amount was, it did not go far in providing comforts for all the men. Therefore appeals for gifts of money and kind – socks, scarves, cardigans, comforters, pullovers, capes, candles, chocolates and oxo and any other useful items were launched. Ladies started knitting anything and everything that would make the men's lives a little more comfortable. Their efforts were appreciated very much. Many letters of gratitude were received by the committee. Among them:

15019 C.S.M. George Townsend to Mrs. Holman
"On behalf of the non-commissioned officers and men of 'C' Company, I beg to tender my warmest thanks for the socks, note-paper and envelopes, and playing cards which your committee has sent us.
"Under ordinary circumstances, Government issues of socks would be ample, but here the trenches are in such a 'treacley' state that one cannot have too many pairs, so that your gifts are verily 'Godsends'.
"Every recipient is truly grateful and sends his best wishes to you and your committee, wishing its members a happy New Year; hoping that before another year has elapsed , the battalion will have done its share and return home."

Lt. Beckett
"It was exceedingly kind of you to send the books and they are very highly appreciated. If you had seen the men huddled up in little groups, sitting on straw in barns, reading them by the light of a flickering candle, I am sure you would feel more than repaid for all your labours."

Lt. R. Hosegood
"The Christmas puddings were so appreciated on Christmas Day. When I went around my men in the trenches, they gave me a taste, and it was very excellent."

Several relatively minor incidents occurred before the battalion's stay at Maricourt ended.

On 29th December 2nd/Lt. Fitzgerald – who was to become renowned throughout the battalion for his daring trench raids – with Sgt. Pope and two men from 'B' Company, attempted to bomb an enemy sap on the Perrone Road. It was unsuccessful.

The second incident occurred only two days before the battalion was due to leave the area. At about 3 a.m. on 6th January the enemy sent a bombing party to attack an outpost, in the form of a large bush, in which were a number of sentries. The enemy's approach was detected and the post evacuated, just as the attackers hurled their bombs into the bush. The sentries replied with bombs and rifle fire and, after having driven off the attackers, returned to their post.

Captain Colt had joined the battalion in September 1914. He had previously served in the Royal Navy and was to become known as a fearless leader on the battlefield. On one occasion, at night, he went out in front of the trenches and, on returning, was challenged. Either the sentry did not hear or he did not wait for a reply, for he fired at Captain Colt at almost point blank range, and missed. When Captain Colt returned, by a safer route, he asked who had fired. The sentry answered, and was told that he was a rotten shot – using words of a somewhat colourful nature to that effect.

Due to the Maricourt trenches being in a 'quiet' sector, casualties were light, but inevitable. The first fatalities occurred on the 10th December: 14903 Pte. Alfred Stanley Lewis of 'C' Company, ironically not to enemy action. He died when a shelter collapsed and crushed him. On the same day, 14861 Pte. Walter Gilbert Collins, again, of 'C' Company was the victim of a sniper.
On 11th December, 16882 Pte. Frederick Edwin Cook was dangerously wounded by a trench mortar and died the same day.

1915 – France

On 13th December, 14042 Pte. Henry Hurley Denning of 'A' Company was sniped. Pte Denning had proved to be an excellent shot during training and was allocated 'special' work which amounted to sniping. He was a tall man and this probably was his undoing. While scanning across no-man's land for enemy movement, he himself was sniped.

On 14th December, 16738 Pte. George Henry Collier of 'B' Company was the battalion's third victim to enemy snipers.

On 16th December, 16620 George Henry James of 'A' Company, who was attached to the West Spring Gun Battery, was killed by a shell.

On 31st December, 14491 Pte. Walter Ernest Davis of 'C' Company died in a base hospital in Rouen. He had been accidentally shot in the foot by 14914 Pte J.G. Place on 11th December. He died due to infection.

On the 8th January, 14763 Pte. Harold Arthur Rich of 'D' Company was killed by a shell.

In addition, three men were wounded.

The men had been prepared to expect death and wounding. Even so, when it happened it was a shocking new experience. Particularly so when, the victim was a pal. Death was never far away. The general attitude was either the fatalistic, 'If it's got your name on it……' or the more trustful 'What is to be will be.' There was a light heartedness in the acceptance of the risk. Humour was found and a very warm comradeship resulted.

13986 Cpl. Robert Anstey
"The first casualty in our Company 'A' was a well liked fellow named Henry Denning, who was shot through the head, at a place in the trench where it came to a dead end. Just before 'stand-to' Lt. Parr came to me and said, "Anstey, you know about Denning. The fellows are a bit shaken. I'm not going to make it an order, but it would be a great help to them if you would take your fellows and change places."

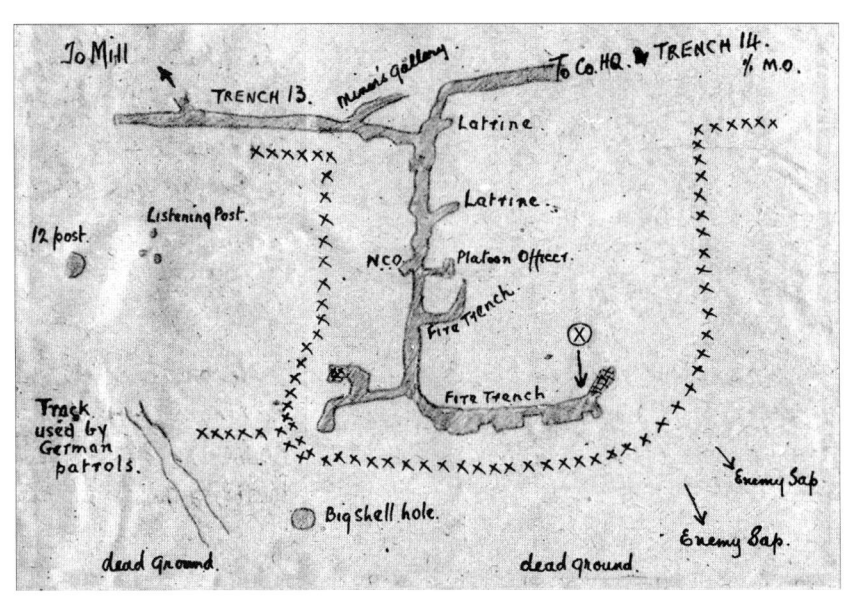

Trench sketch drawn by Lt Parr of 'A' Company's positions at Maricourt. Pte Denning killed where marked 'X'

Chapter VII

1916 – Anybody's Own

Britain's Western Front offensives of 1915 were ill-conceived and poorly planned and lead. Britain was not prepared, either tactically or industrially, during 1915 to engage in any offensives. The battles of Neuve Chapelle in March, Festubert and Aubers Ridge in May and Loos from September until October were all costly, disastrous failures.

However, it was believed that the rising tide of Britain's new armies and its increased munitions supplies by the end of the year promised the means for an offensive far larger in scale than any before to break the trench deadlock.

Britain's armies in France had grown to 36 divisions by the end of 1915. By that time voluntary enlistments, though massive, had nevertheless proved to be inadequate to meet Britain's needs and so, on 27th January 1916, by means of the Military Service Act, voluntary service was replaced by conscription.

Early in January the battalion left the Maricourt Sector. During the rest of the month and February, time was spent in marching and resting. Whilst at Allonville for the first half of February, the battalion was issued with the new 'tin helmets'. They were at first regarded with some amusement and not a little disfavour as being not at all comfortable. In time, however, the benefits were appreciated as an asset affording a certain amount of protection from flying debris that had before caused some serious injuries.

2nd/Lt.'s Hosegood and Allen in a trench at Arras. 2nd/Lt. Allen is fashioning his newly issued steel helmet

14780 L/Cpl Ralph Smith
"We were at Allonville near Amien for a few days. As it was so near Amien, the C.O. granted passes to a few men to visit it. There were only about twenty passes divided among the four Companies. I happened to be lucky to be given one by our Company commander. The C.O. had issued a warning that anyone contracting VD, if single he would personally inform the parents, if married inform the wife, also there would be a forfeiture of pay.

"Three of us from my Company went with the intention of sight seeing. When we passed through there were a dozen or more little children all chanting the only English I think they knew; "Anglais soldat.... my sister 2 francs follow me." They did no business with us. Several street girls would call to us from upstairs windows."

20089 Pte. William James
"We were back for a rest now for a bit before making another move. The weather was very mild there but still wet. We were in a part mentioned in recent fighting in the papers. Up till then everything was going pretty smoothly, although, we had lost a few of our brave lads. It might sound rather callous, but they were soon forgotten over there, as it was a fact of life for us that we had expected and had to get used to.

"It was pleasing to see the lads going about their daily business with indifference to the dangers, laughing and joking as if they were safe in England."

Capt H.A. Colt
"While here, an interesting light was thrown on the financial status of the men of the battalion. So well off were they, having not spent any of their pay, they refused to touch the food provided for them, preferring to purchase most of their meals from the villagers; the amount of letters and parcels too, that came for the battalion gave a most terrific shock to the postman of the other unit billeted in the village – the 1st D.C.L.I.

"The 5th Division had created, some time earlier, a Divisional concert party with a view to entertaining its troops when the opportunity arose. It was named the 'Whizz-Bangs' and its entourage consisted of men from the units of the Division. The 12th Gloucesters contribution was Pte. Bruce Buchanon, a humorist, and also Pte. Fred Smith a magician, both from 'B' Company.

"Advantage was indeed taken of the period of relative inactivity when a concert by the 'Whizz-bangs' was held in a large barn, property of Mr. Hennessy of brandy fame. Bruce Buchanon had the men of 'Bristol's Own' in uncontrollable laughter and the men of the other battalions of the Division in a state of confusion with his recitals using Bristol slang."

Early days yet, but the battalion had already made a very favourable impression. On 18th January, there was an inspection by Major General C.T Mc M. Kavanagh C.V.O., C.B., D.SO. who was very pleased with what he had seen of the battalion. Also, the C.O., himself a veteran of the Boer War and the early days of the present war, felt it appropriate to write to Col. Burges in praise of the battalion that he had inherited from him.

Lt. Col Archer-Shee D.S.O. M.P. in a letter to Col. Burges
"The battalion has now proved its worth at the front and I am extraordinarily pleased with them. We are part of a brigade which comprises, apart from the 12th Battalion, regular army units and all men consider it an honour to be attached to it.

"The men are simply magnificent, having adapted so quickly and eagerly to the discomforts of trench life. Of the officers, I have to say, I believe it would be impossible for me to have a better lot. There is not an inefficient man among them."

At the beginning of February around fifty new drafts were received and 2nd/Lt's. E.L. Hillborne and H.C. Ryland joined for duty, whilst Major F. Wilson-Fox and Captain C.D. Fowler were invalided home as sick and struck off battalion charge accordingly.

One place would be particularly remembered by a few of the men, for it was from Riencourt that the first group of men went on leave on the 24th February. Major Blennerhassett, Captain H.A. Colt and ten men set off.

14780 Pte. Ralph Smith
"I was told that I was to go on leave to England for one week. I was not at all ashamed to admit my nerves were very strained, wondering if my period of life would last out until I made it on leave. Sgt. Radmilovic and I were the only ones from our company, 'C' Company.

"We left the front line when dark, exchanging our French Francs for English money at a Field Post Office to avoid the long queues at kiosks at Victoria station. When we got to Victoria, there were large crowds outside the station to give us a welcome. We then caught a bus to Paddington and a train to Bristol.

"Our compartment became full and we were the centre of attention. We spoke to some people who said our relatives would be excited to see us. I told them they didn't know, so they took my address and promised to telegram when they got off at Reading.

"I'm glad to say my sisters and brother-in-law were at the station waiting for me, while my mother and father anxiously waited at home. Sgt. Radmilovic lived at Weston-Super-Mare so we arranged to meet on our return.

"It was so nice to be at home and sleeping in a comfortable bed after having to sleep with my clothes on for so long. The time passed much too quickly so the time came for departure. But I never told them anything about my experiences at the front. I loved my mother too much to cause her any anxiety.

"Wouldn't let my sisters come to the station to see me off, just my father and brother-in-law. I cannot remember much of the return journey. My thoughts were still at home."

Whilst the lucky men who had received leave were on their way home, the battalion was preparing to move to Arras. Indeed, the men who remained would also remember the place and the march from there to Berteaucourt which began on 25th February. Snow had fallen and it had frozen. The first part was covered during a blizzard. Though being only twelve miles distant, the march lasted some three days and was regarded as the worst march the battalion ever did.

20089 Pte. William James
"One day we did the march during a blizzard. It was snowing the whole time and took us several days to complete. It was a dispiriting sight to see the transport struggling along. Those poor mules were slipping and sliding the whole time."

2nd Lt. Ralph Hosegood
"The march occupied three days, and took place in a fierce blizzard of snow which old members of the 5th Division treasured as a war memory ever after. Events were always dated from 'when we went up to Arras and took over from the French in that snow storm.' We marched only twelve miles but it took from 9.30a.m. one day till about 5.00p.m. three days later. It snowed without stop from the time we left till the end of the march, and was freezing the whole time. It was also blowing a regular blizzard. My little battery had to either laugh or cry, so we chose to laugh, and I for one rather enjoyed it, though I was very glad when it was over."

Eventually, on 3rd March the battalion arrived at St. Nicholas, a Northerly suburb of Arras. Here it would remain until early July. At about the same time, Major Lee Warner left the battalion to serve with the 3rd Army head Quarters and Captain Likeman (Adjutant) left for the 3rd Army School as instructor. Neither returned to the battalion. Lieutenant Webb took on the role of acting Adjutant and Captain Robinson took over as O.C. 'B' Company.

13984 Pte. Herbert Francis Allen
"We entered Arras and took over from the French and were billeted in cellars in the shell torn houses in the Grand Place. On entering our allotted cellar, we found lots of straw for lying on but in one corner it was soaking wet and smelling badly. The French had used that corner as a lavatory. I fetched the officer and we all refused to stay there so another place was found. A piano had been taken from one of the ruined houses and placed in a railway archway a short distance away – it had been heavily sand-bagged, so we used to go there when able and have sing songs, some not for publication."

Capt H.A. Colt
"Here we relieved the French. We were the first English troops to hold this part of the line and it was rumoured that the French, attaching enormous importance to the town, had stipulated that only first class troops were to be sent there. It looked as if the rumour were true for once, as the Divisions sent were the 5th, 14th and 51st."

Directly to the front was the Vimy Ridge, from where the enemy was afforded an uninterrupted view of everything the battalion did. Here, again, the position was in a salient, the line running round Arras, from Ecurie in the North to Wailly in the South. To the North-East the front line was as close as 2½ miles from Arras and to the South-East only one mile.

The trenches at Arras were deep and dry. They were solidly constructed with sturdy timber and featured plentiful deep dugouts which, when compared to those at Maricourt, were very comfortable. Up until that time the art of dug-out construction was unknown to the British, though in time they became experts. The battalion's role was that of line holding, as at Maricourt. This time it involved occupation of several redoubts, one of which was named 'Le Redoubt de Bosquet' which was very soon anglicised to 'Bosky Redoubt'. But life here was quite different to what had been experienced at Maricourt. The enemy was very active in its Minenwerfer activities from the 'sausage', the 'rum jar' down to the humble 'pineapple' all of which were intended to make life most uncomfortable. Every so often the enemy would engage in organised barrages on the trenches and blow them in badly. In addition, the area was a hive of underground tunnelling carried out by both sides. The sounds of this subterranean warfare when blowing camouflettes, was often in evidence. But during quiet spells fatigue parties would be sent around to pick up cigarette ends and litter and generally 'tidy up'

13986 Cpl. Robert Anstey
"Thankfully the warfare was of that class which was occasionally designated 'peacetime warfare' when there were only the snipers to shoot you if you showed your head, trench mortars and artillery several times a day to worry you. Or an underground mine to blow the senses out of you. These simple pleasures were mere trifles which marred the Arras trenches of 1916."

A certain projecting portion of the line – the Gridiron – was so constantly and so badly knocked about that it was abandoned and filled in. New wire was put up in front of a trench held by 'C' Company. Sgt. Weeks of 'A' Company and another man were on patrol one night. For some reason the 'C' Company post was not made aware of the fact. When the patrol was near to the post they were seen and were naturally bombed immediately. The pair had a lucky escape. It appeared that the offending post had sent in a report that two Germans, one believed to be an officer, had been seen and bombed to death just outside the barbed wire. To make the report more dramatic, the 'officer' was said to be a 'big man'. Surprise and embarrassment of the bombers, however, resulted when the truth of the matter came from Sgt. Weeks and his companion. The uncomplimentary remarks offered with regard to eyesight and hearing may be best imagined.

14780 Pte. Ralph Smith
"It was in this particular stretch of line I had the unpleasant experience of falling into a 'sump' hole. That is, a deep hole for the rain water to gather in, about 4' 6" deep. The duckboard covering it had slipped out of position. The lads got me out, built a fire in a dug-out, stripped everything off me and dried off all my clothes and equipment. They were fantastic pals. No, not pals – real brothers."

"We all took a dislike and cursed the French mortar section that operated in our area. The procedure was for them to come to the front line, fire a number of mortars and then move off to another part and do the same. We had to endure the ensuing retaliation whilst they were safe somewhere else. But some men believed that the rats knew when there was going to be a heavy bombardment from the enemy lines because they always seemed to disappear minutes before an attack."

2nd Lt. Ralph Hosegood
"Here we became well aquainted with the big German Minenwerfer which was a trench mortar. We had to learn the art of avoiding them by keeping in an open trench and watching their slow murderous flight with care and coolness and moving accordingly."

13984 Pte. Herbert Francis Allen
"It was during our time at Arras that I was hit. The enemy were lobbing trench mortars into our line and we were taking cover as best as we could. During a lull, I was moving from one bay to the next when I heard a distant 'pop'. Before I had chance to do anything it landed very close to me and blew me over.

"At first I didn't realise I had been hit. When I tried to stand, I couldn't. I had caught it in the leg. After a very painful and anxious night I was evacuated down the line, eventually arriving in England. Luckily I kept my leg and after over a year in hospital and convalescence I was discharged 21st September 1917 as being 'No longer physically fit for war service'. My war was over"

Pte. Herbert Allen

2nd/Lt. Herbert Ryland soon became well known for his sense of humour and, being a natural practical joker with a lively temperament, he quickly earned the soubriquet; 'Old fireworks'. It was on 1st April that he decided to play an April fools trick on the Germans. He and Sgt. Risdon crawled out into no man's land at dawn and finding an old, abandoned piece of agricultural equipment began banging it for all their worth. The plan was to get the Germans to look over their parapet and be met with a hail of fire from the platoon riflemen that were waiting for them. They had also rigged up a large sheet containing the slogan, in German saying: 'Sie sind der Kopf eines Schafs' - 'you are a sheep's head' – when translated into German. This being the equivalent of 'April Fool'.

A new draft of two men had an unpleasant welcome. They had been escorted to the front line and from there, directed to their new positions. As they went down the trench, over came a 'Minenwerfer'. Luckily, their former guide had kept an eye on them and they were promptly dug out and sent back down the line on stretchers. It was considered they may have set a record as being with the battalion for the shortest time.

When in support, the battalion was billeted in Arras itself. The old city possessed an extensive network of underground cellars and tunnels which were shell-proof and housed a large proportion of the civilian population. It had been shelled in the early part of the war and, though not generally badly damaged, the beautiful Hotel de Ville and the Cathedral together with the railway station had been completely destroyed.

The only shells to land there during the battalion's stay would be one or two every night at about the time the rations came up. Typical German form, it was possible to set a watch by it. But many of the abandoned houses still possessed much furniture, some of which mysteriously found its way into the numerous dugouts in the front line.

20089 Pte. William James
Arras provided very comfortable billets. When the citizens moved away, they left behind grand houses containing pianos, beds, chairs, tables and other items of furniture. If you did not succeed in procuring yourself a bed you were unlucky, or more than likely, just slow."

Pte. William Smallcombe with Lewis Gun, Arras

One particular street that was used by the battalion as a billet was Rue de St. Quentin. Every house in the street possessed a piano which invariably someone was playing. It was aptly renamed 'Piano Street'.

About this time Captain Colt had a furnished billet and for days a nun had been trying to remove the furniture. She had all the necessary papers. She was, however, persuaded to leave it until the battalion went back into the line. The next day Captain Colt went up to reconnoitre the line prior to taking it over. On returning to his billet, he discovered every stick of furniture had been removed. As he sadly gazed around him his foot struck a hard object embedded in the gap between two floor boards where an old cabinet had been. The object was a small, gold, Indian god that may have originated on a clock or ornament. He adopted the figure as a mascot which remained with him throughout the war.

Many civilians took advantage of the opportunity presented to them by the countless British troops in the town by running various estaminets which served wholesome food, and shops selling various wares including the ever popular silk postcards. Men bought them in their droves to send to mothers and sweethearts

One of the battalion's Lewis Gun Teams, Arras

back home. Movement of soldiers and civilians was kept under strict control by the Town Major and his Military Police or 'red caps'. Shops, and estaminets only coming to life at night.

14138 Sgt. Norman Pegg
"Enterprising shopkeepers still remained behind and derived lucrative profits from the sale of their wares. Actually, it was profiteering on a grand scale. In one place on the Arras–Douai Road, much less than a mile from the line, there was a shop selling everything from biscuits to onions. The proprietors had moved everything into the cellar of the shop to escape the effects of the shells, should they arrive."

The men enjoyed rest periods for other reasons. Contact with women, children and animals reassured them of their continued existence as civilians temporarily in khaki. It wasn't exactly home from home, but it did make them feel a little more comfortable knowing that life went on despite all the horror that surrounded them.

20089 Pte. William James
"It was good when time permitted, particularly in Arras, to see a sort of normal life happening. Normal people, going about their business. After spending much time surrounded by soldiers it was good to see the fairer sex, to know that they still existed. Many were not much to look at but there was a sort of pleasure in seeing them. Sounds ridiculous, but most of us felt the same."

When in rest proper, time was spent further back in a very pleasant village named Agnez-Les-Duisans. Only a few miles to the South-West of Arras it was a very nice location surrounded by clean fields, woods and hedge rows that seemed to the men be in another world. It was most comfortable with all amenities available, from estaminets, shops, barbers and a church. There was also a very able photographer who plied his trade among the British troops billeted there. Most men had their photographs taken in his orchard among the bee-hives and ivy bushes. Also most platoon groups were also photographed there. It really was a delightfull place to stay and very comfortable too.

On the first visit to the village a long lost battalion member rejoined. Jim – the regimental dog that had been the pride of the battalion but went missing at Whitburn came up with the transport. History has not recorded how he made his way from the north east of England to the battalion in Northern France. It was considered he was fortunately associated with the battalion and 'someone' had kindly made the arrangements.

14780 Pte. Ralph Smith

"Rest was not always as it might have sounded. It often meant returning to the front line at night and working with the Royal Engineers' on fatigue parties. They were digging mines under the enemy trenches and the enemy were doing the same under ours. The earth had to be scattered at the back of the trenches out of sight of Fritz. We organised the section as a chain gang, so much distance apart, one man at the face filling the sand-bags, the next man carrying it to the next man until it reached the man emptying them. We worked it so that each man, after a certain time, had his face in the fresh air. As the dawn was nearly breaking on one such detail I stopped the emptying of sand-bags outside and sent for the Corporal in charge and asked where else to empty the earth. He said it was still quite safe outside and I said I wasn't sure. He said he would show me how safe it was. He climbed up at the back of the trench and immediately a sniper's bullet blew his brains out."

Often, when enjoying a little respite during periods in reserve, or even when in rest danger was never far away. Invariably during these times, men would be detailed to return to the front line to 'assist' the Royal Engineers in various forms of activities. These work details were, by their nature quite dangerous and, were extremely unpopular. On the night of 23rd March one such detail was out in no man's land around 3 a.m. involved in mending and replacing wire. Any movement made a certain amount of noise which was unavoidable, no matter how careful it was carried out. The Germans detected something was happening and trained a machine gun in the general direction. One or two random bursts of fire were let off. 14131 Private Arthur Thomas Park of 'A' Company, a September 1914 man, was hit. His comrades got him back to the cover of the trench and did what they could. He died soon afterwards. He was an only son and aged just 19 years of age.

One dawn, our wire patrol carried him.
This time, Death had not missed.
We could do nothing, but wipe his bleeding cough.

Wilfred Owen

Pte. Arthur Thomas Park

During the early part of June the battalion moved to Berneville, another suburb of Arras, to assist the Royal Engineers in making gun emplacements in preparation for an action that never happened. Some working parties, again under Royal Engineers' instructions remained in the line and, while there, the enemy blew three large mines that were named "Cuthbert", "Clarence", and "Claude" which he endeavoured to occupy but was prevented from doing so by the 1st Norfolks and 15th Royal Warwicks. The 12th Gloucesters luckily sustained no casualties.

Both here and at Maricourt and Arras, casualties were light but about them was a curious coincidence or indeed a sad irony. There were six or seven pairs of brothers who landed in France with the battalion the previous November and before four or five months had passed in every case one of the pair had been killed. Another feature was the small number of officers and N.C.O.s whose names appeared on the casualty lists. However, this would change.

Up until the Battle of the Somme, the British High Command displayed little confidence in the citizen soldiers of 'Kitchener's Army. They believed they were not capable of doing anything more complicated than advancing in a series of waves. On 1st July the long awaited 'Big Push' began. After a week long bombardment of the German first and second lines, British troops went over the top at 7.30 a.m. The bombardment had been poorly planned and executed and had not had the desired effect. As a result, the men were cut to pieces by machine gun and shell fire. Over 57,000 casualties were sustained, over 19,000 of whom were dead and the expected breakthrough never happened. What made 1st July particularly noteworthy was that the great majority of attacking troops were New Army battalions and what they had achieved was to prove to the British High Command, that Britain's New 'Kitchener' Armies were capable of fighting with courage, energy and discipline, and it totally dismissed the German opinion that the new soldiers were untrained and useless.

On the 8th July while billeted at Berneville the battalion was warned off to prepare to move when orders were received. The order came on 13th July and a march to Wanquetin was undertaken. While here, time was found in preparing for the coming days. The men's bayonets were collected and taken away for sharpening and equipment was stamped with regimental numbers. Then, to the surprise of the men, a fleet of old London motor buses arrived for the next part of the journey to Puchevillers and conveyed the battalion to a position just outside of artillery range.

14596 William Ayres
"On our marches we were always glad to have the band up in front. They would play through any village. We listened to the tune, for when they struck up the Regimental march, we knew we had arrived at the village where we would spend the night. So we took heart and stepped out."

It was here that an unfortunate incident took place. While sweeping the courtyard of their billet, a young soldier of 'B' Company, set fire to some paper. The wind caught a piece of paper and carried it into a loft full of hay. The highest point was too high to reach without a ladder that was not available anyway. A small engine did, however arrive, from the Brigade pioneers – 6th Battalion Argyle and Sutherland Highlanders, but only a feeble stream of water from a stinking pond resulted. Three houses and six outbuildings were gutted.

A considerable amount of excitement was caused by the fact that the village was *Advanced General Headquarters* for the Somme.

There was recorded, an amusing incident, as was usually the case. One of the battalion officers led a group of Highlanders into one of the burning buildings to rescue 'valuable stores' only to reappear with copious amounts of brandy and champagne. There were other comic occurrences such as an attempt to pull down a house, to prevent the fire spreading, by means of a motor lorry and the efforts of one officer who perched on the roof of an adjacent house and attempted to dowse the flames with the use of a mug of water.

However, there was a happy ending to the adventure. The burned out inhabitants received ample recompense for their loss and the person who caused the fire, Pte. William Yacommeni, went on to be one of the battalion's best runners and was later awarded the Military Medal for his work on the Somme.

Next morning, to the utter relief of the villagers, the battalion moved off, eventually arriving at Becordel-Becourt, or what was left of it where the entire Brigade bivouacked.

Pte. William Yacomeni

Now, the battalion was about to enter its first offensive operation and, as such, had to leave behind, in safety, a cadre of 'dumped personnel'. These were the officers, N.C.O.s and men detailed to remain out of danger so that in the event of the rest of the battalion becoming casualties, a nucleus was available from which to reform the battalion. The following was the main disposition of the battalion at that time:

C.O.: Lt. Col. Archer-Shee D.S.O., M.P.
Deputy 2nd I/C: Captain H.A. Colt
Adjutant: Lt. H. J. Taylor
O.C. 'A' Company: Lt. W.W. Parr
O.C. 'B' Company: Lt. G.R.A. Beckett
O.C. 'C' Company: Captain E.B. Burris
O.C. 'D' Company: Captain T.M. Allison

Somme

Roses are shining in Picardy.
And the roses will die with the summer time.
Frederick Weatherly

Longueval

Since the opening day of the battle on 1st July, ground had been gained in some areas and the line had slowly moved forward. The place, however that was giving the most trouble at the time was Delville Wood where the British line turned at right angles and formed a sharp corner that jutted into the German line.

Delville Wood was a small wood adjacent to the village of Longueval and lay on the right flank of the British line, protecting the approaches to Ginchy and Guillemont, both of which were British objectives. Fighting had begun on 14th July during the Battle of Bazentine Ridge when the 9th Division captured the village and the wood. However, after successive and fierce counter-attacks, both were partially re-taken. It was here that the battalion would see its first action as part of the Somme offensive.

18th July the battalion marched on through the town of Albert to the aptly named 'Death Valley' where it bivouacked for two days and on 21st July moved into support trenches in Caterpillar Valley near Montauban where they suffered heavy shelling from H.E. and lachrymatory shells. The latter were a form of early tear gas and were intended to disable rather than kill. Casualties were sustained and, in the four days in Caterpillar Valley, six other ranks were killed and one officer and 19 other ranks wounded.

Capt H.A. Colt
"We dug ourselves in, in 'Caterpillar Valley' and remained there for four days or so. The first day there was nothing much doing. The Germans shelled pretty heavily just to the rear of us and occasionally put shrapnel over us.

"The next afternoon, however, he made up for this. An aeroplane with British markings had been hovering, over us in a highly suspicious manner, and nothing will ever persuade anyone who was there that it was not a disguised Hun plane.

"Anyhow, the Bosche that afternoon started to shell our trenches severely, while this plane hovered overhead, occasionally dropping coloured lights. The Bosche also put over lachrymatory shells. We had a good many casualties, mostly from 'A' Company. Private Jarman (the younger) was one of a number killed."

14596 Pte. William Ayres
"Beyond Albert the road went through the devastated village of Mametz and on to Montauban. From there, a sunken road ran down to 'Caterpillar Valley' which was the route to Longueval and Delville Wood.

"We marched down the sunken road which was under ceaseless shelling by the Germans, and were put into shallow trenches and dugouts on the far slope of the valley.

"From our trenches we looked back to the sunken road, now on the opposite side of the valley, and could see teams of horses and mules hitched to guns and transport limbers galloping down in an endeavour to beat the barrage. But, even so, we saw team after team caught in the shelling. On our side of the valley we were shelled almost without break with tear gas – lachrymatory shells - they were called. We had little shelter from the gas which inflamed our eyes and made us weep most painfully. We of the signals section were more fortunate as we had been issued with the new box respirator which we wore practically the whole time. For the rest of the men the only protection was the standard cloth gas helmet

"We were in those trenches for three or four days unable to escape the shelling or the tear gas. Though we knew we were going up to the front, it was relief when we finally moved away from there."

14780 Pte. Ralph Ivor Smith
"When we first arrived we were in old German trenches. Their dugouts were very deep and far superior to our own. Some of them were marked 'Foul Gas – Do not enter'. This was because of the dead bodies at the bottom. I'm afraid that during heavy bombardments that was our only shelter."

16588 Pte. Harry Nethercott
"This place was an unhealthy spot, being continuously under shell fire day and night. Shrapnel, high-explosive, gas and tear-gas shells being used. Unfortunately, many horses and wagons bringing up ammunition and food were blown sky high. Evenings we would carry ammunition to the front line. We always went in sections at about 50 yards apart to minimise casualties should a shell land among us."

23rd July the battalion relieved the 1st East Surreys in the front line at Longueval. The men were full of joy at being in a position to 'get its own back'. It remained in the line under very heavy artillery bombardment until the 26th when the battalion moved back down Caterpillar Valley through a Phosgene gas barrage and on to Pommiers Redoubt where it bivouacked. The redoubt had been taken in the early part of the battle and subsequently served as a rest location. 13 other ranks were wounded during the relief. Whilst in the line, casualties amounted to 1 officer and 6 other ranks killed and 3 officers and 110 other ranks wounded.

13986 L/Cpl. Robert Anstey
"We went into the front line in the village of Longueval on the left side of Delville Wood. The fighting in and around the wood and village had been bitter.

"There were still a few isolated walls left standing and on the German side there was a house – 'Machine Gun House' – which for some unaccountable reason had been left almost intact. The wood, which had previously been used as a retreat for German officers who spent their time lounging in wicker chairs, now contained nothing but bare and blacked tree stumps."

14596 Pte. William Ayres

"Delville Wood had been fought over and changed hands more than once. It was, as we found it, a fearsome place. The stench of death lay over everything. The trees were shattered, split and stunted by shellfire. The main trench through the wood was named Orchard Trench – a most inappropriate title. We, of the signal section, worked in threes – three men attached to each Company and Bert Dury, Reggie Phillips and I were frequently together, and I remember one day when we settled into our position, Bert said, "Well, what about something to eat?" to which Reggie Phillips replied; "Oh Bertie, how can you talk of something to eat in this dreadful place?"

"It was while we were there that I was buried by a shell blast over the parapet. And Bert in later years used to recall the incident something like this:-

"When the shell burst, the officer who was resting a few yards away, but not in sight spoke, 'Anyone hurt?' to which Bert replied 'A man buried.' The voice spoke again, "Well get him out, I've got some whiskey here." Some minutes later, Bert was able to report that I was out, and unhurt, "Good." said the voice – "Give him a drink of water."

About the 27th, the 1st Norfolks captured the greater part of the village of Longueval and the following evening the battalion returned, relieving the 1st Cheshires, this time to positions slightly further forward. On the way in there was a hold-up in the communication trench as the battalion was going in. If an attack had developed at that time, things would have become very uncomfortable. In an effort to straighten out the tangle, Lt. Parr jumped out on top. The Germans threw everything at him at short range, rifle fire, machine gun fire and even 'whizz-bangs'. By some miracle he was not hit and besides, appeared quite unconscious of the fusillade going on around him.

Here the trenches were merely scratches and the order was given to dig in which the men did with a will. This was fortunate as the next morning a very heavy barrage was put down on them causing further casualties.

Earlier in the day the 1st East Surreys had captured some strongpoint but were forced to relinquish their gains and fight their way back to their own lines due to their flanking unit from the Suffolks being beaten off. As a result of this, the enemy was intent on counter-attacking and on several occasions large numbers were spotted moving along the road from Flers and among the trees of one of the orchards in Longueval. On each occasion, accurate rifle fire and British artillery prevented the attacks from materialising.

Although the German counter-attacks had dissolved in the British barrage it was not long before they retaliated. Countless S.O.S. signals were sent up then the shells came crashing down onto the battalion's positions.

During these terrible bombardments, and under cover of darkness, many D.C.L.I. and East Surreys crawled into the battalion's trenches. All were wounded and some had their arms and legs smashed. They had been lying out in no-man's land for five or six days since those battalions had attacked.

The enemy barrage was extremely heavy and without abatement. The men of the battalion always considered that on no occasion, before or after, did they experience heavier shelling than that received at Longueval.

14780 Pte. Ralph Ivor Smith

"We moved off towards Longueval at night. As we did so the Chaplain was standing to one side praying over us as we passed. That upset a lot of the men. During the night we were subjected to very heavy shelling. We were told to expect a German counter-attack so we lined the trenches with rifles trained on the enemy lines. The next thing I knew was an almighty explosion and the whole section of our trench was blown

in, and we found ourselves completely buried. The ambulance section worked terribly hard and got out the killed and wounded. I could feel blood running from my arm, leg and head and as my arm had been shattered above the elbow I could only feel the stump so I thought it had been blown off."

14134 Pte. Harold Hayward

"During the attack I was acting as a runner. Lt. Beckett passed me a message explaining that because of an outflanking movement on our right, due to a failed attack, he was forced to give up the position. I set off with the message clutched in my hand and on the way I was caught in the blast of two shell bursts. I wasn't hurt but the piece of paper carrying the message was gone, and I had to convey the message to the C.O. verbally.

"The worst part of the journey to battalion H.Q. was the sunken road near the site of the old mill. It was heavily swept by machine gun fire and I'm not ashamed to say I had considerable 'wind up' while negotiating it."

20089 Pte. William James

"One morning shortly after day break, we heard a rush of shells going just over our heads, onto the German lines which were around 300 yards away. The shriek of the shells and sound of the explosions were deafening, and we could see the devastating effects as the shells crashed upon the enemy position. We knew they were heavy shells, we were told later that they were from 9" naval guns brought up for a special bombardment, and we'd had no previous warning."

Battalion Headquarters was situated several hundred yards to the rear near a sunken road not far from a mill, or where once a mill had stood. It appeared on the trench map but had long since ceased to exist. The sunken road was constantly swept by machine gun fire and it was here that Lt. Ralph Hosegood was killed on 23rd July. At the time of his death, he was attached to the 95th Brigade Trench Mortar Battery and had been caught by a machine gun while observing forward. Lt Hosegood was the first original officer to be killed, having joined the battalion in September 1914 as a private soldier, receiving his commission in March 1915. His body was removed and buried near Montauban, a rough cross marking the spot.

2nd/Lt. Bate 9th M.G.C.

"After wishing for months to meet Ralph, I did so on one Sunday morning at dawn, before an attack at Longeuval. He was with his Trench Mortar Battery. As the infantry got near their objective the T.M.B. had to cease fire. I saw Ralph for some hours while the attack was progressing helping wounded men up a sunken road towards the dressing station. He was quite regardless of personal safety, considering only others. Then heavy machine-gun fire caused a slight retirement of part of our line. My machine guns were near his battery, very busy. After the counter attack had been repulsed I went to find Ralph, intending to have a little chat for a few minutes, only to find that he had lost his life in trying to save others. When he heard the infantry were retiring he wanted to give them covering fire with his guns, but was afraid of hitting our own men. So he was looking over the parapet to see when he could open fire and a machine-gun caught him."

Saturday 29th July was a hot day. The C.O. visited all trenches at 6.00 am He ordered that 'C' Company's trenches should be deepened further by two feet. During the afternoon the bombardment became more intense particularly over 'B' Company's position in 'Duke Street'. The position was very crowded and they were being shelled by 8" and 11" howitzers. They were ordered out and into the next company's trench which was not being so badly damaged.

13986 L/Cpl. Robert Anstey

" I shall not easily forget the thrill I received as I saw the C.O. running across open ground, utterly unconcerned in the midst of some very heavy shelling, in order to move 'B' Company to a less exposed position"

"Platoon H.Q. was in a shallow dug-out. Lt. Parr came up out of the dug-out and said 'I'm coming out into the trench with you Anstey: if I have to be killed I won't be killed like a rat in a trap'.

"I was in some hot corners later on but never experienced a more intense shelling. During the *attempted enemy counter-attack, I was slightly wounded. A bullet went right through my helmet and ploughed a groove in my scalp. I am very pleased it wasn't an inch or two lower, it was a fairly near escape."*

Orders were received to attack several enemy strong points.

O.C. 'C' Company received the following order:
"It is possible that we may be ordered to take posts 'A', 'B' and 'C' this afternoon. Please reconnoitre post 'A' with a view to occupying it if ordered. Further orders later."

O.C. 'B' Company O.C. received the following order:
"Expect that we are to be ordered to take posts 'B' and 'C' this afternoon at 3.30 p.m. If we have to do it in daytime will detail your Company to do it. Suggest that you send two platoons via bank running along hedge on map and advance from there. There are two old German trenches running from 'B' and 'C'. Do not expect opposition until we come under view of German posts marked on map. 'C' Company will go forward and occupy post 'A'.

"It is proposed to do this under cover of heavy artillery fire. I have suggested it would be easier to do it at night, and the matter is not finally settled.

O.C. 'C' Company received the following order:
"The Brigade has been ordered to attack and take the line shown in red on the enclosed plan. Your work is to take point 'A' and consolidate. It is understood that a trench already exists to this point which only needs deepening but, if not, occupy post and consolidate if possible. Send by return your requirements in sandbags, wire, bombs (if necessary).

"O.C. BINDER (12th Gloucesters) does not consider that you should use more than a platoon at the outset to carry out this work. If you cannot quite attain point 'A' then dig in at the nearest point which you can obtain.

"Please be careful to send forward before artillery barrage lifts to see whether any portion of your advance is threatened by M.G. fire."

11 Platoon, 'C' Company. Lt. H. C. Ryland centre second row

At 1.30 p.m. further orders were received that the Brigade would attack after half-an-hour's preliminary bombardment. The 1st East Surreys to be on the right the 12th Gloucesters on the left. The 1st East Surreys were to take a further two posts: posts 'D' and 'E'.

At the allotted time, from left, 'C' Company sent 11 Platoon under command of 2nd/Lt. H. C. Ryland to point 'A', and 'B' Company sent 6 Platoon under 2nd/Lt. E. L. Hillborne and elements of 5 Platoon under 2nd/Lt. R. J. Fitzgerald to points 'B' and 'C' respectively.

At post 'A' 2nd/Lt H. C. Ryland and his party successfully established themselves and set to consolidating. The 'B' Company parties lead by 2nd/Lt.s Hillborne and Fitzgerald dashed forward under cover of the barrage and established themselves at posts 'B' and 'C' without incurring any casualties.

On the right, Lt. Fitzgerald's party was in place by 3.31p.m. and found it to be an old German trench which had been obliterated by shell fire. They were subsequently fired on by a machine gun but were able to dig themselves in. The party consisted of 17 men The other half of the platoon attempted to reach them but were caught by the same machine gun and those who were left, took shelter in a shell hole around 100 yards away.

The party of the 1st East Surreys nearest, advanced at the same time but could not be seen from point 'C' once they got down. At 4.00 p.m. one officer and three men joined Lt. Fitzgerald. They were not shelled or fired upon again until after 9.00p.m.

The centre party under Lt. Hilborne established themselves at point 'B' at about 3.32p.m. and found the trench had been hastily vacated by the Germans leaving loaded rifles, bombs ready for use and some bodies lying around that had been killed by artillery fire. The trench was fairly deep and, when the remainder of his party arrived, the position was consolidated well. The enemy put down a barrage behind points 'B' and 'C' and fired on Lt. Hillborne's position with machine gun fire. His men returned fire and hit several of the enemy who showed themselves in getting into cover. He took 33 and incurred 9 casualties.

The main consolidation party, whilst approaching post 'B' under 2nd/Lt. E. B. Huddy was caught. Out of 36 men, 18 became casualties including Lt. Huddy who was killed.

14265 Alfred Coombs
"I was in Lt. Huddy's platoon somewhere near the orchards at Longueval. We went over the parapet to attack at about 4.00p.m., Lt. Huddy leading us. When we had got forward about 250 yards they turned machine guns on us and the line was held up for a while. I and my mate were wounded and rolled into a shell hole and Lt. Huddy, who was not hit at the time, jumped into the same hole with us. After a while he asked us if we were not going on to which I replied that we were wounded. He said, "Well I'm going on anyhow" and jumped up calling to his men to come on. The moment he was out of the shell hole he was shot dead and fell back into it. We lay there with him until 10.00p.m. before crawling back to our own line."

Sergeant Harris and twelve men of 'B' Company managed to reach a post forward and to the right of post 'C' near to the 1st East Surrey's positions and dug themselves in with four shovels and entrenching tools. They were heavily shelled but remained there. On the 30th, one officer and three men of the 1st East Surrey's had orders to retire, but Sgt. Harris, not having received such orders, remained in position. They were relieved by a party of 14th Royal Warwicks on the evening of the 31st.

Having come under fire at post 'A', 2nd/Lt. Ryland was badly wounded in the buttock. He was immediately treated as best as could be done and four of his men began carrying him back to comparative safety. Shortly after they set off, they were caught by a machine gun burst which killed Pte's. Charles Blake and Nelson Griffin. 2nd/Lt. Ryland received a second wound to the thigh, but was eventually evacuated.

14134 Harold Hayward
"The casualties that day were bad. Many of the wounded were stranded in no-man's land and there was nothing we could do for them. I helped a group of stretcher bearers evacuate some men to the aide post. One incident stuck in my memory. We picked up a badly wounded man and on the way back he got out a fag, put it between his lips and lit it, totally unconcerned that his intestines were exposed.

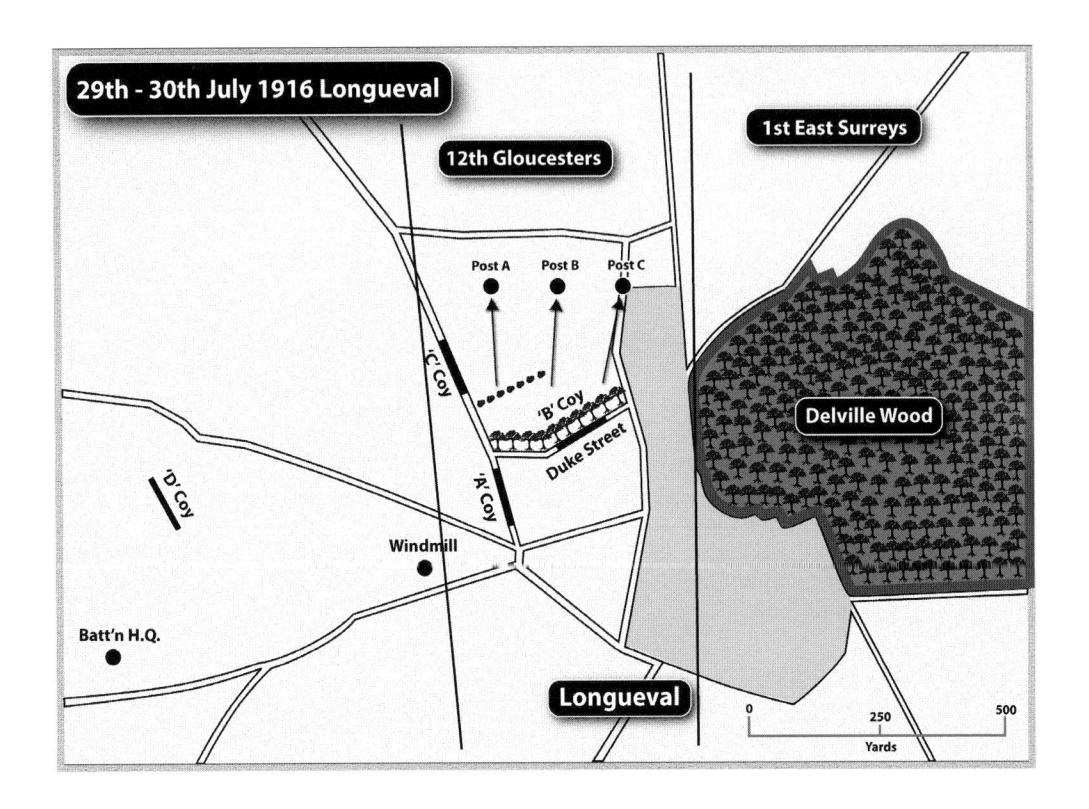

"On one occasion, five or six men who had been lying out in 'no man's land' crawled in. All were surrounded and not until several attacks had been made did they get back into touch with our troops. They stated that our troops attacked the post actually held by them but luckily no casualties were sustained."

Capt H.A. Colt

"About two days later we were agreeably surprised by the arrival of the missing party who had attacked the German strongpoints on the 29th. It appeared they had taken their objectives but had been surrounded and not until several attacks had been made did they get back into touch with our troops. They stated that our troops attacked the post actually held by them but luckily no casualties were sustained."

Brigadier General Lord Esme Gordon-Lennox Commanding 95th Brigade in a letter to Lt. Col Archer-Shee D.S.O.:

"I have much pleasure in asking that you will have recorded against the names of the N.C.O.s and men of your battalion not only my admiration, but also the admiration of the 95th Brigade and the 5th Division for the splendid courage and devotion to duty which they displayed on July 29th, 30th and 31st, in holding onto the advanced post at Longueval, in a very critical situation. I know you must be proud to have men of this stamp in your battalion, equally am I proud to have them in my Brigade."

The following men, all of 'B' Company, were commended for their action in holding onto the advanced post until relieved on the 31st:

9405 Sgt. J. Harris
14435 Cpl. E.J. Warren
16805 L/Cpl. H.V. Weatherhead

14398 Pte. E.S. Streets
26134 Pte. R. Gray
20184 Pte. F.J. Dymock
14416 Pte. C.H. Taylor
20083 Pte. A.H. Room
20284 Pte. H. Clarke
14339 Pte. A.F. Lewtas
14331 Pte. G. Keeler
16635 Pte. W. Thyer
25308 Pte. A. Scribbens

Sgt. Harris and L/Cpl. Weatherhead were both awarded the Military Medal for their part in the aforementioned action.

The evening of the 30th July the battalion was relieved and proceeded, again, to Pommiers Redoubt. Here it remained for two days until moving, on the 2nd August, to a tented camp outside the village of Dernancourt, where it was reunited with the 'dumped' personnel. Two days later, after a long wait at Mericourt station, during which time the men amused themselves by throwing cigarettes into the German prisoners' cage, the battalion moved to Airaines and after a short march arrived at Vergies for an extended period of rest. Here the usual re-fitting and re-drafting with officers and men took place, plus of course the usual training. Vergies was provided as a rest village and the battalion stayed for seventeen days. It was a very comfortable village where the men were able to rest and recover from the terrific shelling they had received at Longueval.

Pte. William Smallcombe kept a notebook on which he recorded daily observations. In it, in indelible pencil, he wrote what came to mind on the 29th July at Longueval.

15066 William Smallcombe

"Murder! Murder! Everywhere! Gracious God! How can it be allowed? My comrades lie around – on the parapet – just in front – dead – discoloured and oh God so lonely. Some dear son, of a weeping mother. How she must long to know where he is – but to see him laying cold and dead would break the heart of any parent. Death is coming every few seconds taking its horrible toll. We dodge and duck to escape that death dealing shrapnel – but it claims its victims. One poor lad tries to rise but utters a cry of pain as the shrapnel bites into his back. We drop again and find ourselves lying by another poor lad who was killed five minutes ago. Into the trenches – those of us left."

Some of the men recently wounded would make their way back to the battalion, many would not. And more would be discharged from the army as being "No longer physically fit for war service" or, disabled.

Private Sam Bollom had fought hard to get into the battalion in 1914 despite the doctor telling him he had a weak heart. He was hit by a bullet that blew out part of his collar bone and damaged his lung. His war was over. While Private Ernest Shanks, who had originally been rejected due to the height restriction, collected a lot of shrapnel in his back. He eventually recovered and was posted to the Royal Berkshire Regiment. L/Cpl Gilbert Hooper was hit in the hand. After treatment he was posted to the R.F.C.

2nd/Lt. Herbert Ryland was hit in the buttock and thigh. After time in hospital and convalescence he recovered but was disabled and for the rest of his life wore a high boot.

British Campaigns in France and Flanders - Sir Arthur Conan Doyle

"July 1916 the 1st Norfolks were relieved on the 27th by the 95th Brigade, who took the final posts on the north and east of the houses, 1st East Surreys holding the Northern Front.

"The 12th Gloucesters particularly distinguished themselves on this occasion, holding onto three outlying captured posts under a very heavy fire. The three isolated platoons maintained themselves with great constancy, and were all retrieved, though two out of four officers and the greater part of the men had

Pte. William Ayres - 1916

become casualties. This battalion lost 320 men in these operations, which were made more costly and difficult by the fact that Longueval was so exaggerated a salient that it might more properly be called a corner, the Germans directing their very accurate artillery fire from the tower of Ginchy church.

"It should not be forgotten in our military annals that though the 99th Brigade actually captured Delville Wood, their work would have been impossible, had it not been for the fine advance of the 95th Brigade of the 5th Division upon their Longueval flank."

Vergies

14596 William Ayres
"After Longueval, we rested, for about three weeks, in a village well away from the front, and I remember this incident while we were on the journey there. In the German dugouts we had found many of the Picklehaube spiked helmets which the Germans wore and some were brought away as souvenirs.

"Now, Reggie Phillips had picked up one of these helmets and that was the cause of the trouble. To get to our resting village, the battalion went by train. But some of us of the signallers covered the journey on bicycles which took us two days. Reggie had lost his forage cap in the excitement of war, and decided to don the German Picklehaube which he did to the delight of the various villagers we passed on our way. But not so the brass hats. For a staff car passed us and the officers took a dim view of it. They stopped and looked at Reggie with stern disapproval. They told him he was disgracing his uniform by wearing a helmet of the German army. Reggie was thoroughly told off, and we were left deflated."

Vergies was 50 miles away from Longueval. The contrast between the peaceable conditions there and the terrific shelling experienced at the place they had just left was immeasurable. The countryside around Vergies was very pretty with plenty of woods, alternating with the growing crops of varying colours, and it was the best time of year to be there.

The schoolmaster of the village, who had been wounded at the beginning of the war, spoke good English and was very friendly. He did much to make the battalion's time there as happy as possible.

On the first Sunday, a memorial service was held at which the names of the officers and men who had been killed in and around Longueval were read out. This was the battalion's first heavy casualty toll.

Officers killed:

2nd/Lt R. Hosegood
2nd/Lt. E.B. Huddy
2nd/Lt. H.S. Painter
2nd/Lt. N.F.K. Richards

Officers wounded:
Captain E.H. Burris
2nd/Lt. H. Bennett
2nd/Lt. R. Cooper

2nd/Lt. B. H. Ellison
2nd/Lt. H. E. Lambert
2nd/Lt. N. F. Ryder
2nd/Lt. H.C. Ryland
2nd/Lt. G. H. Thomas
2nd/Lt. S. Wilkins

Other ranks:
Killed/died of wounds: 58
Wounded: 254

14134 Harold Hayward
"I have a good recollection of this service and how stunned I was when names of so many I knew in each Company were read out. This was about a week after pulling out from Longueval when what remained of the battalion was paraded by Companies. At the time I was still detained at battalion H.Q. and so saw the parade both from the front and the flank. Every platoon with only a few men left, and hardly an N.C.O. or officer. A cold feeling sent through me."

Soon afterwards, Harold was released from battalion H.Q. for the time being and instructed to assist 2nd/Lt. G.E.R Gedye in compiling various statistics concerning billeting, depth of wells, accommodation for the mule transport, etc. During which time they were both invited to dine with Mr. Le Maire, who had only just returned from convalescent leave. After sampling the best hospitality and a certain amount of locally produced Calvados, an apple brandy, 2nd /Lt. Gedye was a little the worse for wear. True to form, Harold continued to carry out his orders and quietly and discreetly assisted 2nd/Lt. Gedye back to his quarters.

A good deal of training was accomplished whilst at Vergies. Musketry, the attack and wood fighting. Also new drafts of officers and men arrived to replace those lost. Lt. Wilmot, the transport officer, whose spirit was stronger than his body, was forced to go sick and was invalided home. A year later, however, he contrived to persuade the medical authorities to allow him to return.

Prior to the action at Longueval it had been promised that home leave would be given soon afterwards. However, the course of General Haig's 'Big Push' was not going exactly to plan. Every possible man would be required and so home leave was cancelled. By way of consolation, both officers and men were allowed two or three days leave at Le Téport on the Normandy coast. As might be imagined, a good number took advantage of the opportunity.

14780 Pte. Ralph Ivor Smith
"In lieu of the 'Blighty' leave we had been promised before going into action at Longueval, a chance to have a couple of days at a town on the French coast was substituted. I was among those lucky to be offered this privilege and, wearing side arms, we travelled to LeTréport to make the most of 48 hours' leave. We were given the addresses of hotels that were on payment and prepared to take us in for a couple of nights.
"The weather was beautiful and the sea calm. I bought a pair of swimming shorts and spent most of the time on the sea shore as none of my particular pals were among the lucky party.
"On the forenoon of the first day there I noticed a young lady, around my age, trying to swim a few strokes and I shyly offered, in my best schoolboy French, to teach her the rudiments. This was met with a very distinctly English, "No thank you." I saw her again the next day but, too timidly I now think, did not make any further approach. I could not at first think that an English girl would have been allowed an exit permit as there was no holiday traffic in 1916!"

14178 Albert Thompson in letter to his wife Tuesday 8th August 1916
"...Well, darling, it was not my intention to tell you but, now I see from your letters that you know, I may just as well tell you that we have been in the thickest of it for some time now, but now we are brought back away from it all for a quiet rest and we arrived here yesterday and a very well change it is too after the

continual fighting and sound of the guns, which was tremendous. In fact, to sum it all up, dearie, if the Devil ever has to make hell a worse place than it was up where we were fighting then he's got a stiff job on, and I should be more than sorry for anyone who went there. I am very thankful to say that the Almighty above has guarded over me and brought me out of that inferno safely, without as much as a scratch."

The battalion remained at Vergies until 23rd August when it entrained for Dernancourt. From there it moved into support trenches near its old 1915 positions at Maricourt. The trenches were in a filthy condition and swarmed with fleas. However, apart from the occasional burst of shrapnel, things were quiet. An operation was planned for this area but was cancelled due to heavy rain and so the battalion moved into tented accommodation at nearby Bronfay Farm. While here a bomb exploded in an incinerator, wounding one man. To save moving him, the improvised court of enquiry assembled near him while he was being treated. As the court finished, another bomb exploded, very nearly damaging the court.

Some of those that died as a result of the fighting during July 1916

Pte. Charles Blake.
KIA 29th July

Pte. Francis Bond.
KIA 21st July

Pte. Herbert Byrne.
DOW 24th July

Pte Norman Case.
KIA 24th July

Pte. Arthur Cottrel.
KIA 27th July

Pte. Ernest Dyer.
KIA 29th July

1916 – Anybody's Own

Pte. Clifford Fabian.
KIA 29th July

Pte. Charles Farndell.
KIA 29th July

Pte. Henry Fear.
DOW 6th August

Pte. Stanley Fletcher.
KIA 29th July

Pte. Nelson Griffen.
KIA 29th July

Pte. William Griffey.
KIA 21st July

L/Sgt. William Hodgson.
KIA 29th July

2nd/Lt. Ralph Hosegood.
KIA 23rd July

2nd/Lt. Edward Huddy.
KIA 29th July

1916 – Anybody's Own

Pte William James.
KIA 29th July

Pte. William Jefferies.
DOW 13th August

Pte. Charles Love.
KIA 29th July

Cpl. Herbert Lumbard.
KIA 29th July

Pte. Percy Ogden.
KIA 26th July

2nd/Lt. Henry Painter.
KIA 29th July

Sgt. John Phillips.
KIA 24th July

Pte. Robert Powell.
KIA 21st July

Pte. Joseph Skinner.
DOW 1st August

Pte. Ernest Thornett.
KIA 29th July

Cpl. Benjamin Whittock.
KIA 29th July

Guillemont

Orders were received 2nd September stating that the battalion would relieve the 1st East Surreys in the line near Guillemont that evening. All ranks were warned to be economical with water due to difficulty in getting fresh supplies.

Further orders received at 1.00p.m. stated that the 95th Brigade would be taking part in a general attack upon the German positions South of Guillemont the next day, Sunday September 3rd. The 1st D.C.L.I. would be on the left, with the 12th Gloucesters on the right. 'A' and 'C' Companies would form the first waves of the assault, with 'A' Company on the right and 'C' Company on the left. Therefore, on the evening of the 2nd the battalion marched to its jump off positions, order of march being Companies 'C', 'A', 'B' and 'D'. The following was the disposition of the battalion that went in:

C.O. Lt/Col Archer-Shee D.S.O., M.P.
Deputy 2nd I/C Captain H.A. Colt
Adjutant: Lt. J. P. Webb
O.C. 'A' Company: Captain E.A. Robinson
O.C. 'B' Company: Lt. R. J. Fitzgerald
O.C. 'C' Company: Lt. C. Barrington
O.C. 'D' Company: Captain T.M. Allison

During the morning of the 3rd, the enemy shelled the support lines heavily with shrapnel. R.S.M. Healy and several H.Q. orderlies were killed this way, while Lt. Col. Archer-Shee was hit on the arm by a spent shell case.

14134 Harold Hayward
"Against my wishes I had been seconded to battalion H.Q. as a runner. I was feeling quite sorry for myself as I wanted to be near my close pals, Harold Howell and Tom Webber. Major Beckett had been instructed to nominate one man from each Company and had put forward my name as one of his former Colston School pupils. I even protested to the C.O. himself, but he was adamant. A number of his H.Q. staff had been evacuated with shell shock and they had to be replaced before the battalion went into action and

I could not be spared. I was disappointed but had to accept. Battalion H.Q. was situated in Assembly Trench. The shelling was particularly heavy above us and I was sheltering with many of the H.Q. staff, orderlies, signallers etc. On my one side was Arthur Bacon from Weston-Super-Mare. On my other side was R.S.M. Healy. A shrapnel shell burst immediately over our trench sending a shower of lead balls down on us wounding a number of men and killing outright Arthur bacon and the R.S.M. Miraculously, I was unscathed but pinned beneath the body of the R.S.M. whose blood had run all over me."

The British barrage opened up at 08.30a.m. and the attack began at midday. The men advanced behind a creeping barrage advancing at the rate of 50 yards per minute. They were instructed to keep within 25 yards of the landing shells!

On high ground, above and to the right of the ground over which the two Companies attacked, was a German fortified position known as Falfemont Farm. In front of the position was a cliff above a chalk pit, directly overlooking the battalion's objectives on the edge of which were sited several machine guns. It was clearly realised that unless these positions were neutralised, the attack of the 95th Brigade would be under severe threat. The problem was artillery or, more to the point, the lack of it.

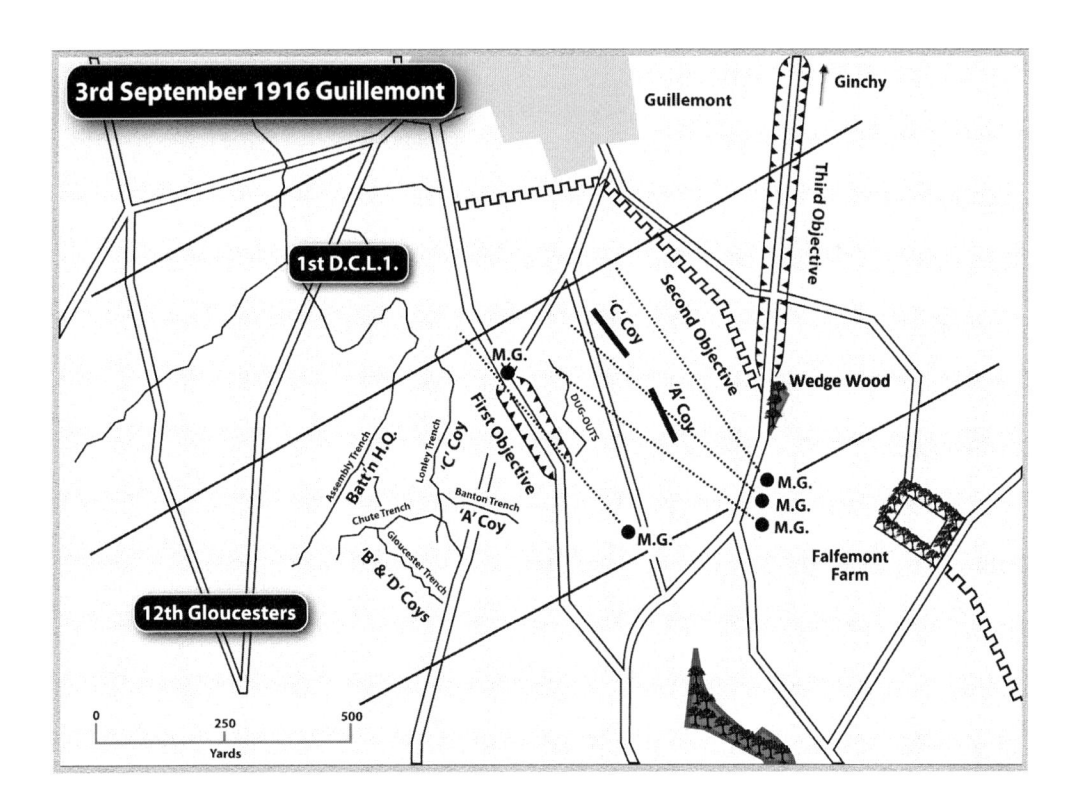

The key to successful operations was adequate artillery and effective artillery tactics to neutralise enemy positions. The B.E.F. in 1916 was short of guns and its artillery tactics were in their infancy. Thus the British artillery was spread far too thinly and was unprepared for the tasks it had been set. The opening of the Somme battle had shown that. The threat, represented by the existence of the Falfemont Farm positions, was intended to have been eliminated before the attack of the 95th Brigade began. Due to the shortage of guns, the French agreed to provide the necessary artillery support.

And so the Falfemont Farm positions were attacked at 08.50a.m. on the 3rd by the 2nd Battalion K.O.S.B.'s. But the gallant attempt was an utter disaster. The French, on the K.O.S.B.'s right were held up by machine gun fire and the artillery, intended to support the K.O.S.B.'s, had been, at the last minute, re-directed toward a German attack that had developed further South. Regrettably news of the re-direction had not been transmitted and the infantry attack proceeded. The K.O.S.B.'s suffered many casualties and Falfemont farm remained intact. As such, the subsequent attack by the 12th Gloucesters was, therefore, doomed to misfortune before it began. It was fated to be at the mercy of heavy machine gun fire.

14596 William Ayres

"We were due to go over at noon. And spent three hours in shallow trenches, so shallow that only by sitting tight at the bottom of the trench could we get our heads under cover. Throughout those three hours we were under constant shelling. It was with relief that we started off at twelve o'clock."

The first objective was a sunken lane followed by several dugouts in an embankment and a machine gun covering the dugouts. The initial obstacle to be dealt with was easily overcome and the dugouts 100 yards further on were found to be unoccupied. But off to the right was a lone machine gun which did some damage. It had to be neutralised. A section of 'A' Company, with Capt. E. A. Robinson present, rushed it. Six men, all pals who had joined together in September 1914, were brought up against the gun at close quarters. They rushed it and were all killed in the space of a moment. Capt E.A. Robinson was hit in the chest and his trusty batman, Pte. Percy Edwin Fisher, killed. The gun was put out of action but at a cost.

14134 Pte. Harold Hayward

"Soon after the attack began, I heard Captain Robinson had been wounded. I waited until the stretcher bearers brought him in under cover. I escorted him the length of the support line talking to him on the way. He had been hit in the chest but seemed very cheery and was smiling and talkative and asked of the welfare of his batman Pte. Fisher. He was surprisingly cheerful and talkative. I imagined that once he got treatment he would be alright. But he died of his wounds around a week afterwards I think.

Eric Robinson had been a Private soldier with 'A' Company to start with. When he asked Major Stansfield about a commission he was told he wasn't really suited as to be an officer a substantial income was required. Unknown to Major Stansfield, Eric Robinson was a director of the paper firm E.S & A. Robinsons of Bristol. Eric was commissioned into the battalion.

From 12.50p.m. with the first objective successfully taken, the main advance to the second objective began. The distance between the first and second objectives was around 300 yards. The machine guns around Falfemont Farm, that covered the ground over which the advance took place remained intact, 'A' Company was subsequently taken in direct enfilade and suffered accordingly.

The German second line between Wedge Wood and the southern extremities of Guillemont village itself formed the second objective. Although the ranks had been savagely cut down the remaining men took this position with vengeance in mind and with few problems. The remains of 'A' Company, which had been most badly mauled, held this line as 'C' Company moved on toward the third objective, which was simply a case of wheeling right.

The third objective was the sunken lane leading from the corner of Wedge Wood running northwards along the sunken lane leading toward Ginchy. This should have been a relatively easy and inexpensive move. However, an unfortunate incident took place involving 'C' Company. Wedge Wood and the sunken road, which should have served as a guide, although marked on the maps, had been completely destroyed by shell fire and were no longer features on the landscape. In the confusion of battle, the remains of Leuze Wood, which was further on was mistaken for Wedge Wood and some of the attackers went too far and were caught by their own artillery and had to fall back sharply.

Capt. H. A. Colt
"A party of 'C' Company under Sgt. Hughes went a good bit beyond their objective owing to the obliteration of landmarks. This party had a bad time from our final protective barrage."

By 2.50p.m. all objectives had been successfully taken. Consolidation took place and 150 German prisoners from the 73rd Fusiliers and the 164th Regiment were sent back.

16588 Pte. Harry Nethercott
"We formed a line and walked slowly forward. We had only gone a few yards when my mate was hit. Lines of men were just disappearing. The Germans' machine guns fired at us like it was target practice. It was sheer slaughter

"I got machine gun bullets in both arms and my right ankle and was quite unable to move. There were six of us in one shell-hole. The ones I remember were SollyLevy, Norman Spafford as wounded and William 'Boty' King dead. We were hit around 1.30p.m. Sunday the 3rd. At 7.00p.m. on Tuesday 5th a Sergeant gave me a drink of water and I was eventually sent down the line to a casualty clearing station".

20089 Pte. William James
"We were smelly, unshaven and sleepless. My uniform was rotten with other men's blood and partly spattered with a friend's brains. It was horrible.

"I remember thinking that if we survived, it would be a miracle. After a couple of hours we got into a shell-hole and there was a youngster in it, crying. He was obviously in a state of terrible shock as he flung himself on us and threw his arms round my neck".

14138 Sgt. Norman Pegg
"At Guillemont on 3rd September, two or three machine guns caused most of the damage. But the men were undaunted in their spirit."

14107 Sgt.Reginald MacFarlane
"The attack was marked by the remarkable resolution with which the men carried it through. Following the opening of the British bombardment, which seemed to make the earth boil, we hopped over the parapet full of confidence, but the German machine gunners were steady men, and their aim was good. The ground was pitted with innumerable shell holes, large and small, and to reach the enemy's positions we had to descend these holes and come up on the other side of them. We were, in this way greatly impeded in our progress and while we were approaching the lines of German defences, whole waves seemed to melt away, for men were falling fast. In many of the shell holes badly wounded men had to lie for many hours and in some cases days without water or shelter before help could be sent to them. I remember many men covered by ground sheets, too badly hit to move, lying among dead and dying comrades."

14138 Sgt. Norman Pegg
"It is the recollection of scenes of the kind witnessed at Guillemont which causes me to read, or listen to, with a deep sickening feeling some of the glib descriptive writing or public speaking, official and unofficial, which have from time to time thrust themselves on the people who have stayed at home. To the man who underwent the experience, a battle is not gay, glorious or frivolous, but devilish and murderous."

14178 Albert Thompson an 'A' Company man, had written a letter to his wife on 8th August during his time in rest at Vergies. Speaking of his time at Longueval, he had ended the letter saying:

"I am very thankful to say that the Almighty above has guarded over me and brought me out of that inferno safely, without as much as a scratch."

Private Thompson was wounded at Guillemont on the 3rd September. He died of his wounds four days later on the 7th September.

Of the officers who went over that day, Lt. Fitzgerald was the only one who came out unhurt. At the end of the fighting the battalion consisted of two parties of men: 'B' Company under Lt. Fitzgerald with the remnants of 'A', 'C' and 'D' Company. For his action of gathering the remnants of the battalion and consolidating the objectives gained Lt. Roy James Fitzgerald was awarded the Military Cross.

14134 Pte. Harold Hayward

"The C.O. had promised me that I would go up. He said, "I'll send you out to see how far the battalion has gone forward. Just do you work here now and I'll let you go up to the front tomorrow". I knew he meant when things had quietened down.

"We went up to the line the next morning. It was fairly safe because we were only going to the line our boys were supposed to have occupied and there were other troops ahead of them. But all the way up, as it got lighter, we could see people lying all over the ground. I was shocked to see people I knew well. That was terrible.

"At first, when we got to the line, we couldn't find the battalion. There was nothing but a motley array of men in the trenches, not just people from other battalions of our own brigade, but people from other divisions I'd not even heard of. It was an awful mix up. Eventually we did find our own boys and, by a miracle, I found my pals Tom and Harold. They were in the aid post. A shell had come over and buried Harold when they were going forward and men ran over him while he was down with all this earth and stuff on top of him. It was a miracle he got out. Tom was completely shell-shocked. We'd lost a lot of our N.C.O.s and many officers.

"There was a gap – a big gap beyond the right of our line, and the ground was hidden so we couldn't see anybody at all. The C.O. wanted to know who was there and what they intended to do. It was all quiet then, so he told me to run down and find out. We were standing there, quite exposed, and I had just stepped away from the C.O. and turned round when suddenly I was hit by a bullet that came from behind us, from one of the line of trenches we had overrun. There must have been a German sniper still holding out there and, of course, the C.O. presented a good target, standing there with his stick and badges of rank and medal ribbons, but the sniper got me instead – right in the groin."

The bullet that got Harold had first pierced his tobacco tin before entering him. The steel jacket of the bullet broke in two, the lead inner part being just inside the wound.

On the C.O.'s instruction he was carried back to the temporary battle H.Q., a captured German engineers' dug-out, where Lt. Fitzgerald extracted the bullet and bandaged the wound. Harold was evacuated to the C.C.S. and eventually back to England where the remainder of the debris was removed and he made his recovery.

At the same time Harold had moved forward with the C.O., the 1st Devons moved up in front of the battalion positions, attacking and capturing German trenches in front of Leuze Wood. Meanwhile the tattered remnants of the 12th Gloucesters sat tight in their captured trenches until the evening of the 6th when relieved by a battalion of the London Regiment. The men moving away, to camp at Happy Valley.

Capt. H. A. Colt

"All Companies but particularly 'A' Company had very heavy casualties. Among the dead I remember seeing Pte.'s Dearlove and Shorto, both of 'A' Company, and remember thinking that the men of the type we lost at Longueval and Guillemont would not easily be replaced.

"On the evening of the 6th we were relieved. On our way out, the Germans made a big bombing attack on our front line posts in front of Leuze Wood and we were nearly called back. As it was C.S.M., at this time acting R.S.M. Bailey, was obliged to guide two Companies of the relieving unit to counter-attack.

"We marched back to camp near the Citadel where we remained some days, during which time what was left of the Brigade paraded for a highly congratulatory address from the Corps commander."

Thus dearly bought the battalion gained a high reputation for their work and the gallant manner in which the attack was carried through. For the success it had achieved that day, the battalion paid a very heavy price. The casualties sustained in a very short space of time were terrible. Whole sections were wiped out.

When the roll-call was taken the full truth became known. A very large proportion of the battalion had become casualties:

Officer killed:
2nd/Lt. L.C.H. Vincent
Officer died of wounds:
Capt. E. A. Robinson
Officers wounded:
Capt. T. M. Allison,
2nd/Lt. S. Reynolds
2nd/Lt. G. E. R. Gedye
2nd/Lt. E. L. Hillborne
2nd/Lt C. Barrington
2nd/Lt. L. C. Evans
2nd/Lt G. B. Hall
2nd/Lt. A. Laird
2nd/Lt. F. C. Howard

Other Ranks Killed: 76
Other ranks died of wounds: 32
Other ranks wounded: 277
Total: 396

In terms of military gains the attack on the 3rd September had been a success. In terms of human suffering and sacrifice, it had been a severe loss. The few remaining officers were to be kept busy over the few days of rest given to the battalion. The saddest and most dispiriting task at hand for them was the writing of letters which had to be written and written as soon as possible to the relatives of the men who had been killed. No available officer was spared this unenviable task. With so many letters to write and so many faces to remember, it became usual to use standard phrases to cushion the blow to the families at home.

Dear Mrs. Beacham, I want just to send you a line to express my sympathy.....Dear Mr. and Mrs. Elson.....he lived to see the advance carried to its final point. Dear Mr. and Mrs. King, ...it may be a consolation to know......Dear Mrs. Simpson....I regret to inform you.......he lies where he fell in a soldier's grave.......killed while advancing and, I believe, instantaneously....He could have suffered no pain, and not before he saw victory crowning our efforts.......killed while gallantly attacking the German trenches.........etc., etc.

The letters made it appear that men died without suffering pain, they died gloriously and willingly. The aim of the letters, in every case, was to preserve the illusion of heroic death, of a clean fight, of a quick death and clean wounds. The ugly truth was unthinkable and never considered suitable or appropriate for the delicately balanced, bereaved families.

Phillip Gibbs, a correspondent representing the London Daily Chronicle Dispatches was able to witness the battalion's attack. His report was published in the New York Times, 7th September:

"It was great fighting that gained this ground and the men were their own generals. The West Country lads were not moved like marionettes pulled by strings from headquarters. It was, after the first orders had been given, a soldier's battle and its success was due to the young officers, non-commissioned officers and men, using their own initiative, finding another way round when one failed and arranging their own tactics in the face of the enemy to suit the situation of the moment".

Letter from Lt. Col. Murray, C.O. 14th Royal Warwickshire Regiment to Lt. Col. Archer-Shee. C.O. 12th Glosters
September 1916

"I think you would like to hear from an independent witness of the magnificent advance of the 12th Gloucesters on the 3rd September last. I happened to be in a position from which I could see every detail of their advance to the 2nd and 3rd objectives.

"The battalion came on in their extended lines as steadily as if on parade and without wavering and, although suffering heavy losses, passed through a German barrage in a most valiant manner. The lines were very much troubled also by long range machine gun fire from the direction of Falfemont Farm, but though gaps appeared and the lines were rapidly thinning out, I never saw the slightest sign of wavering. On that day your men covered themselves with glory, and no troops could have carried through such a difficult task with more dash, or indifference as to consequences."

Lieutenant Ernst Jünger Füsilier Regiment 73

"It was the days at Guillemont that first made me aware of the overwhelming effects of the war of material. We had to adapt ourselves to an entirely new phase of war. The communications between the troops and the staff, between the artillery and the liaison officers, were utterly crippled by the terrific shell-fire. Despatch carriers failed to get through the hail of metal, and telephone wires were no sooner laid than they were shot to pieces. Even light-signalling was put out of action by the clouds of smoke and dust that hung over the field of battle. There was a zone of a kilometre behind the front line where explosives held absolute sway.

"I was wounded and evacuated before the English attacked. My Company suffered severe losses during its time at Guillemont. It was attacked from all sides owing to the large gaps in the line. Little Schmidt, Fähnrich, Wohlqemut, Lieutenants Voqel Sievers - in fact, nearly the whole Company - had died, fighting to the last. A few survivors only, Lieutenant Wetje among them, were taken prisoners. Not one man got back to Combles to tell the tale of this heroic fight that was fought to the finish with such bitterness. Even the English army command made honourable mention of the handful of men who held out to the last near Guillemont. I was no doubt glad of the chance shot that withdrew me as if by a miracle from certain death on the very eve of the engagement."

British Campaigns in France and Flanders - Sir Arthur Conan Doyle

"The advance of the 95th Brigade upon the left of the 5th Division had been a very gallant one, though the objectives which were so bravely won were nameless lines of trenches and a sunken road. The first line of the attack was formed by the 1st DCLI on the left and the 12th Gloucesters on the right, closely followed by the 1st Devons and the 1st East Surreys.

"They were in close touch with the 59th Brigade of the 20th Division, who were attacking Guillemont village on their left. Within two hours of the first attack, all three objectives had been captured, and the remains of the victorious battalions were digging in upon the line Ginchy-Wedge Wood. The losses were heavy in each battalion, but particularly so in the 12th Gloucesters. For a time they were under fire from both German and British batteries. Yet they held on to their ultimate objective and the following extract, from the impression which they produced on an experienced regular lot, is worth quoting, if only to show the pitch of soldiering to which our amateur volunteers had reached:

'Gloucestershire was once the favourite forcing ground for the champions of the British ring. The old fighting breed still lives.'

One of the battalion's young casualties. Killed at Guillemont 3rd September 1916   (IWM)

Grave of Pte. Ernest 'Piggy' Fry. He was buried by his comrades in Wedge Wood 3rd September 1916

1916 – Anybody's Own

Sorting the packs of the dead and wounded at Guillemont 4th September 1916   (IWM)

Awards for the action of the 3rd September:

M.C.
2nd/Lt. R. J. Fitzgerald

M.M.
Sgt. A. Hammond
Sgt. L. Hughes
L/Sgt. W.L. Gage
L/Cpl. F. Boobyer
L/Cp. W. Yacomeni
Pte. W.E. Dunsford
Pte. F.G. Taylor

And when thinking of the battalion's actions, at Longueval and Guillemont, one verse of 'Bravo Bristol' seems so apt:

*It's a rough long road we're going,
It's a tough long job to do.
But as sure as the wind is blowing,
We mean to see it through!
And what though your ranks are thinning?
You fight on just the same
You fight for the sake of England,
And the honour of Bristol's name!*

Some of those that died as a result of the fighting at Guillemont 3rd September 1916

Pte. Arthur Allen.
KIA 3rd September

Pte. Albert Babb.
KIA 3rd September

Pte. Arthur Bacon.
KIA 3rd September

Pte. John Ball.
KIA 2nd September

L/Sgt. Montague Baugh.
KIA 3rd September

Sgt. Arthur Beacham.
KIA 3rd September

Pte. Charles Bennison.
KIA 3rd September

Pte. William Bruton.
KIA 3rd September

Pte. Henry Cash.
KIA 3rd September

1916 – Anybody's Own

Pte. Ernest Cook.
KIA 3rd September

Pte. Frederick Curtis.
KIA 3rd September

Pte. Francis Day.
KIA 3rd September

Pte. Francis Dearlove.
KIA 3rd September

L/Cpl. Leslie Elson.
KIA 3rd September

Pte. Percy Fisher.
KIA 3rd September

L/Cpl. Sidney Foss.
KIA 3rd September

Pte. James Friend.
KIA 3rd September

Pte. Ernest Fry.
KIA 3rd September

1916 – Anybody's Own

Pte. Henry Gerrish.
KIA 3rd September

Sgt. William Harman.
KIA 3rd September

RSM Charles Healey.
KIA 3rd September

Pte. William Iles.
KIA 3rd September

Pte. Frank James.
KIA 3rd September

Pte. Herbert Jelly.
KIA 3rd September

Pte. William King.
KIA 3rd September

Pte. Frederick Lewis.
KIA 3rd September

Pte. Harold Osborne.
KIA 3rd September

Pte. Thomas Price.
KIA 3rd September

L/Sgt. Carl Radford.
KIA 3rd September

Pte. Cyril Rogers.
KIA 3rd September

Pte. Arthur Sampson.
KIA 3rd September

Pte. Leonard Shorto.
KIA 3rd September

Pte. Tomas Stocker.
KIA 3rd September

Pte. Gerald Sumsion.
KIA 3rd September

Pte. William Thyer.
KIA 3rd September

Pte. Charles Wheeler.
KIA 3rd September

1916 – Anybody's Own

Pte. Herbert Williams.
DOW 3rd September

Pte. William Williams.
KIA 3rd September

Pte. Frank Young.
KIA 3rd September

Pte. Frank Channing.
DOW 4th September

Pte. Francis Hitchins.
DOW 11th September

Pte. Richard Middle.
DOW 8th September

Capt. Eric Robinson.
DOW 10th September

Pte. Norman Spafford.
DOW 1st October

Pte. Albert Thompson.
DOW 7th September

Morval

The battalion was, by this time, a severely weakened force of around 200 men and apart from the company commanders, only five officers were available. The battalion spent the next ten days at Ville-sur Ancre, a few miles behind the line, resting and re-organising. New drafts arrived to replace a small proportion of those lost at Longueval and Guillemont. Ironically, one of four subalterns who arrived on 17th September was 2nd/Lt. L.C. Robinson, a cousin of Captain Eric Robinson who had recently died of wounds received at Guillemont. A total of four officers and 112 other ranks joined during this time.

Capt. H. A. Colt
"The situation was:- The division who had come into the line when we went out after the battle of 3rd September at Guillemont had experienced great difficulty in acquiring their next objectives – which included the infamous 'Quadrilateral' – and it was necessary, therefore, to relive them.

"During our stay at Ville-sur-Ancre we had been told, first, that we should not have to go into the battle of the Somme again; later that if we did, however, have to go in, it would only be to hold the line for a day or two. Finally, of course, we did go in and were then told to capture Morval."

Between the 21st and the 24th of September time was indeed spent in support trenches in front of Ginchy not far from the *'Quadrilateral'*. Working parties were provided to help dig assembly trenches. During this time, an amusing controversy occurred.

2nd/Lt. Atkins, while leading a working party in the darkness, stumbled into an old barbed-wire entanglement; the resultant lacerated wounds set up some form of blood poisoning and the officer was sent down the line. Our orderly room returned him as 'sick'. Brigade, on the other hand, said he was 'wounded' and pointed out that the Field Ambulance reported him as suffering from 'multiple wounds'. It was explained that the term 'multiple wounds' was a surgical one and did not mean that the officer had been damaged by the enemy. The matter was referred to the A.D.M.S. of the Division who gave the following Solomon-like decision: *"Had this officer collided with our own barbed-wire he would be 'sick'. As, however, he was damaged by German barbed-wire he is 'wounded."* It was then triumphantly pointed out that though the barbed-wire in question had been erected by the Germans it had been in British possession at least a week. His casualty return was accordingly amended.

An incident occurred while here. Several officers ventured into Leuze Wood in the hope of securing a pheasant or two for supper. The story goes that that they did in fact hit a couple of birds with their revolvers! But the shooting party was rudely broken up when the German artillery decided to put down a violent barrage on the wood. The remaining pheasants and the officers sought safety elsewhere.

To the South East of Ginchy stood the village of Morval. The task of taking this village fell to the 95th Brigade and so on the evening of the 24th the battalion moved up, not in order to 'hold the line' for a day or two, but to take part in the capturing of this village. This came as no surprise to anyone.

At 12.35p.m. 25th September, the Battle of Morval got under way. This time the lead units were 1st Devons and 1st East Surreys, with 12th Gloucesters and 2nd K.O.S.B.s following up. So at the start of the action the battalion were in support. After the first and second objectives, German trenches in front of Morval village were taken, the 12th Gloucesters and 2nd K.O.S.B.s took the village itself, moving right through the village and dug in on the south side.

At this time the enemy may have been described as confused as well as weakened in this area resulting in the battalion suffering relatively few casualties. An interesting feature here was that a large number of Germans, while escaping from Combles lost their way and gave themselves up to the battalion.

14138 Sgt. Norman Pegg
"The next adventure, after Guillemont, was rather a happier one. It was at Morval which had been a very pretty village, situated on a hill, and the capture of this commanding position on 25th September was one of the reasons for the downfall of the German stronghold of Combles. In this battle the Germans

displayed unmistakeable signs of lowering morale. Casualties at Morval were, by comparison with Longueval and Guillemont, very light."

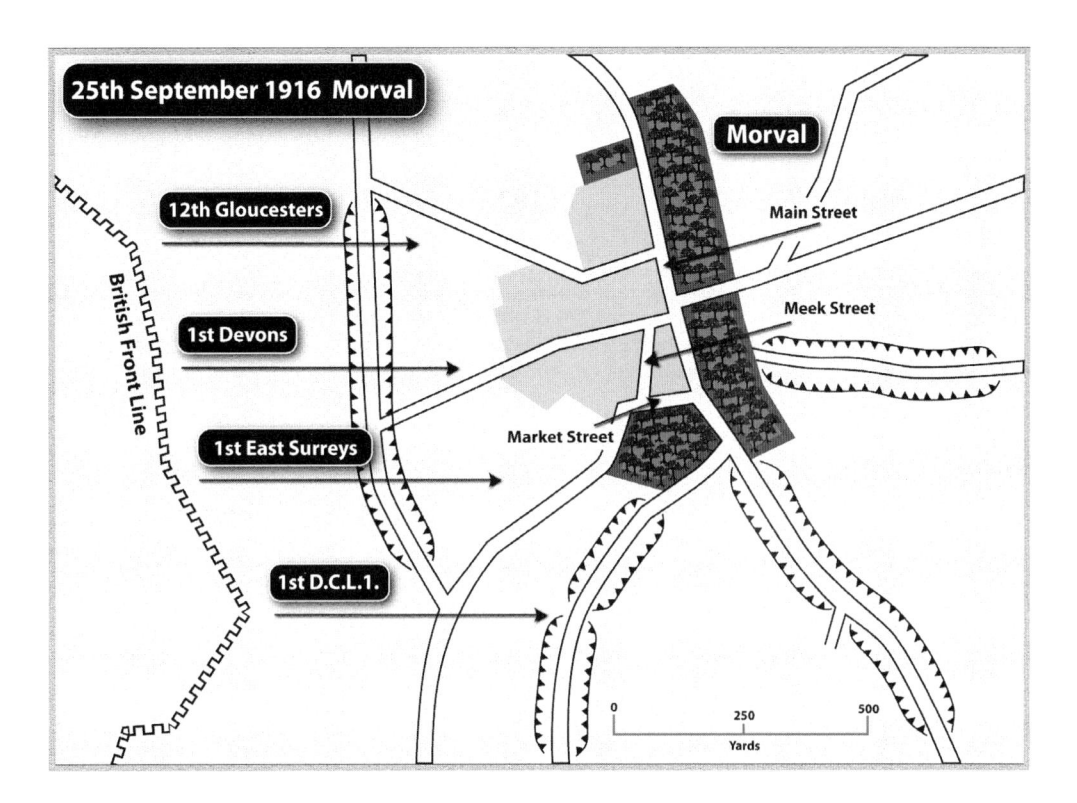

Men of 'B' Company advancing in support, Morval 25th September 1916 (IWM)

Capt. H. A. Colt
"At the beginning of the attack, we were in support, but at the end we swept up through the village and orchard and formed a new front. It should be mentioned that the orchard was a depression devoid of any signs of a tree or any other vegetation.

"Tanks were used in this battle, though they were, however, of no assistance to us as they got 'bellied' in the mud. Later one came back across our line and caused a bit of a commotion."

Casualties at Morval:

Officers wounded:
2nd/Lt. R.C. Cox
2nd/Lt. L.C. Robinson (returned to the battalion three days later)
Other ranks killed or died of wounds: 12
Other ranks wounded: 59

Private George Stanley Hawker, a member of the Ambulance Section, was giving water to a wounded German soldier when a shrapnel shell burst nearby taking off his left hand. In a badly shell-shocked state, he was evacuated to a C.C.S. and then base hospital then a hospital back in England. Shortly after his arrival he received the following letter from Captain John Lang R.A.MC who commanded the Ambulance Section:

"My dear Hawker, I was glad to have news of you today and to learn that things were going satisfactorily. I wish you to know that I have recommended you for the Military Medal in recognition of your splendid work, not only during the last fight, but during the whole time I have been with the battalion and I know, whether you get the award or not, both your fellow stretcher bearers and myself fully realise that your bravery has well earned even a higher award than that."

Decorations were few on the Somme, but in all fifteen Military Medals and one Military Cross were awarded. Three of the MM's went to Ambulance Section members; Privates Dunsford, Taylor and Hawker. The M.C. going to Lt. R.J. Fitzgerald for his part in the attack of 3rd September at Guillemont.

On the night of 26th September the battalion was relieved and proceeded to march to Oxford Copse, a camp in Happy Valley. Here it bivouacked for a couple of days. Its stay was uneventful save one night an enemy aircraft bombed them, though no casualties resulted.

After the capture of Morval, the 5th Division's involvement in the Somme battle was over. The 12th Gloucesters was now mearly a shadow of what it had been a year earlier.

British Campaigns in France and Flanders - Sir Arthur Conan Doyle
"The 95th Brigade carried the trenches to the West of Morval. This dashing piece of work was accomplished by the 1st Devons and the 1st East Surreys. When they had reached their objective, the 12th Gloucesters were sent through them to occupy and consolidate the South side of the village."

The 5th Division received the following communiqué on 30th September:
H.Q. Fourth Army
30th September 1916.

"The conspicuous part that has been taken by the 5th Division in the Battle of the Somme reflects the highest credit on the Division as a whole and I desire to express to every Officer, N.C.O. and man, my congratulations and warmest thanks.

"The heavy fighting in Delville Wood and Longueval, the attack and capture of Falfemont Farm line and Leuze Wood and finally the storming of Morval, are feats of arms seldom equalled in the annals of theBritish Army. They constitute a record of unvarying success which it has been the lot of few divisions to attain, and the gallantry, valour and endurance, of all ranks have been wholly admirable.

"The work of the Divisional Artillery in establishing the barrages and supporting the infantry attacks, is deserving of the highest praise and proves that a very high standard of training has been reached. It is a matter of great regret to me that the division is leaving the Fourth Army, but after three strenuous periods in the battle front, they have more than earned a rest.

"In wishing all ranks good fortune for the future, I trust I may one day again, have this fine division under my command."

H. Rawlinson,
General,
Commanding Fourth Army

Lt. Col. Archer-Shee

"The casualties were terrible. The flower of the 12th was lost on the Somme. Of the 950 members of the battalion who entered the Somme battles, some 736 became casualties. Although there was still a proportion of 'old originals' in the battalion when, after some months, some of the wounded returned from hospital, the necessary large re-enforcements meant that the character of the battalion had changed.

"After the Somme it was never, in quite the same way, that 'band of brothers' the battalion of 'business and professional men'. Because of this, those originals who remained were drawn still closer in comradeship, for many of us I believe, would say in thinking of the Battle of the Somme and our dead comrades."

The Battle of the Somme of 1916 marked the end of an age of innocence and of vital optimism in British life that has never fully recovered.

Some of those that died as a result of the fighting at Morval 25th September 1916

Pte. Charles Mansfield
DOW 3rd October

Pte. Norman Oakhill
DOW 14th December

Pte. Reginald Pople
DOW 25th September

Pte. Grantley Skuse
DOW 27th September

Pte. Albert Weeks
DOW 26th September

The battalion moved by train and by foot to Bethune where residence was taken up at the Ecole des Jeunes Filles, a girls' school that had been requisitioned. This was home for four days, at the end of which time the 95th Brigade was tasked to take over the line at Givenchy which was immediately north of the La Bassee Canal, Festubert which was north of Givenchy and Cuinchy which was just south of the canal. Collectively, the three areas were summed up as the Festubert Sector. Here the battalion remained until March 1917.

Festubert

This was slightly North of Givenchy and very wet. The reason for the water was that drainage was difficult due to the many drainage ditches having been destroyed by shell fire. This was decidedly reminiscent of the 'Old Bill' type of warfare. The trenches were not trenches but breastworks, erected on what were locally called 'islands' or plots of ground two or three inches above the surrounding water. Breastworks were above-ground trenches. Earth, rocks, sand-bags, masonry, tree trunks and any other material that could be found in the area was used to provide cover. Every eight yards there was an island traverse, a great mound of earth and sandbags strengthened by revetting, around which the trench wound. This was intended to localise the effects of shell explosions or prevent an enemy who might reach the flank being able to pour fire right down the length of a trench. Dugouts were made by leaving a space for a shelter and covering it with 'wriggly tin' and earth. There were numerous communication trenches. Moving from one post to another meant wading. Mud was plentiful. But there were no mines and the shelling was not severe. Accommodation, if one was lucky, was a leaky, damp shelter.

Givenchy

This sector was noticeably dryer than at Festubert. The front line, however, was very muddy owing to it constantly being blown in. Along most of it, extended a series of mine craters each of which had a name, such as 'Red Dragon', 'White Horse' etc. Trench mortar fire here was heavy. The support line was almost entirely destroyed by this means during the battalion's stay. A good deal of patrolling went on without much success. Near the Givenchy church was a spring that proudly advertised that it produced the best water in the Pas de Calais.

In the trenches, dugouts were impossible. Men lived in shelters made by roofing over a portion of the fire bay. When it rained, the trenches were usually water-logged for days. Some unknown genius had, previous to the battalion's arrival, constructed a 'dug-out' in Oxford Terrace, the support line. It was not very deep. Its occupants one night awoke to find the place a foot or so deep in water, while the roof was one glorified shower bath. Poking his head outside, one of the men found, as he had expected, it was raining.

Cuinchy

This was south of the canal. It was connected about one hundred yards in the rear to the front line, to the Givenchy sector by a foot bridge that was a couple of feet under water. There was also a lock further back and a bridge (iron road) about a mile back adjacent to the reserve line.

The principle scenery here was the 'Brickstacks'. Some belonged to the enemy but most to the British. The area had been an extensive brick field area. The large neat stacks of bricks were all that remained of the brick factory that once dominated the area. As in the Givenchy Sector the defences were breastworks due to the high water table. However, compared to previous quarters the ground here was slightly dryer. These breastworks ran in and out of the huge thirty feet high stacks of bricks. The lines at this point were quite close together with the British and the enemy sharing the stacks, with each side's snipers making full use of them. Between these ran a closely connected line of mine craters - 'Lunatic', 'Stirling', 'Argyle & Sutherland Highlanders' - were among the most notable of these. The front line here was blown in with unfailing regularity in front of the 'Brickstacks' each day. So too was 'Edgware Road', the extreme right communication trench. This sector was favourable for raids and small patrols.

So much for the front line, when in support the battalion was usually accommodated either in the support line, near the reserve line, or better, in 'Marley Street' which still boasted of a little battered housing. From here, as was usually the case, working parties went back up the line each night either carrying or digging.

As might be expected, the battalion on arrival here, was very weak in numbers. Since the Somme battles, only 150 drafts had been received. Nor was the battalion up to the same high pitch of efficiency and moral that had enabled it, without flinching, to endure the terrific shelling at Longueval, the devastating machine gun fire during at Guillemont and the 'last kick' in the capture of Morval. Many of the well trained, 'beginning-of-the-war' men had become casualties. They had been replaced by a small number of badly trained, humble spirited drafts who represented conscription. Having said that, in time, the new drafts did pick up a resolute and soldierly spirit and eventually became worthy imitators of their predecessors in the battalion.

Four days of each sixteen were spent in reserve at small villages three or four miles to the rear. Le Quesnoy and Gorre were usually occupied by the battalion. Occasionally, the whole brigade would be relieved and would then go back further to Bethune. That was always very popular as some form of normal life could be resumed for a short while, in the way of washing, cleaning and eating.

14596 Pte. William Ayres
"We spent some time in the La Bassee Canal zone. When in support, we were usually billeted in the village of Cuinchy near Bethune. At one time we signallers were in the house of two sisters, one married whose husband was serving with the French forces and one a widow. There were four daughters and one son. They looked after us well, bringing mattresses for us to sleep on and serving us with coffee, eggs and chips. When the serving husband came home on leave they gave us a splendid meal. They had previously lived further up along the canal where our front line, at that time went through their former home."

14138 Sgt. Norman Pegg
"After Morval we moved to another part of the line, Festubert and the La Bassee brickfield. The six months spent here were of the ordinary trench-holding sort, with little more exciting than had happened to us at Arras. It was a district as slimy and slushy as the Somme marshes were the previous winter. At Festubert there were several 'islands' which were the last word in discomfort. A few inches down and you came to water so that instead of trenches, parapets or breastworks were the order. The great feature about the parapet was that it was easily knocked down by a well-aimed shell and that in this way the damage caused in a fraction of a second took a few hours to repair at night-time. The whole of the country hereabouts was waterlogged.

"In the brickfield at Cuinchy, which is the other side of the famous La Bassee Canal and railway, conditions were a little better and, underneath the huge stacks of bricks, safe dugouts had been constructed. A marvellous system of tunnels, extending for miles, had been bored by the Royal Engineers. It was, in fact, a great place for underground life, in spite of its very close proximity to the watery land around Festubert. There were in Cuinchy, Canbrin and other villages clustered together many cellars which were habitable and they were utilised to house troops. Within a hundred yards of the line these cellar dugouts were used to a considerable extent.

"The brickfield and the immediate neighbourhood had been a great district for trench mines of all sizes, the earth hereabouts giving the appearance of having been blown up several times over. There were huge craters extending for a long line, generally in 'No-Man's-Land' but, during our time amid the brick-stacks, mining activity had thankfully quietened down a little."

This, of course, was regarded as a 'quiet' sector and despite the battalion's weak state it had no bearing on the amount of line that was to be held. Consequently, the line was held by a series of small posts around 200 yards apart.

On 22nd October, after the battalion had been a fortnight in this part of the line, Lt. Col. Archer-Shee went home on leave to have a bullet – an old wound from 1914 – removed. Major Blennerhassett took over temporary command of the battalion until 20th November which saw the arrival of Lt. Col. R. I. Rawson of the 1st Gloucesters to take over command of the battalion during Col. Archer-Shee's absence.

The relatively quiet nature of life in the Festubert Sector was a welcome change for the men who had suffered and survived the conditions on the Somme. Though rather depleted in numbers the gradual return of wounded men and new drafts allowed the battalion to sit back and gather itself whilst continuing to carry out its normal duties.

13986 L/Cpl. Robert Anstey

"I had been wounded during July at Longueval and had spent three months recovering. When I rejoined the battalion in November they were in trenches on the banks of the La Bassee Canal. I went up one evening with the rations.

"It was a sadly altered 'A' Company I found, and as I sat in the 'dug-out' with young Sgt. Major McFarlane asking after one and another of those fellows I had grown to love, only to hear that they had passed on, a black feeling of depression came over me for the first time in my army life. After about twenty minutes there was a voice at the entrance and in walked Lt. Parr. Those months had altered him, but there was the same steady smile. He said he was glad to see me back, and as we shook hands we looked into each other's eyes. I don't think it was imagination on my part when I felt that rank didn't exist. We were brothers under the skin.

"The Sgt. Major soon went out on duty and for a while we sat and talked of those great hearted fellows we should see again no more. Then he got up and said, "We've have received some reinforcements, but they are different from the good fellows we have known. But we must carry on." And then, after a pause, he looked me in the eye again and said, "I'm relying on you Anstey, to back me up." That was just what I needed to throw off my depression at what seemed the tragic futility of it all."

Casualties during the remainder of 1916 were understandably light. Those that there were, were caused by the odd shell or trench mortar round. One such unfortunate incident occurred on 30th October when Private Ernest Bowring from Barton Hill, Bristol became a victim. An original battalion man originally of 'F' Company and then of 'B' Company, his mother received the following letter from one of his pals:

15066 L/Cpl. William Smallcombe

"It is with the deepest regret and profound sorrow that, on behalf of the Lewis Gun section and myself, I have to convey to you the sad news of your son's death. He was the best and bravest comrade whom we had – never a sign of fear in the face of the most terrible dangers. Always he was bright and cheery. It was cruel fate that in the last hour which we were in the trenches, a German trench mortar shell wrecked the 'dug-out' and crushed your dear son. His death must have been instantaneous for, although parties worked for a long time, they could not get to him. You can rest assured that every effort will be made to recover his body and have it buried in the soldiers' cemetery. We all send our heartfelt sympathy to you and trust God will give you strength to bear this great burden. Later when peace is declared, I will endeavour to let you know where your dear son and our brave comrade met his death."

Private Bowring's body was eventually recovered and buried at Gore British Military Cemetery very close to where the battalion had its reserve billets.

1916 – Anybody's Own

On the 3rd November the battalion marched from its rest quarters at Le Quesnoy to relieve the 1st D.C.L.I. in the line at Cuinchy. This was its first time at Cuinchy. The very next night, November 4th/5th a small enemy force succeeded in raiding one of the battalion's posts. The raid was well planned and ably carried out. A party of men of 'C' Company manning a left post was surprised. Before the men could react they were clubbed, a number taken prisoner and another left bleeding from several knife wounds. The enemy then proceeded to bomb along the defence line towards a post on the right. A Lewis gunner at this post was killed by a bomb. The enemy retired immediately the support arrived and were fired on by Lewis guns as they crossed 'no man's land'. The battalion's losses were one killed, three taken prisoner and four wounded. The Lewis gunner killed by the bomb during the raid was 14858 Pte. George Frederick Percy Bryant, aged 22, of 'C' Company. He was an original volunteer who enlisted September 1914.

The remainder of 1916 was relatively uneventful. Before Christmas, the battalion marched back to the girls' school billets that it had enjoyed at the end of September last.

Battalion signallers at the Ecole des Jeunes Filles, Bethune, Christmas 1916

At this time the 12th battalion was quite prominent in the brigade as Col. Rawson was also commanding 95th Brigade. The old grouse of the D.C.L.I. was: *"It isn't that the Gloucesters have joined the brigade, but the brigade that has joined the Gloucesters."*

The men spent a very happy Christmas. Not only were they out of the line but they also took advantage of fine food provided by the Comforts Committee and the large grants made to each company from the canteen funds. While at Bethune, the many open shops and estaminets provided a pleasant distraction to the men, as did no less than two concerts held by the 5th Divisional Concert party, the 'Whizz-Bangs', at theatres in the town.

14138 Sgt. Norman Pegg
"A description of events in the Festubert-La Bassee district would be incomplete without a reference to the town of Bethune. From a tired infantryman's point of view, it was a health resort. It was five or six

miles from the line and at the time we were there it had not suffered greatly, there being only a few shell-shattered houses and civilians remained behind in large numbers. Its main fascination was in the numerous well-stocked shops, where food and drink could be obtained at reasonable prices. The great idea of most men immediately coming from the line for a rest in the town was, after getting cleaned up, to dash off and have a good, hot meal. Steak, chips and onions, eggs and chips and various other morsels were greatly in demand – and available."

Poster advertising the 5th Divisional Concert Party - The Whizz-Bangs.
December 1916, Bethune   (IWM)

      Rather more tedious, however, was the last Sunday of the year when there was first a church service, then a lecture lasting an hour and a half from a G.H.Q. Staff Officer on censorship, followed in the afternoon by a compulsory meeting with a dozen or more chaplains to talk over the future of Post Bellum religion.

      After the battles of 1916 the battalion was in a weakened state and the war was entering its third year. There was no sign that it would end soon. What lay in store for the coming year, was anyone's guess.

Chapter VIII

1917 – Soldier on

For the British Army, 1916 was dominated by the Battle of the Somme which started disastrously on 1st July. There followed nearly five months of attrition during which the Fourth Army of General Henry Rawlinson and the Fifth Army of General Hubert Gough advanced about seven miles (11 km) for a cost of 420,000 casualties. The French, the British and the Germans paid a heavy price for the fighting, though none of the contending parties knew the exhaltation of victory. Despite the losses, the British Army under Haig had grown in size and experience to such an extent that it was now regarded as an equal partner to the French Army on the Western Front.

In February 1917 the German Army performed a tactical withdrawal and re-grouped at a new defensive line – *The Hindenburg Line*. It was this formidable defencive system that the British Army would face during its next offensive, the Battle of Arras in April.

The lessons learned during the Somme campaign appeared in two official pamphlets: SS143 – *Instructions for the Training of Platoons for Offensive Action* and SS144 – *The Normal Formation for the Attack*. They both represented a significant step forward in tactical doctrine. They discussed the re-organisation of the platoon as a major tactical unit giving more flexibilty and firepower in terms of riflemen, Lewis gunners and bombers. The lessons were absorbed and applied to future training.

The year started with the news that Capt. Colt and Lt. Parr had been awarded the MC in the New Years Honours and Capt. Colt had been gazetted Major. During the next two months Major Colt was given temporary command of the battalion while the C.O. was away.

During January little of interest occurred, except that two men performed the almost incredible feat of stealing a jar of rum from a party of Highlanders. The Highlanders were a working party on a communication trench and had brought their dinners – including the rum. The enemy started to shell and the Highlanders took cover. While this was going on, the two men crept forward and pinched the rum. Luckily for them, the Highlanders had no idea of what had happened to their rum.

At the end of January the battalion moved slightly south to Cuinchy where it remained for the rest of its time in the Festubert Sector.

The weather was very cold and concealed braziers were allowed to the men's delight. Not only did this concession allow them to warm themselves and dry their socks but it allowed then to cook the chestnuts provided - in lieu of so many ounces of potatoes – by a thoughtful Government with the 'wind up' about a potato famine.

Col. Archer-Shee returned toward the end of January: however, it was to be a relatively short stay. He had been finding the combined pressures of running the battalion and carrying out his parliamentary duties too much. On 10th February, he handed in his resignation. On 25th February, during a particularly quiet month, he proceeded on leave prior to relinquishing command of the battalion. He was not to return to the battalion and was sorely missed by the remaining original men who had known and respected him since he joined the battalion in August 1915. The battalion hit a low spot with, during August 1915, the loss of their beloved C.O., Lt. Col. Burges. But, in the event, his replacement, Lt. Col Archer-Shee D.S.O., proved a most excellent C.O. who, both at home and overseas, enjoyed as high a respect as it would be possible for any Commanding Officer to enjoy. There was no doubt that the good reputation which the battalion earned in the line, up to the conclusion of the Somme battles, was due very largely to him.

1917 – Soldier on

Men washing in the Le Bassee Canal

March was an eventful month in one respect: on the 5th a most successful raid was mounted by 'A' Company, under the command of Capt. W. G. Chapman who had joined the battalion from 1st Gloucesters six weeks previously. 'A' Company was sent back to Le Quesnoy for a full week in order to rehearse for the action.

Zero was at 5 a.m. and was launched from the bottom of 'Argyle' crater. Even though the event had been postponed one week from the original date due to bright moonlight, the moon was, on the night, near its full. Luckily, however, its light grew dim as zero approached and, by a stroke of luck, snow began to fall.

The raid was carried out under a barrage, while smoke was used to prevent any action on the part of the enemy machine guns in their brick-stacks. It proved very effective. From zero until the last man was back in, the raid took twenty minutes. On their return, among the stream of men with blackened faces were two terrified Germans. They looked as if the least they expected was instant execution.

Our casualties were very light. Two men wounded in exploding the second Bangalore torpedo-for making a gap in the enemy wire–and one man slightly scratched on the cheek by a comrade's bayonet in the rough and tumble of 'going over'. The enemy's casualties were estimated at six killed when entering their trenches and fifty killed by mobile charges dropped into their dugouts – judged by the number of rifles standing outside.

This was the most successful raid carried out by the 95th Brigade up until that time. After this one, in order of merit came that of the 1st D.C.L.I. who inflicted the same enemy casualties but themselves suffered thirty killed and wounded. In retaliation, the enemy attempted several small raids here. All were miserable failures.

Among those awarded honours for this action were Capt. Chapman, the Military Cross and Sergeant Macfarlane the Distinguished Conduct Medal.

13986 Sgt. Robert Anstey

"'A' Company carried out a successful raid on 5th March at Cuinchy. The whole Company went over into the German trenches, took two prisoners, did an immense amount of damage and got back with only a few lightly wounded.

1917 – Soldier on

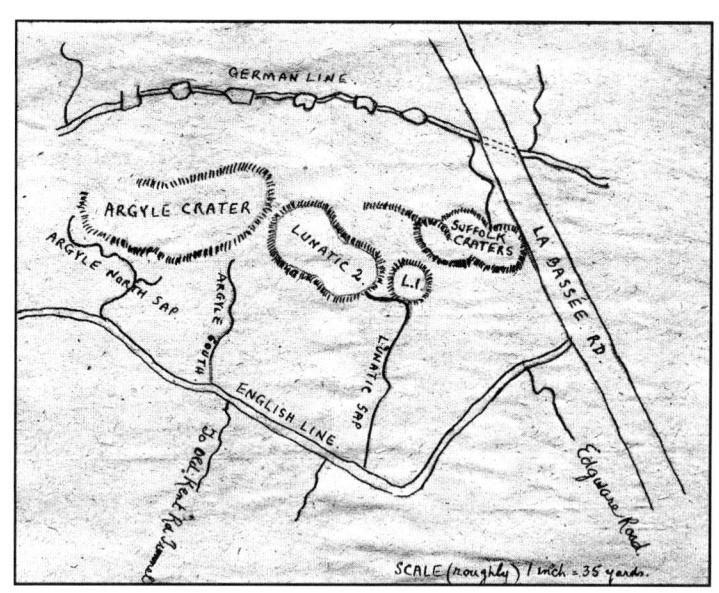

Sketch map of area covered by the raid

"The Company assembled in Argyle crater, while I had the job of being let down on a rope by two other men in order to deal with a German listening post in Lunatic crater No.1, (L1 in the above sketch) before moving on to the German line."

Lt. Col. Rawson returned from brigade and from 18th March took full command. Soon after the battalion was in billets at Burbure, a small mining town surrounded by huge slag heaps. As a very strenuous training regime was undertaken at this time, full use was made of these slag heaps for Lewis gun and rifle fire and rifle grenade and bombing practice. Unfortunately whilst practicing bombing one bomb exploded prematurely and blew off the thrower's hand also wounding Lt. E. M. T. Burges. While there, another regiment used the slag heap area for a grimmer purpose – the execution of a deserter.

During this period several new officers from the 66th Division, then in England, were attached to the battalion for instructional purposes. The most notable of these was a captain who was prepared to reduce his rank to 2nd/Lt. in order to join the 12th Gloucesters. Also drafts of other ranks were received signifying an approaching action and, sure enough, on 7th April the 5th Division was ordered to provide a reserve for the Canadian Corps in their successful attack on Vimy Ridge on Easter Monday.

The Canadian's attack on Vimy Ridge was a complete success in the centre and on the right. However, on the left they had been held back. As a result, on 20th April the 5th Division relieved the Canadian division affected.

14138 Sgt. Norman Pegg
"But good things come to an end some time, and at the end of March we bade farewell to Bethune and the brickfields. A short time was spent near Lillers 'resting' during which period we did an incredible amount of drilling – marking time in the mud – for instance. We then joined the Canadians near Vimy. The Ridge had been captured by the Canadians on Easter Monday.

"South of Lens is a large village – Avion; and it was here that we had our first experience of the pleasure of Vimy Ridge. The houses, many of which seemed quite new, had not been badly knocked about and, like all French dwellings, they possessed cellars. Unfortunately, Fritz knew all about these cellars and, guessing that they sheltered troops, shelled them.

> "Near Avion was a small village named Fresnoy, a name which, when combined with the date, 8th May is particularly odorous in the nostrils of those who were misfortunate enough to have been there at that time."

Capt. H. A. Colt
> "The weather was abominable while we were at Bois des Alleux, a good deal of snow falling and making the mud worse than before – if that was possible.
>
> "On the 14th we relieved a support battalion of the Canadian 19th Brigade in quarries east of Souchez near Cabaret Rouge. Shelter was in the form of tunnels. About a mile away from our destination, voices in the dark enquired whether 'Old' Sam Farrington was still with us. Investigation was promptly made as to the identity of the persons so familiar with the battalion. They proved to be the 129th Heavy Battery who shared H.Q. at Bower Ashton with us in early 1915. L/Cpl Farrington had been the M.O.'s orderly at that time, whence their intimate knowledge of him. During this time battalion headquarters suffered several casualties as it picked its way over the 'duckboard' track across the river.
>
> "About the 18th we were near the Bois l' Hirondelle. Everyone one who was there will remember this place, through Angres and the railway bridge. It was a nasty place. Here the battalion had a rough time, especially from shelling. One platoon of 'A' Company being blown up by a shell that penetrated their cellar.
>
> "About a week was spent here at a small village (Petit Servins) nearby, when the battalion moved up to Maison Blanche, near the Labyrinth of evil fame. The transport moved to a spot midway on the Arras–St. Eloi Road. Next morning they were badly shelled by a heavy, high velocity gun – believed to be a 12.2." These shells did not give the customary warning of their approach. About twenty being fired one falling in the middle of the camp making a hole in which an ordinary police station could have been placed, with ease."

When the shell landed in the camp, Captain Taylor was sitting in his bath while Captain Parr was shaving. Casualties, however, were light. One man scalded by having a 'dixie' of boiling water upset on him and two men injured by large clods of earth.

14596 William Ayres
> "On that day Jo Clifford was killed on his way up to the line. His body was brought back and we buried him in the valley."

Casualties mounted as a result of the increasing artillery fire raining down on the battalion's positions. On the 24th relief came and the following nine days were spent in the comparative safety of 'Niagra' camp doing the usual cleaning and training. And, of course, there were the inevitable church parades. But every man enjoyed the added luxury of a hot bath – a very rare occurrence for the front line soldier.

The following was the disposition of the battalion at this time:

C.O. Lt/Col R.I. Rawson
2nd I/C Major H.A. Colt
Adjutant: Captain J.H. Allen
O.C. 'A' Company: Captain W. G. Chapman MC
2nd I/C Lt. R.J. Fitzgerald MC
O.C. 'B' Company: Captain W.W. Parr
2nd i/c Captain H. Jeune
O.C. 'C' Company: Captain J. P. Webb
O.C. 'D' Company: Major T.M. Allison

Fresnoy

The small village of Fresnoy, best described as 'a pimple on a salient', was situated 3½ miles east of Vimy Ridge. To its right, the line ran back well west of Oppy – which had defied all efforts by the Canadians to capture it – while on the left, the line ran back well west of Lens. It was under complete observation, for on the rising ground near the Chez Bontemps – a large quarry on the hillside – it was possible to look down into the area. On 3rd May the 2nd battalion of the 1st Brigade of the 1st Canadian Division attacked and captured the village. It was stated that 20 Canadians had actually captured Fresnoy, but that 500 had become casualties trying to hold it. There was good reason for this. It was part of the Queant Drocourt line, which the Germans were quite attached to.

The 1st Canadian infantry battalion was relieved by the 12th Gloucesters on the 4th May. The relief was difficult as the ground could not be reconnoitred in daylight and the 'trenches' were no more than a series of overlapping shell holes connected by ditches. The Germans continued shelling all night.

The order of battle of the 95th Brigade at this time was:
Front line right: 1st East Surreys
Front line left: 12th Gloucesters
In support: 1st D.C.L.I.
In reserve: 1st Devons

The 1st Battalion East Surreys were to the right of the battalion and the 19th Canadian battalion to the left. From that date onward, the enemy concentrated all available hate on Fresnoy. The situation thus far was that the Canadians had pushed forward as far as possible and the Germans were prepared to fight back. Positions were flattened by an incessant bombardment and enemy aeroplanes harassed the defenders with their machine guns. Although retaliatory artillery support had been constantly asked for, very little was forthcoming. On the evening of the 7th May Brigade H.Q. were warned to expect an attack.

On the night of May 7th/8th the Companies in the front line were relieved by 'A' Company on the right, under the command of Lt. R. Fitzgerald, and 'C' Company on the left under command of Capt. J. P. Webb. 'B' Company going into support and 'D' Company into reserve. 'A' Company's trenches had been totally obliterated, the men having to move into shell holes to the rear of the line.

A good deal of rain fell during the night and in the morning there was a heavy mist. At 3.45a.m. a very heavy enemy barrage started on all lines and battalion H.Q. situated to the front left of Arleux. The rain formed mud which was liberally distributed over the rifles and Lewis guns during the relief, due to both the slippery mud causing men to fall and the shells throwing soil and mud everywhere.

With the arrival of the 5th Bavarian Division, brought up expressly to win back the position, now complete, the German attack was imminent. If the Germans were feeling strong, the 12th Gloucesters were feeling unfit and weak in numbers, its losses of the previous year never fully made up. A large proportion of the replacements received were partially trained conscripts and men from other regiments who had been wounded and were out to the front for a second and even third time.

At dawn the battalion was attacked in force while gas shells were dropped in quantity on the supporting artillery. Due to heavy mist it was not possible to see more than 50 yards. S.O.S. flares were fired but not seen by the artillery and all communications cables had been cut by enemy shells. The first attack was repulsed by the front line Companies. However, the second attack managed a foothold in the front line trenches. 'B' support Company under Capt. Parr immediately counter-attacked and ejected the Germans from the battalion's trenches. The battalion was outnumbered and, during the third attack, small pockets of enemy worked around to the rear of the line and so the battalion was being attacked from three sides. Things were not going well. 'A' Company had practically ceased to exist in the first enemy attack. The remnants of 'C' Company had fallen back with a mixed crowd of Canadians to the sunken road occupied by battalion H.Q. Two wounded officers of 'C' Company reported that the Canadians on their left had fallen back, exposing their flank, carrying with them some of 'C' Company. They also reported that casualties were heavy.

14138 Sgt. Norman Pegg
"The defences around Fresnoy and the small wood adjacent, which had just been taken, had not undergone any form of consolidation. It consisted of shell-holes connected by a few glorified ditches, and in these lay the battalion, to face hordes of Germans, who came over the top in the early morning of 8th May 1917.

"During the previous night heavy rain had fallen. This caused much mud which, in turn, clogged and choked the rifles and Lewis guns. It was necessary to work in pairs – one man firing, the other cleaning. When the myriads of Germans appeared in the early morning they had what might have appeared an easy task. But we put up a good hand-to-hand fight with bomb and rifle and even rifle butts and for a time held the attackers at bay. But we were very much outnumbered and gradually forced back. But in small groups the men fought stubbornly until wounded or killed."

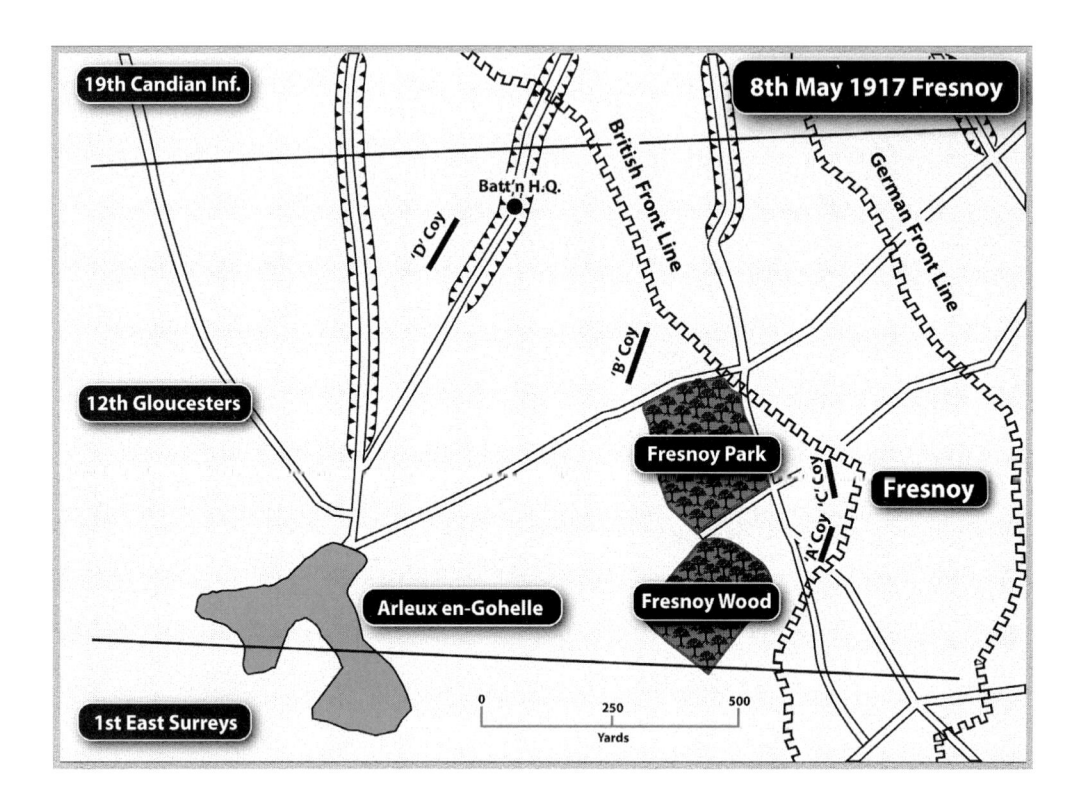

Lt. Col Rawson, C.O. immediately ordered Capt Kendall – 'D' Company D.C.L.I. to take his Company and 'C' Company 12th Gloucesters and counter-attack to regain the front line. However, within an hour Capt. Kendall had returned and reported that it was hopeless counter-attacking without a supporting barrage which he could not get.

At 07.30 'D' Company, under command of Major Allison, was the final Company to be committed and moved forward to make ground beyond the sunken lane where the remnants of the 12th Gloucesters, 1st D.C.L.I. and various groups of Canadians had retired to. The rain had made the ground very slippery, making progress slow and it was a long way to the front line. After some distance they met the enemy. At 08.00 Major Allison reported back that his Company was held up by machine gun fire and were being heavily barraged. By 09.45 the situation took a further turn for the worst when it was reported that 1st East Surreys had fallen back to Arleux. 12th Gloucesters original position was now completely outflanked, forcing them to fall back also. No further impression could be made against the enemy. Around 11.30 Major Allison, who had himself been wounded, and 'D' Company fell back and arrived in the sunken lane. As a last ditch effort, Lt. Col. Rawson himself re-organised about 150 men in six platoons, got their weapons clean and with three Lewis guns was able to establish a line by 3.00p.m. Nor, may it be added were the 1st Devons and 1st Norfolks any more successful when they mounted a counter- attack some sixteen hours later.

Lt. Col. R.I.Rawson
"The position remained thus until evening when Lt. Col. Blunt of the 1st Devons arrived to take over. An S.O.S. signal was sent up by the Canadians on our left who reported 600 enemy north of Fresnoy Wood. This time we got a good barrage which broke up the enemy attack. At 10p.m. the remains of the 12th Gloucesters were relieved by the 1st Devons."

Capt. H. A. Colt
"By the time the battalion was relieved only one officer – 2nd/Lt. G.H. Gillard – besides the C.O. and Adjutant came out unwounded. The battalion was very much depleted and filled with a savage hate against the Hun."

By this time there was not a single Company officer left in 12th Gloucesters. The support Company, 'B' Company had fought to the last. None of the officers, including Capt. W. W. Parr, 2nd Lt.s W. T. Burges, A. W. Merrell and J. T. Ryde was ever seen or heard of again. Furthermore, 2nd Lt. D. N. Leicester was killed; Lt R. J. Fitzgerald was wounded and missing; Major T. M. Allison, 2nd Lt's. E.M.T. Burges, C. J Houlston, A. Metcalf, R. C. Cox, C. H. Culpin, D. D. Herring, G. F. Ticehurst and were wounded. Of the rank and file, 87 men were dead and 201 wounded.

Lt. R. J. Fitzgerald
"The Germans counter-attacked at dawn. I was cut off with a number of others, all of whom were wounded. I must have been rendered unconscious as the next thing I remember is coming round and being in the enemy's hands. I was taken to a German field dressing station where bullets were removed from my arms and shrapnel from my face without anesthetic. But this was due to the rush and any suffering was not intentional. From here I sent a postcard to my wife back at Warmley, Bristol, which reached her through the Red Cross about six weeks later.

"On May 11th I arrived at a hospital at Rastatt in Germany where my wounds were seen to. I had been hit nine times. They took X-ray photographs and I do believe they really did their best for me. By June 8th I was considered well enough to move and was transferred to Strohen prison camp."

14997 Pte. Richard Amesbury
"The night was characterised by a heavy rainfall which diluted our spirits and the mud clogged our rifles. Both the rifles and Lewis guns were choked. Some of our Lewis guns and gunners were knocked out so that when the hordes of Germans attacked at daybreak they had an easy task. But we put up a good hand to hand fight with bomb and rifle and, for a time held them back. There was lively work at close quarters, the butt ends of the rifles being used to good effect. Quite a few of our own chaps were stunned in this way only to be taken prisoner when they gained consciousness. A number of chaps who were actually surrounded escaped, others were rescued. A few escaped by acting as a 'guy' which was to feign death. It was a very dangerous practice, but a few, by waiting for their opportunity got away with it."

24429 Pte. Bert Hickery
"The trench was like thick rice pudding. As soon as you took the cover off your rifle it was clogged up – useless. I remember Sgt. Bouskill saying, "They are massing up for another attack." I missed that attack, luckily, as I was detailed with another man to relieve two brigade runners. On the way there, I remember seeing our field gunners who had been gassed. That explained the lack of artillery support. The Germans knew of the conditions in our trenches and kept up a constant barrage. If we had continued to counter-attack I am sure we would have won back the position, but the battalion was too badly decimated.

"Sgt. Bouskill was badly wounded in this attack and, subsequently died of his wounds later that day."

20089 Pte. William James
"I took a draft of reinforcements up the line to Captain Parr. By the time I got back to battalion H.Q., all those men and Captain Parr had been reported as missing."

Lt. Col R. I. Rawson
"Before the enemy's infantry attack, most of the Lewis guns in the front line had been blown up, but two were kept going, in each case the Nos. 1 being the only men remaining of the team. One gun was responsible for wiping out four waves of Germans with 15 drums firing point blank at fifty yards. The German losses were stated by my men to have been very heavy. Their bodies piled in lines on the ground."

In addition to these two guns was one operated by 2nd/Lt.. E.M.T. Burges, a relative of Lt. Col Burges, who kept a gun going until himself wounded. The Lewis gun to which Lt. Col. Rawson refers was being operated by Cpl. Civil of 'C' Company.

20193 Cpl. Harry Civil
"On the evening of May 4th 1917, we took over the front line trenches at Fresnoy to the right of Vimy Ridge, our portion being at the head of a salient, and as it had been raining previously our trenches were in a very muddy state. Before dawn on May 8th the Germans put up a terrific barrage and we 'stood to'. Through the dim light we saw the enemy advancing in mass formation and immediately, as number 1 of my Lewis Gun section, I opened fire. I kept firing and saw the Germans going down in crowds. They were so thick that each bullet probably accounted for two or more of them. They were such mass formation and so near that I could not miss them.

"Someone in the rear was shouting "go back, quick, retire" and glancing quickly round I saw that I was alone. I strained my eyes as far as I could see to my front – through the dim light I could see about 80 to 100 yards – and could only see a few Germans running back at whom I fired off the remaining few rounds in mypan, replacing it with a full one – which was about the sixth.

"It was not long before the Germans attacked again; they seemed to come from a trench about 100 yards away. I took aim and pulled the trigger but the gun jammed after a few rounds. Bullets were hitting the ground all around me, splashing, with a sting, the mud into my eyes, face, ears and hands. The enemy came on to the accompaniment of hooters, whistles and loud shouts, and it was only when the foremost wave was on me that I got my gun working again. I fired at them point blank, about four or five pans until there was nothing left alive along about 150 yards of my front.

"My steaming gun jammed again. It was very hot. Setting it right again I saw the enemy advancing on two flanks. I opened fire on the extreme left and slowly traversed to my front and diagonally from the right where there was a raised road running diagonally from the enemy lines to ours. The Germans were advancing in apparent column of route along this road so I took sight on the nearest position to our line and traversed slowly. I was able to take a very good aim and the Germans were now silhouetted against the now lighter sky. I could see the effects of my shooting. My gun was then damaged by an enemy bullet which had hit under the pan, burring up the feeding arm. It now ceased working altogether. Something exploded nearby - probably a grenade – and the force of the explosion combined with my, none too firm foothold flung me backwards into the trench. I got to my feet and abandoned the position.

"There was no sign of life along my front, the number of enemy dead was high, and I knew that at that time the trench was still in our hands. I resolved that the best thing would be to go back and gather any stragglers and man this trench that had not been lost. On my way back I found only the dead and dying. One poor fellow, badly wounded, asked me for water. As I attempted to help him a bullet took him through the throat and he died in my arms. I stumbled on – it was hard going through the glutinous mud and I was fairly exhausted – until I came to a sunken road where there were a number of men gathered together. They consisted of our men and Canadians – about 100 in number. I pulled out a handkerchief and tore it into strips giving some men a portion with which to clean the mud from the bolts of there rifles. I conveyed the message that the trench I had just left was not in German hands and I led the way forward again. But by then the enemy had occupied the trench and began sniping us as we approached. Our counter-attack was a 'wash out' and as far as I know I was the only unwounded man who returned to our reserve trenches."

As referred to by the C.O., Cpl. Civil's Lewis gun had been heard from the reserve line and it was

Lewis Gun as used by Cpl. Civil

also known he had done effective work. A few days later Cpl. Civil was summoned by the C.O. He was asked details of his action with his Lewis gun and of his rounding up an improvised counter-attack.

In the course of a few weeks he was promoted Lance Sergeant and then full Sergeant. Eventually he was presented with a Certificate of Honour bearing the dates of this 8th May engagement and that of a previous engagement of 13th–18th April 1917. Notice was given that a record was kept and entered in regimental orders.

Cpl. Civil's actions that day were remarkable. He should have been awarded, in the very least, the Distinguished Conduct Medal (DCM) in recognition for his work. However, as the action was not considered successful, no awards were made despite his 'effective work'.

After the end of the war it was proposed that, quite rightly, he be awarded the VC for his valour at Fresnoy. However, it was not pursued due to the length of time which had elapsed since the event.

Lt. Col. R.I.Rawson Commanding 12th Gloucesters
"This disaster was due to the following:
(1) Attempting to hold an impossible salient as a defensive position.
(2) Lack of aeroplanes.
(3) Lack of artillery support of any kind.
(4) Was largely contributed by the bad weather.
(5) The thick dust forming into mud at once and visibility being NIL."

M. Henri Bidon - French critic
"Fresnoy was captured by the Canadians on May 3rd. We indicated then the extreme difficulty of holding this place as an isolated point. In fact it is situated right inside the German position and is hemmed in to the north and south by unconquered ground. Acheville on one side and Oppy on the other. Our allies consequently occupied at this point a sharp salient beyond the general line of advance. The ground also lent itself badly to defence. Fresnoy, lies in a hollow, with rising ground on three sides. These heights were captured on May 3rd but we are not sure whether our allies succeeded in retaining this ground. Even so, these heights themselves were dominated by others held by the enemy, from which their concentric fire could be directed against Fresnoy."

A Canadian officer later said:
"We are full of praise for the English Bristol lads, who held on in spite of the frightful fire, served their machine guns to the last and only fell back from their advanced lines when Fresnoy village, by then a heap of ruins, became a death trap in which no man could stay alive."

Among the many men killed that day was Capt. W. W. Parr. He was 45 years of age and had only got into the battalion by constantly badgering the Recruiting Committee. He finally convinced them that even at the age of 42 he had a lot to offer. He was right. He rapidly made his way up to Sergeant and in early 1915 was commissioned. He was an extremely popular officer among all ranks. At the front, he was quickly recognized as being a very brave soldier and excellent leader of men. At Fresnoy he had led 'B' Company in a counter-attack and tried desperately to rally the shattered remnants of 'A' and 'C' Companies. He was last seen, fighting a group of Germans with a shovel.

Letter from Capt. C.S. Petheram to Mrs. Parr
B.E.F. May 12th 1917,
"Dear Mrs. Parr,
It is with the deepest regret that I have to write and tell you that your husband, Captain W.W. Parr, is missing. He took his company over in a brave attempt to gain, by an immediate counter-attack, some ground which had been lost. He was seen by an NCO walking about among his men, helping and encouraging them. His men absolutely worshipped him and would follow him anywhere. Every single officer loved him, and he was absolutely the life and soul of the mess. Always he was ready to make jokes at any time. When I first joined the battalion in September last I was posted to his company, and was his only subaltern for a long time. I went over the top first with him and stayed with him nearly all the time in this battalion. In this way I may say that I got to know him and count him as one of the best friends I have ever had. I am now commanding the company he last took over and shall endeavour to run it on similar lines to what he did. I do not know what to say, Mrs. Parr, to give you any hope. I leave that to God and the future. I can only sincerely console with you in such especially distressing circumstances. If he is dead, he died as he always lived, like a hero, and if he is alive - I cannot hold much hope of that - no one will be gladder than I. If I can do anything to help in any investigation, or can assist in any way out here, please command me. Believe me, yours very sincerely, C.S. Petheram."

Capt. Wilfred Parr M.C.

Lt. Col. R. I. Rawson
"Dear Mrs. Parr,
………………About three weeks ago when we were in a very unpleasant situation, I went up to see your husband and to visit a forward post. While there it was shelled and I sat down under the bank in front to get cover. Your husband came and stood in front of me deliberately and when a shell burst somewhat close, he leant over and pretended to light his pipe. That will tell you better than anything how I personally felt about him".

13986 Sgt. Robert Anstey
"Many good fellows 'went west' at Fresnoy on 8th May. Among them was Capt. W. W. Parr MC, who was an outstandingly brave soldier, a man of character and of a fine, dry wit. Anyone who has read 'Journey's End' - by R. C. Sherriff - will remember the character of the older officer – Mr. Osborne. This was Parr to the life. He was one of the finest men I have known. The C.O. was right when he described him as the best loved man in the battalion".

Capt. H. A. Colt
"Considering its very weak state, the courage and devotion to duty shown by all ranks during the operation at Fresnoy ranks equal to the Battle of 3rd September 1916 at Guillemont. What more can any man do than to sacrifice his life in the defence of his trenches and his comrades?"

In loving memory of Pte. William Quarterly, 12th Gloucester Regiment,
Killed in action 8th May 1917.
Youngest son of Mr. and Mrs. Quarterly.

Softly at night the stars are gleaming upon that silent grave.
Where there lieth without dreaming. One we loved, but could not save.
God will grasp that broken chain, clasp it till we meet again.
No father or mother saw him die,
no sister or brother to say goodbye,
no friend or relative to clasp his hand.
But we hope to meet again one day in that promised land.

For those who suffered the experience and survived the war, the mention of Fresnoy, was to evoke memories of ill omen for the rest of their lives.

The following was the disposition of the battalion at this time:

C.O. Lt/Col R.I. Rawson
2nd I/C Major H.A. Colt

Adjutant: Captain Maywood
O.C. 'A' Company: Captain W. G. Chapman MC
O.C. 'B' Company: Captain B. B. Kirby
O.C. 'C' Company: Captain G.R.A. Beckett
O.C. 'D' Company: Captain H. J. Taylor

Some of those that died as a result of the fighting at Fresnoy 8th May 1917

Sgt. Percy Bouskil
DOW 8th May 1917

Pte. Charles Brooks
KIA 8th May 1917

Pte. Frederick Clark
KIA 8th May 1917

Pte. Ewdin Cook
KIA 8th May 1917

Pte. Joseph Hewlett
DOW 8th May 1917

Pte. George Norman
KIA 8th May 1917

Pte. Lestock Palmer
KIA 8th May 1917

Capt. Wifred Parr
KIA 8th May 1917

Pte. Harold Parsons
KIA 8th May 1917

1917 – Soldier on

Battle of 3rd Ypres

After Fresnoy, the battalion spent over a month re-organising in the pretty village of Diéval. Time was spent in cleaning equipment and very hard training. So hard was it that the only spectator who appeared at a 'Whizz-Bangs' divisional concert party in Diéval itself was a man from the 1st East Surreys. And he walked five miles to see it! The Gloucesters and Devons took the opportunity to get some sleep instead.

On 9th June they returned to the line at Arleux, the area to which they had been pushed back at the time of the Fresnoy attack, where the 2nd King's Liverpools were relieved. In front could be seen the remains of the village of Fresnoy. It seemed, however, as though both sides were more or less satisfied with the damage they had inflicted on each other. When taken over, the front line consisted of a series of scattered rifle pits with the odd strand or two of wire in front of them. Full advantage was taken to give the enemy as much trouble as possible. The enemy certainly had a rotten time opposite us. He was constantly bombarded with gas and burning oil. Though he did not return much gas, the front line was usually badly shelled after one of these actions and very many casualties thus resulted.

Time out of the line was marked with hard, intense training and hard graft with Royal Engineers working parties of well over one hundred men at a time being detailed off regularly. The 12th Gloucesters were always remarkably good at hard work and when, at the end of August we handed over the trenches to the 31st Division, they took over a highly organised and excellent trench system with functional communications trenches running back towards Vimy. Also, while there, the battalion was constantly sapping forwards and bringing the front line closer to the enemy.

In early August, the battalion lost a very likeable and able officer in the form of Capt. G. R. A. Beckett who was appointed second in command of the 4th Leicesters. Capt. Beckett, pre-war, had been a master at Colston's School in Stapleton, Bristol. He joined as a private soldier in September 1914 and was soon afterwards granted a commission within the battalion. He never returned to the battalion, his new division refusing to part with him.

In and out of the line including spells in Brigade reserve took up August, during which excellent weather was enjoyed. At the end of August the battalion marched to Mazieres. A strenuous time was spent there, interspersed with hard work and training. In the spare time available were also sports, concerts, boxing tournaments. The amount of field practice, trench-to-trench attacks, rifle practice, bombing and physical training was at a very high level. The men naturally considered what might be in store for them.

On 31st July the 3rd battle of Ypres had begun. This battle eventually became more popularly known by the name of its final objective - the village of Passchendaele. Field Marshall Haig, through his uncontrollable optimism, was convinced that the German army was now close to collapse and once again made plans for a major offensive to obtain the necessary breakthrough.

This was, indeed, what was in store for the battalion and, on 25th September, it marched to St. Flochel for entraining on the first part of its journey to Bayenghem, about twenty miles south of Calais. After several days of heavy marching over hard roads in very hot and sultry conditions they arrived at Meteren. The 12th Gloucesters were proud that of all four battalions in the brigade, they had the fewest men fall out during the gruelling march.

Leaving Meteren at 8 a.m. on 1st October, by motor lorries this time, the battalion proceeded to the Ypres-Menin Road and took up a position near Stirling Castle.

Almost as soon as it arrived there, it was subject to a severe gas shell bombardment and 'D' Company suffered many casualties, including three out its four officers. On 4th October an attack was mounted on the enemy's line. The 1st Devons were on the right and the 1st D.C.L.I. on the left. The 1st East Surrey's were in close support and 12th Gloucesters in reserve. The attack began at 6a.m. and at 6.40a.m. the battalion, less 'A' Company which had been detailed for carrying, moved forward to take up the position occupying the line vacated by 1st East Surreys. At this time the enemy's artillery was very active and 'B' and 'D' Companies suffered heavy casualties just moving into position. At 10.10a.m. orders were received to send 'C' Company forward to reinforce the 1st Devons. Casualties again were heavy.

20193 Sgt. Harry Civil

"We had heaps of gassed soldiers. I wish those who called it a holy war could have seen the poor things burnt and blistered all over with great mustard-coloured, festering blisters, with blind eyes all sticky and glued together, always fighting for breath with voices a mere whisper, saying their throats were closing and they would choke."

14138 Sgt. Norman Pegg

"During the attack on the 4th October some of us had a very unpleasant experience. For practically the whole of the day the enemy put down a very heavy barrage and we were engaged the whole time carrying boxes of rifle ammunition, bombs and rifle grenades a distance of about 1,000 yards forming a series of small dumps. This was done, of course, under the very nose of the enemy who, seeing what was being accomplished, promptly shelled the new dumps as they were started."

Next day, the shelling continued and the battalion withdrew to Sanctuary Wood in the evening. However, due to the darkness and the appalling state of the ground, it was not complete until 8a.m. on the 6th. Shelter in Sanctuary Wood took the form of shell holes and shallow dugouts. 'Duck-board's were constantly shelled and destroyed. Movement during the day was limited as the enemy could observe every part of the position.

Lt. Col. R. I. Rawson

"We were in the line at Gheluvelt, just off the Menin Road. The surrounding countryside was very flat and consisted mostly of shell holes and water, around which wandered duckboard tracks broken here and there by shell fire. Spots marked on the map as 'Sanctuary Wood' or 'Inverness Copse' presented no different appearance to spots indicated on the map as flat open country."

The principal feature in that part of the world at that time was shells. There were at least three definite barrage lines and the shelled area ran back to well past Zillebeke. The amount of shells landing in this part of the world was extremely plentiful. But even further back was not safe. The first night in this area, no less than two men, and thirty five horses and mules of the 95th Brigade Machine Gun Company were killed by bombs dropped from enemy aeroplanes. One of their officers, Lt. Davidson had a narrow escape. As he was sleeping with his head on an air pillow, suddenly his head bumped to the ground. A splinter from a bomb had pierced the pillow!

The Ypres sector was generally agreed among the men as being the worst place on earth. The countryside was very badly knocked about with practically nothing remaining of villages and woods. Of the villages, literally to say there was not a brick left on top another was an understatement. There were no bricks left. Most distinctive was the smell, being a combination of gas, cordite, petrol and the putrefying dead.

In peacetime, the low lying countryside had been covered in drainage ditches or 'bekes'. The shellfire had destroyed these with the affect that the whole area was a marshland, completely impassable in certain areas. The roads had shared the same fate as the villages. They were on the maps but nowhere else. The remains of the woods, just blackened tree stumps, all had British names - well, according to the maps they did: 'Glencorse Wood', 'Inverness Copse', 'Polygon Wood' and 'Sanctuary Wood' to name a few. Dotted about the area were 'pill boxes', reinforced concrete strongholds, most of which were built by the Germans. These were always heavily fought over as they were the only places which afforded any degree of safety. They were always over-crowded.

Among these 'pill boxes' was a small, ill-smelling one named 'Jerk House'. It served as battalion H.Q. due to its one outstanding feature: it had been very well built by the Germans and defied all types of shells that

1917 – Soldier on

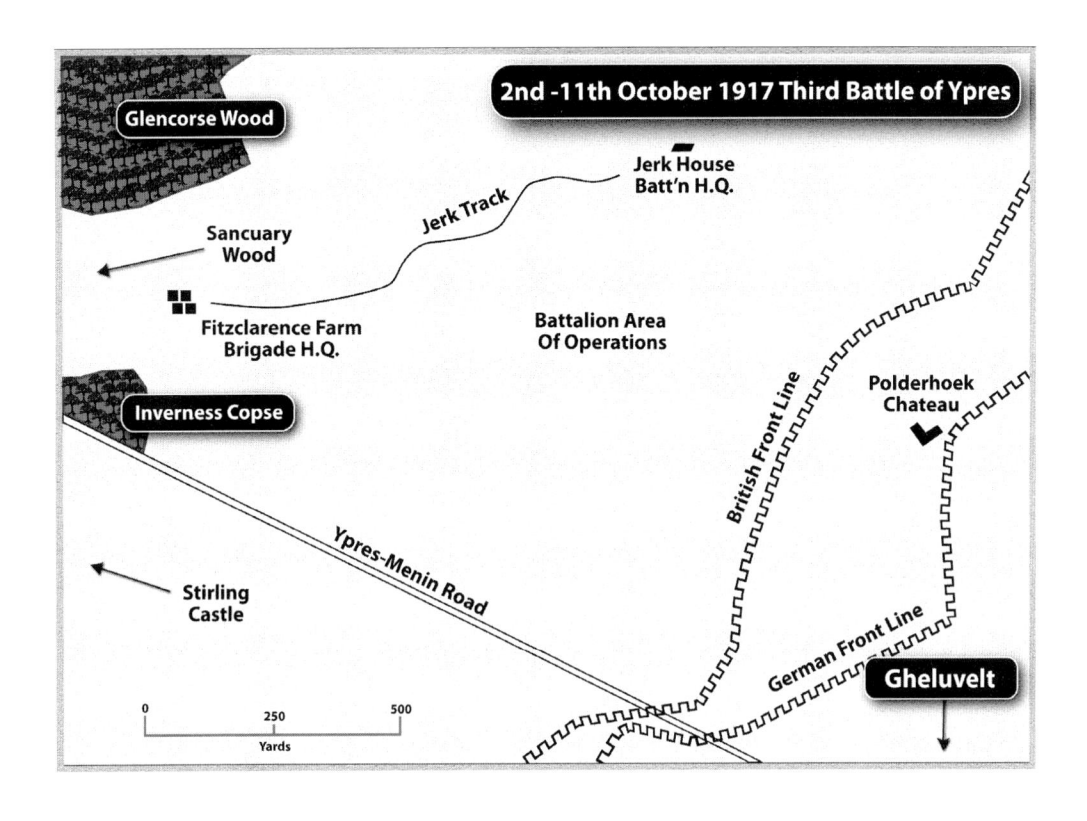

Map: 2nd - 11th October 1917 Third Battle of Ypres

Locations shown: Glencorse Wood, Sancuary Wood, Jerk Track, Jerk House Batt'n H.Q., Fitzclarence Farm Brigade H.Q., Battalion Area Of Operations, Inverness Copse, British Front Line, Polderhoek Chateau, German Front Line, Ypres-Menin Road, Stirling Castle, Gheluvelt. Scale: 0 – 250 – 500 Yards.

hit it. Rumour had it that even 8" shells just bounced off it so its inhabitants did not mind its drawbacks, such as the need to constantly bale the water out and the dead German under the sand bag steps. It was very cramped and dirty and it smelled bad, but it was a welcome haven.

Leading from the line back to Brigade H.Q. was the infamous and aptly named 'Jerk Track', a duckboard track, broken and slivered by shell fire with innumerable curves where new duckboards had been laid between shell holes. The shell holes were death traps. Men were particularly careful in stepping around them as to fall into one was certain death. They were all filled with mustard gas contaminated water. Many men were known to have drowned in them. By the side of the track lay corpses or pieces of corpses of both British and German soldiers. The track was around a mile long, though most men that encountered it would have sworn it was more like ten miles. It offered no shelter. In fact it was raised above the level of the surrounding country due to the water.

Capt. H. A. Colt

"An objective was Polderhoek Chateau or what remained of it. It had been a fair sized building on a low rise. This was strongly and stoutly held by the Germans, as was Gheluvelt immediately to the south of it. Three separate attacks were made by our division on the Chateau. The first attack captured the place but the enemy immediately re-took by a counter-attack. The second also got home but was repulsed by counter-attack. The third failed to take the objective. In none of these attacks, however, were the 12th Gloucesters directly involved. Their role was that of support or reserve on each occasion. This entailed all the arduous work of carrying and moving from position to position through heavy barrages. As a consequence, we lost a very large number of men without getting any particular kudos other than that of being able to withstand the maximum amount of punishment"

1917 – Soldier on

14596 William Ayres
"At this stage in the war, it was required that, when entering upon any major conflict, a portion of each battalion should be left in the transport lines. A part of each platoon and Company and of the headquarters sections – which included the signallers – was left with the transport, so that if the battalion was wiped out, there was the nucleus to start again. They also, of course, were available for support. The men left behind were known as the 'dumped personnel' We went to Ypres in October to take part in the third battle of Ypres. When the battalion went into the line, I was one of the 'dumped personnel'.

"The battalion did their spell in the line and returned to support and when the time came, they prepared to go up to the front line again, I should have been with them. But on the very evening before we were due to set out, I was detailed to go on a six weeks signal course at Cassel which was the Second Army Headquarters."

14138 Sgt. Norman Pegg
"During our adventure here it poured with rain most of the time and, what we referred to as trenches, were in fact inland waterways. In these circumstances, there was no chance of drying your feet which stayed wet the whole time. The result of this was that when we were relieved, we were able to march out at the rate of around one mile per hour. Neither had we been able to wash in that time. Even basic washing and shaving was out of the question as all the water laying had been affected by gas. Despite these disadvantages, there was still time for a laugh occasionally. One lad had a weakness for rum – when he could get it. He discovered a large rum jar which, judging by its weight was full. He uncorked it and took a large mouthful, swallowing all of it. But he took no more. It was whale oil."

Remaining in the area in and out of the front line but never out of range of artillery shells until 11th October, the battalion spent most of the time providing carrying parties to carry ammunition and rations to the front line and even parties for retrieving and burying the dead. It was relieved by the 12th Battalion Durham Light Infantry at 10a.m. on the 11th and marched to Ridge Wood.

Coming out of the line along 'Jerk Track' for the final time the battalion suffered a number of casualties. One of these was 14375 Corporal Claude Cecil Parry, a stout hearted original member of the battalion that had enlisted on September 17th 1914. Lying, with his back broken by shell fire, by the side of the track he flatly refused to be moved. He cheered his comrades as they reluctantly passed by. He was aged 22 and his body was never recovered or certainly not identified. His name lies on the Tyne Cott Memorial to the Missing, near Passchendaele and also on the Fishponds War memorial in Bristol.

Some twelve days were spent in reorganising, refitting and resting the battalion before its next foray. At this time some considerable advances were made in the efficiency of the regimental band. The original band had been formed in Bristol during 1915 and was of quite a high standard. Further instruments had been purchased by Lt. Col Archer-Shee D.S.O. M.P. during early 1916 and the band was always popular among the brigade.

Most of these original band members, however, had since become casualties and these had been replaced, on an ongoing basis since. It has to be said that, though the instruments remained, the new players lacked the right combination. In fact, they were usually referred to by the envious battalions of the brigade - none of whom possessed their own bands – as the 'Terrible Ten'. As fortune would have it, Sgt. Underwood, an organist by profession, joined the battalion at this time. He took the band in hand. More instruments and music were purchased and, within three months, it rivalled the divisional band.

Another organisational change took place when, at the end of October, Lt. Col. Rawson left the battalion for a six month tour of duty in England. He eventually rose to the rank of Brigadier general. His place was taken by Lt. Col. Colt who had joined the battalion in September 1914. He was a very brave, very capable officer. He was extremely popular among the men and his appointment was well received.

On 25th October six subalterns joined. Back in the front line on the 28th 2nd/Lt. Wilfred Dann, one of those subalterns, was caught by shellfire near battalion headquarters and was badly wounded. He died on 30th

October. His time with the 12th Gloucesters lasted just five days, two of which he spent in hospital.

Lt. Col H. A. Colt

"Towards the end of October we again went into the line. This time two Companies held the line between Reutelbeke and Polderbeke, still in sight of Polderhoek Chateau. The two Companies were in support to other battalions of our brigade. Here we spent four or five days.

"After being relieved from here we went back to Ridge Wood, where we were billeted in huts and again, re-organised. Coming out through the shell fire, we again suffered many casualties. We were then clear of the salient and did not return. Later we moved to Divisional Reserve at Bedford House and soon after on 12th November Aragon camp near Westoutre and then on to another camp at the small village of Henneveux around twelve miles due east of Boulogne."

After leaving the Ypres sector on 12th November, the battalion rested for the remainder of the month. Usually rest periods were anything but. Another name was relief: However, such relief was rarely looked forward to as relief from the trenches. In fact, it came to the point where the trenches were a relief from the drill and training. But this period was pleasantly different. Whilst the usual cleaning up and re-organisation happened, there was little drill or training. It was a pleasure for the men to be able to enjoy the unspoilt countryside and woodlands at a very nice camp just east of Boulogne. With showers, clean clothing and bedding, pleasant quarters and their pay of five francs weekly, a well deserved rest was had by all.

14596 Pte. William Ayres

"At the time the battalion was at rest I was at Cassel attending a signals course. It was a delightful town and a particularly pleasant place to spend six weeks. Actually, all the places behind the line were good because there was no aerial bombing and you were beyond the range of artillery shelling. The countryside was green and quiet and pleasant.

"As each course came to an end, it was the practice to retain, certain of the 'students' as instructors for the next course and I was chosen to be given one of these posts. But before the next course could commence, the movement of troops to the Italian Front got under way and those of us who belonged to those divisions affected were sent back to our units."

Casualties sustained for period of **1st October – 7th November:**

Officers killed: 4
Officers wounded: 6
Officers gassed: 4
Other ranks killed: 59
Other ranks wounded: 177
Other ranks gassed: 91
Total: 14 officers and 327 other ranks

2nd/Lt. William Mills was from the 1st battalion and attached to the 12th. He arrived with the battalion on 7th August. He was killed by shell fire on 4th October aged 26. Just short of two months spent with the battalion.

2nd/Lt. William Henry Mills
KIA 4th October 1917

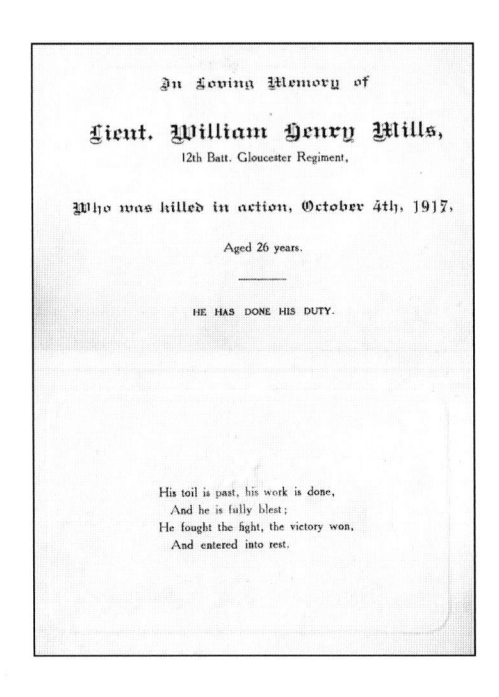

In Loving Memory of

Lieut. William Henry Mills,

12th Batt. Gloucester Regiment,

Who was killed in action, October 4th, 1917,

Aged 26 years.

HE HAS DONE HIS DUTY.

His toil is past, his work is done,
And he is fully blest;
He fought the fight, the victory won,
And entered into rest.

1917 – Soldier on

Some of those that died as a result of the fighting during the Battle of 3rd Ypres - Passchendaele October and November 1917

PTE. Ernest Anning
KIA 2nd October

Pte. Ernest Champman
KIA 4th October

Pte. William Dyte
KIA 4th October 1917

Pte. George Hobbs
KIA 13th October

Pte. Francis Leonard
DOW 7th October

2nd/Lt. William Mills
KIA 4th October

Pte, Edward Williams
DOW 29th October

1917 – Soldier on

Italy

The Western Front was certainly regarded by the British Government and the General Staff to be 'the only real front.' However, fortunes on other fronts had a bearing. From the first Russian Revolution in February 1917 when the opposing factions were fighting among themselves, the Germans involvement in Russia had diminished. The second Russian Revolution of November 1917 effectively ended their fight with Germany. This would have far reaching consequences on the Western Front in 1918.

Whilst the Battle of Paschendaele slogged on relentlessly, the situation in Italy had become serious with the joint Austro-Hungarian and German offensive at Caporetto.

The Italian Front traced its way through 400 miles of tumbled mountain-side. Only the extreme Eastern sector of about 50 miles along the River Isonzo had invited attack by the Italian army, mainly because 15 miles beyond the Isonzo lay the great Austrian Naval base of Trieste. In all, the Italians launched eleven offensives on the Isonzo, taking them half way to Trieste at a cost of over one million casualties. The last and biggest such offensive, in August and September 1917, brought the Italian infantry to the edge of moral collapse. Mutinies and plummeting morale were crippling the Italian army from within. The soldiers had been engaged in attack after attack that often yielded minimal gain. The Austrians too would have been unable to withstand further Italian attacks and so, having received desperately needed reinforcements in the form of seven German divisions, gambled on a swift counter-stroke.

The counter-offensive was led by the German General Otto von Below and smashed home on the 24th October in rain, snow and cloud on the Caporetto Sector: a huge artillery barrage followed by infantry using new 'Hutier' tactics. These were new infiltration tactics introduced by the Germans leading to the creation of small groups of soldiers with a certain degree of autonomy, capable of penetrating enemy territory on missions of sabotage and misdirection using localised initiative. Directed under a creeping barrage, enemy strong-points were easily bypassed allowing the Italian rear to be attacked. Resistance was easily overcome and the Italian Second Army, a formation poor in discipline and morale, collapsed in utter rout which then retreated westward. What then followed was a series of actions which shattered the Italian army. At the end of the first day, the Italians had retreated 12 miles. The retreat stopped at the River Piave where a defensive line was established, just a few miles north east of Venice.

The Italian army was in a state of total disarray with 10,000 killed, 30,000 wounded and 293,000 prisoners lost, while a further 400,000 deserters had dissolved into the surrounding towns and villages.

The remaining Italian troops along the Piave were barely strong enough in numbers to defend such an important position and there was no reserve to support the shock of an attack at any other point. Like the French at Verdun, the Battle of Caporetto was a battle from which the Italian army never truly recovered.

At an allied conference held on 5th November, the Italian government asked the British and French for assistance in the form of 15 divisions. It was imperative that Italy be kept in the war. If she was defeated, vast numbers of Austrian and German troops would be released for involvement on the Western Front which, it was felt, may well have tipped the balance against the already overstretched Allies.

After careful consideration and at the request of the Allied Supreme War Council, as an effort to stiffen Italian resistance to enemy attack after this recent disaster, a strategic and political move was agreed by the British and French governments. The response was to immediately move troops to Italy in the form of nine infantry divisions – four French and five British. The four British divisions were the 5th, the 7th, the 23rd, the 41st and finally the 48th (South Midland) Territorial Force Division. By chance, these divisions included three Bristol battalions: the 4th, 6th and 12th Gloucesters.

After the turmoil of the Ypres Salient, the 12th Gloucesters moved to a camp at Le Parcq, near the town of Hesdin. Here they went through the usual routine of cleaning up, re-fitting and training as was usual after a major engagement. On the 1st December the battalion was awaiting instructions to move. All had been recalled from leave. While here everyone was amazed when Lt. Fitzgerald showed up. He had been wounded and left for dead at Fresnoy back in May. He had subsequently been taken prisoner by the Germans who had treated his wounds. He eventually ended up at Strohen prison camp in Germany. While there, he teamed up with Lt. Harding of the R.F.C. and escaped, eventually making their way to Holland then England. At 2.30p.m. on the 30th November he entertained the whole battalion with a lecture on 'his recent experiences in Germany'.

Lt. Fitzgerald shortly after his escape
from Germany

    From here, in order to ease the burden of the rail network, 'A' and 'C' Companies with half of battalion H.Q. and half the transport but with the entire band, under the command of Lt. Col Colt, entrained at Hesdin. The remaining half of the battalion under Captain Maywood was due to follow some time later. In fact, their departure was postponed due to events at Cambrai. The Battle of Cambrai had initially been a huge success where on 20th November 476 tanks attacked and caught the Germans by complete surprise, gaining ground to a depth of up to four miles. The advantage, however, had not been followed up and, as the British momentum dwindled, the Germans counter-attacked. Until the situation became clear, 'B' and 'D' Companies were under orders to move at a moment's notice. In the event, the German counter-attack petered out by 3rd December and on the night of 4th/5th the British withdrew to a new line.

1917 – Soldier on

14596 William Ayres
"After completing the signals course at Cassel, I found the battalion near Boulogne: well, half of it. The battalion had been split in two, the first half having already left for Italy. Then came the battle of Cambrai and there was a time of some uncertainty as to the course of the battle and we, the second half of the battalion, were held back until the line became stable. But at last we were put into trains to wander most enjoyably down through France round the Mediterranean coast to Genoa and across northern Italy."

Lt. Col H. A. Colt
"We were fairly comfortable in the train. Two officers were allocated to each compartment and 20-25 men to each covered van. Strict orders were given as to discipline while in the train, including the removal of boots and puttees and the daily rubbing of men's feet with whale oil.

"An elaborate programme of 'Haltes Repas' was worked out, whereby one hour in ten would be spent stopped so as to enable the stretching of one's legs. Unfortunately, however, there were so many troops, both British and French, going to Italy that our train got behind and all the 'Haltes Repas' vanished into thin air. However, at one point our train broke down and we were able to go for a short route march.

"Our journey lay past Paris and included Marseilles, Nice, Cannes and Menone. Just before we reached Genoa we turned north through Parma until we reached Ests, our detraining station."

The train journey took six days with the half battalion arriving at Este on the 7th December. It was a relatively comfortable and interesting journey in that it was through pleasant countryside untouched by war. During an uneventful journey, the only thing of note was that 'Jim' the Regimental dog went AWOL - again. He left without the permission of the N.C.O. in charge of his truck and missed his train. Luckily he was brought along later by another train. It has not been recorded whether he was charged.

The whole experience for the men was unlike anything they had experienced before, whether considering their civilian life or certainly their service life. At every Italian station of any size the battalion passed through, the train was greeted by great crowds of Italians. Gifts of fruit, flowers and postcards and ribbons of the Italian colours were pressed on the men. There was no doubt the Italians were pleased to see them. At Punta d'Arena the R.T.O. informed the C.O. that an Italian Lt. col. wished to have some coffee with him. In the waiting room, which had been suitably prepared for the occasion, The C.O. and a group of officers were greeted by a Lt. col. of the Italian A.S.C. and seated around a table, each officer with a glass of liquor brandy in front of him. The Italian made a long speech in fluent French amongst which only several words such as 'victore' and 'glore' were understood. This was something of a shock as it was clear that some form of a reply was required. Unfortunately, no officer present was able to offer much more that 'oui' or 'non' or 'merci'. However, the C.O. made a notable effort and stammered out a short speech full of what were intended to be noble and comradely sentiments. The Italian seemed satisfied.

It was bitterly cold when the men bedded down in an old barracks for a few hours before moving again through Noventa Vicentina, Sossano and on to Vicenza and then Sossano, a village about 12 miles from Vicenza. While billeted here an unfortunate incident occured. It was very cold and three men billeted in a small room, lit a brazier of coal and shut all doors and windows to keep themselves warm. Next morning all were ill from fumes and, subsequently, one (28390 Pte. George Reginald Sweeting of Ashton Gate, Bristol) died.

14138 Sgt. Norman Pegg
"Italy after Ypres was a huge contrast. The four months spent in Italy were the happiest and easiest months which it had been the lot of the battalion to have. Some of the troop's notions with regard Italy and the Italians were rather fanciful. They considered that our allies were a nation of organ-grinders and ice-cream merchants and it was a matter of surprise when we arrived that these people were not in evidence. Instead, we found a good natured folk who seemed to regard the British soldier as something of a novelty."

The language difficulty was overcome largely by many of the Italian soldiers who spoke good English with a broad Brooklyn accent. Where this failed, there was a thoroughly British method of dealing with the problem: it was an inspiration of some genius, who found that most Italian words bear a resemblance either to English or French words.

1917 – Soldier on

Lt. B.H. Waddy
"A party of us, on the way to reconnoitre the mountains near Asiago, paid a call at a small country restaurant. Among other things, we wanted cheese. Knowing that the letters 'io' added to the French or English word often produced the Italian equivalent, we demanded of the hostess 'cheesio'. That being a failure, we asked for 'fromagio' which proved eminently successful. The French language was generally more useful than our own, but one might imagine the distorted Italian which was passed out as a result of the English soldier's peculiar ways."

Lt. Col H. A. Colt
"At Sossano we took over a disused local theatre and here the "Whizz-Bangs" held two concerts.
"We were often on the move and on the 15th December marched to Lumagnano and then on the 17th to Arlesega. Both these marches were very trying as the snow had fallen and the transport had a difficult job to keep their horses and mules from falling.
"On the 18th we marched to Villa del Conte where we met the other half of the battalion. Since last we saw them they had a narrow shave of going to Cambrai.
"The conditions here, generally, were very comfortable. Half the battalion was billeted in a large empty house, the other half in the village school. The officers' mess was in another empty house, while the sergeants' mess was in a smaller building. Each morning the battalion paraded in the Village square.
"Five weeks were spent at Villa del Conte during which time a rifle range and an assault course were constructed. From this village parties were sent up to the mountains, for the intention was that the battalion should hold the Brenta Valley near Bassano should the Austrians break through. A good deal of training was carried out and the battalion thoroughly re-organised."

14225 Pte. Bruce Buchanan
"It was while spending the few days in the mountains that we saw some interesting features of the Italian campaign. There were, even at a height of 3,000 or 4,000 feet, tolerably good roads, over which the small lorries used in the Italian army could climb with ease. Another means of transporting food and materials up the mountains was by means of mules. Though the Italian mule seemed comparatively mild in comparison to our own, for we saw time and again, that the transport men, in order to assist themselves up steep roads, hung for miles onto the tails of the animals, who seemed to take it as a matter of course."

Christmas 1917 was remembered as the best spent so far on active service, when the men enjoyed themselves tremendously thanks to the generous gift of £60 being sent by the citizens of Bristol through the Lord Mayor. Concerts were also held despite the makeshift concert hall being rather damp and cold.

24429 Pte. Bert Hickery
"Two days before Christmas we were billeted in a small village from which we could see the mountain tops and at night the fireworks of the guns. The farm cottage my section was in had a loft with stairs going straight up to it. Very comfortable indeed.
"As a surprise on Christmas day: we had puddings and mince pies and also a cask of vin blanc. The fellow sleeping next to me, Impy was his name, could not leave the wine alone even though I warned him of the effects. In no time he was feeling unwell. He was in a very bad way for a number of days and he never spoke to me again."

Chapter IX

1918 – Year of movement

Predominant for the British in 1917 were the battles of Arras, 3rd Ypres and Cambrai. None had produced anything in the way of the expected breakthroughs. At the end of the year, the Germans were presented with a real opportunity to win the war. Russia's collapse released large numbers of men and equipment for use on the Western Front. By the spring of 1918 the Germans were able to deploy 192 divisions, while the combined efforts of the British and French amounted to only 156 divisions.

However, to its credit, the British army had learnt valuable lessons during the costly offensives of 1916 and 1917 and had developed its tactics. During 1917 the U.S.A. had finally entered the war, though their troops, in any significant numbers, would not be effective until around the middle of 1918.

Most of January 1918 was spent in training and preparation work near Padova. Special emphasis was given to route marches and exercises wearing full marching order. Two competition route marches were arranged, the first being won by 'A' Company, the second by 'C' Company.

Acting R.S.M. (C.S.M.) Bailey was awarded the Military Cross in the New Years Honours and Sgt. Watkins, the signals Sergeant was awarded the Belgian Croix de Guerre for his good work at Ypres. This award was the more remarkable as being the only foreign decoration bestowed upon the battalion during the entire war.

As the battalion prepared itself to move off for the front line, Operation Order No. 38 was issued. One point of particular interest in the order was:

<u>II. Cleanliness of Billets</u>
All officers and men are cautioned that the C.O. expects billets be left in a thoroughly clean condition so as not to throw any discredit upon the battalion, observing that the 48th Division (4th & 6th Gloucesters) are about to take over from us.

During the Caporetto offensive, the Austrian army over-ran its own supply lines which obliged it to stop and re-group. This gave the Italians the opportunity to push them back to new defensive positions near Venice on the Piave River.

On 26th January, the battalion relieved, in the trenches along the River Piave, the 215th Italian Infantry Regiment – no less than four battalions. In order to deceive the enemy as to the relief having taken place, every man of the battalion wore an Italian helmet.

14138 Cpl. Norman Pegg
"A very comical effect was thus produced. It was questionable as to whether the C.O. or his orderly – Corporal Hudson presented the quaintest appearance."

The battalion machine gunners did not enter the line until the following night, but there was no lack of machine gun cover as the Italians had no less than 40 machine guns in the part of the line taken over by the battalion and it was jokingly stated that:
"In consequence, had the enemy raided our front line that night, they would not have known that any relief had taken place for there were at least as many Italians as there were English there."

1918 – Year of movement

The line ran in front of the small town of Spreciano along the southern bank to the Piave. The trenches, by comparison with the Western Front, were good and were protected by some of the best wire seen so far.

The surrounding country was flat apart from a hill called the Montello. Square plots of ground were planted with mulberry trees. And there was the river itself. It was not full and in consequence its bed consisted of a series of channels interspersed with pebbly islands.

From time to time the fighting in Italy – by Italian standards – had been bitter. But to men comparing it to scenes they had recently left behind in France and Flanders, it was a mere side show. The main problem faced by the men was the intense bitter cold, made all the worse by the inactivity of the Italian trenches.

20089 Pte. William James
"I received frostbite while in Italy. During my time in hospital recovering I used to steal away to the Expeditionary Force canteen to acquire cartons of Gold Flake cigarettes which I used to sell to the Italians in the town at a vast profit. I continued to do this until they strapped my leg up, due to it not healing, which made me immobile and put an end to my capers."

Eight days were spent in the line, followed by a period in support and a further week spent peacefully in the village of St. Andra, some seven miles behind the line.

On returning to the line on the night of 18th/19th February it was slightly to the north of the previous position. According to the C.O., life was somewhat more active than before:

Lt. Col H. A. Colt
"Here we had a splendid time. On going in we had been told there was positively no ford across the river. And so, for the first two nights, boating operations were carried out. The boat was a crazy old craft that threatened to capsize if one of its passengers as much as winked his eye. In addition to this the current was so strong that one could not row against it. Attempts were made to swing the boat over by rope, using the current as a motive power. In each case the boat failed to reach the opposite shore by some six feet."

In the meantime, the excited voices of Lt. Waddy from the boat and the C.O. from the embankment must have aroused all of Austria!

Wisely choosing to abandon any further water-borne attempts, patrolling returned to a more conventional practice when on the night of the 21st the popular trench raider, none other than Lt. Fitzgerald, led a patrol consisting of himself and Sergeant Pegg of the 12th Gloucesters, Lt. Montanaro and one N.C.O. of the 1st East Surreys. After discovering a ford, they waded across the freezing river and proceeded some 300 yards inland on the enemy side where they discovered an enemy post. They rushed it and captured its two occupants. On returning to their own trenches the two prisoners were parted – 'Algy' falling to the lot of the 1st East Surreys and 'Herbert' to the 12th Gloucesters. Their actual names were unpronounceable.

14138 Sgt. Norman Pegg
"The patrols had some interesting and exciting experiences. On one occasion, four of us were crawling along the low grassy bank and saw two heads bobbing about in one of the small outposts. It was a bright moonlit night and anything within a distance of 70 or 80 yards was plainly visible. The patrol split into two and, dashing over the bank converged on the heads which produced from each a pair of raised arms in typical 'Kamerad' fashion. They were little men and by no means young, and quite harmless looking."

The following night, Lt. Fitzgerald and Sgt. Pegg carried out a similar patrol to the same post which they found empty. They waited until two enemy approached, jumped them and took them prisoner.

Taking advantage of the run of success the next night saw yet another, but larger, patrol set out for the other side. 2nd/Lt. Hale and ten men comprised the patrol which rushed several posts only to find them empty. However, this time the enemy was prepared and the patrol was set upon by around 100 Hungarians. A fight ensued but, due to the odds a withdrawal was decided upon. 2nd/Lt. Hale and three men acted as a covering party for the main group which withdrew successfully, with one wounded man. The covering party itself was withdrawing in pairs when Pte. Tucker was hit and fell forward.

2nd/Lt. Hale
"I tried to help Pte. Tucker who was in a bad way but was immediately surrounded by a group of rough looking Hungarians. My rifle jammed so I fought my way clear with my fists."

A pre-arranged heavy machine gun barrage opened up which checked the pursuit of the enemy allowing the patrol to return safely with no further casualties being sustained.

Although no prisoners were taken nor material captured, it was estimated that quite a number of the enemy were hit during the engagement. It was later learned that Pte. Tucker, who had been left for dead, had been captured and was recovering. 2nd/Lt. Hale was awarded the Military Cross for his night's work.

This was to prove the last such raid across the Piave River that the 12th Gloucesters carried out.

Lt. Col H. A. Colt
"As another brigade was going to carry out a large raid here, we were told that we were attracting too much attention to the spot. The Royal Engineers also complained that our activity interfered with the bridge they were building across the river. By way of consolation the night's activities included suddenly switching on the searchlights and opening up a hot barrage with the Vickers and Lewis guns."

The recent nocturnal adventures had marked the peak of the battalion's activities in Italy. On the 27th February, relief came in the form of the 1st Battalion Cheshire Regiment and the remainder of February and the whole of March were spent in camp or in reserve with the War Diary stating: "Nothing of importance to report."

14138 Sgt. Norman Pegg
"The patrols we had carried out nightly with the greatest impunity would not have been possible against well trained Germans. The Hungarians, whom we were up against, however, were a very inferior crowd. They struck us as being slip-shod soldiers. They carried blankets with then when on outpost duty. Their rifles were as dirty as they themselves. The positions of their outpost trenches reduced them as places of observation to a minimum of utility, and the watch must have been carried out in a very lackadaisical manner. Against them we could not help but have a good time, and it was, therefore, with feelings of great regret that we heard at the end of March that we were to leave Italy, for the nightmare of France."

German Ludendorf Offensive

On 11th November 1917 a conference took place at Mons to decide Germany's strategy for 1918. Ludendorf, who presided, came to the meeting with his mind already made up in favour of staking Germany's last reserves of strength on a grand spring offensive on the Western Front. He saw no alternative: Germany's failing economy and shaky home front ruled out a prolonged defensive struggle. Ludendorf longed for a war of movement.

Germany also understood the potential impact of America's entry into the war. The German High Command hoped to defeat the Allies on the Western Front before the United States could mobilise its full military potential and after more than three years of fighting, a plan was devised to end the crippling stalemate of 'trench warfare' on the Western Front.

1918 – Year of movement

Throughout the winter of 1917-1918 troops were sent by rail from the defunct Eastern Front and, together with selected units withdrawn from the Western Front, trained in new and innovative offensive tactics. Instead of fixed linear objectives there was to be rapid infiltration throughout the enemy defences by storm troops including infantry, machine guns and field artillery. Reserves were to be fed in where the attack was progressing rather than where it was held up. The storm troops were to flow forward by paths of least resistance.

By early March no fewer than 47 special attack divisions and over 6,000 guns were deployed with all their stores and transport behind a front already manned by 28 trench divisions, all with the intention of utmost secrecy. 'Operation Michael' as it was to be known was about to erupt on the British.

The British Army at the time was still attempting to recover after the terrible attrition of Passchaendale. Though General Haig had asked the War Cabinet for fresh drafts of 600,000 men, the Cabinet, in order to curb his wish to take the offensive, had released only 100,000 men. He was also instructed to re-organise his divisions into nine battalions each instead of the usual twelve. By 4th March, 115 battalions had been disbanded. All this on the very eve of the German attack. An attack that proved to be the greatest offensive action the war had seen.

Despite the German measures of concealment, Allied intelligence plotted the build-up of German strength in the west with remarkable accuracy. Although they realised what a hurricane was brewing, they failed to take adequate measures to meet it.

By 18th March, the German army on the Western Front was 37 divisions stronger than in November 1917. On the 21st March, the Germans launched their massive Ludendorff offensive. At 4.40a.m. the Germans began firing one million artillery shells at the British lines held by the Fifth Army. For five hours the British defensive line was blasted by high explosive, shrapnel, phosgene and mustard gas. At 9.40a.m. the Germans switched to a creeping barrage and the storm troops swiftly followed. The paralysis of trench warfare was ended.

The Germans' success was greater than even they had envisaged. By nightfall 21st March on the Fifth Army's front south of the Somme, the attackers had penetrated beyond the British gun lines into open country: a true breakthrough.

By the end of the first day, 21,000 British soldiers had been taken prisoner. Senior British Commanders had lost control of the situation. General Gough ordered the Fifth Army to withdraw. The German attack was the biggest breakthrough in three years of warfare on the Western Front. The British began to fall back in confusion. The 'March retreat' was in full swing and it was into this maelstrom that the 5th Division and the 12th Gloucesters arrived early in April.

Though no details had been released, rumours were plentiful in the last week of March. The fact that something 'was up' was confirmed on the 2nd April when the battalion was ordered to march to Vicenza for entraining for France. The holiday was over.

For the return journey to France the trains were composed as before, the battalion proceeding in two halves: 'A' and 'C' Companies under the C.O. Lt. Col. Colt, and 'B' and 'D' Companies under Captain Maywood. The journey this time took only four days by taking the Mont Cenis tunnel as opposed to the scenic Riviera route.

Nieppe Forest

On 6th April the battalion detrained at Petit Houvin and marched to billets at Iverney. This time the 2nd/12th (as 'B' and 'D' Companies were known) thanks to the train journeys arrived only a few hours after the 1st/12th.

1918 – Year of movement

On the 10th April the battalion set off under dull and miserable conditions on a long march with the intention of relieving the line from the Canadians south of Arras. For the new men in the battalion, who constituted its greater strength, this was just another march. To the veterans of Fresnoy, it brought with it evil memories. A full year had passed and now, almost a year to the day, they were re-tracing the same steps to the same place. When the battalion reached its destination, however, it was ordered back, with much feeling of relief.

Lt. Col H. A. Colt
"On the following day – 11th April – we entrained at Mondicourt. This time the whole battalion and the East Surreys were on the same train. The transport marched.

"The journey was not without incident for we were held up at one place and told that we might not be able to proceed. Getting near a nasty bit of loop line near Bethune, we discovered the reason. The line had just been repaired after being shelled only a few hours before. One shell had hit a cattle truck full of soldiers, parts of whose bodies were lying in the surrounding fields. Bethune looked very much more battered than when we had first seen it in October 1916. About 8.p.m. we detrained and marched to our billets near the village of Bosengham, some three miles away. Next day scores of refugees came streaming through. Orders to be prepared to move at any moment had been received early in the morning.

"At 3.p.m. on the 12th, we moved off, followed by the 1st East Surreys, and at about 6p.m. we reached the eastern, or German side of the Forest of Nieppe near the little railway halt of Coubescure, about two miles west of Merville. Just outside the forest were the 1st D.C.L.I. and the 1st Devons who were to dig in and hold a line about 500 yards outside the forest as soon as dusk fell. We dug in about a 1000 yards inside the forest, in support. The East Surreys in reserve further back."

The situation the BEF found itself in was dire. It seemed so grave that on 11th April Field Marshall Haig issued his famous order:

"Many of us are now tired. To those I would say that victory will belong to the side which holds out the longest.... There is no course open to us but to fight it out. Every position must be held to the last man: there must be no retirement. With our backs to the wall and believing in the justice of our cause each one of us must fight on until the end. The safety of our homes and the freedom of mankind alike depend upon the conduct of each one of us at this critical moment."

Every man had a notice pasted into his pay book:

"KEEP YOUR MOUTH SHUT! The success of any operation we carry out depends chiefly on surprise. DO NOT talk. When you know that your unit is making preparations for an attack, don't talk about them to men in other units or to strangers. And keep your mouth shut especially in public places.

"DO NOT be inquisitive about what other units are doing. If you hear or see anything, keep it to yourself. The success of the operations and the lives of your comrades depend on your silence."

As darkness began to fall and the battalion dug in, all description of men began falling back through – motor transport men, military wood cutters, personnel from the Corps School in Merville and, by the expressions on their faces, seemed very pleased indeed to be getting out of it.

All around the battalion's positions were estaminets and farms, even a chateau – Les Lavriers – abandoned by their owners. Cattle, pigs and chickens strayed about in all directions. Hastily vacated tents and huts yielded such articles as joints of beef and M.T. drivers' sheepskin jackets. Eggs were to be had for the gathering and, for the platoon that could muster among them a countryman, fresh milk. The estaminets contained large stocks of wine and beer and in the chateau of Les Lavriers were a pair of Ming vases. These were destroyed shortly afterwards when the Germans demolished the house with 8" shells. At least for the moment, food was not a problem with any amount of peas, beans and potatoes growing around the front line. Battalion H.Q. even boasted an asparagus bed or two.

14225 Pte. Bruce Buchanan
"We marched up to the Forest of Nieppe, passing on the way various refugees who had been driven

from Merville and its neighbouring villages. Among them were numerous old folk, who had to walk many miles, and footsore youngsters. They were pathetic figures, these people who had had to leave their homes so suddenly and to have to run away hurriedly with nowhere to go. They could take very little with them, but a few managed to struggle away with bundles."

20089 Pte. William James
"We went in the line in the Forest of Nieppe. It was clear the Germans were still coming forward, for the roads were packed with refugees pouring away from the fighting. At nightfall, we took up our positions and, in the morning, the Germans were facing us. We had relieved no other unit, we just filled a gap in the line."

About dawn the next day, the 14th April, the Germans attacked in force. But it was too late. The battalions were well dug in and prepared. The Germans were out for big things and attacked fully laden with packs, their field kitchens well up behind. The objective was the railway junction at Hazebrouck, but their dense masses were so devastated by the withering machine gun fire that they got no nearer than 100 yards in front of the new positions. The attack was successfully repulsed and their casualties very heavy.

'B' Company 12th Gloucesters was ordered up to reinforce the front line as the attack progressed and had to race across several hundred yards of flat, open country. They were caught by enemy machine gun fire and suffered accordingly: 16 being killed and 56 wounded. 2nd/Lt's. G.W. Harris and C.J. Rutland were also wounded.

14997 Pte. Richard Amesbury
"If the Germans ever lost a chance of a breakthrough, they lost it on that occasion. There were several reasons reckoned why they did not, one of a humorous origin, which probably had a great deal to do with it. When the Germans took Merville they found large quantities of whiskey, which they consumed. This proved to be the undoing of a large number of them and greatly hampered operations. One German, however, gained distinction here. Apparently an officer of high rank, he could be seen plainly on a white horse directing his portion of the attack. He was a prominent targetand attracted a lot of fire but, with great good luck for him, he was not hit."

20089 Pte. William James
"It was here that the Germans failed to make a breakthrough. At this time I was an 'A' Company runner and, together with other runners, discovered a wine cellar in the deserted chateau Les Lavriers. Consequently, being the worse for wear after finishing off several bottles in a clearing, I was badly gassed. As a result of the gassing and being temporarily blinded, I spent a couple of months at a base hospital in Calais."

14225 Pte. Bruce Buchanan
"The whole way along the line our division repulsed the Germans with very heavy losses on their part. Incidents were related that these troops were from the Eastern Front. We saw a battalion practising the assault about 1,500 yards from our trenches. Their transport was seen moving in the open in broad daylight within a mile of our line. It was found that bursts of five rounds rapid, well controlled, stopped them every time. That they did not get this from the Russians was very evident."

On the night of the 16th/17th, the battalion was relieved with the intention being that it would move back to the small village of Le Touquet to reorganise. The German artillery, however, had other ideas. It gave the battalion its undivided attention. The bombardment necessitated a hasty journey to the open fields and, after several such excursions, it was decided to move back into the forest and bivouac. On the morning of the 18th, battalion H.Q. was hit by a heavy shell and, although there were no fatalities, the Sgt. Shoemaker and Master Taylor were both wounded.

14997 Pte. Richard Amesbury
"The forest had its obnoxious features. The many days and weeks spent there made you feel down in the dumps. This was because of the large quantities of poison gas dropped on us, for the poison would

1918 – Year of movement

remain in the undergrowth for a long time after it would have disappeared in open country. The cover was, however, taken advantage of to construct rest camps for the troops when out of the line. Unfortunately, the enemy was aware of this and had the annoying habit of shelling the area at one or two in the morning, so that we had to hop nimbly from between the blankest and skiddadle to places of comparative safety."

Back in the line again on the evening of the 21st during another heavy bombardment of both H.E. and gas shells, among the casualties was Captain Anderson R.A.M.C., the battalion M.O. On the 24th, battalion H.Q. was again shelled heavily and many men became casualties. Among those temporarily blinded was the C.O. Lt. Col. Colt.

Le Vert Bois

Since its arrival back in France, the battalion had been on the defensive. On the morning of the 25th, orders were received that this was about to change. The village of Le Vert Bois was to be attacked and captured under a creeping barrage. The objectives included houses, buildings, an orchard and a farm. The farm lay in front of the battalion's line and before it had fallen into German hands had served as a trench mortar school.

It was not known whether the operation would be a success but, pessimism not being one of the battalion's strong points, the name of the farm of Le Vert Bois was immediately altered to the more easily pronounceable and certainly more apt: 'Gloucester Farm'. Whatever the outcome that is how it would remain, on the map.

The main task was allocated to 'A' Company under Captain C.S. Petherham MC and 'C' Company. In reserve were 'B' and 'D' Companies.

All men were ready by night fall and at 21.00 hours 'B' and 'D' Companies moved up into position immediately behind the attacking Companies, 'A' and 'C'.

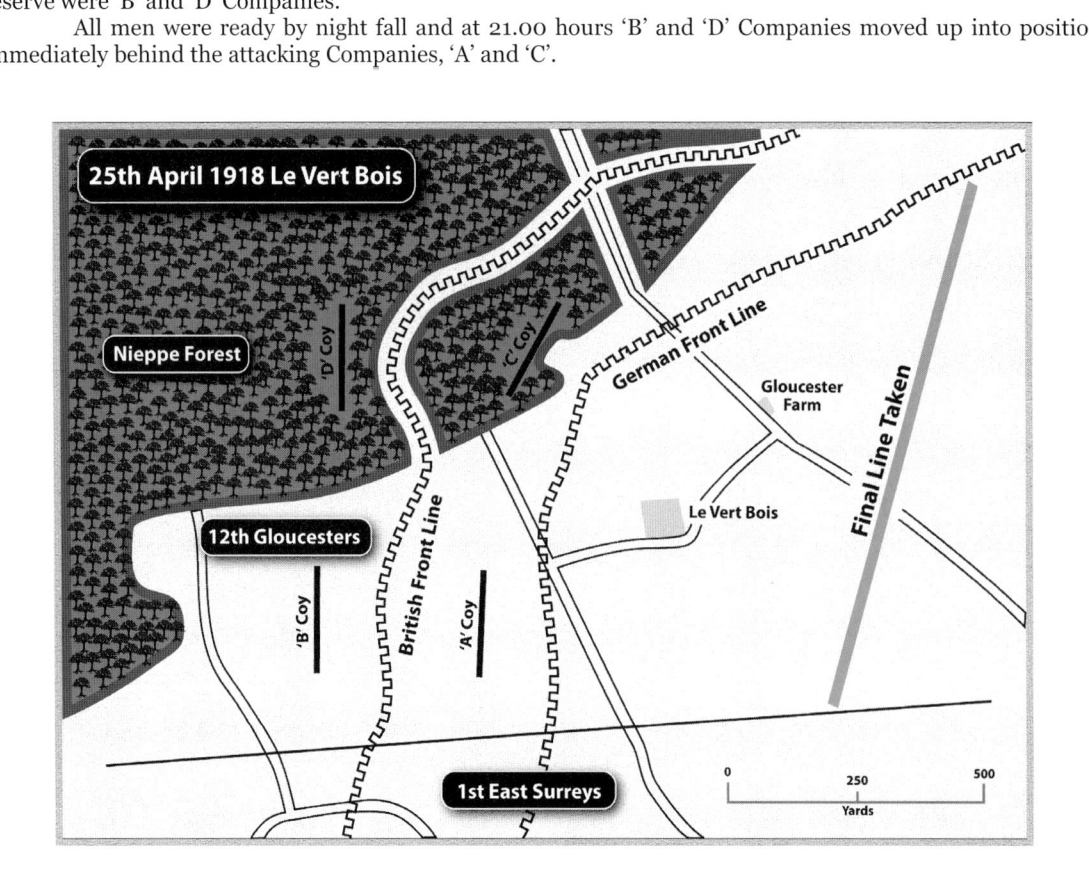

1918 – Year of movement

The barrage opened at zero hour; 9.30p.m. and at 9.33p.m. No. 1 Platoon of 'A' Company under Sgt. Lewis with No. 7 platoon of 'B' Company under 2nd/Lt. G.M. Rogers in close support advanced under the barrage, in fact so close to the barrage that the enemy were completely taken by surprise. All objectives were taken: the group of buildings and the farm itself without serious opposition and, by 10p.m., the men were consolidating on their final position.

On the right of 'A' Company, No. 3 platoon under 2nd/Lt. E.G. Wills attacked from the north over a bridge. No. 2 platoon under Lt. N. Armitage in support also intended to attack from the west over a temporary bridge. However, the bridge had not arrived and an alternative route was taken. Unfortunately, resistance at these two places was heavier. Lt. Armitage was killed and numerous other ranks casualties caused by close range machine gun fire. Shelter was found in a ditch until the gun was put out of action by No. 3 platoon which had met with less resistance, though 2nd/Lt. Wills was wounded. Both platoons joined forces and were reinforced by a platoon of 'B' Company under Sgt. Gosney and advanced to the final objective where they joined up with the left attacking party of 'A' Company around 10.20p.m. 'C' Company, while attacking on the battalion's left flank, met with only slight resistance while taking its objective and numerous prisoners.

While 'B' Company moved up to consolidate the new position, Lt. A. Laird, assisted by Sgt. Smith and one other rank, began systematically searching and clearing the buildings for any remaining enemy. In one cellar was discovered 30 Germans who surrendered without resistance. In the farmhouse, to their great surprise, was found an old woman who had been wounded. She had lived there, practically in no-man's land throughout about a fortnight of war. After her wounds had been attended to, amid much objection, she was conveyed to safety by the only form of transport available: a wheel barrow!

The operation had been a complete success. Among the captures were 3 machine guns, 35 unwounded prisoners, 4 wounded prisoners and a mile of line to an average depth of 500 yards. The War Diary recorded: "Heavy casualties are known to have been inflicted on the enemy." The casualties of the battalion were:

Officer killed:
Lt. N. Armitage
Officer died of wounds:
2/Lt. G.M. Rogers
Officer wounded:
2/Lt. E.G. Wills,
Other ranks killed: 21
Other ranks wounded: 30

General Haking, Commanding XI Corps
"Please convey to Brigadier Generals Oldham and Weston, Lt. Col. Halfield and Major Chapman and all ranks of the 1st Bedfordshire and 12th Gloucestershire Regiments, my congratulations for gaining their objectives last night. It was a most creditable performance and will greatly improve our situation."

Major General R.B. Stephens, C.B., C.M.G., G.O.C. 5th Division
"The divisional commander congratulates PRAY, PILLOW and the divisional and heavy artillery on the exceedingly neat and well arranged operation that was carried out last night. PUG and PEACOCK made a most gallant and successful attack and the determination with which PEACOCK fought their way into Le Vert Bois (Gloucester Farm) is to be especially commended."

PEACOCK was code name for 12th Battalion Gloucestershire Regiment.

For these exploits, Captain Petherham received a bar to his MC, and Lt. A. Laird and Lt. R.E. Guise the MC; also Sgt. J. Lewis was awarded the DCM.

From that time until late June, the battalion varied its time between rest, support and front line duty near Merville, with very little to report apart from the usual casualties caused by shelling and gassing. That

1918 – Year of movement

was, apart form an unfortunate incident which took place on the 6th June, in the front line, when 2nd/Lt. E. E. Shepherd, C.S.M. J. Lewis and Sgt. F.C. Smith were killed by a heavy trench mortar. Both C.S.M. Lewis and Sgt. Smith were original battalion members who had joined in September 1914. Sgt. Smith had also been a stalwart member of the 5th Divisional concert party, the "Whizz-Bangs" since its early days.

On the 25th June, while again in the line in the neighbourhood of Caudescure, two newly-joined officers attempted a daylight reconnaissance of a supposed enemy house. One officer, 2nd/Lt. Drew, and an accompanying N.C.O. both were killed. The other officer, 2nd/Lt. Abbott, gallantly attempted to rescue them but found himself in open country under heavy rifle fire at close range. It was certain death to move, so he had to lie 'doggo' hoping to get away at dusk. The Germans, however, had him under good observation, stalked him at dusk and took him prisoner. This was not known and he was considered dead also.

That night the battalion was relieved and rested for a few days in camp in the forest. On the night of the 27th/28th June, the battalion found itself in the line at Caudescure again. On its way in, the enemy gave it a hearty welcome in the form of a very warm barrage. All sorts of H.E. and gas landed on and around them. That resulted in the battalion losing 47 men as casualties.

Cornet Perdu

On the morning of the 28th, the battalion got its revenge. The battalion took part in a two brigade attack. Penetrating to a depth of over 2,000 yards the small village of Cornet Perdu was taken. 'C' Company pushed forward patrols to the Plate Becque River. A considerable number of prisoners were taken, whilst the battalion sustained relatively light casualties. The wounded, though, were later difficult to find as the corn was waist high.

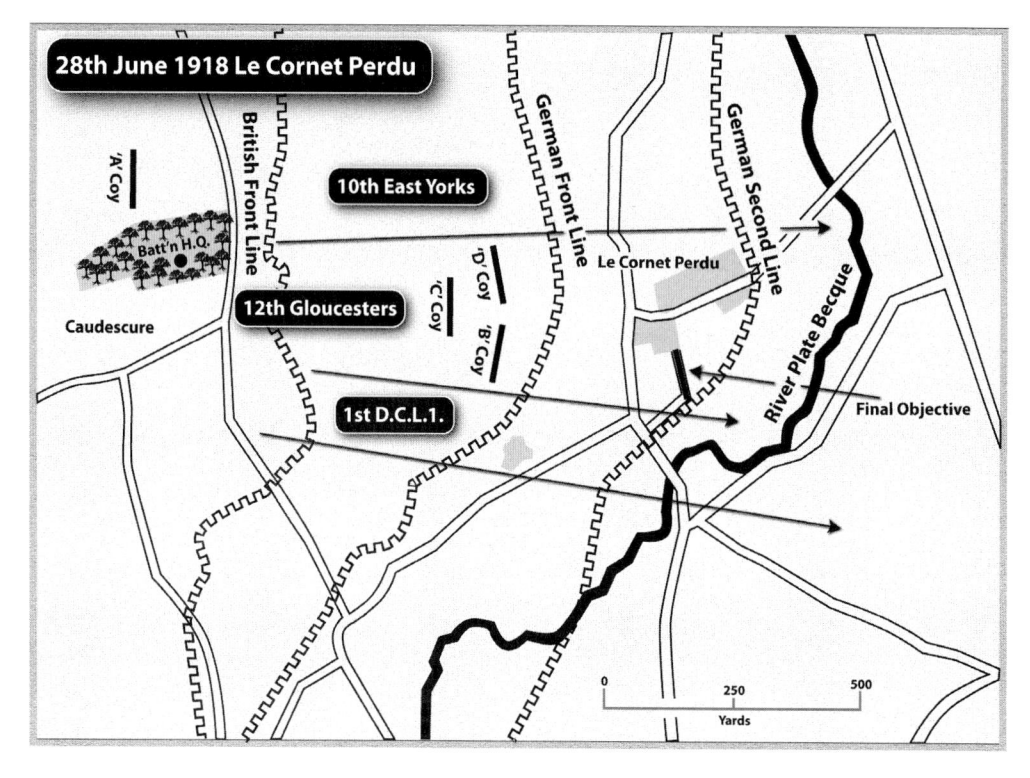

1918 – Year of movement

During the afternoon, the Germans attempted a counter-attack, but it was severely repulsed and just seemed to melt away under the battalion's heavy and accurate return fire. More prisoners were taken.

37831 C.S.M. George Pine
"We attacked and took the village of Cornet Perdu. In fact, all objectives were taken for a relatively small number of casualties. The next day, I accompanied Lt. Reginald Guise forward of our position in order to reconnoiter the enemy positions. It was at this time that the enemy began shelling us heavily. Lt. Guise took a hit to the head and was killed instantly. It was a real shame as he was a good man."

Among the honours awarded for this action were: Captain Bray, Lt.s Greenhalgh and Coombs and the Rev. Harrison the M.C. Also four 'A' Company stretcher bearers did some very gallant work bringing in the wounded and were awarded M.M.'s.

A curious incident arose from this action. The 1st D.C.L.I. on the right of the battalion attacked over the ground the battalion had held three days previous and where two officers were killed as had been supposed. A photograph in a captured camera, on being developed, showed one of these officers sitting in a trench surrounded by Germans: it was 2nd/Lt. Abbott.

Major General R.B. Stephens, C.B., C.M.G., G.O.C. 5th Division
"I wish to convey to you and your staff and to thank all ranks of the Division my appreciation and thanks for the very successful operation carried out by them on the 28th June.
"The task of the 95th Brigade under Brigadier General Norton, D.S.O., involved an advance of nearly 2000 yards and the capture of the farms of L' Epinette and Le Cornet Perdu. The energy, dash and determination with which the 1st D.C.L.I. under Lt. Col. Kirk, D.S.O. and the 12th Gloucesters under Lt. Col. Colt, MC fulfilled their tasks is deserving of the highest praise."

At the end of June the battalion welcomed back one of its original September 1914 men. Robert Anstey had been wounded at Longueval in July 1916 then rose to the rank of Sergeant. He had been granted a commission and on the morning of 8th May 1917, during the ill-fated Fresnoy action, had been ordered off by the then Captain Colt should harm come to him.

Having gained his commission, he had been posted to the 2/5th Gloucesters and had been with them during the launch of the German offensive back in March when he had received his second wound.

2nd/Lt. R.H. Anstey
"I returned to France towards the end of June and, on arrival at the base at Rouen, found I was posted back to my old battalion, the 12th Gloucesters in the 5th Division.
"During my absence they had gone to the Ypres Salient and had taken part in the Passchendaele battle, where they had 241 casualties in 11 days. Then there was Italy and then when the German attack developed in March, they were rushed back to France in April. They had been successful in holding up a strong German attack in the Nieppe Forest area.
"I rejoined the old battalion at Steenbeque. The Commanding Officer was then Lt. Col. H. A. Colt MC who, as Captain Colt, had been my Company commander when we first went to France in November 1915. A fine soldier, he had been awarded the MC early on and had several times been 'mentioned in despatches'.
"In a letter to my wife at this time I wrote: "The C.O. was very decent indeed….He said "I suppose for sentimental reasons you would like to go back to the old Company" Of course I agreed, so behold, me now a Platoon Commander in the Company where I once stood in the ranks as a 'Tommy' ."

Early in July news reached the battalion that Lt. R. J. Fitzgerald, famed character of many a daring trench raid had been killed in action on the 1st July. He had been attached to the Royal Air Force as an observer in a F2B Bristol Fighter. Having been attacked by an enemy aircraft the pilot managed to return the aircraft to it's home base. Unfortuneately it was discovered on landing that Lt. Fitzgerald had not survived the attack. He was buried in Vignacourt Cemetery near Amiens.

Grave of Lt. Roy James Fitzgerald M.C.

Things seemed to be going well for the battalion. But at the back of each man's mind was the possibility of leave. It was arranged based on a man's service, or time at the front. This was unfortunate for men newly posted to the battalion as men with the greater service came first. Even so, opportunities for leave periods were few. Those who were fortunate enough to get away for a few days noticed that things at home were not what they expected.

20089 Pte. William James
"I was granted five days' leave around July 1918. I was fortunate as the battalion was busy at the time and I hadn't been home in almost two years. The people back home were pleased to see me, but they were different. I never spoke about life at the front, but what really surprised me was that no one was interested in anything about my pals in the battalion or in me. They were full of their own problems about shortages and rationing. There was more interest and talk of obtaining sugar than what our boys were going through in France. It seemed to me that patriotism had worn completely threadbare. By the time my leave was over, I felt pleased to be going back to people I understood."

14138 Sgt. Norman Pegg
"Arriving home on leave I went to my aunt's home and I found that people wanted to take me out to dinners and theatres and didn't seem to want to know much about what we were doing at the front. I didn't tell them anything of the horrors but I did explain to them that the conditions were really terrible and the food not good at all. But they didn't seem to want to know at all."

1918 – Year of movement

14225 Pte. Bruce Buchanan
"When you stepped off the leave train, the first effect was that you were just home for a holiday, but soon that began to wear off. I felt there was something unreal about leave. I'm bound to say that I got myself into a state of mind that it was the trenches that were the real world and it was home, and my family that were unreal."

Nothing very much of interest occurred During July. A good deal of time was spent though in worrying the Germans, in testing his line and in hard work in the line working on trenches.

In the early part of August the battalion were relieved by the 2/5th Gloucesters. Whether the news that there were even more Gloucesters in this part of the line upset the Germans or whether the great attack further south on the 5th of August caused it, one thing is certain, the enemy vacated his line and went back within two days of the relief.

Irles

At the end of the first week of August the battalion found itself in a tented camp outside a small village. While there, Captain Petherham MC left for a six months tour of duty in England.

Here, every opportunity was taken to re-organise the battalion and to practise the new skills of open warfare attack. A few lessons were impressed upon the men that were very soon to be of great value to them. Several concerts were held, the stage being constructed of material from a bridging pontoon kindly provided by the R.E. from a neighbouring camp.

Much of August was spent moving from one place to another until the 19th when the battalion arrived in the neighbourhood of Hebuturne. The next morning was spent in reconnoitring the front line and that evening moved into the line near Bois de Biex in reserve to the 95th Brigade, the front line being held at that time by the 37th Division. At this moment the composition of the battalion was as follows:

C.O.: Lt. Col. H.A. Colt MC
Adjutant: Captain J. H. Maywood
Inteligence Officer: Lt. A Laird
Signalling Officer: Lt. A. Bracher
O.C. 'A' Company: Captain N. R. Hathaway
O.C. 'B' Company: Lt. T. C. Greenhalgh
O.C. 'C' Company: Captain B. A. Russell
O.C. 'D' Company: Captain J. P. Webb

The situation was that the line in front of the battalion was held by the 37th Division. On their right was the New Zealand Division.

2nd/Lt. R.H. Anstey
"As Captain Petherham, O.C. 'A' Company had been posted back to England, the Company was temporarily under the command of Captain Hathaway,
an officer recently transferred from the A.S.C. As soon as the next show started, he handed over command to me."

At daylight on the 21st August the 37th Division attacked and captured the enemy's front and support lines including the villages of Puisieux au Mont and Bucquoy. Shortly after, the 63rd (Naval) Division on the left and the 5th Division on the right pushed through on the frontage of the 37th Division to exploit their success. In our brigade this attack was carried out by the 1st Devons and 1st East Surreys. The 1st D.C.L.I. were in support and the 12th Gloucesters in reserve.

The attack was carried out in dense fog, the supporting tanks became bewildered and lost, as did the attacking troops. No troops moved forward to the right of the battalion since the New Zealanders were ordered not to move until we had reached our final objective, which was three miles distant. They were then to sweep forward, swing half right and join up our right flank to the stationary part of the line to the south.

1918 – Year of movement

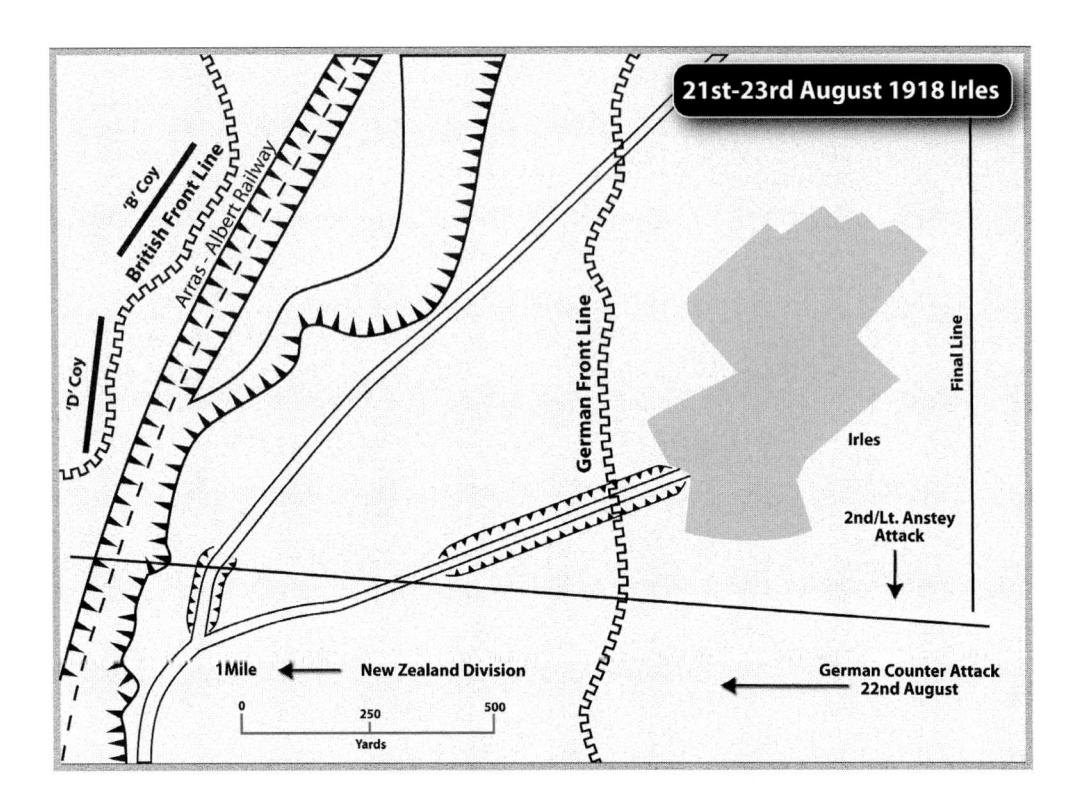

At noon – the fog having cleared by 11a.m. – the situation was very obscure, as no reports as to progress made had been received by the 95th Brigade.

The battalion was accordingly sent forward to clear up the situation or to take and hold the final objective. On the right was a small valley, on the far side of which the ground rose slightly. Not surprisingly, the Germans held this rising ground, on which they had numerous machine guns sited and firing. 'B' and 'D' Companies were ordered to attack, with 'C' in support and 'A' in reserve.

Without any sort of supporting barrage and without tanks the battalion went forward with great success, using its Lewis guns to provide covering fire. They worked their way over open, undulating country for a further mile, under very heavy machine gun fire and a certain amount of shelling from the enemy, to whom their advance was perfectly visible from the rising ground. Here the battalion was held up and had to dig in.

14596 William Ayres
"It was August and the weather was hot. Because of the heat I had drunk all the water from my water bottle. As I passed a dead soldier, I was glad to find his water bottle was full. So I took his, and threw mine away. I discovered later that the water bottle I had taken was full of rum – and I wanted water!"

1918 – Year of movement

The battalion, moving forward at Irles August 1918   (IWM)

The situation was now that the 12th Gloucesters held most of the brigade front line, with the 1st East Surreys holding the remainder. The whole of the right flank was open, save for a defensive flank some 100 yards in length. This, however, was considered safe as the New Zealanders were positioned a mile to the rear and the 1st D.C.L.I. now in support could easily be swung around to form a further defensive flank. Also, about a mile to the battalion's rear was the 1st Devons who were in line with the New Zealanders. To the battalion's front was rising ground from which enemy machine guns were still very active.

Among the casualties were Captains Webb and Russell wounded. Captain Webb, another battalion original, subsequently died of his wounds. Captain Russell, having been moved to the safety of a shell hole, was later hit again by a stray bullet as he sat between the C.O. and the Adjutant.

At dawn on the 22nd the Germans put down a heavy barrage and then counter-attacked immediately on the battalion's right – open – flank. There being no one to oppose them – other than the flanking fire of the battalion's few Lewis guns there – he, swept on past battalion H.Q. which was around ¾ of a mile distant till brought up against the New Zealanders.

This movement left their right flank exposed and 2nd/Lt. Anstey with two platoons of 'A' Company was accordingly ordered to attack it.

Going forward in a most gallant manner, this party cut off a large number of Germans from their 1st, 2nd and 3rd waves. The remainder retired. In their confusion, some 200 were driven into the arms of the 1st Devons and captured, while 2nd/Lt. Anstey and his 40 men returned with 105 prisoners and 5 enemy machine guns.

2nd/Lt. R.H. Anstey
"In spite of a stubborn resistance, 21st August had proved a successful day and we advanced further during the night. The 12th Gloucesters were on the right of the 5th Division, with the New Zealanders on our right, further back.

1918 – Year of movement

"Soon after dawn on the 22nd, a big gap was discovered on the New Zealand front. The Germans threw two battalions of storm troops into this gap in an attempt to turn our flank. 'A' Company was acting as reserve Company and I received urgent orders from the C.O. to take 2 platoons and hold an embankment - map references supplied – 'at all costs'. The total strength of my two platoons was 40 men and 2 Lewis guns. I was fortunate enough – with the aid of a bit of bluff – to be able to hold up the counter-attack and 380 Germans in total surrendered with six machine guns. 105 prisoners and 5 machine guns falling to my own action

"Everyone seemed pleased. Later in the morning the N.Z. general visited my position. He said some complimentary things – saying that he had watched the operation through his field glasses from a nearby hill and told me that the New Zealanders were proud to be working with us."

On the 23rd orders were received to attack the final objective – the village of Irles. At 11a.m. the attack was launched with the 1st East Surreys on the left and the 12th Gloucesters on the right.

The Arras–Albert railway line ran in front of the British line, as did a natural feature with steep side. It was not realised how deep and steep-sided the cutting through which this ran in one place on the Gloucester's front. Going down this and up the other side 'D' Company got too far behind the creeping barrage. As a result, the German machine guns held up this part of the attack and caused many casualties. Soon, however, a flanking movement restored the situation.

14596 William Ayres

"We had taken up a position along a railway line and by that time, the men were parched with thirst. There was, a little way away, a shell-hole filled with green and slimy water. But it was water and, one by one the men would edge their way to the shell-hole to drink the water, repulsive and unpleasant though it was. We soon realised we were overlooked from the German positions and, in particular, there was a sniper with his sights trained on the spot. And here, let me say a word for an unknown but chivalrous German sniper. When he could see, due to bandages, or limping, that a soldier moving towards the shell-hole was wounded, his rifle would remain silent. But let a fit man endeavour to approach the place, then, his shooting would be deadly."

In front of the village of Irles the battalion was, again, held up by machine gun, rifle and trench mortar fire. The village was strongly held by the enemy and it took six hours to clear them, doing so by 07.30p.m.

Soon afterwards the battalion was relieved by the 1st West Kents, whose first effort was to claim the capture of the village. This claim, however, was withdrawn on it being pointed out to them that their first storming party – 1 officer and 2 men – reached the village ten minutes after the Gloucesters had passed through it. Twenty officers had gone into the line on the night of the 20th/21st August. By 8p.m. on the 23rd, three remained.

2nd/Lt. R.H. Anstey

"Late at night on the 22nd I joined the other two platoons of 'A' Company with my men and, just after midnight received orders for the renewed attack next day.

"It was a stiff fight, but we eventually crossed the railway line, climbed the hill and stormed the village of Irles. Lt. Col. Colt did some fine work here, rallying and personally leading the attack which captured the village. He was seriously wounded in doing so.

"My Company came out of this action with 1 officer and 34 men. We again, captured a large number of prisoners and machine guns. I was wounded here for the third time – a machine gun bullet in my left shoulder."

14596 William Ayres

"During the afternoon I was standing at the entrance to a dug-out (as it was a captured German dug-out the entrance faced the wrong way) when a sniper took a shot at me. I do not know how near to my head the bullet went – but to this day, I can hear the crack of it, as it hit the wooden frame of the dug-out just

1918 – Year of movement

behind me. Maybe, a fraction of an inch away from my head. The next day, we went forward in the face of heavy machine gun fire, not only from our front, but also with enfilading fire from our flanks. I received a bullet wound in my leg. It was my long awaited 'blighty' a few days later I was off to England.

"By that time, another deliverance had come to light. While on my way to hospital, I discovered that the bible I had carried in my left breast pocket, had been pierced by a bullet. The bullet had passed right through the bible, and must have gone away under my arm. Some pencils in the same pocket were smashed to pieces. The bible, torn right through by the flight of the bullet, is still with me."

During the operations 21st–23rd August the 12th Gloucesters captured some 9 officers and 300 other ranks as prisoners. 1 Howitzer, 2 field guns and some 40 machine guns. Casualties caused in so doing amounted to:

Officer killed:
Captain Maywood Adjutant (1st D.C.L.I.)
Officer died of wounds:
Captain J.P. Webb
Officers wounded:
Captain B.A. Russell, D.S.O.
Lt. T.C. Greenhalgh, MC
Lt. A. Laird, MC
Lt. F.H. La Trobe, MC
2nd/Lt. R.H. Anstey
2nd/Lt. G.G.L. Dicks
2nd/Lt. J.D. Geake
2nd/Lt. L.W. Halse
2nd/Lt. L.S. Holman
2nd/Lt. J. Ibbotson
2nd/Lt. J.T.W. Miles
2nd/Lt. B.E.L. Monk
Other ranks killed: 31
Other ranks wounded: 269

Among the honours awarded for the operations carried between the 21st to the 23rd of August were:

Lt. Col H.A. Colt, MC – the D.S.O.
Lt's Anstey, Benjamin and Ibbotson - the MC

On the 24th Major W.G. Chapman assumed command of the battalion and 2nd/Lt. A. Bracher took over duties of adjutant. About 10.30p.m. the battalion withdrew to reserve. Here it remained until the end of the month. Other attacks were planned but in the event came to nothing.

On the 14th September the battalion moved into the line at Neuville and relieved part of the New Zealand Division. The enemy had moved up two new divisions and was preparing to attack. The attack was expected at dawn. However, thanks to a very heavy British barrage the expected attack failed to materialise. In retaliation, the enemy shelled the battalion's positions with gas from 8p.m. onwards.

The remainder of September saw the battalion in the line the whole time. Several attacks were planned but again did not materialise. On the 1st October the battalion left the trenches for the last time near Metz and marched to hutments in Velu Wood. Battalion War Diary reported: "Weather fine. Nothing to report."

1918 – Year of movement

In the spring of 1918 as part of a British Army reorganisation, it was ordered that each division, comprising three infantry brigades, would reduce its complement from twelve infantry battalions down to nine. Subsequently, as previously stated, by 4th March 115 battalions had been disbanded. The 5th Division decided to ignore the directive.

And so, the 5th Division had successfully contrived to evade the stipulated reduction of its infantry brigades to the required three battalions each. However, the authorities eventually caught up and demanded that prevarication should cease and the specified changes be executed. The division was thus obliged to lose three of its existing twelve battalions. It was clear that none of the regular battalions would be under threat and, therefore, the axe would fall on some of the division's Territorial Force or Service battalions. The existing pioneers were the 6th Argyll and Sutherland Highlanders. This battalion was promptly returned to its old division, the 51st. Following on, along with the 15th Warwicks, the 12th Gloucesters were disbanded. The 14th Warwicks took over as divisional pioneers. Four officers and the greater part of 'D' Company of the 12th Gloucesters were transferred to this battalion as pioneers. What skills, it was considered, they possessed for pioneering work may only be guessed at.

On the 5th October orders were received for disbandment to commence on Sunday 6th. On that day at 10 a.m. a ceremonial church parade was held, after which disbandment commenced. Other ranks were transferred to other units of the 5th Division. Disbandment was completed on the 19th when Captain and Adjutant A. Bracher went to the 1st D.C.L.I. and Lt. S.H. Gillard went to the 1st Devons.

20089 Pte. William James
"On returning to the battalion and disbandment, I was posted to the 1st Devons. I was disgusted and as a protest, immediately reported sick due to my gassing. I did not go in the line again."

Bitter irony cannot get any more so than the case of 16624 Private Charles Edward Butler of 'C' Company. He had enlisted in the battalion during December 1914. He had been wounded at least once at Morval, Somme, 25th September 1916. He survived his time with the 12th Battalion throughout the war and was posted to the 1st Devons on the disbandment of the battalion on 6th October. He was killed in action with the Devons two weeks later on the 20th October.

From a sentimental standpoint, it seems distinctly unfair that the battalion was not allowed to survive the remaining month of the war. It had experienced much of the unprofitable and adverse side of it, and had played such a prominent part in the actions of the 5th Division and the 95th Brigade and, just when the enemy was being hurled back with a vengeance, it was disbanded.

The battalion never returned to anything like its full strength after its mauling during the battle of the Somme in 1916 and the battles of Arras at Fresnoy and later the 3rd Ypres in 1917. This, however, had no bearing on what was expected of it and, it continued, right until the end, to carry out its duties well aided by its superb leadership in the hands of its officers and NCOs and, the initiative of its men. With this in mind, it was all the more remarkable that, during the whole of 1918, the 12th Battalion Gloucestershire Regiment, a Service battalion, held the distinction of attacking more frequently than any other Regular battalion of the 95th Brigade.

Of the 990 men who landed with the battalion in November 1915, just under ten percent of them remained with the battalion at the time of disbandment in October 1918. Of those original men, 205 had died with the battalion and over 100 more died after being posted to other units. Approximately one third of its November 1915 strength had died. Taking into account later postings into the battalion, the total number of officers who served and died with the battalion amounted to 32. The total number of men, 756.

When the men left the city, amid all the furore and excitement, in June of 1915, they did so as part of a strong organisation, a true 'band of brothers'. The Lord Mayor, John Swaish, had said jubilantly: *"May we have the pleasure at no distant date of giving you a joyous return on your welcome home.* And, spoken

1918 – Year of movement

earlier during the first public showing of the new battalion on Monday 21st September 1914, *I am quite sure you will do your part, and when you come back we will have another meeting in the Colston Hall to welcome you."*

When the remaining original men were finally demobilised in 1919 from other units, they returned home alone, to a world they did not recognise, to people they did not know or understand. The war was over and many of the original men were either dead or wounded and displaced throughout the length and breadth of the country or, had been discharged as disabled. The battalion no longer existed. There was no 'joyous return or even a welcome home.'

The patriotism that was prevalent during the heady days of 1914 and 1915 had long since evaporated. The world was now a different place. Too many men had died and too many had been disfigured by the war, both physically and mentally. People at home were intent on forgetting the terrible war, and in putting it behind them. They didn't want to be reminded of it. 'Bristol's Own' was part of that war and by then, a memory that people wanted to forget.

The old Lie:
Dulce et decorum est Pro patria mori.

Some of those that died as a result of the fighting during 1918

Pte. Charles Butler
KIA with
1st Devons
20th October 1918

L/Cpl. Arthur Crossman
KIA 25th August 1918

Cpl. George Greening
KIA 25th June 1918

1918 – Year of movement

Pte. Albert Hopkins
DOW 31st August 1918

Cpl. Robert Lewis
KIA 25th April 1918

Pte. Rginald Matthews
KIA 20th June 1918

Pte. Reginal Naish
DOW 4th May 1918

Sgt. Frederick Smith
KIA 6th June 1918

Pte. Frank Sydenham
KIA 25th August 1918

L/Cpl. James Thould
DOW 11th March 1918

Capt. Jack Webb
DOW 22nd August 1918

Chapter X

Old Comrades' Association

Very soon after the end of the fighting an idea occurred to Mrs. Blennerhassett of the Comforts Committee, the wife of Major Blennerhassett, the first 'Second in Command', to organise a reunion of past battalion members. The first reunion, meeting in the Soldiers Room at the city museum, was necessarily a small affair. The second meeting was larger and the third meeting, held on Saturday 4th January 1919, was attended by no less than 35 officers and 268 men.

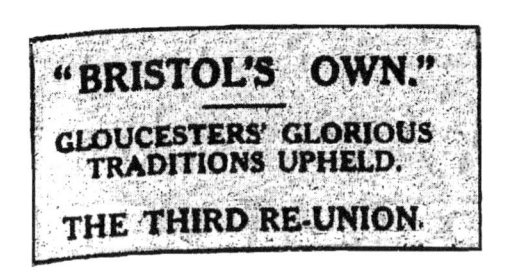

> **"BRISTOL'S OWN."**
> GLOUCESTERS' GLORIOUS TRADITIONS UPHELD.
> THE THIRD RE-UNION.

Lt. Col. W.E.P. Burges presided and prominent among the attendance were: the Lord Mayor; Mr. H.W. Twiggs; Lt. Col. Archer-Shee; Lt. Col. Russell-Kerr (who was first adjutant); Lt. Col. Likeman; Major J. Carr; Major G.R.A. Beckett; Major Wilson–Fox; Major Logan; Major Hooper (the first quartermaster); Captain Leschalles; Captain Burris and Lt. H.C. Ryland.

A great number of the men were de-mobilised ex-soldiers, but there were also a good number of officers and men still in uniform, including several who had only recently been released from captivity in Germany.

Lt. Col. Burges announced that he had received apologies for absence from Lt. Col. and Mrs. Blennerhassett and Lt. Col. and Mrs. Colt. He also announced that it would be the last entertainment given by the Comforts Committee which, as the war was ended, would cease to exist. The debt of gratitude which they all owed that committee was a very big one as many of the officers and men who had been at the front knew, at first hand, what the efforts of that committee had meant. On behalf of the gathering, he tended grateful thanks for their valued efforts to Mrs. Holman, Mrs. Robinson, Mrs. Blennerhassett, Mrs. Wilson-Fox, Mrs. Ostler and others. To Mrs. Holman, the Honorary Secretary, he handed, from 'the boys' of the old battalion, a small souvenir of their gratitude: a silver ink stand bearing the back badge of the Gloucesters and inscribed – "To Mrs. Holman, from the boys of the 12th Battalion Gloucestershire Regiment, in grateful recollection of all she has done for them."

Whilst reminiscing of the early days of the battalion, Lt. Col. Burges said it was not very pleasant sleeping in the 'White City' buildings as they tended to be very draughty. The battalion would never have accomplished what it had, had it not been that every man was there for the purpose of doing his job and learning to the best of his ability. During their course of musketry at the seaside they had only 40 old rifles, but still they came out on top. He said the training of the battalion was the happiest time he had ever spent in his life, for he had the inestimable pleasure of seeing the battalion grow, not only in numbers, but in efficiency. At the farewell smoking concert at the Colston Hall he had said that they had in their keeping the honour of the Gloucestershire Regiment and that he felt convinced that that honour would be upheld to the very end by the men of the battalion. Well, they had done it. It had upheld the traditions of the two line battalions, the 1st and the 2nd – furthermore, the 12th had been in the forefront. Now there was the nucleus of a battalion Old Comrades Association and he hoped every man of the battalion would join and support it. In conclusion, Lt. Col. Burges asked for two minutes' silence while they thought of 'Fallen Comrades'.

The Lord Mayor continued by saying that 'Bristol's Own' represented the patriotism, the courage and the efficiency of Bristol generally during the Great War. His Lordship quoted from an official report with reference to the work of the battalion on 3rd September 1916. The officer who made the report stated that under fire the battalion proceeded as steadily as if on parade and they went through a heavy German barrage in the most gallant manner. After noting that they faced heavy machine gun fire, the officer wrote: "I never saw the slightest sign of wavering. That day your men covered themselves with glory and no troops could have carried through such a difficult task with more dash or more indifference to consequences." He mentioned that the battalion had lost over 700 men and that they would be remembered that evening in the midst of their rejoicing and that they would be glad to think that their lives had not been sacrificed in vain.

Lt. Col. Archer-Shee stated that 'Bristol's Own' had incurred 735 casualties during the Somme battles, out of the 990 that went over in November 1915, and that the Somme was only the beginning of it. He had handed over command to another officer who was later succeeded by Lt. Col. Colt. He had had the privilege of meeting the battalion again last summer, when they were conducting themselves as if going to a tea party, instead of into a very serious fight in which, however, they were very successful. Those who had fought in the war had the satisfaction of knowing that they had taken part in the greatest war in history and that England had never stood higher in the estimation of the whole world than she did at that moment. He said that he had been a member of the 12th Battalion Gloucestershire Regiment and that there was nothing he was more proud of than the fact that he once had the honour to be their commanding officer. It was on this day that the 12th Battalion Gloucestershire Regiment Old Comrades Association was formed.

One of the ladies of the former Comforts Committee, in 1925, paid a visit to some of the battlefield sites of the Somme well-known to the battalion. In a letter to Mr. E.E. Shanks, the acting secretary of the Old Comrades' Association, she regarded scenes familiar to those who were in the battalion in the stirring days that, at that time, seemed so long ago:

"Having recently visited the Somme I wish to tell you of my findings. Longueval, it may interest you to hear, is mostly grass grown. The high banks on either side of 'Duke Street' or the sunken road are down to four feet only, and the village is rebuilding with tin and wooden huts. The trenches are still to be seen and shell-holes and wire are left as they were in 1916.

"We passed through Guillemont and saw the trenches. The ground is partly cleared and the shell-holes filled in, but of the village there is not a stick or a stone to show there was once a village. It is all grass.

"We passed though Suzanne. The chateau is still standing and would be habitable with a few repairs carried out."

Around Easter of 1930 a long-awaited, Old Comrades' Association battlefield re-visit took place over a five day period. Approximately 50 men attended and H.Q. for the tour was the Hotel Du Commerce in Arras.

Places visited included: Arras, Bethune, Cabaret Rouge, The Somme, Morbecque, Suzanne, Agnez Les Duisines, Fresnoy and other places. The main party split into separate smaller parties which were designed to cover various battle-field areas depending on what parts the men wished to see.

Whilst at Longueval it was discovered that a cross had been erected in memory of the battalion. Mr Sam Bollom said: *"It was strange as we had no idea it was there or who had placed it there."*

A superb photograph album depicting much of the battlefield re-visit was created by one of the men. This was handed down through the years and eventually given to the author. It covers most of the 'old haunts' of the battalion. For example a photograph of men in Piano Street, Arras where, still visible on the window sill was '1st Battalion D.C.L.I.'; Bethune War Memorial; Cabaret Rouge cemetery; visiting the grave of A. R. Milne at Morbecque Cemetery; a G.S. Wagon on the road between Thilloy and Arras; Quarry Cemetery; Somme looking over the wall at the stretcher bearer's dugout in the quarry; the Gloster Cross at Longueval and many other locations so well known to the men. Memories of the visit remained for many years afterwards.

Robert Anstey, an original battalion member, had a letter published in the Western Daily Press on 13th November 1934:

"Sir, it is armistice night, and I am wondering if I may send a greeting – through you – to the men of my old battalion, 'Bristol's Own'.

"Fate has ordained that some of us who served in her ranks should live hundreds of miles from the old city, but at this season our thoughts turn Bristol-wards, and to the great-hearted fellows who shared with us those strange experiences of the war years.

"Any attempt to glorify the ghastliness of war leaves me stone cold, but what we shall never forget are the great moments we shared, the comradeship born of mutual hardship and suffering, the wonderful understanding of each other, the unfailing loyalty, the sacred fellowship between man and man – all filling the temple of memory with an everlasting fragrance.

"To you all, my comrades, I wish good fortune and courage to sustain you in these testing days as in those. Hail and farewell."

Members of the O.C.A. had decided that a lasting memorial to the battalion should be on display in Bristol. The culmination of much arrangement and subscription by association members was the service held on the 28th January 1951 in the Crypt of St. Nicholas Church, Bristol. Many members attended the service during which a fine bronze plaque was unveiled by F.P. Burton ('A' Company) and dedicated by Canon J.M.D. Stancomb, R.D.

Old Comrades Association

During an Old Comrades' gathering shortly before his death in 1935, Lt. Col. Archer-Shee stated that the men sat before him were honorary members of a proud regiment and had been honourable members of it for an important time in the history of their country. He said that 'Bristol's Own' had added a great deal to the battle honours of the regiment and that the Gloucestershire Regiment ought to be the proudest infantry regiment in the British Army because of those honours. They had meant loss and suffering, and pluck, and grit, and everything that went to make the greatest and manhood of England. It was only when he thought of that, that he realised what those honours meant. He reflected that some people had said they wanted to forget the war, as if there was something not honourable in fighting. But it was their tradition which, handed down, inspired those who followed them. England would always be great as long as she had her sons to fight for her, not in an aggressive but defensive spirit. When he heard talk of there being no more war, he said: but let them see that they were ready for it in any case and determined to do as well as they had done in the past.

Last post for the old soldiers

After 57 years of unbroken annual meetings the few remaining members of the Old Comrades' Association of the once proud 12th Battalion Gloucestershire Regiment held their final meeting on 8th June 1976. That year, Mr. Sam Bollom, secretary, sent off 73 letters to all the men still on the list of members. But he only got 30 responses. He received many letters saying this man has recently died or this man is too ill to attend. By that time, the men no longer wore their medals to the meeting, considering that no one was interested anymore. Recently the association's chairman, Mr. Bill Craddock had died. Mr. Bollom rang 17 members but was only able to find six to attend the funeral.

The association's meetings ended where they had began: in the city's Art Gallery with just a handful of proud, old gentlemen.

The remembrance of the fallen and the comradeship of their brethren that formed the O.C.A. was summarized by the following verse:

"When War broke out in City, Town,
Battalions formed of great Renown.
In this fair City, one well known,
Became the famous 'Bristol's Own'.
And men from every walk of life,
Determined yes what'ere the strife.

Many a Mother, Sweetheart, Wife,
Now mourns the man who gave his life.
That Wars would end and fighting cease,
So that we all might, all might live in peace.

A noble sacrifice tis true,
They died for England, yes, and you.
A finer bunch you could not find,
Our thoughts are with those left behind.

On foreign soil so rich and deep,
At last they've found eternal sleep.
A sacred silence every year,
We keep for those we hold most dear.

Time marches on, the years roll by,
True comradeship will never die.
At our Re-union every year,
We meet to greet and spread good cheer.

Bruce Buchanan
'B' Company
'Bristol's Own'

Chapter XI

Consecration of the Colours

The 12th battalion Gloucestershire Regiment had never, along with all the Service battalions formed during the war, received battalion colours. During the forming of these battalions, during the stirring days now past, only essentials were considered. After the wars end, an Army Order was issued stating that colours should be presented to the Service battalions who took part in the war, the colours to be disposed in accordance with the decision of the last commanding officer.

Lt. Col. Colt DSO, MC, being the last commander of the 12th, decided that as the Bristol Citizen's Recruiting Committee had raised the battalion, the colours should be handed over to that body. And so the ceremony was arranged for Thursday November 4th at 2.40 p.m. in Bristol Cathedral.

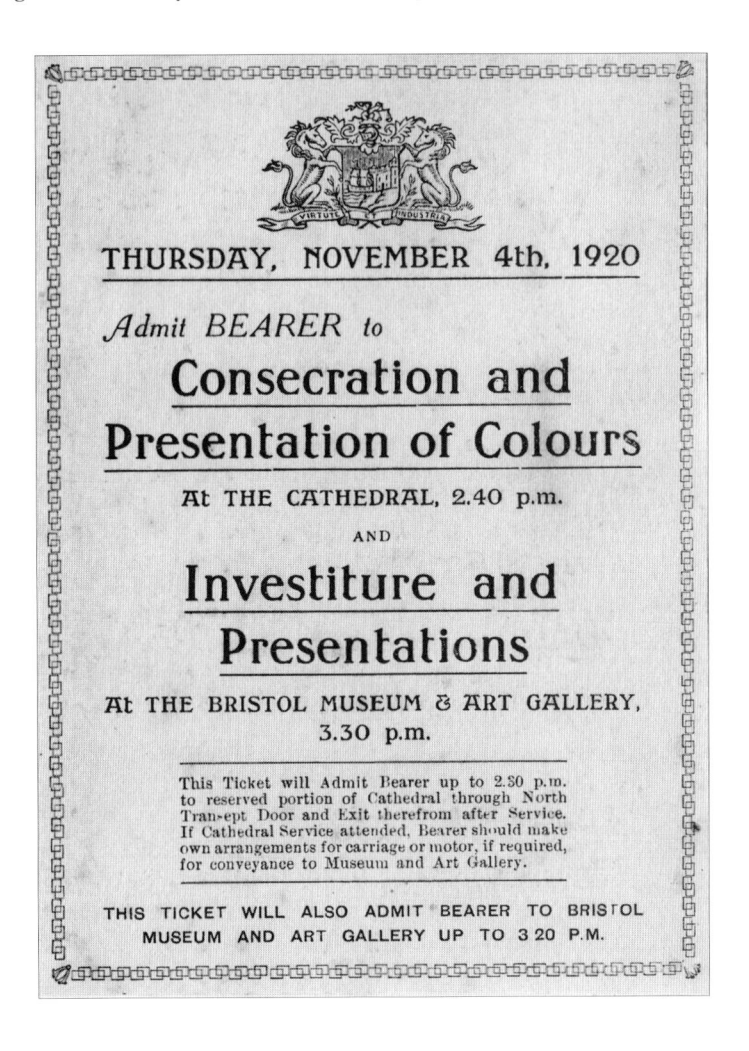

THURSDAY, NOVEMBER 4th, 1920

Admit BEARER to

Consecration and Presentation of Colours

At THE CATHEDRAL, 2.40 p.m.

AND

Investiture and Presentations

At THE BRISTOL MUSEUM & ART GALLERY, 3.30 p.m.

This Ticket will Admit Bearer up to 2.30 p.m. to reserved portion of Cathedral through North Transept Door and Exit therefrom after Service. If Cathedral Service attended, Bearer should make own arrangements for carriage or motor, if required, for conveyance to Museum and Art Gallery.

THIS TICKET WILL ALSO ADMIT BEARER TO BRISTOL MUSEUM AND ART GALLERY UP TO 3.20 P.M.

Consecration of the Colours

```
                                    33 Corn Street,
                                    BRISTOL,
                                    13th October, 1920.

Dear Anstey,
        On the 4th of next month we are consecrating and
handing over the Colours of the 12th to the Lord Mayor.

        As you have played a somewhat prominent part in the
doings of the Battalion, I give you the first offer of
carrying the Colours of the 12th on this occasion.

        Will you let me know as soon as possible whether you
are able to do this or not.

        Hoping you are well and with Best Wishes,

                                    Yours sincerely,

                                    (Sgd) H. A. Colt.

Lieut. R.H. Anstey, M.C.,
23, Brynland Avenue,
Bristol.
```

Letter from Lt. Col. H. A. Colt D.S.O, MC. requesting the services of 2nd/Lt. R. H. Anstey

Ex-officers, N.C.O.'s and men of the battalion mustered in College Green early in the afternoon in preparation for the consecration service at the Cathedral. Many officers as well as junior rank wore their war scarred uniforms, the sleeves and breasts of their tunics bearing ample evidence of their war service.

The Gloucestershire Regiment Depot at Horfield provided a band and a special detachment, including a colour party and paraded under the command of Lt. Feldon, M.C. The ranks of the ex service men of the 12th Battalion Gloucestershire Regiment were made up of a large and representative body of, now, civilians, all of which sported their ribbons and medals.

The parade formed fours and marched into the Cathedral taking their seats in the nave. Seated near the chancel were a large number of prominent citizens including: The Lord Lieutenant of the County, the right Hon Earl Beauchamp, K.G., the Lord mayor and lady Mayoress, The Sheriff of Bristol, Sir William Howell-Davies, M.P., Mr. G. B. Britton, M.P., Sir E. James. Capt. Claude Dobson, V.C., D.S.O., R.N., Sir Frank Wills, Mr. Claude fry, Master of the Society of Merchant Venturers, and a number of Aldermen and City Councillors and, Mr. A. Risely, the hon. Secretary of the Bristol Citizens Recruiting Committee, upon whose shoulders the arrangements of the days proceedings fell.

The Dean and canons took up their positions and, at a roll of drums from the west end came, from the organ a fanfare of trumpets. Simultaneously the colours of the battalion were borne along the naïve by Lt. R. H. Anstey M.C. and handed to the late commanding officer of the battalion; Lt. Col Colt D.S.O., M.C. who placed them on the Communion table. After the service, the colours were taken and handed back to Lt. R. H. Anstey M.C. and were marched out of the Cathedral while the National Anthem was sung.

The question as to where the colours should be placed for safe keeping had received much consideration. One option was a desire to preserve them in the Cathedral. This would have been an excellent choice. Another option was the Council Chamber. However, the option chosen, as favoured by most including a fare proportion of original surviving battalion members was the Museum and art gallery. As we shall see later, this was an unfortunate choice.

Consecration of the Colours

2nd/Lt. R. H. Anstey M.C. bearing the
colours outside of the Cathedral

Outside the Cathedral crowds of people had assembled. To the order of "Present arms", the colour party, with fixed bayonets, took up its position amidst the escorting troops. Mounted police with drawn swords, led the procession, headed by the Lord Mayor's coach. The band played the familiar strains of the Gloucestershire Regimental March and large numbers of people followed the procession up Park Street to the Art gallery.

There were a series of presentations at the Art Gallery, and these took place in the presence of the Lord Mayor, the Lord Lieutenant of the County, the sheriff and many prominent citizens. Alderman Twiggs, in presenting the Roll of Honour of Bristol men who had fallen, and of those who had received honours and distinctions said Bristol had raised between 55,000 and 60,000 men for the forces during the war, and they mourned the loss of 5,601, whose names would be found recorded.

The colours were presented to the Lord mayor who remarked the battalion had not only upheld the honour of Bristol, but the wonderful traditions of the Gloucestershire Regiment.

The final resting place of a proud battalion's colours should have ensured that those colours would remain intact in their original form for many years. The Bristol Cathedral was, most probably, the best choice in this respect as many Service battalions laid up their colours in this way.

The choice of the art Gallery was, perhaps, a worthy one in terms of accessibility to the public. The problem was, the colours were hung high up in the roof, immediately adjacent to large sky lights. The resultant ultra violet rays from the sun over the years did the damage. The colours stayed in this isolated position for seventy years . They were eventually taken down before they fell down. The clours no longer exist.

Not, at all, a fitting memorial to a very proud battalion.

Chapter XII

Gloster Cross

Lt. Col Archer-Shee was the C.O. of the battalion at the time of its first major offensive actions during the Battle of the Somme. A time at which many of its original members became casualties. Though he left the battalion early in 1917 to devote more time to his parliamentary responsibilities, he soon regretted his decision and later returned to command other battalions. He always followed the battalion's fortune.

In 1921, he had erected, at his own expense, an oak memorial cross at the crossroads outside of the village of Longueval, overlooking the site of the battalion's first attack of the 29th July 1916. It was a purely personal act that he considered did not need to be publicised and so, few of the O.C.A. members knew anything of it, until the battlefield re-visit in 1930. The 'Gloster Cross' was born and remained until sometime during WW2 when it disappeared.

Original Cross in 1921. Notice the ammunition containers and boxes in the foreground

In 1983 the author was given the photograph album, mentioned in Chapter XI containing photographs of the Old Comrades' Association battlefield re-visit in 1930, by the widow of Pte. Ernest Shanks. The knowledge of the battlefield re-visit was down to three men: the man, who took the photographs and created the fine album whose name is unfortunately not known; when he passed on, the husbandship was taken up by Bill Cradock; when Bill passed on, the album passed to Ernest Shanks; and, shortly after Ernest passed on, it was given to the author. Without it, the knowledge of the memorial cross at Longueval may so easily not have come to light.

Among many photographs in the album was several photographs showing men standing around the 'Gloster Cross' at Longueval, Somme.

Gloster Cross

Old Comrades around the cross in 1930

Sam Bollom, Jack Rutherford and Ernest Shanks in 1930

It was, however, by 1982 no longer standing. On the next visit to the Somme the following year, the exact position of the original cross was identified and, immediately, the decision was taken to replace it. Over the next few years, permission was sought and obtained from the land-owner, the farmer and the Mayor of Longueval. Bristol City Council was approached and agreed to manufacture the cross from English Oak, British Aerospace and Thornton's Travel of Filton generously agreed to meet the travel and incidental costs of the project.

Site of the original cross in 1983

The Lord Mayor of Bristol, Mr. J.M. Bosdet, three original battalion members; Mr. Harold Hayward M.C., Mr. William Ayres and Mr. Ewart Hale, together with friends and family of the author and the cameras and a reporter from H.T.V., attended a rousing send-off from the Council's Wellington Road Depot on Friday 4th April 1986.

Next day, the author, his father, Mr. Roy Marks and friend, Nick Fear, whose grandfather served with the battalion and died of wounds received on the Somme, set off in their car with a very heavy oak cross attached to a specially constructed roof rack. Foundations were quickly dug and, thanks to the services of the local Longueval builder, a quarter of a ton of concrete was poured into the hole around a steel foundation tube.

The cross was erected on Wednesday 9th April. It was very moving to see a cross standing again where the original had stood so many years before.

On returning home, moves were immediately put in place to arrange a consecration service for the Cross. The Regimental Association kindly arranged for a representation from the 1st Battalion Gloucestershire Regiment and the services of the Rev. Sam Davies were secured. Sam was a famous man: he had been padre to the 1st Battalion Gloucestershire Regiment at the Imjin River, Korea in 1951 - Remaining behind with the wounded, he was subsequently captured by the Chinese and spent two years as a P.O.W.

The service was set for Sunday 12th October 1986. The party consisted of sixteen people in a minibus and the weather was atrocious. The rain was torrential all the way from Bristol to Albert and the sea crossing was rough!

At the send off 4th April 1986. Three original battalion members:
Harold Hayward M.C., Ewart Hale and William Ayres

The Rev. Sam Davies was approached during the evening prior to the planned service with various observations regarding the weather for the next day. His answer was simply that all would be fine. The very next day the sky was pure blue with no cloud. Clearly, Sam had been in touch with forces upon high requesting good weather for the ceremony. It certainly worked.

The Gloucestershire Regiment had kindly sent their Second in Command, Major Cable, the R.S.M. WO1 Wright, a trumpeter and several other men as back-up. All had covered the many miles, by road all the way from Berlin! From Bristol came a British Legion Standard Bearer, the author and family, friends and associates and the daughters of Pte. A. C. Summons. Also in attendance were Mr. and Mrs. Tom Fairgrieve, CWGC wardens of Delville Wood. That was from the British side. From the French side, practically the whole of Longueval village turned out in their Sunday best, plus a sizeable number of gendarmes to control the roads, ably backed up by men of the local fire brigade.

It turned out to be a marvellous and memorable experience for all who attended and was more than ably conducted by the Rev. Sam Davies. After the ceremony and wreath-laying at the cross, the whole entourage proceeded the 300 yards back to the centre of the village where a wreath was laid and words spoken at the village war memorial commemorating the fallen from the village of Longueval.

Of course, no such occasion would be complete without refreshments. In the weeks leading up the ceremony Tom Fairgrieve was asked what was the best things to provide as refreshments. With no hesitation, "Boiled fruit cake and whiskey" came the reply. And so it was. The author's wife, mother and mother-in-law all set to producing copious amounts of boiled fruit cake.

The village Marie was provided for the event and it was packed. The fire brigade took a liking to the copious amount of Whiskey that had been provided and the home-made boiled fruit cake was disappearing fast. After an hour or so, people began leaving. When the place was practically empty, it was noted that just one piece of boiled fruit cake remained. Before any comment could be made relating the fact, the door flew open, a young lad of around seven or eight ran in, snatched it up and equally quickly disappeared.

1986 is now twenty-five years ago. During that time, the popularity and interest in visiting the World

Gloster Cross

Trumpeter 1st Gloucesters, Major Peter Cable 1st Gloucesters, The Rev. S. J. Davies, WO1 Brian Wright 1st Gloucesters

Gloster Cross back in place 1986

War One battlefields has grown exponentially. The effect of the Gloster Cross standing at the crossroads at the edge of the village of Longueval has associated that small corner of France with Bristol, with the Gloucestershire Regiment, but more particularly to the mercantile and professional young men who made up the 12th Battalion the Gloucestershire Regiment, 'Bristol's Own'. It has placed those associations firmly on the map and is now part of the itinery for many of the coach tour Companies. There are always wreaths and poppy crosses at the base of the Cross. It is in people's minds.

The final thing is to say that nothing is really final. After many years of research and family and work issues, the author has finally completed this book. Concurrent with writing and finishing the book, the author was also busy replacing the replacement Cross. The position of the cross is extremely exposed to the extremes of the seasons' weather. The Cross that was erected in 1986 unfortunately succumbed to damp infiltration which caused the joints to begin opening which exasperated the problem. A new Cross in beautiful English Oak with a hand engraved inscription was funded and manufactured. After some initial problems with removing the 1986 Cross from the steel foundation tube, the new one was put in place during October 2009.

Gloster cross, steps and base, 2010

Since then a red brick base and steps from the road have subsequently been provided to finish off the project and make it easier for people to get to the Cross. Furthermore, a feature has been built into the base: a square of cobblestones at the top of the steps. The cobblestones are special: they are from an old Bristol street. When you visit the Cross, you may be stepping on stones that some of the men from the battalion once stepped on.

The unknown man who took the photographs and beautifully mounted them in the album all those years ago could have had no idea that what he was doing would one day prove to be of key importance to the memory of the battalion. Until it came to light, the one-time existence of a memorial cross to the battalion was unknown. The existence of the photograph album made the subsequent replacement of the Cross obvious, ensuring the battalion be remembered and the name of 'Bristol's Own' kept alive, approaching one hundred years after its formation, and for many years thereafter.

Gloster Cross

Chapter XIII

Vignettes

2nd Lt. Ralph Hosegood

In 1914 Henry and Ellen Hosegood had three sons and one daughter. Their eldest son; Arnold was killed in action 24th February 1915, their second son; Ralph of the 12th Gloucesters was killed in action 23rd July 1916 and their youngest son; Gilbert was killed in action 10th September 1916.

Ralph came from a Methodist home which was a formative influence on him. He was a delicate boy and the victim of nervousness. This, he resolutely set to work to conquer from an early age. He went to Ley School and secured a place in the first Cricket IX. Cricket was one of his enthusiasms. He was a steady bat, with a strong drive when set, and played for two seasons before the war, for Clifton 1st. He was not without hopes of attaining a place in the county team, as he scored at least one century for his club and was a fine field at point – his long reach proving a great asset.

On leaving school at the end of 1910, he was articled to a Bristol firm of solicitors, and became as brightly interested in his profession as in sport. The senior partner became much attached to him and regarded him as 'a first rate pupil and a very dear friend.'

Religion was always very close to Ralph and with his developing gifts of speech it was natural that he should become a local preacher and a Sunday school teacher. His first sermon was preached at the little chapel at Brentry on Whit Sunday, 1912. He loved children and became much interested in a children's play hour on Wednesday evenings at Broad Plain, one of the poorer parts of Bristol.

When war broke out he did not leap into khaki. The idea of fighting was extremely repulsive to him. The general trend of public opinion counted for little. There was a hard struggle to pass through and he offered himself a willing sacrifice to what he felt to be the divine call. Many of his friends were receiving commissions and joining the O.T.C., but Ralph did not consider himself as good soldier material and enlisted as a private on 5th September into the newly forming Bristol Battalion.

The rough and tumble of a private's life and the foulness of speech was hard for him but his genuine friendliness and his keen sense of humour carried him smiling through. Despite his own misgivings, he worked conscientiously at his task, and determined to become a model private, so much so that he gradually overcame his reluctance to take a commissioned rank, and was honoured by the offer of a commission into his own battalion by the commanding officer Lt. Col. Burges. He was gazetted 2nd Lt. on 29th March 1915. To his colonel he was 'my favourite subaltern in the 12th, such a delightful boy, and so companionable; one of those whose whole object was to learn to do his best'

Once at the front, as bombing officer, Ralph was attached to the 95th Brigade's West Spring Gun battery when in the line at Maricourt in December 1915. The West Spring Gun was a wretched machine which was used to fling bombs two or three hundred yards into the enemy trenches. On 23rd March 1916 his battery was broken up and he returned to his beloved 'A' Company. But the brigade had an eye on him and on 30th April he began a course at a light trench mortar school eventually taking up a post with the 95th Brigade T.M.B.

Time at Arras led to the greatest offensive thus launched by the British and French. The Battle of the Somme which began on 1st July. As we have previously discussed, Ralph met his death on 23rd July. It is said he finished his course. From one of his favourite texts, 'I have fought a good fight, I have finished my course, I have kept the faith.' His religion was a subject of chaff and affection among his fellow officers. But it is deeply moving to understand how these men and those that served with him in the ranks had such warm feeling towards him.

One of his last kind thoughts before his death was to make arrangements, through his twin sister, on the closing night of playroom last session, for the children to have a "cocoa feast," and he also sent a letter from the front, "My dear little friends at Broad Plain. Here I am ten feet down in under the ground, feeling just like a rat. Wouldn't I give a lot to be with you tonight, playing musical bumps, fox and geese, and making the dollies as well?........."

One of his former Sunday school pupils had subsequently been posted the 12th Gloucesters in France in 1916 after Ralph's death and was himself badly wounded at Fresnoy the following year. He wrote, 'I have been greatly impressed since I arrived at this battalion to find what a fine tribute every fellow gives to the late 2nd Lt. Hosegood...........I have often thought since how proud I am to think he was my Sunday School teacher and what a fine example of a Christian soldier he was.'

2nd Lt. Herbert Ryland From Stow-on-the-Wold, had come from a very religious family that saw the war as very wrong. Herbert was working in Kingston, Jamaica but returned immediately war was declared. With his first aid skills and a strong feeling that he preferred not to harm anyone, he joined the R.A.MC as a private. Although ostracised by his family, he went to France in 1915 and did good work and was wounded in the arm. At one point, he was listening to a wounded man in no man's land and decided to go out to get him in. His sergeant forbade him to do so but his conscience took over and he went out and rescued the man to which the sergeant marched him off to put him on a charge. After the story had been explained to the officer in charge, he was delighted to hear it. He eventually gave Herbert a choice: he would recommend him for an award or a commission, it was his choice. Herbert considered his options. He felt that as many of his friends had 'gone west', and, perhaps a change of scenery would do him some good. He elected to take the commission.

After completing his officer training, Herbert was asked to which unit he wished to be posted. Of course, he stated the Gloucestershire Regiment and, fortunately, his wish was granted when he was duly posted to 'C' Company of the 12th Battalion in February 1916. Herbert was proud of his new regiment and battalion. He fitted in well.

On 29th July 1916 at Logueval, the task of capturing and holding post 'A', as part of the battalion's orders, fell to 2nd/Lt. Herbert Ryland. He and his party were successful in driving the Germans out of the post. One German, being caught by surprise, dropped his weapon and threw his hands in the air shouting 'Kamerad'. Momentarily incensed by the terrible shelling they had received, Herbert lost his usual compassion and shot the man dead. Herbert regretted that act for the rest of his life.

Soon after taking and consolidating the position, Herbert received a bad wound to his buttock and became a casualty. His wound was attended to and a makeshift stretcher arranged in order to get him back to 'C' Company lines. Four of his men carried him and, having almost achieved their objective, the group was caught by a burst of machine gun fire. Herbert was again wounded, this time in the thigh, and Privates Blake and Griffin were killed.

Vignettes

16694 Pte. C. J. Blake
Eldest of thirteen children, Charles C. Blake resided at Milton, near Weston-Super-Mare. He was formerly in charge of the Weston terminus of the Weston and Clevedon light railway and joined 'Bristol's Own' upon its formation.
Pte. Blake met his death at the hands of a German machine gunner. At the time of his death he was acting voluntarily as a Company stretcher bearer. He was killed while helping a wounded officer to safety.

Lt. Barrington of 'C' Company says, in a letter to his parents;
"…….His conduct while under my command was absolutely without blame and his loss will cause a vacancy in the Company which cannot easily be filled. I always noticed his coolness and bravery under fire, and his extreme willingness to do anything that might be required. The only consolation I dare offer you is that he died a hero's death trying to do good to others and serving his King and Country in a most gallant fashion."

16564 Pte. Nelson Frank Griffin
Private Nelson Frank Griffin, of Coaley, Gloucestershire, was killed in action on 29th July at Longueval whilst attempting to rescue his badly wounded platoon officer, 2nd/Lt. H.C. Ryland.
Private Griffin was 20 years of age and employed at Listers. He was a member of the Coaley Church choir and was a bell-ringer, as well as playing in the Uley brass band and the Listers works band before enlisting on 27th December 1914. His Platoon sergeant wrote to Mr. Griffin:

"Dear Mr. Griffin,
I am writing to you on behalf of the Platoon of which your son Private N.F. Griffin was a member, to express to you their deep sympathy on the loss of your son. "I can assure you that we have all felt his loss most acutely, as he was quite one of the most popular boys in the Company. "Speaking for myself, I can only tell you that I always found your son one of the very best; he was always cheery and willing; and never showed the slightest fear, even when we were exposed to hot fire.
"I may not tell you where he was killed, but I may say that at the time he met his death he was helping to get our platoon officer, Lt. Ryland, who was badly wounded, under cover.
"I am afraid I have not expressed very well how much we miss your son, or how deep our sympathy is for you and Mrs. Griffin, but I hope you will excuse me for this, and will try and understand our feelings. We must hope that the war will soon be over, and then you will meet some of our boys, and they will be able to tell you more than I am allowed to write.
"I will conclude by asking you to accept my own deep sympathy with you, because as sergeant of your son's platoon, I knew him well and always had a great liking and admiration for him.
        Yours truly,
        Sergeant Risdon"

Pte. Griffin was one of a number of men, 2nd/Lt. Ryland included had special identity discs made up and put on a bracelet. All details were beautifully hand engraved on a neat oval disc and attached to a chain to wear around the wrist. The issue identity tags were made from fibre, which is a hard compressed paper. It was not long before these dissolved. This is the main reason why so many men that died are unknown. Their identity discs suffered in this way, leaving the remains unidentifiable. None of the men that died on or around 29th July at Longueval were found or identified with the exception of three men discovered in 1935. They were identified by items found on them that were engraved with their names and numbers. It is a bitter irony that, though acting in good faith, Sgt. Risdon removed Pte. Griffin's identity disc and sent it to his parents. Perhaps if he had not done so, Pte. Nelson Griffin would have a known grave.

Vignettes

Pte. Nelson Griffin's identity disc

A good friend of Nelson, Private T. M. Horell had been wounded during July and was recovering in St. Georges Hospital, Hyde Park Corner, London when he learned of Nelson's death. He wrote:

"*Dear Mr. Griffin,*

It was with great sorrow that I read, this evening, of the death of your son, Nelson. The news was conveyed to me by letter from one of the boys. I convey to you my heart-felt sympathy to you in your loss. There is one great comfort to know that he died as he lived, a true British gentleman. He gave his life for others and 'Greater love hath no man than this, that he lay down his life for his friends'.

"*Nelson and myself were as brothers and I had ample opportunities of noticing his great worth. It was he who stood by me the day I was wounded and, despite the great danger to himself, he helped me to the collecting station. He died, as I am told, giving aid to others. Such a glorious end to such a good life. May God be near you in your great trouble and cheer you and one great day we shall all meet again.*

"*I felt I must write these few lines as I myself feel a personal loss in Nelson's death. Again, expressing my great sorrow.*

I remain,
Yours sincerely
T.M.Horrell"

The wife of one of the men attempting to carry 2/Lt. Ryland to safety wrote to Mrs. Griffin on the 31st August:

"*Dear Mrs. Griffin,*

Pardon my writing to you but my husband – 14922 Pte C.E. Rogers of 12th Glosters, desired me to do so, as your son was next to him when he was killed, and he says if he is spared he will visit you to tell you any particulars. They will soon again be in action. It is a terrible time for us all. You have my sincere sympathy, one lives in dread from day to day.

Believe me,
Yours truly
Amy F. Rogers"

Private C.E. Rogers was killed in action at Guillemont four days after the date of this letter.

2nd/Lt. Herbert Ryland was eventually evacuated and got back to England where his recovery began.

Though he remained in the Army, Herbert was effectively disabled and unfit for further war service. On joining the battalion, he had rapidly forged a firm friendship with the C.O., Lt. Col. Archer-Shee, so much so that after the war he became his private secretary. Martin Archer-Shee also became godfather to Herbert's daughter, Moira. To Moira, the C. O. was always uncle Martin.

Soon after his wounding, from his hospital bed on the 10th August, he penned letters to the parents of Private's Charles Blake and Nelson Frank Griffin. The following letter was received by Mr. Griffin of Coaley, Gloucestershire:

"Dear Mr. Griffin,

I am writing to offer my belated but deepest sympathy on the death of your son. The reason I have not written earlier is because I was talking to him when he was killed and was severely wounded myself from the same machine gun.

"He was one of the very best boys in my platoon – always smiling, no matter how depressing the conditions and a great favourite with his comrades. A brave boy too, who never once showed that he knew what fear meant.

"He was killed after we had taken a German trench and death was almost instantaneous. We shall all miss him very much. He was one of the sort we can ill afford to lose.

"Once more, on behalf of the platoon and also of myself, assuring you how deeply we feel his loss and how much we sympathise with you in your deep sorrow.

> *Believe me to be,*
> *Yours sincerely*
> *2nd/Lt. Herbert Ryland*
> *O.C. No. 11 Platoon"*

Such was Herbert's feelings of admiration, gratitude and heart felt sympathy toward the two men who had given their lives in attempting to save his, he placed each year on the anniversary of the action, from at least the early 1920's, an In Memoriam notice in the Daily Telegraph:

"To the memory of my comrades of the 12th Battalion Gloucestershire Regiment (Bristol's Own) who gave their lives for King and Country in the 1914-18 War and, in particular, Privates Blake and Griffin, of 'C' Company, killed on 29th July 1916, while carrying their wounded officer to safety. Greater love hath no man than this."

Herbert died in 1960. His wife Margaret continued to place the In Memoriam notice until shortly before her death in 1977.

14440 Pte. William Yacomeni
Born in Lewisham, Kent on 18th June 1896 William was possibly the eldest of seven children. The family moved to Tannery House, Bishops Street, Bristol where William was raised. He was educated at the Merchant Venturers and took up a position as a civil servant in 1912. He enlisted into the New Bristol Battalion on 19th September 1914.
William sailed for France with the battalion on 21st November 1915. His qualities were quickly recognised and he was promoted Lance Corporal on 3rd February 1916. During the Somme and the battle of Guillemont 3rd September 1916 he acted as battalion runner and did good work. As a result, he was awarded the Military Medal and was promoted Corporal on 28th October 1916. Soon afterwards he applied for and was granted a commission. Leaving for England on 21st December 1916.

Vignettes

After officer training, William was asked if he had a preference as to what unit he should be sent. His reply was simply "Any one except the unit I am present serving." As such he received a commission with the 3rd Battalion The Kings Own Royal LancasterRegiment.

During April 1918 he was captured. His statement regarding circumstances which led to capture reads:

"With 2/Lt. Alexander and 30 O.R. I was in command of Route 'A' Keep on the night of 22nd/23rd April 1918. This Keep was an advanced post and had been captured and re-captured three times previous to my occupying it. The garrison should have been 2 officers and 60 O.R.s. We had no wire, no S.O.S. , no bombs, no reserve of S.A.A. and no very lights. A company of German Storm Troops attacked us just before dawn under a barrage of 5.9s minnenwerfers and M.G.s. The trenches, previously badly knocked about were rendered untenable except in parts; and 13 O.R.s managed to get back to the main line of defence – without orders from myself. 2nd/Lt Alexander and myself remained in our part of the keep, firing on the enemy until we were outflanked and forced to surrender. 15 O.R. were captured with us."

2nd/Lt Yacomeni was unwounded when he was captured. He spent the remainder of the war in captivity in Mainz, Germany. He was repatriated 29th November 1918. Moving with his unit to Ireland. He received his gratuity and re-enlisted for one year.

A board of enquiry into his capture exonerated him from any blame. He finally relinquished his commission 1st January 1920 being demobilised on the 9th.

He soon went to London to find work. But the war and his captivity had had an adverse effect on him. 17th February he booked into the Washington Hotel, Eastborne Terrace, Paddington where he shot himself with his service revolver. The inquest was held 25th February. The verdict; "Suicide during temporary insanity."

Yacomeni family around 1906. William stood centre rear

Vignettes

16th December 1915
Mr. and Mrs. Thomas James of Yorkley Wood, near Pillowell, experienced a severe blow in the death of their third son, George Harry James, a private in the 12th Gloucesters. The unwelcome news was contained in a letter written by Lt. Co. Archer-Shee, stating that he was killed by an enemy shell whilst on duty in the trenches working a bomb throwing gun.

10th March 1916
The late Private William B. Bradford, who joined the 12th Battalion Gloucestershire Regiment when it was first raised. He was in 'A' Company and was just 24 years of age when he met his death in France. He was on sentry when a shot came through the sandbags and penetrated his head. He passed away without regaining consciousness. He was buried with full military honours. Pte. Bradford, prior to joining the 12th, was an assistant to Mr. Dunn, tobacconist, of Stokes Croft. He was one of the old boys of St. Augustine's Working Men's Club. Pte. Bradford resided at 617 Gloucester Road, Bishopston.

23rd March 1916
Sgt. F.W. Pyman of Bristol's Own, who was recently killed whilst serving King and country. Sgt. Pyman's wife, who resides at 15 Manor Road, Bishopston has received the following letter from Lt. Col. Archer-Shee: "Dear madam, I deeply regret to inform you of the death of your husband, No. 14551 Sgt. Pyman F.W., Gloucestershire Regiment, who was accidentally shot and died of the wound shortly afterwards, on 23rd March. He has been buried at Habarcq, near Arras."

24th March 1916
Pte. Arthur T. Park of the Gloucestershire Regiment, who was recently killed in action. From the time of leaving school until he joined the Gloucestershire regiment on 12th September 1914, Pte. Park was employed by Mr.Drew, provision merchant, North Street. He was the only son of Mr. and Mrs. W. Park, of 2 Gloucester Street, Eastville and at the time of death was 19 years of age.

24th May 1916
Mr. J.G. Edmonds received news of the death in action of his son Pte. Jack Edmonds. The gallant young fellow, who was only 26 years of age, was educated at the Forum School, Bath and was at Stothert and Pitt's for a short time and then emigrated, having been in South Africa and the United States. He returned from America at his country's call and enlisted in the Gloucesters.

29thJuly 1916
Mr. and Mrs. Dyer of 35 Summerhill Road, St. George, Bristol had already lost two sons, one at Loos in 1915 and one on the 1st July on the opening day of the Somme offensive. They then received news of the death in action, on 29th July, of Ernest, who had been killed whilst carrying a message to one of the advanced posts.

Mr. Edward Bond had been the nephew of Pte. Francis Bond who had been killed in action on 21st July 1916 near Longueval. Like his uncle, Edward had taken up a post in an insurance office in Corn Street, Bristol. In the same office was George Randall of 'B' Company 12th Gloucesters, a senior member of staff. Due to their connection with the battalion, they became close acquaintances.

George had been badly gassed during 1918 and suffered accordingly. On a cold and foggy night in the early 1930's Edward was leaving the office late one evening. On the steps outside he discovered George huddled and coughing badly. He attempted to comfort George and eventually called a taxi to take him home. George never returned to work and died shortly afterwards.

In 1935, a farmer was tending some ground adjacent to the crossroads outside the village of Longueval. During his work he opened a shallow grave containing the remains of five men, four wore the 'Gloster' shoulder title. The Imperial War Graves Commission identified three of the men as 15018 Walter

Vignettes

Holborow of 'A' Company, 16558 Charles Love of 'D' Company and 14768 Henry Ridley of 'D' Company. The forth man was not identified but was clearly 12th Gloucesters, the fifth man was a German soldier. All five men were exhumed and reburied with honours at the nearby London Cemetery in front of 'High Wood'. The men were buried as found. The 12th Gloucesters men were buried as two pairs, either side of the German soldier.

During 2007, two Dutchmen, walking the fields around Longueval happened upon the remains of a World War One soldier. The remains were found very near to post 'B' which was attacked on 29th July 1916 and, among the items found with it, was a brass 'Gloster' shoulder title still on its épaullete. News quickly reached the author who began talks with the M.O.D. and the C.W.G.C. Though it was not an easy task, after many months of correspondence, telephone calls, negotiations and preparation of evidence to both parties, the M.O.D. finally agreed to identify the soldier as an unknown soldier of the Gloucestershire Regiment and the C.W.G.C. agreed to bury the remains not only in London Cemetery but in the empty grave, once occupied by the German soldier, between his battalion comrades who were interred there in 1935.

On Tuesday 8th April 2008 the unknown soldier of the 12th Battalion Gloucestershire Regiment, who died on 29th July 1916 was finally laid to rest among around 50 mourners including a New Zealander piper. His 'Gloster' shoulder title was very kindly returned by the two Dutchmen and replaced with his remains before burial.

During the 1980s an old lady passed away. She had lived alone in a small cottage in the Mendips. Her fiancé was Corporal Frederick Chappell of 'C' Company.

Frederick's war began on 21st November 1915. He successfully got through his trench warfare initiation and even survived the terrible battle of the Somme. He and his sweetheart exchanged many letters during that time. He trying not to tell her of the horrors he witnessed daily and she telling him of her ordinary life and in her desperation trying to cheer him up by saying say how things would be better when this terrible war was over and they might marry and raise a family.

1916 ended and 1917 began. Not satisfied with the slaughter of the Somme, the High Command was busying itself with plans for the next debacle. An attempt would be made to dislodge the Germans from their new defensive position, the *Hindenberg Line*. There was to be a new battle around the town of Arras in France.

The 12th battalion arrived in the area on 1st May and were placed in what remained of the Front Line, east of the devastated village of Fresnoy, on 4th May. We have previously spoken of the terrible events surrounding the battalion's involvement at Fresnoy on 8th May. 288 men and 13 officers becoming casualties that day.

Back home, Frederick's sweetheart was unaware of the particular danger being faced by the men in France. She wrote to Frederick and simply awaited his return letter. She waited and she waited. No letter arrived. In time, she learned that Frederick had been killed in action on that day. His body was never recovered, and so he is regarded as one of the missing. His name now rests among 35,942 missing officers and men on the Arras Memorial in Faubourg d'Amiens Cemetery.

Frederick Herbert Chappell was only 24 when he died. His fiancée mourned him. For the rest of her life, she remembered him. She often considered what might have been had fate not taken the course it had. But, at the going-down of the sun and in the morning, he was there, with her. She looked at his photograph beside her while she drank her lonely cups of tea. She never forgot Frederick and remained unattached for the rest of her life, dying a spinster.

Perhaps

Perhaps some day the sun will shine again,
And I shall see that still the skies are blue,
And feel once more I do not live in vain,
Although bereft of You.

Perhaps the golden meadows at my feet
Will make the sunny hours of spring seem gay,
And I shall find the white May-blossoms sweet,
Though You have passed away.

Perhaps the summer woods will shimmer bright,
And crimson roses once again be fair,
And autumn harvest fields a rich delight,
Although You are not there.

Perhaps some day I shall not shrink in pain
To see the passing of the dying year,
And listen to Christmas songs again,
Although You cannot hear.

But, though kind Time may many joys renew,
There is one greatest joy I shall not know again,
Because my heart for loss of you
Was broken, long ago.

Vera Brittain

Appendix I

Officers Roll

Original battalion Officers shown in bold type

Surname	Christian/Intls	Rank	Comments
Abbottt	W.J.S.	2nd/Lt.	1918
Alderick	F.R.	2nd/Lt.	1915-
Allen	**J.H.**	**Captain**	**M.I.D. 1914-1918 Adjutant 1917**
Allison	**Thomas Mcgregor**	**Major**	**1914-1918**
Andrews	F.H.	2nd/Lt.	1917
Anstey	R.H.	2nd/Lt.	M.C. 1918
Archer-Shee	**Martin**	**Lt. Col**	**D.S.O. M.P. C.O. 1915-1917**
Armitage	N.	Lt.	Attached from 2nd/3rd Scottish Horse 1918
Atkins		2nd/Lt.	1917
Atkinson	**E.R.**	**2nd/Lt.**	**1915-**
Bailey	Donald William	2nd/Lt.	Attached from 1st battalion 1917
Baines	H.P.B.	2nd/Lt.	1915-
Baker	S.G.R.	2nd/Lt.	1915-
Balston	**Thomas**	**Captain**	**1915 - 1917**
Barrington	**C.**	**2nd/Lt.**	**1915-1916**
Barnes	A.	2nd/Lt.	1916

Surname	Christian/Intls	Rank	Comments
Bayliss	J.J.	2nd/Lt.	1918
Beckett	**G.R.A.**	**Major**	**M.C. 1914-1917**
Beadle	L.A.	2nd/Lt.	1918
Beer	Robert Alexander	2nd/Lt.	1917
Benjamin	T.J.	2nd/Lt.	1917-1918
Bennett	S.G.	2nd/Lt.	1916-1917
Bingham-Hall	**T.B.**	**Captain**	**1914-1916**
Blennerhassett	**W.A.R.**	**Major**	**2nd In Command 1914-1917**
Bloodworth	N.C.	2nd/Lt.	1917-1918
Box	C.H.	2nd/Lt.	1918
Bracher	A.	2nd/Lt.	1918
Bradbury	E.A.	2nd/Lt.	1917 Attached from 3rd battalion M.C.
Bray	W.	Captain	Attached from 1st battalion 1917-1918
Bridgeford	T.R.	2nd/Lt.	1918
Burges	E.M.T.	2nd/Lt.	1917-1918
Burges	**W.E.P.**	**Lt. Col**	**Original C.O.**
Burges	Walter Travers	2nd/Lt.	Attached from 3rd battalion 1917
Burris	**E.H.**	**Captain**	**1914-1918**
Calvert	M.	2nd/Lt.	1917
Chapman	W.G.	Lt. Col.	M.C. O.C. 1918
Charsley	C.	Lt.	1918

Officers Roll

Surname	Christian /Intls	Rank	Comments
Chate		2nd/Lt.	1917-1918
Clare-Smith	**A.R**	**2nd/Lt.**	**1914-**
Clifford	**A.W.**	**Captain**	**1914-1917**
Clifton	F.J.	2nd/Lt.	1918
Cole	**B.S.**	**2nd/Lt.**	**1914-**
Cole	H.A.	Captain	
Coombs	W.H.	Lt.	1918
Colt	**H. A.**	**Lt. Col.**	**D.S.O. M.C. 1914-1918 C.O. 1917-1918**
Cooper	**H.D.**	**2nd/Lt.**	**1915-1916**
Cornock	W.B.	2nd/Lt.	1917-1918
Cox	R.C.	2nd/Lt.	1916-1918
Cox		2nd/Lt.	1918
Crocombe	C.	Lt.	Q.M. 1915
Culpin		2nd/Lt.	1917
Dann	W.	2nd/Lt.	
Davidson	N.D.	2nd/Lt.	M.C. 1917-1918
Deglar	F.	Lt.	1918
Dicks	G. G. L.	2nd/Lt.	1918
Digby		2nd/Lt.	
Drew	R.W.	2nd/Lt.	Attached from 3rd battalion
Druett	G.O.	2nd/Lt.	1918
Ellison	A.W.	2nd/Lt.	Attached from 11th battalion 1916-1918
Evans	L.C.	2nd/Lt.	1916

Officers Roll

Surname	Christian/Intls	Rank	Comments
Eyers		2nd/Lt.	1917
Farrington	G.W.	2nd/Lt.	Attached from 3rd battalion
Fearman		2nd/Lt.	1918
Feden	R.	2nd/Lt.	1916
Fitzgerald	**Roy James**	**Lt.**	**Attached to R.A.F.**
Fitzmaurice	**W.H.**	**2nd/Lt.**	**1915-1916**
Fowler	**C.D.**	**Captain**	**1914-1916**
Fowler	George Edward	2nd/Lt.	kia 28/10/17
Geake	J.D.	2nd/Lt.	1918
Gedye	**G.E.R.**	**2nd/Lt.**	**1914-**
Gillard	S.H.	Lt.	1917-1918
Greenhalgh	T.	Lt.	1918
Guise	R.E.	Lt.	kia 29/6/18
Gunning	T.P.	2nd/Lt.	1918
Gurney	**F.E.**	**Lt.**	**1914-1916**
Haggart	W.J.	Lt.	kia 31/8/18
Hale	E.L.	Lt.	Attached from 13th battalion 1916
Hale	W.J.	2nd/Lt.	M.C. Attached from 3rd battalion 1918
Hall	G.B.	2nd/Lt.	1917
Hall	G.H.	2nd/Lt.	1916
Halse	L.W.	2nd/Lt.	1918
Harris	G.W.	2nd/Lt.	1918
Hathaway	N. R.	Capt.	1918

Officers Roll

Surname	Christian /Intls	Rank	Comments
Herring	D.D	2nd/Lt.	1917-1918
Hicks	A.K.	2nd/Lt.	1918
Hillborne	E.L.	2nd/Lt.	1916-18
Holman	L.S.	2nd/Lt.	1918
Hooper	**A.**	**Captain**	**1915-**
Hathaway	N.R.	Captain	From A.S.C.
Hosegood	**Ralph**	**2nd/Lt.**	**Attached Brigade T.M.B.**
Houlston	C.J.	2nd/Lt.	1917-1918
Howard	F.C.	2nd/Lt.	1916-1918
Huddy	Edward Burnside	2nd/Lt.	Attached from 11th battalion
Ibbotson	J.	2nd/Lt.	1918
Ingram		2nd/Lt.	1917
Ireland	James Balleny	2nd/Lt.	1917 Attached from 11th battalion
Jeune	Hugo St. Hellier	Captain	Attached from 9th battalion
Kerr	**R.J.**	**Captain**	**Adjutant 1914-1915**
King	A.F.	Captain	
Kins-Higgs	D.	2nd/Lt.	1916
Kirby	B.B.	Major	M.C. 1918
Laird	A.	Lt.	M.C. + Bar 1916-1918
Lane		Lt.	Q.M. 1917
Lambert	**H.E.**	**2nd/Lt.**	**1914-1916**
Lane	**A.H.**	**Lt.**	**Q.M. 1915-1917**
Lang	J.	Lt.	M.D. from R.A.M.C.

Surname	Christian/Intls	Rank	Comments
Latrobe	F.H.	Lt.	M.C. 1918
Lee-Warner	**C.B.**	**Major**	**1914-1916**
Leicester	Donovan Nicholas	2nd/Lt.	Intelligence officer 1916-1917
Lemon	**R.J.**	**2nd/Lt.**	**1915-**
Leschallas	H.P.	Captain	
Likeman	**J.L.**	**Captain**	**1915-1916 Adjutant 1915**
Lee-Warner	**C.B.**	**Major**	**1914-**
Lewis	**G.S**	**2nd/Lt.**	**1914-**
Lodge	H.	2nd/Lt.	1918
Logan	**P.N.**	**2nd/Lt.**	**1915-**
Lloyd	**S.**	**Lt.**	**1915-**
Machon	**R.E.**	**Lt.**	**1914-**
Mainstone	James Francis	2nd/Lt.	Attached from 1st battalion
May	L.C.	2nd/Lt.	1917-1918
Maywood	J.H.	Captain	1918 Attached from 1st D.C.L.I. Adjutant
Metcalf		2nd/Lt.	1917
Merrell	Arthur Walter	2nd/Lt.	Attached from 1st/2nd battalions
Merrell	W.T.	2nd/Lt.	1917
Metcalf	A.	2nd/Lt.	1917-1918
McShane	H.B.	2nd/Lt.	1917-1918
Miles	J.T.W.	2nd/Lt.	1918
Millard	W.K.J.	2nd/Lt.	1918

Surname	Christian /Intls	Rank	Comments
Mills	William Henry	2nd/Lt.	Attached from the 1st Battalion 1917
Milton	L.	2nd/Lt.	1917
Monk	B.E.L.	2nd/Lt.	1918
Murray	A.N.	Captain	
Painter	Henry Septimus	2nd/Lt.	Attached from 16th battalion 1916
Parr	**Wilfred Wharton**	**Captain**	**kia 8/5/17**
Pearson	E.	Lt.	Q.M. 1918
Petheram	C.S.	Captain	M.C + Bar 1916-1918
Phillips	S.R.	2nd/Lt.	1918
Poole	**A.G.**	**2nd/Lt**	**1914-1915**
Ratcliffe	G.E.	Captain	M.C. 1918
Ransom		Major	1918
Rawson	R.I.	Lt. Col.	C.O. 1917
Rawlins	F. McC.	Lt.	1917
Reade	G.	Lt.	Attached from 3rd battalion
Reed		2nd/Lt.	1915-
Reed	W.H.	2nd/Lt.	Attached from 11th battalion 1916-1918
Reynolds	S.	2nd/Lt.	1916-1917
Richards	Norman Frederick Kynaston	2/Lt.	kia 24/7/16
Rider	**N.F.**	**2nd/Lt.**	**1914-1916**
Roberts	D.J.	2nd/Lt.	1918
Roberts	R.G.	2/Lt.	1918

Surname	Christian/Intls	Rank	Comments
Robinson	Eric Arthur	**Captain**	**Dow 10/9/16**
Robinson	L.C.	2nd/Lt.	1916-1918
Rogers	Godfrey Marcus	2nd/Lt.	Attached from 1st battalion dow 28/4/181918
Russell	B.A.	Capt.	D.S.O. 1918
Rutland	C.J.	2nd/Lt.	1917-1918
Ryde	John Titcombe	2/Lt.	Attached from 1st Battalion Bedfordshire Regiment
Ryland	Herbert C.	2nd/Lt.	1916-1918
Sandbach	L.D.	2nd/Lt.	1917-1918
Sants	**H.E.V.**	**Captain**	**M.C.**
Shephard	W.E.	2nd/Lt.	M.I.D. kia 6/6/18
Shewell	**A.V.**	**Lt.**	**1914-1918**
Slight	**H. St. G.**	**Lt.**	**1915-**
Smith	M.G.H.	2nd/Lt.	1917-1918
Stansfield	W.B.	Major	1914-
Templ	B.	2nd/Lt.	1917
Thacker		2nd/Lt	1917
Ticehurst	G.F.	2nd/Lt.	1916
Thomas	G.N.	2nd/Lt.	1916-18
Vincent	Lionel Charles Henry	2/Lt.	1916
Waddy	B.H.	Lt.	1918
Waldron		2nd/Lt.	1917

Surname	Christian/Intls	Rank	Comments
Webb	**Jack Purnell**	**Captain**	**1914-1918**
Weir		2nd/Lt.	1917-1918
Wicks	G.G.L.	2nd/Lt.	1918
Wilkins	S.T.	2nd/Lt.	1916-1917
White	H.H.	2nd/Lt.	1918
Williams	E.J.	2nd/Lt.	1918
Williams	F.	2nd/Lt.	1917-1918
Wilmott	**T.A.**	**Lt.**	**Battalion transport 1914-1918**
Wills	E.G.	2/Lt.	1917-1918
Wilson-Fox	**F.W.**	**Major**	**1914-1916**
Wood	H.	2nd/Lt.	1917

Appendix II

Roll of Honour - Officers

Original battalion officers shown in bold type

Surname	Christian name(s)	Rank	Comments
Allison	**Thomas McGregor**	**Major**	**kia 30/05/18 (Attached 8th batt'n)**
Armitage	Noel	Lt.	kia 25/04/18
Bailey	Donald William	2nd/Lt.	kia 04/10/17
Beer	Robert Alexander	2nd/Lt.	kia 05/10/17
Bradbury	Ernest Alfred	2nd/Lt.	dow 02/04/17
Burges	Walter Travers	2nd/Lt.	kia 08/05/17
Dann	Wilfred	2nd/Lt.	kia 30/10/17
Drew	Richard William	2nd/Lt.	kia 25/06/18
Farrington	George William	2nd/Lt.	kia 28/06/18
Fitzgerald	**Roy James**	**Lt.**	**kia 01/07/18 (Attached R.A.F.)**
Fowler	George Edward	2nd/Lt.	kia 28/10/17
Guise	Reginald Edward	Lt.	kia 29/06/18
Haggart	William Jackson	Lt.	kia 31/08/18
Halse	Lionel William	2nd/Lt.	dow 17/10/18
Hosegood	**Ralph**	**2nd/Lt.**	**kia 23/07/16**
Huddy	Edward Burnside	2nd/Lt.	kia 29/07/16
Ireland	James Balleny	2nd/Lt.	kia 05/05/17
Jeune	Hugo St. Hellier	Captain	dow 12/05/17
Mainstone	James Francis	2nd/Lt.	kia 04/10/17

Roll of Honour - Officers

Original battalion men shown in bold type

Surname	Christian/Intls	Rank	Comments
May	Leo Cuthbert	2nd/Lt.	kia 27/06/18
Maywood	James Henry	Captain	kia 23/08/18
Merrell	Arthur Walter	2nd/Lt.	kia 08/05/17
Mills	William Henry	2nd/Lt.	kia 05/10/17
Painter	Henry Septimus	2nd/Lt.	kia 29/07/16
Parr	**Wilfred Wharton**	**Captain**	**kia 08/05/17**
Richards	Norman Frederick Kynaston	2/Lt.	kia 24/07/16
Robinson	**Eric Arthur**	**Captain**	**dow 10/09/16**
Rogers	Godfrey Marcus	2nd/Lt.	dow 28/04/18
Ryde	John Titcombe	2/Lt.	kia 08/05/17
Shephard	Ernest Edward	2nd/Lt.	kia 06/06/18
Vincent	Lionel Charles Henry	2/Lt.	kia 03/09/16
Webb	**Jack Purnell**	**Captain**	**dow 22/08/18**

Appendix III

June 1915 Nominal Roll

'A' Company

Number	Name	Rank	Number	Name	Rank
13981	Ackland F.R.	Cpl.	15040	Bodman C.W.	Pte.
13983	Aiers E.N.	Pte.	14002	Bond F.W.	Pte.
13984	Allen H.F.	Pte.	14004	Boyd H.J.	Pte.
13984	Anstey E.N.	Pte.	14005	Bradford A.J.	Cpl.
13987	Ashman S.P.	Pte.	14006	Bradford W.B.	Pte.
16466	Babb A.E.	Pte.	14008	Bray F.W.	Pte.
13989	Bacon E.G.	Pte.	16574	Bromwich J.	Pte.
13992	Baker F.J.	Pte.	14009	Brooks C.W.	Pte.
13993	Baker P.S.	Pte.	14010	Brown G.W.	Pte.
13994	Bancks C.G.	Pte.	16656	Brown W.A.	Pte.
13995	Banks C.M.	Pte.	14011	Bryant H.H.	Pte.
13991	Bailey A.	Sgt.	14013	Burgess S.G.	Pte.
13977	Baker E.W.	C.Q.M.S.	14014	Burton F.P.	Pte.
13996	Barker H.V.	Cpl.	14015	Byrne H.F.	Pte.
13997	Battagel F.	Pte.	16470	Byrt S.H.	Pte.
13998	Beale H.	Pte.	16626	Carey S.	Pte.
16740	Bennett T.	Pte.	14016	Case C.A.	Pte.
16553	Berry E.J.	Pte.	14018	Chapman G.D.	Pte.
16587	Blackmore A.	Pte.	15050	Chate C.G.	Pte.
14000	Block P.H.	Pte.	14019	Cheston H.L.	Pte.

June 1915 Nominal Roll – 'A' Company

Number	Name	Rank	Number	Name	Rank
16662	Church G.	Pte.	16551	Dearlove F.C.	Pte.
16594	Clark F.W.	Pte.	14040	Denham A.J.	Cpl.
14020	Clark F.J.	Pte.	14041	Denning E.E.	Pte.
16769	Clark H.G.	Pte.	14042	Denning H.H.	Pte.
14021	Clark L.A.	Pte.	16658	Dimond W.L.	Pte.
16593	Clark W.J.	Pte.	14043	Dingle H.	Pte.
14023	Clarkson R.T.	Pte.	14044	Dix W.L.	Pte.
14024	Clegg A.S.	Pte.	14046	Dunkin C.W.	Pte.
14025	Clifford G.A.	Pte.	15022	Elley R.	Cpl.
14026	Cocks E.J.	Pte.	14047	Elmes A.E.	Pte.
14027	Coggins S.	Pte.	14048	Elson L.N.	Pte.
14028	Cole C.P.	Cpl.	14051	Everson A.E.	Pte.
16705	Collins W.T.	Pte.	20099	Fairchild A.	Pte.
16476	Cook A.B.	Pte.	14053	Fear A.J.	Pte.
14031	Coombs W.J.	Pte.	16718	Forte E.	Pte.
16490	Cox A.	Pte.	16691	Forte N.S.	Pte.
16485	Cox S.A.	Pte.	14056	Ford W.J.	Pte.
15039	Cozens H.	Pte.	16657	Fouracres H.	Pte.
14032	Craddock W.A.	Pte.	14057	Fowles J.H.	Pte.
14033	Crane J.F.	Pte.	14058	Friend J.E.	Pte.
16040	Cruse R.W.	L/Sgt.	14671	Gage W.F.	Pte.
14036	Davis P.T.	Pte.	14060	Gay N.V.	Pte.
14037	Davies P.	Pte.	14061	Gerrish H.H.	Pte.
14038	Davis W.E.	Pte.	16591	Giddings A.J.	Pte.
14039	Denby E.W.	Pte.	14062	Godfrey S.	Pte.

June 1915 Nominal Roll – 'A' Company

Number	Name	Rank	Number	Name	Rank
14063	Gouldsworthy A.V.	Pte.	16620	James G.H.	Pte.
16763	Gowan F.	Pte.	14082	Jayne R.W.	Cpl.
14064	Graham G.	Pte.	16518	Jones A.W.	Pte.
14065	Griffey W.H.	Pte.	14087	Jones A.S.	Pte.
16714	Hadley F.	Pte.	16519	Jones J.H.	Pte.
14066	Hardy N.	Pte.	14088	Jones T.	Pte.
16525	Harper A.V.	Pte.	14085	Johnstone K.J.	Pte.
14068	Harrington J.H.	Pte.	14084	Justham R.	Pte.
14075	Haynes C.G.	Pte.	14092	King A.	Pte.
14069	Hemmens F.C.	Sgt.	14091	King W.M.	Pte.
16506	Hemmings J.H.	Pte.	14093	Lamb E.G.	Pte.
16607	Hennessey H.	Pte.	14096	Lethabee A.H.	Cpl.
14039	Higgins A.G.	Pte.	14095	Lethaby H.	Cpl.
14070	Hill G.E.	Cpl.	14097	Levy L.	Cpl.
15018	Holborow W.	Pte.	14098	Levy S.	Pte.
14071	Holten J.F.	Pte.	14101	Lodge C.H.	L/Cpl.
14072	Hore F.G.	Pte.	14102	Lord F.B	Pte.
14074	Hostler A.C.	Pte.	14101	Lothiam L.S.	Pte.
16512	Howell F.H.	Pte.	14106	Luckwell S.G.	Pte.
15062	Huntley R.S.	Pte.	14109	Mallett G.B.	L/Sgt.
16479	Hutchings H.J.	Pte.	14112	Mattock W.	Pte.
16592	Hynan H.C.	Pte.	14100	Lewis J.	L/Cpl.
16590	Ireland S.R.	Pte.	14107	MacFarlane R.A.	L/Cpl.
14080	Jaggard M.G.	Pte.	14114	Miles W.Y.	Pte.
12952	James F.	Pte.	14119	Moore G.J.	Pte.

June 1915 Nominal Roll – 'A' Company

Number	Name	Rank	Number	Name	Rank
16491	Moore H.	Sgt.	16768	Powell R.	Pte.
14118	Moore L.A.	Pte.	14145	Price F.R.	Pte.
16667	Moore N.C.	Pte.	16501	Pritchard O.	Pte.
14120	Morrish G.E.	Pte.	14147	Purchase C.A.	Pte.
14122	Nash A.L.	Pte.	14148	Ratcliffe C.J.	Pte.
15025	Newman H.	Sgt.	16673	Rayford W.	Pte.
14123	Nichols W.F.	Pte.	15064	Reed H.A.	Pte.
14123	Northam W.M.	Pte.	16614	Reed H.J.	Pte.
14127	Ogden P.E.	Pte.	16612	Rex P.E.	Pte.
14128	Osborne H.C.	Pte.	14149	Rice A.E	Sgt.
14129	Owens J.T.	Pte.	16600	Rick L.G.	Pte.
15005	Page W.T.	Sgt.	14152	Robbins W.A.	Pte.
14131	Park A.T.	Pte.	14154	Rocket W.L.	Pte.
14132	Parker H.W.	Pte.	14155	Rogers J.C.	Pte.
16741	Parsons A.V.	Pte.	14385	Rowbotham J.C.	Pte.
14133	Parsons G.	Pte.	14157	Saffin H.A.	Pte.
14134	Payne W.H.	Pte.	16488	Sage A.E.	Pte.
14135	Pearce F.R.	Pte.	14158	Sage F.E.	Pte.
14136	Pearce L.W.	Pte.	14159	Saise A.J.	Pte.
14138	Pegg N.R.	Pte.	14160	Salter G.L.	Pte.
14139	Percy G.	Sgt.	16720	Sargent A.	Pte.
15031	Phillips J.H.	Sgt.	14161	Saunders R.	Pte.
14140	Pildren R.J.	Pte.	16710	Sellars	Pte.
16474	Pomeroy P.W.	Pte.	14162	Selway D.W.	Pte.
16468	Poole A.O.	Pte.	14163	Sheppard H.C.	Pte.

June 1915 Nominal Roll – 'A' Company

Number	Name	Rank	Number	Name	Rank
16536	Sherman A.R.	Pte.	14186	Turner J.	Pte.
14164	Shorto L.R.	Pte.	14187	Tutton C.C.	Pte.
14165	Sims S.O.	Pte.	14190	Walker G.J.	Pte.
16595	Small J.	Pte.	15037	Watkins J.	Pte.
16673	Smith J.	Pte.	14191	Way R.P.	Pte.
14168	Smith M.G.	Pte.	14194	Weeks R.W.	Pte.
16675	Smith T.E.	Pte.	14192	Webb C.B.	Pte.
14169	Spafford N.R.	Pte.	14196	White L.G.	Pte.
16484	Steer J.N.	Pte.	14433	Whittard A.G.	Pte.
14172	Stokes D.M.	Pte.	14197	Wickens J.H.	Pte.
14173	Stratton R.P.	Pte.	14201	Wilkens J.	Pte.
14174	Stockman R.C.	Pte.	16507	Williams A.E.	Pte.
14175	Summers R.E.	Pte.	14198	Williams A.F.	Cpl.
16492	Thomas R.G.	Pte.	16730	Williams A.J.	Pte.
14177	Thomas W.J.	Pte.	15034	Willoughby A.J.	Pte.
14178	Thompson A.E.	Pte.	14202	Wingfield A.T.	Pte.
14179	Thompson R.H.	Pte.	14203	Withers H.G.	Pte.
14180	Thyer A.C.	Pte.	16628	Woodfield F.	Pte.
14181	Tottle W.A.	Pte.	14204	Worswick J.A.	Pte.
15019	Townsend G..	C.S.M.	14260	Wright E.	Pte.
16504	Tratman A.W.	Pte.	14207	Yeates F.W.	Pte.
14182	Treble H.	Pte.	14208	Yeatman E.H.	Pte.
16683	Tuckey R.J.	Pte.	15013	Yelling J.T.	Pte.
14183	Tudball F.	Cpl.	14209	Yeoman R.H.	Pte.
14184	Tuplin W.C.	Pte.			

'B' Company

Number	Name	Rank	Number	Name	Rank
16552	Abrahams E.R.	Pte.	16527	Blanning J.	Pte.
14220	Addicott A.	Pte.	14228	Bodman H.W.	L/Sgt.
14445	Allen A.A.	Pte.	16612	Bollom S.J.	Pte.
14221	Allen A.J.	L/Cpl.	14968	Bouskill P.J.	Sgt.
16749	Andow E.W.	Pte.	14240	Bolton G.	Pte.
16463	Attwood M.W.	Pte.	14239	Boyce R.W.	Sgt.
14219	Avent A.G.	Pte.	14229	Brain G.	Pte.
16533	Babbington L.G.	Pte.	14235	Bray C.N.	Pte.
16646	Bailey W.H.	Pte.	16649	Bryant C.A.	Pte.
16643	Baker H.T.	Pte.	16509	Bryant G.	Pte.
14224	Ball C.E.	Pte.	14234	Bubb H.G.	Pte.
14230	Banfield H.M.	Pte.	14225	Buchanan B.M.	Pte.
16636	Banwell W. F.	Pte.	14446	Buchanan G.	Cpl.
14244	Barnes A.F.	Pte.	14618	Burnell W.F.	Pte.
16505	Barnes S. V.	Pte.	14236	Burrington H.W.	Pte.
14226	Barnfield G.E.	Pte.	16689	Burt T.H.	Pte.
14231	Bastin F.C.	L/Cpl.	14238	Bushell W.A.	Pte.
14227	Beaven A.G.	Pte.	14265	Carter V.C.	Pte.
14243	Beaven W.G.	Pte.	14260	Challenger H.C.	Pte.
14540	Bellamy J.	Pte.	16247	Chapman E.S.	Pte.
14242	Bennison C.	Pte.	14270	Chapman V.S.	Pte.
16634	Binding F.A.	Pte.	16248	Chappell L.E.	Pte.
14588	Bishop H.	Pte.	14248	Chapple W.H.	Pte.

June 1915 Nominal Roll – 'B' Company

Number	Name	Rank	Number	Name	Rank
14259	Chaplin A.	L/Sgt.	16522	England F.	Pte.
14246	Clifford A.E.	L/Cpl.	14442	Evans J.W.	L/Cpl.
14253	Close E.A.	Pte.	15044	Farndell C.	Pte.
16534	Cleaves J.	Pte.	16508	Feltham W.	Pte.
15057	Clements E.	Pte.	14285	Fisher P.E.	Pte.
14255	Clake P.V.	Pte.	14286	Foss S.G.	L/Cpl.
16738	Collier G.H.	Pte.	16573	Franklin S.	Pte.
16596	Cook J.	Pte.	14287	Furness W.E.	Pte.
14262	Cooke E.	Pte.	14299	Gardiner E.C.	Pte.
16745	Cooper E.	Pte.	14294	Glendall A.H.	Pte.
14251	Cottrell A.B.	Pte.	14289	Gliddon H.W.	Pte.
14268	Cousins G.R.	Pte.	14587	Godden G.V.	Pte.
14264	Cowardhayes F.	Pte.	15052	Godfrey E.J.	Sgt.
14256	Cox H.W.	Pte.	14296	Godfrey H.T.	L/Cpl.
14257	Cronin J.F.	Pte.	14291	Gosney W.E.	L/Cpl.
14261	Cross E.	Pte.	14290	Gove J.H.	Cpl.
14269	Cross W.G.	Pte.	16622	Green G.H.	Pte.
14249	Curtis F.A.	Pte.	14293	Green R.C.	Pte.
14278	Dancey H.S.	L/Sgt.	14443	Greenland F.J.	Pte.
14274	Dewfall F.G.	Pte.	16701	Hall A.W.	Pte.
14273	Dyer E.	Pte.	14306	Harding W.J.	Pte.
14275	Dyte W.L.	Pte.	14300	Harman W.C.	Cpl.
14280	Elliott A.E.	Pte.	14307	Harvey E.G.	Pte.
14281	Emery C.L.	Pte.	14312	Hathway F.L.	Pte.

June 1915 Nominal Roll – 'B' Company

Number	Name	Rank	Number	Name	Rank
14314	Hayward H.J.	Pte.	14333	King W.F.	Pte.
14320	Hedges F.	Cpl.	16712	Kingman G.	Pte.
14301	Hewlett G.W.	Pte.	14334	Kingston L.J.	Pte.
16764	Hicks J.H.	Pte.	14967	Knight E.A.	Pte.
14313	Hill F.J.	Pte.	14337	Lacey T.E.	Pte.
14355	Hitchens H.J.	Pte.	14334	Legge H.	Pte.
14317	Hodges W.P.	Pte.	14347	Leonard J.R.	Pte.
14302	Holloway E.H.	Pte.	14336	Leversuch A.H.	Pte.
14308	Hooper G.W.	L/Cpl.	14341	Lewis A.G.	Pte.
14319	Hodgson W.T.	L/Cpl.	15072	Lewis G.	Pte.
14311	Howell H.S.	Pte.	16604	Lowis R.C.	Pte
14321	Hughes A.E.	Pte.	14340	Lewis T.	Pte.
16631	Hutchings H.J.	Pte.	14339	Lewtas A.F.	Pte.
14316	Hutton A.B.	Pte.	14346	Lovell H.	Pte.
14328	Jackson T.	Pte.	14343	Lumbard H.J.	L/Cpl.
14325	Jeffrey W.	Pte.	14355	Maggs C.A.	L/Sgt.
14324	Johnson G.F.	Pte.	14348	Mann H.E.	Sgt.
14217	Jones P.A.	Pte.	14349	Mappin W.H.	Pte.
14217	Jones R.H.	Pte.	14350	Matthews E.L.	Pte.
14323	Jones R.H.	Cpl.	16648	Matthews W.R.	Pte.
14326	Jordan A.	Pte.	14360	McLean W.G.	L/Cpl.
14327	Jordan J.H.	Pte.	14358	Milne A.R.	Pte.
14331	Keeler G.F.	Pte.	14351	Monks E.F.	Pte.
14332	Kift R.P	Pte.	16543	Morgan L.T.	Pte.
16579	King J.B.	Pte.	14356	Morley G.A.	Pte.

June 1915 Nominal Roll – 'B' Company

Number	Name	Rank	Number	Name	Rank
16757	Morton A.D.	Pte.	14383	Phipps A.F.	Sgt.
14357	Munslow A.R.	Pte.	16503	Poole C.B.	Pte.
14369	Naish E.A.	L/Cpl.	14372	Pope R.G.	Sgt.
14363	Naish R.P.	Pte.	14376	Powell C.J.	Pte.
14364	Nelmes	Pte.	14213	Pretty W.H.	C.Q.M.S.
14969	Newey E.R.	Pte.	16538	Pride H.G.	Pte.
15028	Newton H.	Pte.	14378	Puglsey A.A.	Pte.
14367	Norris J.	Sgt.	14589	Purnell H.E.	Pte.
14364	Norman G.H.	Pte.	14386	Randall G.H.	Pte.
16565	Notton C.	Pte.	16523	Rex B.E.	Pte.
16572	Notton W.	Pte.	14387	Robbins W.A.	Pte.
14370	Oakley C.E.	Pte.	16586	Rogers F.J.	Pte.
16639	Osborne R.	Pte.	14388	Rogers W.A.	Pte.
14379	Palmer L.C.	Pte.	16650	Roper W.	Pte.
15058	Panting J.	Pte.	3266	Russell T.	C.S.M.
14375	Parry C.C.	Pte.	14409	Sargant H.C.	L/Cpl.
14374	Peet H.B.	Pte.	14395	Scraise T.	Pte.
14382	Pearce A.O.	Pte.	14406	Shanks E.E.	Pte.
14373	Pearce F.S.	Pte.	14396	Short H.	Pte.
14740	Pearce G.T.	Pte.	14392	Short F.R.	Pte.
14380	Perrett G.S.	Pte.	14394	Shortman A.G.	L/Cpl.
14444	Peters A.E.	Pte.	14411	Sims A.L.	L/Cpl.
14317	Phillips H.E.	Pte.	14404	Skardon G.	Cpl.
14583	Phillips J.	Pte.	16486	Slocombe T.J.	Pte.

June 1915 Nominal Roll – 'B' Company

Number	Name	Rank	Number	Name	Rank
15066	Smallcombe W.A.	Pte.	16625	Truckle F.E.	Pte.
14440	Smith A.W.	Pte.	14415	Tucker A.A.	L/Cpl.
14399	Smith F.C.	Pte.	16526	Tugwell A.	Pte.
14391	Smith F.G.	Pte.	16542	Venning H. G.	Pte.
14397	Smith W.	Pte.	16671	Vicker G.	Pte.
14408	Southron H.C.	Pte.	16709	Vowles E.F.	Pte.
14389	Speare R.S.	L/Cpl.	16752	Vowles F.H.	Pte.
14393	Summons G.	Pte.	14423	Vowles W.R.	Pte.
16684	Still F.	Pte.	14427	Ward A.	Pte.
15073	Stock A.E.	Pte.	14435	Warren E.J.	L/Cpl.
14398	Streets E.S.	Pte.	14431	Watkins G.J.	Pte.
16743	Storror G.S.	Pte.	16514	Watkins G.W.	Pte.
16696	Summerill W.A.	Pte.	14437	Webb R.W.	Pte.
14410	Symonds C.C.	Pte.	15063	Weeks S.	L/Cpl.
14416	Taylor C.H.	Pte.	16746	Wickenden R.	Pte.
14418	Taylor H.J.	Sgt.	16478	Williams E.H.	Pte.
14414	Thomas E.L.	Pte.	15068	Williams F.	Pte.
14413	Thomas G.H.	Pte.	14434	Williams R.S.	Pte.
14417	Thompson H.W.	Pte.	16589	Williams W.	Pte.
14419	Thornborrow F.C.	Pte.	16753	Williams W.F.	Pte.
16750	Thornett E.L.	Pte.	16727	Wiltshire A.	Pte.
16748	Thornett L.	Pte.	14436	Wiltshire A.	Pte.
16635	Thyer W.	Pte.	14966	Woodland	Pte.
14421	Townsend J.E.	Pte.	14425	Wooles E.H.	Pte.

June 1915 Nominal Roll – 'B' Company

Number	Name	Rank	Number	Name	Rank
14429	Wright C.H.	Pte.	16569	York W.	Pte.
14440	Yacomeni W.	Pte.			

'C' Company

Number	Name	Rank	Number	Name	Rank
16659	Abraham A.	Pte.	16605	Bessell C.H.	Pte.
14598	Ackland E.G.	Pte.	14850	Blick H.E.	Pte.
14456	Adams T.J.	Pte.	14876	Blick P.H.	Sgt.
14842	Allen A.	Pte.	14466	Bonshor J.L.	Pte.
15012	Allen C.F.	Pte.	14857	Braddon E.R.	Pte.
14592	Amos A.	Pte.	14849	Brett F.J.	Pte.
14843	Anderson W.	Pte.	16751	Brice L.	Pte.
14458	Arnold E.A.	L/Cpl.	14468	Brine A.G.	L/Sgt.
14840	Ashford G.E.	Pte.	14848	Brooke F.E.	Pte.
14841	Atherton J.	Pte.	14470	Brooke G.L.	Sgt.
14460	Auton W.T.	Pte.	14847	Bruton W.C.	Pte.
16719	Baber G.	Pte.	14858	Bryant G.F.	Pte.
14464	Bacon L.	Pte.	16576	Burden C.	Pte.
14461	Bailey W.G.	Pte.	14472	Burkett F.J.	Pte.
14859	Bainton P.L.	Pte.	14463	Burnett W.C.	Pte.
14844	Baker O.R.	Pte.	16624	Butler C.E.	Pte.
14853	Ball C.G.	Pte.	14473	Butterfield F.	Pte.
14846	Ball E.H.	Pte.	14453	Caburn J.W.	C.Q.M.S.
14854	Bannister G.A.	Pte.	14477	Carter E.H.	Pte.
14462	Barr G.	Pte.	15032	Case N.G.	Pte.
16758	Barrett F.C.	Pte.	14479	Chappell F.H.	Cpl.
14465	Beacham A.	L/Sgt.	14475	Clarke H.E.	Cpl.
14852	Bennington O.	Pte.	14478	Clifford J.E.	Pte.

June 1915 Nominal Roll – 'C' Company

Number	Name	Rank	Number	Name	Rank
14481	Coles T.A.	Pte.	14495	Doody F.W.	L/Cpl.
14863	Coles E.	Pte.	14874	Drake M.E.	Cpl.
14861	Collins	Pte.	14496	Dury H.J.	Pte.
14868	Cooper P.	Pte.	16677	Eamer F.	Pte.
14488	Cossans S.	Pte.	14660	Edwards F.C.	Pte.
16736	Cottle E.V.	Pte.	14498	Edwards G.P.	Pte.
14860	Cox H.S.	Pte.	16516	Edwards J.G.	Pte.
14484	Cromack J.A.	L/Cpl.	16729	Edmonds J.	Pte.
14485	Cross C.J.	Pte.	14499	Extance L.F.	Pte.
16521	Cross R.E.	Pte.	14875	Eyers R.G.	Pte.
14864	Crossman A.E.	L/Cpl.	14500	Farr F.C.	Pte.
14487	Croydon J.H.	Pte.	14879	Field S.F.	Pte.
14476	Clarke F.H.	Pte.	14880	Fletcher S.R.	Pte.
16532	Curtis A.	Pte.	15070	Flower J.	Pte.
14493	Dalton W.	Pte.	14878	Forden L.A.	Pte.
14871	Davis J.W.	Pte.	14881	Fowler G.E.	Pte.
14490	Davis H.	Pte.	14877	Fowles G.L.	Pte.
14872	Davis V.G.	Pte.	16469	Fricker H.A.	Pte.
14491	Davis W.E.	Pte.	16737	Fry C.	Pte.
14783	Davies A.M.	Pte.	14502	Fuller M.A.	Pte.
14492	Davison A.	Pte.	14882	Gibbs A.	Pte.
16618	Day J.	Pte.	14506	Gould E.	Pte.
14494	Dayment A.F.	Pte.	14507	Green A.	Pte.
14869	Diaper H.L.	Pte.	14883	Green H.	Pte.
14870	Dicks R.C.	Pte.	15008	Gregory A.V.	Pte.

June 1915 Nominal Roll – 'C' Company

Number	Name	Rank	Number	Name	Rank
16564	Griffen N.F.	Pte.	16489	Holpin H.G.	Pte.
16548	Groves T.R.	Pte.	14518	Hopkins C.W.	Pte.
14295	Guy P.	Pte.	16700	Horrell T.	Pte.
14511	Haggis A.	Pte.	14894	Horsell T.	Pte.
14509	Hale E.G.	Pte.	14517	Horsford A.	Pte.
16487	Hall B.	Pte.	14520	Howland E.	Pte.
14885	Hall G.H.	Pte.	14890	Hughes L.	Sgt.
16645	Hallett P.J.	Pte.	16715	Hurdman C.	Pte.
14884	Ham A.W.	Pte.	14519	Hurdman W.t.	Pte.
14510	Harris R.B.	Pte.	14889	Hussey W.G.	Pte.
14892	Hart G.	Pte.	14521	Jacobs H.W.	Sgt.
14512	Harvey H.C.	Pte.	14522	Jones F.T.	Pte.
14887	Hazzel D.H.	Pte.	16513	Jenkins G.L.	Pte.
14452	Healy C.E.	C.S.M.	16685	Jefferies W.J.	Pte.
16663	Hearn W.J.	Pte.	14524	Jones L.	Pte.
14891	Hedges G.	Pte.	14896	Jones R.J.	Pte.
14888	Hemmens G.E.	Pte.	14899	Justham F.V.	L/Cpl.
14513	Hemmings F.G.	Pte.	14525	Keates W.C.	Pte.
14886	Hibberd A.G.	Pte.	14526	Kendall H.J.	Pte.
14893	Hicks W.C.	L/Cpl.	14901	Kingston C.S.	Pte.
14514	Hilbourne E.J.	Pte.	14902	Lane H.G.	Pte.
14700	Hine F.C.	Pte.	14528	Langley A.G.	Pte.
14516	Hodges R.G.	Pte.	14529	Leach A.E.	Pte.
16770	Hooper J.F.	Pte.	14531	Leslie J.	Pte.
16499	Holder C.	Pte.	14903	Lewis A.S.	Pte.

June 1915 Nominal Roll – 'C' Company

Number	Name	Rank	Number	Name	Rank
14904	Lewis A.J.	Pte.	14549	Pollard T.F.	Pte.
14905	Lewis W.C.	Pte.	16524	Poole W.J.	Pte.
14907	Linger F.E.	L/Cpl.	14916	Pope A.G.	Pte.
16681	Love J.	L/Cpl.	14550	Powell H.	Pte.
14533	Lucas H.E.	Pte.	14919	Prance W.	Pte.
14534	Malthoff E.J.	Pte.	16734	Price T.	Pte.
14908	Martin F.C.	Pte.	16735	Prossor A.S.	Pte.
14536	Matthews R.H.	Pte.	14552	Rawlings A.	Pte.
14911	Meats A.G.	Cpl.	14923	Risdon T.O.	Sgt.
14537	Middleton S.T.	Pte.	14924	Rodway H.A.	Pte.
16766	Mills E.	Pte.	14922	Rogers C.E.	Pte.
166089	Milsom L.J.	Pte.	14553	Roper N.H.	Pte.
14538	Milstead E.H.	Pte.	16668	Rugman G.	Pte.
14539	Molter E.S.	Cpl.	14490	Salvage W.	C.Q.M.S.
15014	Nash G.	Sgt.	16467	Salvidge W.H.	Pte.
14912	Newton J.H.	L/Cpl.	14554	Sanders A.J.	L/Cpl.
14541	Nicholls J.	Pte.	14556	Seller H.A.	Pte.
14542	Nyham E.J.	Pte.	14555	Selway W.T.	Pte.
14921	Page F.E.	Pte.	14928	Sevier W.	Pte.
14543	Parfitt J.J.	Pte.	14557	Shearing R.J.	Pte.
14920	Parsons H.J.	Pte.	14558	Short W.A.	Pte.
14545	Pearson G.D.	Pte.	14560	Simons H.	Pte.
14756	Perry H.W.	Pte.	14925	Sims R.E.	Pte.
14548	Phillips R.A.	Pte.	16687	Skinner R.B.	Pte.
14914	Place J.G.	Pte.	14927	Smith C.	Pte.

June 1915 Nominal Roll – 'C' Company

Number	Name	Rank	Number	Name	Rank
14934	Smith E.	Pte.	16500	Tremlin A.P.	Pte.
14167	Smith J.S.	Pte.	14938	Trotman C.	Pte.
14930	Smith R.H.	Pte.	14572	Twiggs W.S.	Pte.
14935	Speed A.	Pte.	14939	Tyley G.E.	Pte.
14926	Stark A.	Pte.	14573	Tyte H.G.	Pte.
14937	Starkes J.E.	Pte.	16531	Vickery E.J.	Pte.
14561	Stephens G.	Pte.	16529	Vowles C.	L/Cpl.
14929	Stinchcombe E.P.	Pte.	14948	Watkins A.E.	Pte.
14931	Strickland W.E.	Pte.	14947	Weare R.H.	Pte.
16660	Stock W.	Pte.	14576	Weeks W.H.	Pte.
14562	Stokes E.	Pte.	14577	Westlake H.M.	Pte.
16515	Sullivan F.	Pte.	14956	White A.F.	L/Cpl.
14564	Talbot B.T.	L/Cpl.	14951	Williamson A.S.	Pte.
14563	Talbot W.H.	Pte.	14199	Williams C.H.	Pte.
14940	Tame W.	Pte.	14957	Williams C.K.	Pte.
14942	Taylor E.H.	Pte.	14579	Williams E.	Pte.
14943	Taylor F.	Pte.	16678	Williams F.C.	Pte.
14567	Thomas C.	L/Cpl.	14575	Williams G.F.	Pte.
14941	Thomas W.C.	Pte.	14822	Williams H.	Pte.
14568	Thring H.M.	Pte.	14438	Woodburn W.	Pte.
14801	Tibbs G.A.	Pte.	16722	Woodman A.J.	Pte.
14570	Tilley A.W.	Pte.	16725	Woodward A.J.	Pte.
14569	Tiley H.	Pte.	16566	Workman H.H.	Pte.
14574	Tomkins W.G.	L/Sgt.	14830	Worswick W.R.	Pte.
14571	Toon E.W.	Cpl.	14946	Wright A.E.	Pte.

'D' Company

Number	Name	Rank	Number	Name	Rank
14597	Adams C.H.	Pte.	14611	Bromfield H.W.	Pte.
16465	Aitken F.	Pte.	16686	Bromfield S.L.	Pte.
14590	Allen W.A.	Pte.	16641	Brooks F.	Pte.
14591	Amos H.T.	Pte.	14622	Brown C.S.	Pte.
14593	Amesbury A.	Pte.	14613	Brown S.	Pte.
14997	Amesbury R.A.	Pte.	15043	Brown R.	Sgt.
14971	Amesbury E.	Pte.	16653	Browning	Pte.
14594	Armstrong R.C.	Pte.	16623	Bryant A.E.	Pte.
14595	Arnold A.C.	Cpl.	16615	Bryant H.G.	Pte.
15001	Atkins P.	Sgt.	14616	Buck S.	Pte.
14596	Ayres W.F.	Pte.	14617	Burrough F.S.	Pte.
14599	Baker J.	Pte.	14620	Buscombe N.	Pte.
14619	Baker L.G.	Pte.	14626	Carter T.	Pte.
16560	Bamford A.	Pte.	14627	Childs S.A.	Pte.
14600	Barnes W.H.	L/Cpl.	14641	Chew A.T.	Pte.
14623	Beard A.C.	Pte.	14994	Channing H.	Pte.
14602	Belston G.	Pte.	16723	Chapman H.H.	Pte.
14604	Birch M.L.	Pte.	15003	Chapman W.W.	L/Cpl.
14621	Bird A.H.	Pte.	14629	Clarke G.H.	Pte.
14607	Bonnet H.	Pte.	14639	Clark J.	Pte.
14608	Bramley H.B.	Pte.	16653	Coffin C.E.H.	Pte.
14609	Brent W.H.	Pte.	14987	Comerford H.H.	Pte.
14610	Brewer W.S.	Pte.	16682	Cook F.E.	Pte.

June 1915 Nominal Roll – 'D' Company

Number	Name	Rank	Number	Name	Rank
14631	Cook R.W.	Sgt.	14662	Fielding J.S.	Pte.
14632	Cottle G.	Pte.	14663	Fisher E.	Pte.
14981	Corner E.G.	Pte.	16702	Francobe T.	Pte.
14984	Corner W.H.	Pte.	14667	Freeman T.K.	Pte.
14640	Coward F.L.	Pte.	16562	Fry A.T.	Pte.
14635	Crouch A.	Pte.	16582	Fry R.E.	Pte.
14636	Crumpton W.V.	Pte.	16651	Gallop V.	Pte.
14643	Dark H.C.	Pte.	14672	Garrett W.	Pte.
14646	Daveridge T.H.	Pte.	16556	Gaston R.	Pte.
14647	Davidson W.H.J.	Pte.	14673	Gibbons H.R.	Pte.
14648	Dawe W.J.	Pte.	14674	Gillingham M.W.	Pte.
14649	Day A.	Pte.	14675	Gisbourne G.H.	Pte.
15069	Dossor F.L.	Pte.	14680	Gillman A.R.	Pte.
14652	Dunsatn J.	Pte.	16719	Glendinning A.	Pte.
14658	Edwards H.W.H.	Cpl.	14676	Golding R.	Pte.
14960	Edwards O.J.R.	L/Cpl.	14677	Green P.	Pte.
14655	Edwards R.H.	Pte.	14678	Greet E.H.	L/Cpl.
14656	Ellard H.G.	Pte.	14679	Gullifer W.E.	L/Cpl.
16777	Ellacott J.	Pte.	14682	Hall E.W.J.	Pte.
14659	England A.R.	Pte.	14684	Hamer W.A.S.	Sgt.
14972	Fear R.	Pte.	14696	Hammond A.F.	L/Cpl.
15054	Farrow H.C.	Pte.	14686	Harding F.	Pte.
14698	Ford A.	Pte.	15061	Harding W.E.	Pte.
14665	Ford J.M.	Pte.	14973	Harper E.	Pte.
14666	Fowler F.	Pte.	14687	Harris W.R.	Pte.

June 1915 Nominal Roll – 'D' Company

Number	Name	Rank	Number	Name	Rank
14688	Hayles E.J.	Pte.	14714	Lancaster E.S.	Pte.
14689	Hedges W.H.	Pte.	14715	Lampard F.G.	Pte.
14691	Hewlett J.	Pte.	14717	Legg G.H.	Pte.
14693	Hill H.L.	Pte.	14530	Leonard S.W.	Pte.
14976	Hobbs G.H.	Pte.	14721	Logan J.	Sgt.
14694	Hodges J.C.	Pte.	16558	Love C.	Pte.
14697	Hodges H.C.	Pte.	14985	Lloyd T.I.	L/Cpl.
14690	Hillier S.T.	Pte.	16598	Lucas H.	Pte.
14695	Hopes A.W.	Pte.	16601	Lucas W.H.	Pte.
16637	Hopkins F.C.	Pte.	14724	March D.W.	Pte.
15049	Hussell W.	Pte.	14724	Matthews A.C.S.	Pte.
14701	Iles H.P.	Pte.	14731	Miller G.J.	Pte.
14702	Inch W.	Pte.	16610	Mills J.T.	Pte.
14709	Jackson P.W.	Pte.	14729	Mountain L.W.	Pte.
14703	James W.L.	Pte.	16597	Morgan A.	Pte.
16633	James P.C.	Pte.	14730	Mullis E.	Pte.
14705	Jelly H.R.	Pte.	14732	Nethercott W.	Pte.
14706	Jennings W.	Pte.	14977	Oliver G.J.	Pte.
14707	Jennings W.E.J.	Pte.	14733	Organ F.G.	Pte.
14961	Jones E.W.	Pte.	14754	Padfield W.M.	Pte.
16557	Kathro E.	Pte.	14763	Parnall L.H.	Pte.
14711	Kendall L.W.	L/Cpl.	14753	Parsons C.J.	Pte.
14999	Kilby C.R.W.	Pte.	14755	Payne A.S.B.	Pte.
14712	Laird A.	Sgt.	14986	Payne C.	Pte.

June 1915 Nominal Roll – 'D' Company

Number	Name	Rank	Number	Name	Rank
16630	Payne O.	Pte.	14764	Richards S.T.	Pte.
14741	Phillpot A.E.	Pte.	14768	Ridley H.L.	Pte.
16611	Pole C.	Pte.	14450	Rimell P.	Pte.
14742	Poole A.H.	Cpl.	14216	Rimell W.C.	C.S.M.
16567	Poole E.	Pte.	16554	Rogers F.A.	Pte.
14743	Poole H.J.	Pte.	14766	Ross H.A.	Pte.
16570	Poole H.P.	Pte.	14790	Seymour C.	Pte.
14744	Pople R.A.	Pte.	14792	Seymour S.J.	Pte.
14745	Porter C.C.	Pte.	16603	Shackson W.	Pte.
14746	Porter C.E.	Pte.	14793	Shearn L.	Pte.
16555	Portlock H.J.	Pte.	14771	Sheppard E.T.B.	Pte.
16606	Powell P.	Pte.	14789	Sheppard G.E.	Pte.
14752	Preedy G.	Pte.	14772	Shirley J.	Pte.
14748	Prewett C.E.	Pte.	15023	Short F.	Pte.
14751	Price C.J.	Pte.	14773	Shute S.G.	Pte.
14750	Price P.R.M.	Pte.	14775	Skuse G.S.	Pte.
14749	Prossor A.E.	Pte.	14776	Slocombe W.A.	Pte.
14757	Radford C.	L/Cpl.	14778	Slowley W.D.	Pte.
14993	Radmilovic J.	L/Cpl.	14779	Small F.W.	L/Cpl.
14758	Raggett R.J.	L/Sgt.	14780	Smith R.J.	L/Cpl.
14762	Redston T.V.	Sgt.	14974	Solway B.J.	Pte.
14760	Reece H.G.	Pte.	14996	Sperring H.	Pte.
14761	Reed T.F.	Pte.	14781	Spice G.	Pte.
14769	Reeves F.H.	Cpl.	14787	Stacey E.J.	Pte.
14763	Rich H.A.	Pte.	16632	Staple H.E.	Pte.

June 1915 Nominal Roll – 'D' Company

Number	Name	Rank	Number	Name	Rank
14982	Stephens L.H.	Pte.	14809	Waldron R.G.	C.Q.M.S.
14788	Stevens H.J.	Pte.	16577	Walker D.	Pte.
14782	Stock W.G.	Pte.	14810	Walker R.B.	Pte.
20052	Stokes F.E.	Pte.	16690	Walters O.C.	Pte.
14980	Stroud A.G.	Pte.	14992	Ware R.C.	Pte.
14774	Summons A.C.	Pte.	14811	Warfield A.E.	Pte.
14785	Sutton C.A.	Pte.	14836	Watts F.	Pte.
14786	Swenson J.E.	Pte.	14814	Webb B.A.	Pte.
14797	Sydenham F.	Pte.	16563	Webb T.W.	Pte.
16679	Tandy W.G.	Pte.	14815	Webber E.A.	Pte.
15055	Taylor H.	L/Cpl.	14816	Weeks F.G.	Pte.
14795	Taylor R.A.	Pte.	14817	Weeks A.E.	Pte.
14799	Thorne C.R.	Pte.	14837	Weeks A.J.	Pte.
14798	Thould J.	Pte.	16621	White A.H.	Pte.
16654	Trayhurn A.E.	Pte.	14819	Whitewell C.C.	Pte.
14802	Tripp H.H.	Pte.	14818	Whittaker A.J.	Pte.
14803	Trott R.H.L.	Pte.	14834	Whittock B.	L/Cpl.
14978	Tucker C.	Pte.	16613	Whittock S.C.	Pte.
14805	Turner A.	Pte.	14825	Wilcox H.	Cpl.
16541	Turner E.	Pte.	14820	Wilkins F.G.	Cpl.
14808	Vallis L.J.	Pte.	14995	Wilkins J.F.	Sgt.
16580	Vizard J.	Pte.	14821	Williams N.	Pte.
14807	Vowles E.	L/Cpl.	14829	Wood A.R.	Pte.
14837	Wadman H.B.	Pte.	16627	Woodbine H.	Pte.
14812	Waite E.	Pte.	14827	Woodman R.A.	L/Sgt.

June 1915 Nominal Roll – 'D' Company

Number	Name	Rank	Number	Name	Rank
14813	Wonnacott E.	Pte.	14831	Wyllie A.	Pte.
16472	Worth C.W.	Pte.	14839	Young E.H.	Pte.
16473	Worth F.W.	Pte.			

June 1915 Nominal Roll – H.Q staff attached to 'D' Company

H.Q. staff attached to 'D' Company

Number	Name	Rank	Number	Name	Rank
14970	Addis F.	L/Cpl.	14156	Rowlands H.W.	Pte.
13978	Barber H.C.	O.R. Sgt.	14828	Woods K.J.T.	Pte.
14569	Britton A.E.	Cpl.		**Grooms**	
14250	Cooke W.B.	Sgt.	14099	Lewis J.R.	Pte.
13975	Cotterell J.	R.Q.M.S.	16510	Marsh H.	Pte.
14035	Darlington	L/Cpl.	14826	Winstone C.M.	Pte.
14284	Farringdon S.	L/Cpl.		**Ambulance Section**	
14451	Greenwood W.	Sgt.	14851	Ballinger F.H.	Pte.
14454	Gregory W.	Sgt.	14585	Barnes R.C.	Pte.
14713	Lane A.H.	R.S.M.	16550	Brace V.	Pte.
14540	Morgan J.	Cpl.	14865	Cash H.W.	Pte.
14353	Morrish W.H.B.	L/Cpl.	14045	Dunsford W.E.	Pte.
14551	Pyman F.W.	Sgt.	16629	Haile T.A.	Pte.
14448	Sloper F.H.	Sgt.	14315	Hawker G.S.	Pte.
14975	Toogood E.W.	L/Cpl.	14699	Hopcroft J.C.	Pte.
16785	Watkins F.C.	Sgt.	14983	Hunt J.C.	Pte.
	Signallers		14089	Kemp-Welch R.	Pte.
14958	Bacon A.G.	Pte.	14330	King B.	Pte.
14628	Clark D.A.	Pte.	14719	Lewis F.	Pte.
14645	Davis E.G.	Pte.	14342	Lewis R.J.	Pte.
14497	Dugdale A.	Pte.	14727	Mills R.	Pte.
14368	Newton A.C.	Pte.	16747	Skinner J.P.	Pte.
15004	Owen	Pte.	14796	Taylor F.G.	Pte.

June 1915 Nominal Roll – H.Q staff attached to 'D' Company

Number	Name	Rank	Number	Name	Rank
14915	Powell E.A.	Pte.	14193	Weeks A.J.	Pte.
16704	Rutherford J.	Pte.	14832	Wescombe W.R.	Pte.
14791	Seymour A.F.	Pte.	**Machine Gun Section**		
Pioneers			14001	Boddie R.C.	Pte.
14626	Chandler C.	Pte.	15071	Boobyer F.	Pte.
14283	Elliott C.E.	Pte.	14441	Clement S.A.	Pte.
14298	Gover A.	Pte.	14055	Fonceca H.J.M.	Pte.
14304	Holloway H.	Pte.	14566	Thorn F.J.	Pte.
14345	Lewis R.T.	Pte.	14953	Willatt R.L.	Pte.
14952	Watkins A.E.	Pte.	16481	Wiltshire R.J.	Pte.

'E' Company

Number	Name	Rank	Number	Name	Rank
16619	Aitken E.	Pte.	20129	Bowman L.	Pte.
20093	Almrott J.	Pte.	20068	Boulton F.M.	Pte.
20056	Anstey J.	Pte.	16732	Bright J.J.	Pte.
14457	Archer J.S.	Pte.	16665	Bressington P.	Pte.
20054	Attwood G.	Pte.	20080	Brett W.E.	Pte.
20094	Aubrey F.	Pte.	20104	Brimble R.J.	Pte.
13990	Bacon H.R.A.	Pte.	16744	Browne J.	Pte.
14223	Barnard H.G.	Pte.	20103	Bull R.C.	Pte.
20087	Barnes S.J.	Pte.	20113	Burnell W.	Pte.
20106	Barnes S.T.	Pte.	16638	Butcher A.T.	Pte.
20120	Barnes W.G.	Pte.	20105	Carr R.E.	Pte.
16483	Bascombe W.S.	Cpl.	20118	Carroll W.J.	Pte.
20067	Bater A.J.	Pte.	20074	Cavill C.A.	Pte.
16733	Baugh M.H.	Pte.	16756	Charley G.T.	Pte.
16726	Beadle B.S.	L/Cpl.	20117	Cheeseman G.E.	Pte.
20079	Bellamy W.H.	Pte.	16480	Clifton W.A.	L/Sgt.
20064	Bellet t A.E.	Pte.	14480	Cohen D.	Pte.
16694	Blake C.J.	Pte.	20086	Collins A.K.	Pte.
16697	Bleaken C.	Pte.	20119	Combs H.E.	Pte.
14845	Bond H.M.	Pte.	14867	Cox E.J.	Cpl.
15027	Cox F.	Pte.	16809	Curry G.	Pte.
15067	Crew C.	Pte.	16695	Dando C.V.	Pte.

June 1915 Nominal Roll – 'E' Company

Number	Name	Rank	Number	Name	Rank
16707	Davies J.A.S.	L/Sgt.	16711	Greenwood E.	Pte.
20126	Davis A.	Pte.	20132	Groves H.	Pte.
20109	Day F.J.	Pte.	16792	Gulwell W.	Pte.
20115	Dowling H.E.	Pte.	20102	Hale S.J.	Pte.
15046	Duggan D.	Pte.	20058	Hallett A.E.	Pte.
16812	Dunn A.	Pte.	20098	Hancock H.J.	Pte.
16475	Dury W.J.	Cpl.	16644	Harris C.G.	L/Sgt.
20173	Edwards B.J.	Pte.	20130	Hayman A.	Pte.
16482	Evans C.R.	Cpl.	16616	Hayman G.C.	Pte.
16780	Evans R.L.	Pte.	16547	Heales J.G.	Cpl.
14292	Excell T.G.	Pte.	20090	Hillman A.G.	Pte.
16775	Flay A.A.	Pte.	14515	Hodge F.S.	Pte.
16528	Fletcher F.	Pte.	20121	Hodges L.I.	Pte.
16599	Ford	Pte.	20065	Holland E.	Pte.
16804	Forrester J.	Pte.	20071	Hooper G.J.	Pte.
20101	Franklin S.	Pte.	16793	Hudson W.G.	Pte.
16781	Fulford W.H.	Pte.	14303	Hudson W.J.	Pte.
20096	Gallop A.C.	Pte.	16664	Hughes H.	Pte.
16806	Garland A.C.	Pte.	16495	Hunt A.C.J.	L/Sgt.
14503	Gay W.R.	Pte.	16582	Hunt G.	Pte.
16699	Gibbs A.	Pte.	16539	Hunter W.B.	L/Cpl.
20084	Godfrey H.R.F.	Pte.	20081	Hurd H.E.	Pte.
16754	Gordon C.B.	Pte.	20076	Iles W.J.	Pte.
20097	Green G.	Pte.	20089	James W.	Pte.
20114	Greenland A.	Pte.	14704	Jarman A.E.	Pte.

June 1915 Nominal Roll – 'E' Company

Number	Name	Rank	Number	Name	Rank
14708	Jarman L.V.	Pte.	14121	Mundy H.B.	Pte.
16721	Jefferies A.	Pte.	20138	Musty J.	Pte.
16786	Jenkins C.D.	Pte.	20063	Neale T.E.	Pte.
16713	Jordan J.H.	L/Cpl.	16588	Nethercott H.A.	Pte.
20131	Kingman J.	Pte.	16801	Newman S.H.	Pte.
20055	Knight W.E.	Pte.	16537	Newman W.C.	Cpl.
20051	Lambert F.G.	Pte.	20078	Newport A.	Pte.
20062	Lewis S.P.	Pte.	16608	Newton J.T.	Cpl.
14722	Levatino C.	Pte.	20124	Nicholls R.	Pte.
16693	Longman W.	Pte.	20123	Oliver W.	Pte.
16530	Love F.	Cpl.	15058	Palmer G.	Pte.
20110	Lowe W.A.	Pte.	14215	Parish H.J.	C.Q.M.S.
20135	Luker H.J.	Pte.	16584	Parker F.	Sgt.
20066	Macmullon W.J.	Pte.	20085	Parsons S.J.	Pte.
16724	Maggs G.	Pte.	16617	Patch O.	L/Sgt.
20082	Mann G.	Pte.	15035	Paulton H.	Pte.
16807	Massey T.M.	Pte.	20234	Pester E.J.	Pte.
16680	May P.	L/Cpl.	16790	Pester F.G.	Pte.
16802	McClean R.	Pte.	16796	Perks G.	Pte.
16758	McIntyre J.	L/Cpl.	16774	Pike F.J.	L/Cpl.
14352	Meredith A.E.	Pte.	20057	Pobjoy W.	Pte.
16767	Mills G.E.	Pte.	14990	Porter W.	Pte.
20112	Mitchell A.C.	Pte.	20091	Powell H.J.	Pte.
16755	Moorcroft R.J.	Pte.	16771	Pritchard F.	Pte.
15045	Moore H.	Pte.	16810	Pritchard G.	Pte.

June 1915 Nominal Roll – 'E' Company

Number	Name	Rank	Number	Name	Rank
16798	Punter E.T.V.	Pte.	20077	Sweeting T.	Pte.
16787	Ranger W.M.	Pte.	16794	Thomas A.E.M.	Pte.
16784	Richards R.	Pte.	16672	Thompson J.	L/Cpl.
20125	Robins W.	Pte.	20108	Till G.E.O.	Pte.
20083	Room A.H.	Pte.	20134	Tilley F.W.	Pte.
16773	Roper J.S.	Pte.	20075	Tucker T.C.	Pte.
20107	Rugman H.C.	Pte.	14584	Tuckwell B.	Pte.
16698	Sage G.E.O.	Pte.	16808	Vernon E.A.	Pte.
16788	Sampson A.	Pte.	20072	Vernon J.F.	Pte.
13979	Scaife A.	C.S.M.	20116	Veryard R.	Pte.
20095	Scott G.	Pte.	20128	Viner W.	Pte.
16791	Seaman E.	L/Cpl.	16799	Vizzard J.	Pte.
15056	Shipton M.W.	Pte.	20122	Walters G.	Pte.
16666	Short H.	Pte.	20092	Watts A.V.	Pte.
16647	Sinclair W.A.	Pte.	16805	Weatherhead H.V.	Pte.
20111	Skidmore H.	Pte.	16669	Weekes G.O.	Pte.
20059	Slade H.	Pte.	16783	Wheeler C.W.	Pte.
20127	Slade R.	Pte.	16494	Whithers F.	Pte.
16776	Smith M.	Pte.	16559	Wilkey G.C.	L/Cpl.
16674	Smith P.F.	Pte.	16789	Williams H.D.	Pte.
16708	Starkey J.	Pte.	20137	Willie H.	Pte.
20070	Stocker T.M.	Pte.	20083	Wilson W.	Pte.
20061	Stone .E.F.	Pte.	16800	Wood W.B.	L/Cpl.
16778	Stringer E.N.	Pte.	16751	York E.	Pte.
20281	Styles F.	Pte.	15024	Young I. of G.E.A.	Sgt.
20280	Styles R.	Pte.			

June 1915 Nominal Roll – 'F' Company

'F' Company

Number	Name	Rank	Number	Name	Rank
20172	Allen G.	Pte.	20229	Buxton W.	Pte.
20203	Anning E.	Pte.	20230	Bugler H.	Pte.
20293	Baddeley F.	Pte.	20136	Butchart D.	Pte.
20178	Baker E.R.	Pte.	20165	Butler A.	Pte.
20153	Baker H.	Pte.	20161	Butler W.	Pte.
20147	Ball J.	Pte.	20260	Calt J.	Pte.
16496	Barrett F.	C.Q.M.S.	20301	Carr C.	Pte.
20201	Bate F.T.	Pte.	14017	Cavell C.V.	Pte.
20243	Beale L.W.	Pte.	20295	Chivers N.C.	Pte.
20160	Bedgood E.	Pte.	20193	Civil H.	Pte.
20250	Beynon P.W.	Pte.	16581	Clark H.	Pte.
20217	Bishop A.E.	Pte.	20284	Clark H.	Pte.
20257	Booth W.	Pte.	20254	Clarkson R.W.	Pte.
20181	Bowden F.V.	Pte.	20141	Compton E.	Pte.
20253	Bowen W.	Pte.	20232	Cornock G.	Pte.
20170	Bowman W.	Pte.	20176	Cotton W.	Pte.
20199	Bowring E.G.	Pte.	20275	Coombs D.W.	Pte.
20167	Bowyer S.W.	L/Cpl.	20225	Coward W.L.	Pte.
20289	Brace J.	Pte.	20182	Critchley W.E.	Pte.
20207	Breakwell P.L.	Pte.	20157	Cullimore H.	Pte.
20198	Brewer A.L.	Pte.	20224	Curtis A.G.	Pte.

June 1915 Nominal Roll – 'F' Company

Number	Name	Rank	Number	Name	Rank
20296	Curtis F.J.	Pte.	20154	Hackwell J.	Pte.
20244	Davis G.W.	Pte.	20179	Hale G.	Pte.
20247	Davies D.J.	Pte.	20146	Hartshorne R.W.	Pte.
16760	Delaney M.P.	Sgt.	20163	Haskins G.H.W.	Pte.
20196	Durbin A.	Pte.	20155	Hatherwell E.	Pte.
20285	Dyer H.A.	Pte.	20202	Hellier L.	Pte.
20184	Dymmock F.J.	Pte.	20151	Hendy J.	Pte.
20279	Dymond F.W.	Pte.	20149	Hillman F.	Pte.
20278	Dymond .T.E.	Pte.	20300	Hitchings C.W.	Pte.
20210	Eales R.	Pte.	20298	Hook S.D.	Pte.
20297	Evans D.T.	Pte.	20206	Hooper P.H.	Pte.
20220	Ewens A.	Pte.	20219	Horsford J.	Pte.
20158	Ford A.H.	Pte.	20152	Janes A.	Pte.
20180	Fowler T.	Pte.	20215	Jones F.	Pte.
20238	Gage B.	Pte.	20216	Jordan H.	Pte.
20231	Gigg W.H.E.	Pte.	20277	Khan P.R.	Pte.
20194	Goddard C.	L/Cpl.	20162	King D.	Pte.
20272	Goodlife F.W.	Pte.	20205	Knowles S.J.E.	Pte.
20200	Goodlife W.A.	Pte.	20249	Laing T.	Pte.
20241	Green C.H.R.	Pte.	20168	Leonard F.	Pte.
20274	Gregory W.G.	Pte.	20288	Leonard W.G.	Pte.
20174	Griffen R.	L/Cpl.	14720	Lifton A.	Sgt.
20226	Griffiths O.	Pte.	14214	Lloyd F.S.	Sgt.
20236	Grinter F.	Pte.	20171	Lloyd H.	Pte.

June 1915 Nominal Roll – 'F' Company

Number	Name	Rank	Number	Name	Rank
20213	Locke A.	Pte.	20302	Pountney B.	Pte.
20187	Long G.	Pte.	15021	Pritchard T.	Cpl.
20271	Mann G.E.	Pte.	20166	Putt E.	Pte.
20140	Mansfield C.	Pte.	20273	Roberts G.W.	Pte.
20143	Marsh G.	Pte.	20276	Rose E.V.	Pte.
20222	Marshall C.J.	Pte.	16692	Rose H.E.	L/Cpl.
20237	McGill A.W.	Pte.	20050	Rowe H.E.	L/Cpl.
14535	McLeod A.	Pte.	20188	Sharman J.L.	Pte.
16544	Mead H.G.	Cpl.	20233	Sharp S.F.	Pte.
16762	Medhurst W.	Cpl.	20175	Shaw A.W.	Pte.
20169	Middle R.	Pte.	14212	Shelper A.E.	C.S.M.
20256	Mills G.	Pte.	20145	Sheppard T.E.	Pte.
20245	Mitchell S.	Pte.	20221	Shewan V.	Pte.
20286	Mizen J.S.	Pte.	20255	Sims S.G.	Pte.
20136	Noble B.	Pte.	20242	Smale C.W.H.	Pte.
20139	Noble S.	Pte.	20192	Smith H.	Pte.
20197	Notton A.	Pte.	20248	Stamper J.	Pte.
20261	O'Connor W.	Pte.	20204	Stephens A.E.	Pte.
20133	Oerton F.	Pte.	20228	Stribling A.E.	Pte.
20270	Osborne R.A.	Pte.	20159	Sutton A.	Pte.
20214	Parsons J.	Pte.	20208	Sweeting B.	Pte.
20287	Payne F.S.	Pte.	20150	Tilley C.	Pte.
14377	Perkins F.	L/Cpl.	20283	Tomkins F.	Pte.
20227	Plumley J.	Pte.	20189	Turner C.	Pte.

June 1915 Nominal Roll – 'F' Company

Number	Name	Rank	Number	Name	Rank
20209	Wakefield N.E.	Pte.	20144	Wood W.O.	Cpl.
20251	Way A.J.	Pte.	20164	Worgan B.	Pte.
20177	Whittingdon W.	Pte.	20223	Wright L.	Pte.
20240	Williams F.	Pte.	20195	Wyatt F.H.	Pte.
20292	Williams T.	Pte.	20183	Yandell S.J.	Pte.
20252	Wills C.H.	Pte.	20148	Young F.	Pte.
14581	Winters W.	Cpl.			

Appendix IV

Other Ranks Roll of Honour

Original battalion men shown in bold type

Number	Surname	Christian name(s)	Rank	Comments
14456	**Adams**	**Thomas John**	**Pte.**	**kia 03/09/16**
44420	Adcock	Samuel James	Pte.	kia 25/04/18
21330	Alder	Reginald	Pte.	Kia 29/09/18
16128	**Aldous**	**Leonard**	**L/Cpl.**	**kia 21/04/17**
200337	Alexander	Frederick	Pte.	kia 04/10/17
14842	**Allen**	**Arthur Charles**	**Pte.**	**kia 03/09/16**
29259	Amess	William George	Pte.	dow 24/08/18
25255	Ancrum	Ernest James	Pte.	kia 03/09/16
201917	Andrews	Albert George	Pte.	kia 02/10/17
20203	**Anning**	**Ernest**	**Pte.**	**kia 02/10/17**
13850	Apperley	Reginald Wallace	Pte.	kia 08/05/17
201100	Ashley	Herbert Thomas	Pte.	kia 20/09/18
39729	Ashwin	Percy Arthur	Pte.	kia 14/04/18
28324	Atkinson	Frederick	Pte.	died 30/06/18
20054	**Attwood**	**George**	**Pte.**	**kia 03/09/16**
204002	Avens	Bertie Norman	Pte.	died 03/08/17
22747	Ayres	George	Pte.	kia 03/09/16
16466	**Babb**	**Albert Edward**	**Pte.**	**kia 03/09/16**
14958	**Bacon**	**Arthur George**	**Pte.**	**kia 03/09/16**
37557	Baddeley	Richard	Pte.	kia 05/05/17

Number	Surname	Christian name(s)	Rank	Comments
40101	Bailey	Eric Thomas	Pte.	dow 01/09/18
11578	Bailey	Thomas	Sgt.	kia 25/04/18
36551	Baker	Frederick	Pte.	kia 04/10/17
39914	Baker	George	Pte.	kia 25/08/18
238050	Baldwin	James	Cpl.	kia 25/04/18
14853	**Ball**	**Christopher George**	**Pte.**	**kia 03/09/16**
20147	**Ball**	**John**	**Pte.**	**kia 02/09/16**
202520	Ball	Maurice Brynmor	Pte.	Kia 28/06/17
39057	Banner	Victor	Pte.	kia 25/04/18
24712	Banning	William	Pte.	kia 20/08/16
16636	**Banwell**	**William Henry**	**Pte.**	**kia 08/05/17**
23249	Bartlett	Herbert	Pte.	kia 03/09/16
37829	Bartlett	Percy	Cpl.	kia 17/07/18
28249	Barton	Arthur	Pte.	kia 08/05/17
22809	Bater	John Henry	Pte.	kia 08/05/17
32512	Bath	Arthur	Sgt.	kia 08/05/17
16733	**Baugh**	**Montague Hardinge**	**L/Sgt.**	**kia 03/09/16**
32083	Baxendale	Robert	Pte.	died 01/10/17
14465	**Beacham**	**Arthur**	**Sgt.**	**kia 03/09/16**
16726	**Beadle**	**Bertram Stephen**	**Cpl.**	**kia 08/05/17**
20243	**Beale**	**Leonard Wesley**	**Pte.**	**died 12/08/16**
38170	Beattie	Charlie Christopher	Pte.	kia 23/08/18
16540	**Bellamy**	**James**	**Pte.**	**kia 04/10/17**

Number	Surname	Christian name(s)	Rank	Comments
27909	Bendall	Albert Edward	L/Cpl.	kia 08/05/17
37594	Bengough	Thomas William	Pte.	dow 23/04/17
11040	Bennett	Frank Percy	Cpl.	kia 08/02/17
14242	**Bennison**	**Charles**	**Pte.**	**kia 03/09/16**
260421	Bethell	Albert Sydney Valentine	Pte.	kia 10/10/17
38041	Betheway	Percy	Pte.	kia 15/04/18
27293	Bevan	Harry	Pte.	kia 17/07/18
21818	Bevan	Thom William	Pte.	kia 21/04/17
28420	Biddel	Oscar	Pte.	kia 08/05/17
38928	Biles	James	Pte.	dow 29/06/18
16634	**Binding**	**Francis Albert**	**Pte.**	**kia 30/07/16**
22639	Black	Leonard William	Pte.	kia 26/07/16
39000	Blackmore	Edward	Pte.	died 30/10/17
16694	**Blake**	**Charles Joseph**	**Pte.**	**kia 30/07/16**
260419	Blake	David	L/Cpl.	kia 28/06/18
235285	Blake	Francis Henry	Pte.	dow 25/08/18
16527	**Blanning**	**Joseph**	**Pte.**	**kia 30/07/16**
240908	Bliss	Jesse	L/Cpl.	dow 10/10/17
14002	**Bond**	**Francis Walter**	**Pte.**	**kia 21/07/16**
14068	**Bouskill**	**Percy John**	**C.S.M.**	**dow 08/05/17**
16511	**Bowen**	**Thomas**	**Pte.**	**died 21/02/15**
20199	**Bowring**	**Ernest George**	**Pte.**	**kia 30/10/16**
14239	**Boyce**	**Reginald William**	**Sgt.**	**kia 30/07/16**
31143	Bracey	Evan	Pte.	kia 11/03/17

Number	Surname	Christian name(s)	Rank	Comments
203371	Bradbury	Albert	L/Cpl.	kia 25/08/18
14006	**Bradford**	**William Benjamin**	**Pte.**	**dow 10/03/16**
37889	Bradley	Ernest William	Pte.	kia 13/04/18
40087	Bradley	Samuel Henry	L/Cpl.	kia 29/09/18
260417	Brayley	Richard Isaac	Pte.	kia 04/10/17
37834	Breen	James	Pte.	kia 08/05/17
27433	Brent	Edward George	Pte.	kia 06/05/17
14849	**Brett**	**Frederick John**	**Pte.**	**kia 08/05/17**
20198	**Brewer**	**Hubert Levi**	**Pte.**	**died 30/08/18**
16751	**Brice**	**Lewis**	**Pte.**	**kia 08/06/16**
260376	Bridge	John Joseph	Pte.	dow 02/09/18
265395	Brine	Arthur Edgar	Pte.	died 12/04/18
37833	Brookman	Frank	Sgt.	died 06/11/17
40130	Brookman	Percy George	Pte.	kia 31/08/18
14009	**Brooks**	**Charles William**	**Pte.**	**kia 08/05/17**
16641	**Brooks**	**Frank**	**Pte.**	**kia 05/05/17**
14622	**Brown**	**Cecil Stuart**	**Pte.**	**kia 26/07/16**
39599	Brown	John Harold	Pte.	kia 30/10/17
37874	Brown	Joseph	Pte.	died 08/05/17
13867	Brown	Raymond George	Cpl.	dow 10/11/17
14613	**Brown**	**Sidney**	**Pte.**	**dow 12/09/16**
260325	Brown	William	Pte.	kia 14/04/18
22631	Brown	William Henry	Pte.	kia 26/09/16
11178	Brownhill	George Thomas	Pte.	kia 08/05/17

Number	Surname	Christian name(s)	Rank	Comments
203381	Browning	Harold	Pte.	kia 08/05/17
14847	**Bruton**	**Wilfred Charlie**	**L/Cpl.**	**kia 06/05/17**
22707	Bruton	William Ernest Husband	Pte.	kia 03/09/16
16649	**Bryant**	**Cecil Albert**	**Pte.**	**kia 25/04/18**
14858	**Bryant**	**George Frederick**	**Pte.**	**kia 04/11/16**
14011	**Bryant**	**Harold Hubert**	**Pte.**	**kia 25/09/16**
5854	Bryant	Harry James	Sgt.	kia 26/04/18
22742	Bryant	Richard	Pte.	kia 03/09/16
38950	Buckley	Herbert	Pte.	dow 30/06/18
40118	Bull	George Herbert	Pte.	kia 29/09/18
39064	Burford	Henry Harold	Pte.	kia 07/11/17
29798	Burns	William James	L/Cpl.	kia 25/08/18
33585	Butler	Ernest	Pte.	kia 08/05/17
32323	Butten	Frederick	Pte.	kia 08/05/17
14015	**Byrne**	**Herbert Fenton**	**Pte.**	**dow 01/08/16**
18642	Cale	Charles Edward	Pte.	kia 04/10/17
38047	Carpenter	Fred	Pte.	kia 28/06/18
22013	Carter	Harry	Pte.	kia 29/06/17
14447	**Carter**	**Valentine Cyril Harold**	**L/Cpl.**	**kia 30/07/16**
37817	Carter	William	Pte.	kia 08/05/17
37997	Carthey	Frederick Henry	Pte.	dcw 30/06/18
22628	Case	James Clifford	Sgt.	kia 04/10/17
15032	**Case**	**Norman George Manning**	**L/Cpl.**	**kia 24/07/16**
14865	**Cash**	**Henry Watts**	**Pte.**	**kia 03/09/16**

Number	Surname	Christian name(s)	Rank	Comments
22214	Challen	George	Pte.	dow 30/08/18
25068	Chamberlain	Frederick James	Pte.	dow 29/08/16
22694	Chamberlain	Wilfred Henry	Pte.	kia 24/07/16
44355	Chanin	Frank	Pte.	dow 22/04/18
14994	**Channing**	**Frank**	**Pte.**	**dow 04/09/16**
33012	Chaplin	Robert	Pte.	died 04/10/17
14247	**Chapman**	**Ernest Charles**	**Pte.**	**kia 04/10/17**
38877	Chapman	Samuel	Pte.	kia 23/08/18
14479	**Chappell**	**Frederick Herbert**	**Cpl.**	**kia 08/05/17**
39066	Chatwin	George Wagstaff	Pte.	dow 15/04/18
44362	Cheverton	George Austin	Pte.	kia 25/04/18
14641	**Chew**	**Albert Francis**	**Sgt.**	**died 23/09/16**
27835	Christopher	Harry	Pte.	kia 23/08/18
14020	**Clark**	**Frederick John Sparks**	**Pte.**	**kia 08/05/17**
14639	**Clark**	**James**	**Pte.**	**kia 03/09/16**
202633	Clark	Walter mark	Pte.	dow 23/08/18
12324	Clarke	Henry	Pte.	kia 03/09/16
200486	Clarke	Richard John	Pte.	dow 25/08/18
15057	**Clement**	**Ernest**	**Pte.**	**kia 05/05/17**
10078	Cliffe	Harry Foster	Pte.	kia 22/04/17
14246	**Clifford**	**Arthur Ernest**	**L/Sgt.**	**kia 04/10/17**
14025	**Clifford**	**Gerald Walter**	**Pte.**	**dow 24/07/16**
14478	**Clifford**	**Josiah Edward**	**Pte.**	**kia 14/04/17**
37648	Coates	Ernest	Pte.	died 05/10/17
14481	**Coles**	**Thomas Alfred**	**Pte.**	**dow 06/08/16**

Roll of Honour – Other Ranks

Number	Surname	Christian name(s)	Rank	Comments
22776	Colley	Charles	Pte.	dow 24/08/16
16738	**Collier**	**George Henry**	**Pte.**	**kia 14/12/15**
39006	Collins	Frederick	Pte.	dow 14/04/18
22788	Collins	Sydney George	Pte.	kia 22/04/17
14861	**Collins**	**Walter Gilbert**	**Pte.**	**kia 10/12/15**
16705	**Collins**	**William Thomas**	**Pte.**	**kia 20/07/16**
16476	**Cook**	**Allan Byron**	**Pte.**	**kia 21/07/16**
14262	**Cook**	**Edwin**	**Pte.**	**kia 08/05/17**
13834	Cook	Ernest	Pte.	kia 03/09/16
16682	**Cook**	**Frederick Edwin**	**Pte.**	**dow 10/12/15**
38953	Cook	Stanley John	Pte.	kia 23/04/18
39067	Cooke	John lane	Pte.	dow 08/11/17
39007	Corbett	Joseph Alfred	Pte.	died 25/08/18
44413	Cork	Edwin Theophilus	Pte.	kia 22/04/18
32084	Cornes	John Henry	Pte.	dow 08/08/18
14632	**Cottle**	**George**	**Pte.**	**kia 08/05/17**
20176	**Cotton**	**William**	**Pte.**	**dow 17/05/16**
14251	**Cottrel**	**Arthur Board**	**Pte.**	**kia 27/07/16**
36149	Cousens	Arhtur John	Pte.	kia 28/06/18
38910	Cownden	Sidney Albert	Pte.	kia 30/10/17
260327	Crease	Frederick	Pte.	kia 31/10/17
31504	Cripps	Willaim Harold	Pte.	dow 03/10/17
16521	**Cross**	**Reginald Edward**	**Pte.**	**kia 20/04/16**
14864	**Crossman**	**Arthur Edward**	**CSM**	**kia 25/08/18**

Number	Surname	Christian name(s)	Rank	Comments
16640	**Cruse**	**Robert William**	**CSM**	**dow 19/05/17**
33655	Cullis	Ernest	Pte.	kia 25/08/18
38416	Cummins	Edwin	Pte.	kia 28/06/18
19367	Cunningham	Edward John	L/Cpl.	kia 28/06/18
16532	**Curtis**	**Alfred**	**Pte.**	**kia 06/05/17**
30656	Curtis	Edwin Colston	Pte.	kia 08/05/17
20296	Curtis	Frederick James	Pte.	kia 03/09/16
32533	Dance	Thomas George	Pte.	kia 22/04/17
200943	Dando	Frederick	Pte.	kia 23/08/18
36151	Davies	Arthur Charles	Pte.	kia 17/07/18
260431	Davies	Goerge Henry	Pte.	kia 09/10/17
37702	Davies	William Ewart	Pte.	kia 25/04/18
25177	Davis	Albert Victor	L/Cpl.	kia 22/04/17
14491	**Davis**	**Walter Ernest**	**Pte.**	**dow 31/12/15**
33605	Dawkes	Charles John William	Pte.	dow 08/10/17
38965	Dawson	William Henry	Pte.	kia 25/04/18
20109	**Day**	**Francis Joseph**	**Pte.**	**kia 03/09/16**
16618	**Day**	**Jack**	**Pte.**	**kia 03/09/16**
16551	**Dearlove**	**Francis Clifford**	**Pte.**	**kia 03/09/16**
14042	**Denning**	**Henry Hurley**	**Pte.**	**kia 12/12/15**
33575	Dimmock	Frank	Pte.	dow 14/04/18
33019	Dingle	William Charles	Pte.	kia 01/10/17
18734	Dinsley	Robert Henry	Pte.	kia 28/06/18
18706	Dobson	John	Cpl.	kia 08/05/17

Number	Surname	Christian name(s)	Rank	Comments
5950	Doherty	John	L/Sgt.	kia 20/04/17
204087	Donnovan	Joseph	Pte.	kia 26/04/18
12881	Driver	George	Pte.	dow 26/07/16
14275	**Duckham**	**Merton**	**Pte.**	**kia 08/10/17**
14497	**Dugdale**	**Alfred**	**Pte.**	**kia 03/09/16**
260507	Duggan	Emlyn	Pte.	kia 04/04/18
37863	Durrant	Montague	L/Cpl.	kia 08/05/17
260309	Dyer	Dudley	Pte.	kia 04/10/17
14273	**Dyer**	**Ernest**	**Pte.**	**kia 30/07/16**
14275	**Dyte**	**William Leopold**	**Pte.**	**kia 04/10/17**
37844	Earle	William	Cpl.	kia 08/05/17
37802	Edgar	Joseph Morris	Pte.	dow 17/05/18
37846	Edmonds	Clifford Leslie	Cpl.	kia 10/10/17
16729	**Edmonds**	**John**	**Pte.**	**24/05/16**
204038	Edwards	Henry Tripp	Pte.	03/09/18
31935	Edwards	William Arthur	Cpl.	05/06/17
23992	Elkins	Edward Percy	Pte.	29/09/18
14280	**Elliott**	**Alfred Edward**	**Pte.**	**20/04/17**
14047	**Elmes**	**Albert Edward**	**Pte.**	**03/09/16**
14048	**Elson**	**Leslie Norman**	**L/Cpl.**	**03/09/16**
36906	Entwistle	Joseph Alfred	Pte.	04/10/17
260436	Evans	Arthur Ethelred	Pte.	02/10/17
37284	Evans	Herbert Charles	Pte.	08/05/17
37690	Evans	William John	Pte.	08/05/17

Number	Surname	Christian name(s)	Rank	Comments
22705	Fabian	Clifford Pike	Pte.	30/07/16
15044	**Farndell**	**Charles**	**L/Cpl.**	**30/07/16**
22651	Fear	Henry	Pte.	06/08/16
1759	Fearnley	Harry	Pte.	08/05/17
18358	Fennell	William	Pte.	03/09/16
14879	**Field**	**Frederick Stanley**	**Pte.**	**03/09/16**
260442	Field	Walter Henry	Pte.	04/10/17
31917	Findley	William George Samuel	Pte.	11/03/17
200301	Firks	John Henry	L/Cpl.	25/04/18
46348	Firth	Harry	Pte.	06/10/18
14663	**Fisher**	**Ernest**	**Pte.**	**08/05/17**
13554	Fisher	George	Pte.	25/06/18
22692	Fisher	Harry	Pte.	08/05/17
14285	**Fisher**	**Percy Edwin**	**Pte.**	**03/09/16**
16528	**Fletcher**	**Frederick**	**Pte.**	**kia 08/05/17**
14880	**Fletcher**	**Stanley Robert**	**L/Cpl.**	**kia 29/07/16**
22790	Ford	Albert	Pte.	kia 03/09/16
266832	Ford	Alfred William	Pte.	kia 31/10/17
16691	**Forte**	**Maurice Stanley Delatons**	**Pte.**	**kia 03/09/16**
14286	**Foss**	**Sidney George**	**Sgt.**	**kia 03/09/16**
37140	Foster	Oswald	Pte.	kia 10/10/17
38945	Fowler	George	Pte.	dow 26/04/18
18194	Fowler	Harry	Pte.	dow 26/08/18
260447	Foxhall	Reginald Stanley	Pte.	kia 28/06/18

Roll of Honour – Other Ranks

Number	Surname	Christian name(s)	Rank	Comments
37861	Freeman	Charles	Pte.	kia 08/05/17
14058	**Friend**	**James Edward**	**Pte.**	**kia 03/09/16**
16562	**Fry**	**Alfred Thomas Guliford**	**Pte.**	**kia 25/09/16**
22649	Fry	Ernest Harold	Pte.	kia 03/09/16
39696	Fry	Reginald Frank	Pte.	dow 13/12/17
26921	Fryer	Charles Christopher	Pte.	dow 03/11/17
240609	Fryer	Raymond Edwin	Pte.	kia 06/11/17
22258	Fuller	Robert	Pte.	kia 20/04/17
25684	Fursland	Joseph Leonard	L/Cpl.	kia 14/04/18
24463	Gabb	Archibold Victor	Pte.	kia 28/06/18
10527	Gadderer	John Frederick	Pte.	kia 05/05/17
34883	Gaines	Lawrence	Pte.	kia 04/10/17
44349	Gale	George William Tom	Pte.	kia 23/08/18
44372	Gamblin	Frederick Charles Edward	Pte.	dow 26/04/18
38975	Garbett	Fred	L/Cpl.	kia 06/11/17
38872	Gardiner	Pelham	Pte.	kia 14/04/18
31513	Gardner	William Alfred Helstone	Pte.	kia 25/04/18
40062	Gardner	William John	Pte.	dow 29/09/18
16806	**Garland**	**Albert Charles**	**Pte.**	**kia 30/07/16**
14061	**Gerrish**	**Henry Heaven**	**Pte.**	**kia 03/09/16**
27903	Gerrish	John William James	Pte.	kia 08/05/17
29383	Gibbins	Hubert Henry	Pte.	kia 08/05/17
16591	**Giddings**	**Arthur James**	**Pte.**	**kia 19/09/16**
40121	Gilbert	Philip	Pte.	kia 29/09/18

Number	Surname	Christian name(s)	Rank	Comments
22712	Gillard	Leonard	Pte.	kia 08/05/17
260384	Gompf	Charles	Pte.	dow 02/07/18
37242	Grant	Albert	Pte.	kia 08/05/17
19217	Green	Alwyn Frederick	Pte.	kia 08/05/17
37849	Green	George peter	Pte.	kia 08/05/17
13705	Green	John Nelson	L/Cpl.	kia 02/10/17
25531	Green	Walter John	Pte.	dow 03/11/17
24016	Green	William	Pte.	dow 11/11/17
12735	Greening	George Henry	Cpl.	kia 25/06/18
27922	Greenslade	Frederick	Pte.	died 05/05/18
202660	Greenway	Frederick	Pte.	kia 17/07/17
39014	Grice	Charles Henry	Pte.	kia 25/04/18
39731	Griffee	Ernest Victor	Pte.	kia 28/06/18
14065	**Griffey**	**William Harold**	**Pte.**	**kia 21/07/16**
16564	**Griffin**	**Nelson Frank**	**Pte.**	**kia 30/07/16**
33607	Griffin	William Henry	Pte.	kia 28/06/18
39715	Griffin	William Thomas	Pte.	kia 28/06/18
39074	Griffith	Owen	Pte.	kia 05/11/17
25350	Griffiths	Leonard Frank	Pte.	kia 02/10/17
20236	**Grinter**	**Frank**	**Pte.**	**kia 09/10/17**
37092	Grisswell	Ralph George	Pte.	died 25/08/18
16792	**Gulwell**	**William**	**Pte.**	**dow 28/07/16**
260289	Gwilliam	Herbert	L/Cpl.	kia 04/10/17
204176	Hacker	Bertram	L/Cpl.	kia 17/07/18

Roll of Honour – Other Ranks

Number	Surname	Christian name(s)	Rank	Comments
44646	Hadland	Frank Nevill	Pte.	kia 23/08/18
28388	Haines	Arthur Stanley	Pte.	kia 06/12/16
17670	Haines	Henry Francis	Pte.	dow 18/03/17
30802	Hall	Frank James	Cpl.	kia 02/10/17
22704	Hall	Percy	Pte.	dow 24/07/16
38036	Hammersley	Percy	Pte.	died 22/08/18
37839	Harding	Gilbert	Pte.	kia 23/04/17
44373	Harding	Henry	Pte.	died 30/06/18
14306	**Harding**	**James Walter**	**Pte.**	**kia 30/07/16**
16715	**Hardman**	**Charles**	**Pte.**	**dow 04/09/16**
14300	**Harman**	**William Cecil**	**Sgt.**	**kia 03/09/16**
21172	Harper	Edward Charles	Pte.	kia 08/05/17
35726	Harris	Henry Joseph Reginald	L/Cpl.	kia 28/06/18
13292	Harris	Robert	Pte.	dow 13/10/16
30569	Hartland	Walter Edward	Pte.	kia 26/04/18
23995	Hatt	Alfred	Pte.	kia 23/08/18
32194	Hawkes	George Herbert	Pte.	died 25/09/18
37608	Haworth	William	Pte.	kia 08/05/17
260390	Hayes	John	Pte.	kia 04/10/17
14688	**Hayles**	**Edwin John**	**Pte.**	**kia 07/05/17**
28709	Hayward	Alfred Victor	Pte.	died 04/04/18
31494	Hayward	Frank George	Pte.	kia 14/04/18
14452	**Healey**	**Charles Edward**	**RSM**	**kia 03/09/16**
260459	Heaven	Godfrey	Pte.	kia 04/10/17

Roll of Honour – Other Ranks

Number	Surname	Christian name(s)	Rank	Comments
15769	Henn	Robert	Pte.	kia 25/08/18
15646	Henry	Ernest	Pte.	kia 29/09/18
2625	Herbert	Abel	Pte.	kia 05/05/17
14691	**Hewlett**	**Joseph**	**Cpl.**	**dow 08/05/17**
25211	Heyden	Arthur	Pte.	kia 08/05/17
21469	Heyden	William Thomas	Pte.	kia 08/05/17
260517	Higgins	George Harry	Pte.	kia 07/11/17
33646	Hill	Ben	Pte.	kia 17/07/18
36679	Hill	Charles	Pte.	kia 20/04/17
36743	Hillier	Robert John	Pte.	kia 23/08/18
37880	Hinder	Percy	Pte.	died 07/08/17
260304	Hine	Donald Goddard	Pte.	kia 02/10/17
22264	Hines	Frederick Charles	Pte.	kia 08/05/17
33591	Hinks	George	Pte.	kia 08/05/17
37248	Hinton	Harry	Pte.	kia 08/05/17
22600	Hitchings	Charles William	Pte.	kia 08/05/17
33069	Hitchings	Percival Leonard	Pte.	kia 25/04/18
14322	**Hitchins**	**Francis Howard**	**Pte.**	**dow 11/09/16**
14976	**Hobbs**	**George Henry**	**Pte.**	**kia 13/10/17**
241786	Hocking	William	Pte.	kia 23/08/18
14694	**Hodges**	**John Charles**	**Pte.**	**kia 30/07/16**
40074	Hodgson	Richard	Pte.	died 19/09/18
14319	**Hodgson**	**William Thompson**	**L/Sgt.**	**kia 30/07/16**
15018	**Holborow**	**Walter**	**Pte.**	**kia 29/07/16**

Number	Surname	Christian name(s)	Rank	Comments
39699	Holloway	Frederick William	Pte.	kia 27/06/18
33096	Holmes	Frederick Victor	Pte.	kia 28/10/17
16489	**Holpin**	**Herbert George**	**Pte.**	**kia 17/07/17**
34903	Holsgrove	Archibold	Pte.	died 30/06/18
31931	Hooper	Albert Lawson	L/Cpl.	kia 08/05/17
12301	Hopkins	Albert Edward	Pte.	dow 31/08/18
39713	Horrell	Francis George	Pte.	kia 22/05/18
44415	Hoskin	William Charles	Pte.	kia 28/06/18
200941	Howell	Harold	Pte.	kia 20/09/18
242379	Howells	Harry lambert	Pte.	kia 28/06/18
260389	Howells	Llewellyn	Pte.	kia 10/10/17
37283	Huggett	Ivor Herbert	Pte.	kia 37283
38011	Huggins	James	Pte.	kia 14/04/18
14321	**Hughes**	**Albert Edward**	**Pte.**	**kia 03/09/16**
32801	Hughes	Ernest	Pte.	dow 28/06/18
33581	Hulett	Albert	Pte.	kia 02/10/17
28311	Humphris	Alfred James	Pte.	kia 20/04/17
25217	Hunt	William Thomas	Pte.	kia 08/05/17
38317	Hunter	Harold	L/Cpl.	kia 21/05/18
16663	**Hurn**	**Walter james**	**Pte.**	**kia 03/09/16**
39016	Hutchings	Glibert	Pte.	died 24/04/18
260366	Hutchinson	Harold	Pte.	dow 15/10/17
37999	Hutchinson	John Hatton	Pte.	kia 28/06/18
24728	Iles	William	Pte.	kia 05/10/17

Number	Surname	Christian name(s)	Rank	Comments
20076	**Iles**	**William John**	**Pte.**	**kia 03/09/16**
36036	Jago	George James	Pte.	kia 25/08/18
12952	**James**	**Frank**	**Pte.**	**kia 03/09/16**
16620	**James**	**George Henry**	**Pte.**	**kia 16/12/15**
14703	**James**	**William Lionel**	**Pte.**	**dow 30/07/16**
14708	**Jarman**	**Leonard Victor**	**Pte.**	**kia 21/07/16**
16685	**Jefferies**	**William James**	**Pte.**	**dow 13/08/16**
14705	**Jelly**	**Herbert Reginald**	**Pte.**	**kia 03/09/16**
260465	Jenkins	Evan	Pte.	dow 02/11/17
14895	**Jenkins**	**Oliver Wilfred**	**Pte.**	**kia 03/09/16**
19283	Jenkins	William	Pte.	kia 27/06/18
260462	Jenkins	William Clynes	Pte.	dow 14/12/17
204262	Jennings	Bert Walter	Pte.	kia 27/04/18
37860	Johnson	Arthur William	Pte.	kia 08/05/17
14234	**Johnson**	**George Frederick**	**Pte.**	**kia 05/05/17**
44380	Johnson	Harry James	Pte.	kia 31/08/18
19379	Joiner	Charles Henry	Pte.	kia 14/04/17
16518	**Jones**	**Alfred**	**Pte.**	**kia 23/04/17**
260468	Jones	Charles	Pte.	kia 14/04/18
13570	Jones	Ellis	Pte.	kia 28/10/17
260392	Jones	Henry James	Pte.	kia 01/11/17
10509	Jones	John	Pte.	dow 26/09/16
260463	Jones	Trevor	Pte.	died 04/10/17
31133	Joyce	Frederick Charles	Pte.	kia 08/05/17

Roll of Honour – Other Ranks

Number	Surname	Christian name(s)	Rank	Comments
14525	**Keates**	**William Cornelius**	**Pte.**	**kia 25/09/16**
37851	Kelley	George Charles	Pte.	kia 08/05/17
203905	Keeling	Ernest James	L/Cpl.	dow 26/04/18
5748	Kemmett	George	Pte.	kia 25/09/16
19837	Kendrick	Frank	Pte.	kia 06/06/18
39512	Kent	Godfrey James Victor	Pte.	dow 23/08/18
44381	Kent	Richard	Pte.	kia 22/04/18
32526	Keyte	Joseph William	Pte.	kia 08/05/17
33584	Kiely	John	Pte.	dow 05/10/17
38973	Killick	Thomas Noah Dicks	Pte.	dow 01/07/18
34909	King	Andrew Bernard	Pte.	kia 23/08/18
27751	King	Frank Edward	Pte.	dow 09/02/17
22627	King	Grantly Reginald	L/Cpl.	died 19/05/16
14091	**King**	**William Mark**	**Pte.**	**kia 03/09/16**
16712	**Kingman**	**George**	**Pte.**	**kia 30/07/16**
19333	Kinnair	William Spence	Pte.	kia 25/09/16
20055	**Knight**	**Walter Edward**	**Pte.**	**kia 03/09/16**
260469	Lamb	John	Pte.	died 30/10/17
20051	**Lambert**	**Frederick George**	**Pte.**	**dow 04/09/16**
15637	Lane	Stephen	Cpl.	kia 25/08/18
33046	Langdon	James	Pte.	kia 25/04/18
260352	Latham	Albert Edward	Pte.	kia 04/10/17
20168	**Leonard**	**Francis Albert**	**Pte.**	**dow 07/10/17**
22773	Leonard	Morton	Pte.	kia 05/05/17

Roll of Honour – Other Ranks

Number	Surname	Christian name(s)	Rank	Comments
14531	**Leslie**	**John**	**L/Cpl.**	**kia 03/09/16**
14338	**Leslie**	**William Norman**	**Cpl.**	**kia 09/10/17**
24022	Letherby	Alfred William Henry	Pte.	kia 29/09/18
14722	**Levatino**	**Caesar**	**Pte.**	**dow 14/09/16**
14904	**Lewis**	**Alfred John**	**Pte.**	**died 02/04/16**
14903	**Lewis**	**Alfred Stanley**	**Pte.**	**kia 10/12/15**
38012	Lewis	Arthur Trevor	Pte.	died 05/04/18
14719	**Lewis**	**Frederick**	**Pte.**	**kia 03/09/16**
14100	**Lewis**	**James**	**A/CSM**	**kia 06/06/18**
14342	**Lewis**	**Reginald John**	**Pte.**	**kia 08/05/17**
16604	**Lewis**	**Robert Cecil**	**Cpl.**	**kia 25/04/18**
38737	Lewis	William	Pte.	dow 24/08/18
7376	Lewis	Wiliam Mark	Pte.	kia 25/08/18
9574	Little	Sidney George	Sgt.	kia 28/06/18
22670	Llewellin	Charles	Pte.	dow 25/07/16
20171	**Lloyd**	**Henry Thomas**	**Pte.**	**kia 26/07/16**
30211	Lomas	William	Pte.	dow 22/08/18
16558	**Love**	**Charles**	**Pte.**	**kia 29/07/16**
17164	Lovell	Arthur Moss	L/Cpl.	kia 23/08/18
32528	Lowe	Herbert William	L/Cpl.	died 25/08/18
38013	Lowes	Thomas	Pte.	kia 04/10/17
38991	Lugg	Frederick William	Pte.	kia 30/10/17
14343	**Lumbard**	**Hubert James**	**Cpl.**	**kia 29/07/16**
204135	MacDonald	Albert Edward	Pte.	kia 06/11/17

Number	Surname	Christian name(s)	Rank	Comments
17738	Mace	Frederick James	Pte.	kia 01/10/17
14351	**Mackan**	**Harry**	**Pte.**	**kia 30/07/16**
14534	**Malthoff**	**Edward John**	**Pte.**	**kia 20/09/18**
32520	Manison	John	Pte.	kia 08/05/17
20271	**Mann**	**George Edward Henry**	**Pte.**	**kia 27/10/16**
22672	Mann	Thomas Herbert	Pte.	dow 07/09/16
20140	**Mansfield**	**Charles**	**Pte.**	**dow 03/10/16**
238026	Markey	Christopher	Pte.	kia 25/04/18
26239	Marks	Thomas Edward	Pte.	kia 21/04/17
238026	Markey	Christopher	Pte.	kia 25/04/18
26239	Marks	Thomas Edward	Pte.	kia 21/04/17
22732	Marsh	Walter John	L/Cpl.	kia 04/10/17
27510	Martin	Charles Henry	Pte.	kia 04/10/17
37256	Matthews	Frederick William	Pte.	dow 09/05/17
14536	**Matthews**	**Reginald Harry Frederick**	**Pte.**	**kia 20/06/18**
34251	May	William Nun	Pte.	kia 14/04/18
26178	Maycock	Charles Frederick	Pte.	kia 04/10/17
32123	McAllister	James	Pte.	kia 04/10/17
22603	McAuliffe	James Carmichael	Pte.	kia 25/09/16
25700	McGrath	Frank	Pte.	kia 14/04/18
18713	Meadows	Richard	Pte.	dow 09/09/16
44350	Merritt	William John	Pte.	kia 25/04/18
266750	Methuen	Lawrence Howard	Pte.	dow 05/09/18
20169	**Middle**	**Richard Henry**	**Pte.**	**dow 08/09/16**

Number	Surname	Christian name(s)	Rank	Comments
201709	Miles	Wilfred Charles	Pte.	kia 02/10/17
34419	Miller	Albert Henry James	Pte.	kia 04/10/17
22610	Mills	Elton Robert	Pte.	dow 17/09/16
16610	**Mills**	**John Tom**	**L/Cpl.**	**dow 20/05/18**
14538	**Milne**	**Arthur Robert**	**Pte.**	**kia 23/04/18**
30739	Mizen	Robert John	Pte.	kia 31/08/18
39527	Mogg	Reginald	Pte.	died 25/08/18
260475	Morris	Alfred	Pte.	dow 03/10/17
34417	Moseley	Frederick Arthur	Pte.	kia 04/10/17
30151	Munro	William	Pte.	kia 05/03/17
14363	**Naish**	**Reginald Paul**	**L/Sgt.**	**dow 04/05/18**
35994	Nash	Albert Stephen	Pte.	died 25/08/18
14122	**Nash**	**Arthur Llewellyn**	**L/Cpl.**	**kia 03/09/16**
23095	Neads	Frederick William	Pte.	died 25/08/18
20875	Newman	John Thomas	Pte.	kia 14/04/18
18076	Nicholson	Lionel George	Pte.	dow 23/08/18
21677	Nixon	Frederick	Pte.	kia 15/06/17
34925	Nobes	Sydney Charles	Pte.	dow 26/08/18
241821	Nokes	William John	L/Cpl.	kia 25/04/18
14364	**Norman**	**George Henry**	**Pte.**	**kia 08/05/17**
44394	Noyce	Frederick	Pte.	kia 17/07/18
25194	Oakhill	Norman	Pte.	dow 06/12/16
260478	Oatley	Gilbert	Pte.	kia 28/10/17
14127	**Ogden**	**Percy Edgar**	**Pte.**	**kia 26/07/16**

Roll of Honour – Other Ranks

Number	Surname	Christian name(s)	Rank	Comments
202514	Orchard	Edward Charles	Pte.	kia 04/10/17
14128	**Osborne**	**Harold Charles**	**Pte.**	**kia 03/09/16**
23474	Osborne	Harry	L/Cpl.	kia 25/08/18
44344	Osman	Harold Henry George	Pte.	kia 25/04/18
38532	Owens	Owen	Pte.	kia 25/08/18
202463	Page	William George	Pte.	dow 29/06/18
24526	Pagett	Leonard George	Pte.	kia 03/09/16
22059	Palmer	Frank	Pte.	kia 25/09/16
44419	Palmer	Harry	Pte.	dow 26/05/18
14379	**Palmer**	**Lestock Clevely**	**Pte.**	**kia 08/05/17**
12068	Palmer	William Albert	Pte.	kia 05/05/17
260356	Panting	Stanley	Sgt.	dow 15/04/18
14131	**Park**	**Arthur Thomas**	**Pte.**	**kia 24/03/16**
39665	Parker	Alfred	Pte.	kia 08/05/17
18257	Parker	John Beetham	C.Q.M.S.	kia 28/06/18
33595	Parkins	Thomas	Pte.	kia 08/05/17
267456	Parkinson	Ernest	Pte.	died 23/08/18
14375	**Parry**	**Claude Cecil**	**Cpl.**	**dow 02/11/17**
29328	Parslow	Joseph Boulton	Pte.	dow 23/08/18
14753	**Parsons**	**Cyril Joseph**	**Pte.**	**kia 03/09/16**
14920	**Parsons**	**Harold John**	**Pte.**	**kia 08/05/17**
23937	Parsons	William Henry	Pte.	kia 04/10/17
21180	Partridge	George	L/Cpl.	kia 25/08/18
44397	Partridge	Percy John	Pte.	died 25/08/18

Number	Surname	Christian name(s)	Rank	Comments
37563	Peacock	Thomas	Pte.	kia 28/06/18
38039	Pearman	Henry William	L/Cpl.	dow 05/10/17
267485	Perry	Ernest James	Pte.	kia 21/05/18
204278	Peters	Bertram	Pte.	dow 02/05/18
18536	Peters	Daniel Nichol	Pte.	kia 28/06/18
28634	Peters	Donald James	Pte.	kia 06/11/17
260401	Phillips	Edgar	Pte.	kia 07/10/17
260483	Phillips	Evan Thomas	Pte.	died 05/10/17
28443	Phillips	Henry	Pte.	kia 02/10/17
15031	**Phillips**	**John Henry**	**Sgt.**	**kia 24/07/16**
34919	Phillips	Thomas Edwin	Pte.	died 08/10/17
238042	Piper	William Arthur	L/Cpl.	kia 28/06/18
44352	Pollentine	Leonard Horatio Hugh	Pte.	kia 25/04/18
16474	**Pomeroy**	**Percival Wright**	**Pte.**	**dow 24/09/16**
2261	Poole	Albert	Pte.	kia 06/05/17
14744	**Pople**	**Reginald Albert**	**Pte.**	**dow 25/09/16**
25402	Powell	Frederick	Pte.	kia 30/07/16
20091	**Powell**	**Henry Joseph**	**Pte.**	**dow 08/05/17**
24679	Powell	Herbert James	Pte.	kia 08/05/17
16768	**Powell**	**Robert**	**Pte.**	**kia 21/07/16**
260343	Powell	Stanley	Pte.	kia 31/10/17
25001	Preen	Albert Edward	Pte.	kia 20/04/17
260400	Price	Albert George	Pte.	kia 06/06/18
20988	Price	Charles	Pte.	died 25/08/18

Roll of Honour – Other Ranks

Number	Surname	Christian name(s)	Rank	Comments
14751	**Price**	**Charles Joseph**	**L/Cpl.**	**kia 05/05/17**
24322	Price	Frank Thomas	Pte.	kia 08/05/17
26369	Price	John	Pte.	dow 08/09/18
14750	**Price**	**Phillip Richard Nicholas**	**Pte.**	**died 22/03/16**
39541	Price	Samuel	Pte.	kia 21/08/18
16734	**Price**	**Thomas James**	**Pte.**	**kia 03/09/16**
22975	Price	Victor	Pte.	kia 03/09/16
34960	Prickett	Edward William	Pte.	died 18/12/17
32128	Prince	James William	Pte.	kia 05/05/17
260482	Pring	William John	Pte.	dow 14/04/18
31889	Provis	Arthur James	Pte.	kia 02/10/17
37414	Pryor	Jasper Henry	Pte.	kia 16/02/17
25693	Pugh	Albert Charles	Pte.	kia 03/09/16
14378	**Pugsley**	**Arthur Augustus**	**Pte.**	**dow 27/03/17**
22647	Pullin	Rowland Alpheaus	Pte.	dow 19/01/17
260351	Pullin	Stuart Augustus	Pte.	kia 14/04/18
9476	Purdy	Gilbert George	L/Sgt.	kia 10/10/17
14551	**Pyman**	**Frederick William**	**Sgt.**	**dow 23/03/16**
37644	Quarterly	William	Pte.	kia 08/05/17
25315	Rabbitts	Reginald Harry	Pte.	kia 04/10/17
14757	**Radford**	**Carl**	**Cpl.**	**kia 03/09/16**
30070	Radway	Henry	Pte.	kia 08/05/17
22368	Ramsden	Hubert	Pte.	dow 14/05/17
20535	**Rawlins**	**Albert**	**L/Sgt.**	**kia 08/05/17**

Number	Surname	Christian name(s)	Rank	Comments
242093	Reader	John William	Pte.	died 25/08/18
32129	Reed	Ernest Ernie	Pte.	kia 08/05/17
24148	Rescorla	George	Pte.	kia 08/05/17
16416	**Restall**	**Sidney Edward**	**Pte.**	**kia 03/09/16**
16612	**Rex**	**Percy Edwin**	**Pte.**	**kia 03/09/16**
260488	Reynolds	Daniel John	Pte.	kia 04/10/17
14763	**Rich**	**Harold Arthur**	**Pte.**	**kia 08/01/16**
30832	Richard	Ernest William	L/Cpl.	dow 24/08/18
39026	Richards	George	Pte.	dow 30/10/17
22656	Richards	Hebert Edward Lloyd	Pte.	dow 28/08/16
14768	**Ridley**	**Henry Lancelot**	**Pte.**	**kia 29/07/16**
22607	Roach	Alexander	L/Sgt.	kia 25/04/18
33577	Roberts	John	Pte.	died 08/05/17
36580	Roberts	Lewis Edwin	Pte.	died 29/06/18
27066	Robinson	Edward	Pte.	kia 03/09/16
14922	**Rogers**	**Cyril Evelyn**	**Pte.**	**kia 03/09/16**
37875	Rollinson	Edward	Pte.	kia 04/10/17
37268	Rooks	James George	Pte.	dow 23/04/18
260349	Roper	Francis Lewis	Pte.	dow 04/07/18
20276	**Rose**	**Edward Victor**	**Pte.**	**kia 03/09/16**
28759	Rose	Kenneth Kingsley	Pte.	kia 21/04/17
11094	Rowe	Edwin	Pte.	dow 08/05/17
32133	Rudge	William Mattey	Pte.	dow 22/04/18
8426	Rummings	Alfred Aloysius	L/Sgt.	kia 03/09/16

Number	Surname	Christian name(s)	Rank	Comments
37269	Salisbury	Frederick Ethelburt	Pte.	kia 08/05/17
16788	**Sampson**	**Arthur**	**Pte.**	**kia 03/09/16**
13252	Sanders	Thomas Henry	Pte.	kia 11/10/16
37826	Sandford	Charles	Pte.	kia 22/04/17
290149	Savage	Leonard William	Pte.	dow 31/08/18
39092	Sawyer	William	Pte.	kia 07/11/17
33017	Scott	George Henry	Pte.	dow 22/08/18
260561	Seaborne	William	Pte.	dow 28/06/18
267509	Sealey	Ernest James	Pte.	kia 25/04/18
260403	Sellwood	James	Pte.	kia 04/10/17
27764	Selway	Arthur George	Pte.	kia 23/04/17
14555	**Selway**	**William Thomas**	**L/Cpl.**	**died 21/02/16**
14792	**Seymour**	**Stanley James**	**Pte.**	**kia 03/09/16**
20233	**Sharp**	**Samuel Feltham**	**Pte.**	**dow 09/05/17**
21711	Shearsby	Edward	Pte.	kia 25/08/18
30779	Shepherd	William James	Pte.	kia 08/05/17
20145	**Sheppard**	**Thomas Edward**	**Pte.**	**kia 14/04/18**
39735	Sheward	Thomas Edward	Pte.	kia 06/11/17
20984	Shirley	Thomas	Cpl.	kia 08/05/17
24906	Shore	Charles	Pte.	kia 08/05/17
16666	**Short**	**Herbert**	**Pte.**	**kia 06/05/17**
14164	**Shorto**	**Leonard Robert**	**Pte.**	**kia 03/09/16**
40002	Shute	Claude Alexander	Pte.	dow 02/09/18
38925	Sibley	Sidney Charles	Pte.	kia 25/04/18

Number	Surname	Christian name(s)	Rank	Comments
37825	Simmons	Joseph Daniel	Pte.	kia 05/10/17
36183	Sivers	Cecil Howard	Pte.	kia 23/08/16
23816	Skinner	Ernest Charles	Pte.	kia 25/09/16
16747	**Skinner**	**Joseph Porteous**	**Pte.**	**dow 01/08/16**
31285	Skinner	Reginald	Pte.	kia 08/05/17
16687	**Skinner**	**Reginald Bertram**	**Pte.**	**kia 08/06/16**
14775	**Skuse**	**Grantley**	**Pte.**	**dow 27/09/16**
25277	Smart	Howard	Pte.	kia 24/07/16
260402	Smith	Alfred John	Pte.	kia 04/10/17
14400	**Smith**	**Arthur William**	**Pte.**	**dow 28/04/17**
14399	**Smith**	**Frederick Charles**	**Sgt.**	**kia 06/06/18**
24092	Smith	George	Pte.	dow 08/08/18
18850	Smith	Gordon	Pte.	kia 08/05/17
16673	**Smith**	**John**	**Pte.**	**kia 08/05/17**
38041	Smith	Thomas	Pte.	dow 30/06/18
37599	Smith	William Geoffrey	Pte.	kia 08/05/17
9233	Smith	William George Thomas	Cpl.	dow 30/06/18
40007	Snow	Walter Frederick	Pte.	died 23/08/18
22779	Spackman	Edward	L/Cpl.	kia 28/06/18
14169	**Spafford**	**Norman Rowley**	**Pte.**	**dow 01/10/16**
37415	Sparrow	Leo Charles	Pte.	kia 23/04/18
12687	Spawton	William Frederick	CSM.	kia 04/10/17
39095	Spencer	Alfred Edward Hollis	Pte.	kia 07/11/17
32522	Starbuck	Samuel Edward	Cpl.	kia 08/05/17

Number	Surname	Christian name(s)	Rank	Comments
16706	**Starkey**	**John**	**Pte.**	**dow 17/10/16**
32135	Stedman	George	Pte.	died 27/04/17
202805	Stewart	Henry Charles William	Pte.	kia 04/10/17
25097	Stiff	Frank George	Pte.	kia 23/04/17
20070	**Stocker**	**Thomas Moorman**	**Pte.**	**kia 03/09/16**
14172	**Stokes**	**Donald Morley**	**Pte.**	**kia 08/05/17**
14562	**Stokes**	**Ernest**	**Pte.**	**dow 06/09/16**
40008	Stokes	John William	Pte.	kia 23/08/18
37854	Stoll	Joseph James	Pte.	kia 02/10/17
22702	Stone	Archie George	Pte.	dow 10/06/16
16778	**Stringer**	**Ernest Nathan**	**Pte.**	**kia 20/04/17**
20281	**Styles**	**Frederick**	**Cpl.**	**dow 02/10/17**
31924	Summers	Edwin Herbert	L/Sgt.	kia 08/05/17
14393	**Sumsion**	**Gerald**	**Pte.**	**kia 03/09/16**
28390	Sweeting	George Reginald	Pte.	died 11/12/17
14979	**Sydenham**	**Frank**	**Pte.**	**kia 25/08/18**
32134	Symonds	Frank	Pte.	kia 21/04/17
14503	**Talbot**	**William Henry John**	**Pte.**	**kia 12/05/18**
14940	**Tame**	**William Charles**	**L/Cpl.**	**died 29/07/17**
39723	Tanner	Percival	Pte.	kia 25/08/18
260498	Tanner	William David	Pte.	kia 04/10/17
34882	Tarr	Frederick George Samuel	Pte.	kia 04/10/17
24060	Taverner	Thomas	Pte.	kia 21/02/18
22810	Taylor	Albert	Pte.	kia 03/09/16

Number	Surname	Christian name(s)	Rank	Comments
203235	Taylor	Arnold Samuel	Pte.	kia 18/06/18
235022	Taylor	Arthur	Pte.	kia 25/08/18
16794	**Thomas**	**Alfred Edward Mervyn**	**Pte.**	**kia 24/07/16**
14507	**Thomas**	**Charles**	**L/Cpl.**	**kia 03/09/16**
260501	Thomas	David	Pte.	kia 02/10/17
38555	Thomas	David Oswald	Pte.	kia 06/06/18
32810	Thomas	Francis Richard	Pte.	kia 28/06/18
2373	Thomas	George	Pte.	kia 30/10/17
260499	Thomas	Jersey Ewart	Pte.	kia 04/10/17
3052	Thomas	Oliver	Sgt.	died 10/08/17
14178	**Thompson**	**Albert Edward**	**Pte.**	**dow 07/09/16**
22657	Thorn	Edward George	Pte.	kia 09/09/16
16750	**Thornett**	**Ernest Lovell**	**Pte.**	**kia 30/07/16**
14798	**Thould**	**James**	**L/Cpl.**	**dow 11/03/18**
16635	**Thyer**	**William George**	**Pte.**	**kia 03/09/16**
38929	Tiffin	Joseph	Pte.	dow 23/08/18
14570	**Tilley**	**Arthur William**	**Pte.**	**dow 26/07/16**
39100	Tirebuck	John Henry	Pte.	died 23/08/18
37859	Todd	William Richard	Pte.	died 27/05/17
39708	Topham	Lawrence	Pte.	dow 25/08/18
38984	Tout	Wallace Victor	Pte.	kia 25/04/18
260496	Trew	Frank	Pte.	kia 29/10/17
44406	Trimmer	Roland Frederick	Pte.	died 25/08/18
39088	Tubb	Francis George	Pte.	kia 25/08/18

Roll of Honour – Other Ranks

Number	Surname	Christian name(s)	Rank	Comments
15695	Tubb	Sidney	Pte.	kia 29/09/18
32137	Tuck	William	Pte.	died 14/04/18
37488	Tudor	Walter James	Pte.	kia 02/10/17
14184	**Tuplin**	**William Claude**	**L/Cpl.**	**kia 03/09/16**
14805	**Turner**	**Arthur**	**Pte.**	**died 09/09/15**
33998	Turner	Cecil Henry	Pte.	died 25/08/18
20636	Turner	Charles Harold	Pte.	kia 23/08/18
14572	**Twiggs**	**Wilfred Sidney**	**Pte.**	**kia 03/09/16**
260017	Twinn	Reginald Charles	Pte.	kia 23/08/18
40110	Uren	James	Pte.	kia 29/09/18
32139	Vaughan	William	Pte.	dow 16/02/17
201010	Viney	Frederick George	Pte.	kia 27/08/18
40096	Wade	John William	L/Cpl.	kia 29/09/18
14837	**Wadman**	**Henry Bracher**	**L/Cpl.**	**kia 03/09/16**
261001	Waite	Ernest Frederick Walter	Pte.	kia 23/08/18
38954	Wale	James George	Pte.	kia 21/05/18
36134	Walker	Frederick Layland	Pte.	kia 25/08/18
38895	Walkling	Joseph Percy	Pte.	kia 25/08/18
32530	Walton	Percy Joseph	Pte.	kia 10/02/17
265411	Warburton	Harold	Pte.	dow 26/08/18
38061	Ward	John	Pte.	kia 28/06/18
260357	Waters	Ernest Griffith	Pte.	dow 07/10/17
38911	Watkins	James	Pte.	kia 28/06/18
203124	Watts	Theodore	Sgt.	kia 25/08/18

Number	Surname	Christian name(s)	Rank	Comments
38042	Watts	Thomas Henry	Pte.	kia 30/10/17
22632	Webb	Albert Alfred	Pte.	kia 07/05/17
33583	Webb	Harry	Pte.	dow 27/05/17
17132	Webster	James Bert	Pte.	kia 28/06/18
14193	**Weeks**	**Albert James**	**Pte.**	**dow 26/09/16**
14816	**Weeks**	**Frederick George**	**Pte.**	**kia 20/07/16**
38056	Went	William Henry	Pte.	dow 05/10/17
32818	West	John Septimus	Pte.	dow 25/08/18
25966	Westbrook	Alfred George	Pte.	kia 23/08/18
38029	Westwood	William Edward	Pte.	dow 18/07/17
16783	**Wheeler**	**Charles William**	**Pte.**	**kia 03/09/16**
17282	Wheeler	George	Pte.	kia 17/07/18
7226	White	Albert Joseph	Pte.	kia 05/07/18
44412	White	William Edgar George	Pte.	dow 18/05/18
11850	White	William Thomas	L/Cpl.	died 08/05/17
18342	Whitehouse	John	Pte.	kia 23/08/18
37828	Whiting	Job Herbert	Pte.	kia 08/05/17
266072	Whitman	Reginald	Pte.	kia 17/07/18
14834	**Whittock**	**Benjamin**	**Cpl.**	**kia 29/07/16**
30770	Wilkey	Frederick Edwin	Pte.	dow 12/05/17
39032	Willcocks	Leonard Victor	Pte.	kia 28/06/18
260505	William	Alfred	Pte.	kia 07/11/17
22784	Williams	Arthur Henry	Pte.	kia 29/07/16
14199	**Williams**	**Charles Hubert**	**Pte.**	**dow 04/09/16**

Roll of Honour – Other Ranks

Number	Surname	Christian name(s)	Rank	Comments
16478	**Williams**	**Edward Humphrey Charles**	**Pte.**	**dow 29/10/17**
14579	**Williams**	**Ernest**	**Pte.**	**kia 03/09/16**
36786	Williams	Fred	Pte.	kia 08/05/17
11358	Williams	Frederick Joseph	Pte.	kia 03/09/16
16730	**Williams**	**Henry Joseph**	**Pte.**	**kia 03/09/16**
16789	**Williams**	**Herbert Dudley**	**Pte.**	**dow 03/09/16**
33097	Williams	John	Pte.	died 31/07/18
37687	Williams	Price	Cpl.	kia 25/08/18
16589	**Williams**	**William**	**Pte.**	**kia 03/09/16**
38027	Wiltshier	Walter John	Pte.	kia 13/08/17
235333	Wintle	Arthur Henry	Pte.	kia 13/04/18
22058	Wolfindale	James	Pte.	kia 17/07/18
14813	**Wonnacott**	**Eri**	**L/Cpl.**	**dow 28/06/18**
28235	Wood	Fred Norman	Pte.	kia 04/10/17
32140	Wood	James	Pte.	kia 08/05/17
37267	Woodcock	Gilbert Francis	Pte.	kia 17/07/17
28252	Workman	John William	Pte.	kia 06/12/16
32515	Wright	David John	Sgt.	kia 04/10/17
13508	Wright	Frank	Sgt.	dow 22/08/18
36841	Yates	John Robert	Pte.	dow 29/06/18
20148	**Young**	**Frank**	**Pte.**	**kia 03/09/16**
24572	Young	Frank	Pte.	dow 07/10/17
35739	Young	Richard Thomas	Pte.	kia 28/06/18

Appendix V

Awards

DSO

Rank/Name — **London Gazette**
Lt. Col. H. A. Colt MC — 07 November 1918

MC

2/Lt. R. J. Fitzgerald	20th October 1916
2/Lt W.W. Parr	1st January 1917
Captain T. Balston OBE	1st January 1917
Lt. Col. H. A. Colt DSO	1st January 1917
Lt. W. G. Chapman	26th April 1917
2/Lt. E. M. T. Burges	17th December 1917
Capt. C. S. Petheram	17th December 1917
" " "	16th September 1918 (Bar)
Capt. G. R. A. Beckett	1st January 1918
13991 CSM A. Bailey	1st January 1918
2/Lt W. J. Hale	22nd April 1918
" " "	8th March 1919 (Bar)
Lt. B. B. Kirby	3rd June 1918
Lt. A. Laird	16th September 1918
" " "	11th January 1919 (Bar)
Lt. W. H. Coombs	15th Oct 1918
2/Lt W. Bray	15th Oct 1918
Lt. T. C. Greenhalgh	15th Oct 1918
2/Lt. R. H. Anstey	11th January 1919
2/Lt. T.J. Benjamin	11th January 1919
2/Lt. J. G. Ibbotson	11th January 1919
2/Lt. F. H. Andrews	19th September 1919

DCM

14107	Sgt. R.A. MacFarlane	26th April 1917
14380	Cpl. G.S. Perrett	4th March 1918
14138	Sgt. N. R. Pegg	1st May 1918

Awards

14100	Sgt. J. Lewis	3rd September 1918
32511	Sgt. W. Smith	3rd September 1918
20200	Cpl. W. A. Goodlife	30th October 1918
14621	Cpl. A. H. Bird MM	30th October 1918
38007	Pte. R. W. Biggs	30th October 1918
13725	CSM. C. H. Carter	30th October 1918
203124	Cpl. T. Watts	30th October 1918
37249	Pte. A.W.H. Hussey	5th December 1918
22624	Sgt. F. J. Paget	5th December 1918
8312	Sgt. F. Bailey MM	5th December 1918
37696	Sgt. T. Palmer	5th December 1918
34821	CSM. G. Pine	03 September 1919

MM

9509	Sgt E.J. Harris	14th September 1916
9574	Sgt. S.G. Little	14th September 1916
14045	Pte. W. E.L. Durnsford	16th November 1916
14440	L/Cpl. W. Yacomeni	16th November 1916
14890	Sgt. L. Hughes	16th November 1916
15071	L/Cpl. F. Boobyer	16th November 1916
14671	Cpl. W. F. W. Gage	16th November 1916
14696	Sgt. A. F. Hammond	16th November 1916
14796	Pte. F.G. Taylor	16th November 1916
16754	Pte. C. B. Gordon	9th December 1916
10030	Cpl. E. Vincent	9th December 1916
16479	Pte H. A. Hutchins	9th December 1916
3179	Pte. J. S. Richards	9th December 1916
14315	Pte. G. S. Hawker	9th December 1916
14194	Sgt. F. D. Weeks	9th December 1916
8312	Sgt. F. Bailey DCM	22nd January 1917
23937	Pte. W. H. Parsons	12th March 1917
27908	Pte. H. Virgo	26th April 1917
15066	L/Cpl. W. A. Smallcombe	11th May 1917
38049	Pte. J. Eason	2nd August 1917
14291	Sgt. W.E. Gosney	2nd November 1917
14621	Cpl. A. H. Bird DCM	12th December 1917
2705	Pte. S. Evans	24th January 1918

Awards

16793	Cpl. W. G. Hudson	28th January 1918
16554	L/Cpl. F. A. Rogers	28th January 1918
16560	Pte. A. Bamford	28th January 1918
14445	Pte. A. Allen	4th February 1918
27587	Sgt. H. Phipps	4th February 1918
16827	Pte. J. C. Bevan	6th August 1918
38882	Pte. L. C. Bush	6th August 1918
32988	Pte W. E. Arnold	6th August 1918
260322	Pte A. Holloway	6th August 1918
39068	Pte. A. R. Cox	6th August 1918
24501	Pte. J. C. Hicks	29th August 1918
266390	Pte. G. W. Leonard	29th August 1918
22673	Pte. G. M. Blanning	29th September 1918
39091	Pte. T. S. Perry	7th October 1918
33017	Pte. G. H. Scott	7th October 1918
9213	Cpl. F. Connock	7th October 1918
32908	Pte. H. Cook	7th October 1918
20023	Pte. G. Rachael	7th October 1918
26517	Pte. W. R. Duffy	13th November 1918
241360	Pte. F. C. Neal	13th November 1918
260373	Pte. M. R. Watts	13th November 1918
34527	Pte. D. S. Stocker	13th November 1918
14326	Pte. A. Jordan	13th November 1918
39689	Pte. R. Ballinger	11th February 1919
37165	Pte. W. J. Isgate	11th February 1919
30749	Pte. W. Holliday	11th February 1919
19408	L/Cpl. J. Watkins	11th February 1919
38121	Pte J.T. Lapworth	11th February 1919
17104	Pte. A. Greathead	11th February 1919
38863	L/Cpl. W. Steward	11th February 1919
32230	Pte. V. Florentine	11th February 1919
38211	Pte. T. Cory	11th March 1919
20401	L/Cpl. J.Leggett	29th March 1919

MSM

14386	Sgt. G. H. Randall	3rd June 1918
14643	L/Cpl. H. C. Dark	3rd June 1918

14083	Sgt. J. F. R. Justham	17th June 1918
14179	CQMS R. H. Thompson	18th January 1919
14809	CQMS R. G. Waldron	18th January 1919
14316	Pte. A. B. Hutton	18th January 1919
14356	Cpl. G. A. Morley	3rd April 1919

MID

	Lt. Col. M. Archer-Shee DSO	15th June 1916
	Capt T.M.G. Allison	4th January 1917
	2/Lt. B. B.Kirby MC	15th May 1917
	Lt. J. H. Allen	15th May 1917
	Lt. R. J. Fitzgerald	30th May 1918
	Lt. Col. H. A. Colt DSO, MC	30th May 1918
	2/Lt. N.D. Davidson	30th May 1918
	Lt. R. G. Roberts	30th May 1918
	2/Lt. A. H. May	27th December 1918
	2/Lt. G. M. Rogers	27th December 1918
	Capt. T. A. Wilmott	27th December 1918
9574	Sgt. S. G. Little MM	15th June 1916
3266	CSM T Russell	15th June 1916
14083	Sgt. J.F.R. Justham MSM	4th January 1917
14325	Pte. C. N. Bray	4th January 1917
14968	CSM P. J. Bouskill	4th January 1917
14107	Sgt. R. A. MacFarlane DCM	4th January 1917
13991	CSM A. Bailey MC	15th May 1917
14265	Pte. A. J. Coombs	18th December 1917
16785	Sgt. F. C. Watkins	18th December 1917
14316	Pte. A. B. Hutton MSM	23rd May 1918
15025	Sgt. W. J. Newman	30th May 1918
14585	Cpl. R. C. Barnes	30th May 1918
16581	Cpl. H. Clark	30th May 1918
33586	Pte E. Tollis	30th May 1918
14513	Sgt. F. G. Hemmings	30th May 1918
14864	CSM A. E. Crossman	30th May 1918
14725	C/Sgt. J. F. Marlow	27th December 1918
20189	Pte. J. M.Turner	27th December 1918
16608	Sgt. J. T. Newton	8th July 1919

Awards

Regimental Certificate of Honour

20193   Cpl. H. Civil   8th May 1917

Belgian Croix de Guerre

16785   Sgt. F. C. Watkins

Appendix VI

Battalion Battle Honours

Somme 1916 – 18
Delville Wood
Guillemont
Fleurs-Courcelette
Morval
Arras 1917 – 18
Vimy 1917
Scarpe 1917
Ypres 1917
Polygon Wood
Broodseinde

Poelcappelle
Passchendaele
Albert 1918
Bapaume 1918
Lys
Hazebrouck
Hindenburg Line
Epéhy
Canal du Nord
France and Flanders 1915-18
Italy 1917-18

Appendix VII

Glossary and Acronyms

2ⁿᵈ I/C – Second in command.

2ⁿᵈ/Lt. – Second Lieutenant

Adjutant - Officer who deals with battalion administrative tasks.

A.S.C. - Army Service Corps.

B.E.F. – British Expeditionary Force.

Blighty – England. From Hindustani Bilayati – foreign land. Blighty wound – serious enough for recipient to be sent back to England.

Brass-Hat – High ranking officer.

Brigade   Made up of four infantry battalions.

Camouflet – In mine warfare. The defenders digging a tunnel under the attackers' tunnel. An explosive charge would be set off to create a camouflet that would collapse the attackers' tunnel.

C.C.S. – Casualty Clearing Station.

Chatting – de-lousing.

Civies/Civvy - Civilian. To be in civvies was to be dressed in civilian clothing rather than uniform.

COY – Company. Approximately 250 men when at full strength.

Cpl. – Corporal.

C.Q.M.S. – Company Quarter Master Sergeant.

D.C.L.I. – Duke of Cornwall's Light Infantry.

D.C.M. – Distinguished Conduct Medal (other ranks).

DOW/dow – Died of wounds. This term referred to men that died after being evacuated from the front line usually at a casualty clearing station, a base hospital or a hospital in the UK.

Division – Made up of three infantry brigades plus supporting arms.

Glossary and Acronyms

Dixie - Large oval-shaped metal pot with lid and carrying-handle for cooking. The lid was often used for baking (e.g. bacon and biscuit pudding) whilst the pot itself was employed to brew tea, heat porridge, stew, rice etc. From Hindustani degchi, small pot.

Drummie – Drum Major.

Dugout - An underground shelter of varying degrees of sophistication.

Estaminet – Establishment found in villages and minor towns for the purpose of eating, drinking and general entertainment of troops. A typical estaminet would have a low roof, an open iron stove and wooden benches and tables. The proprietors would serve wine, cognac, thin beer, coffee, soup, omelettes, steak and the most popular of all French dishes of the time - egg and chips. Very popular with troops when out of the line.

G.H.Q. – General Head Quarters.

Gloster – Gloucester.

Go west - To be killed, to die.

Gum boots - Rubber boots or waders worn in very muddy trenches.

H.E. – High explosives.

H.Q. – Head Quarters.

Hun - German. Kaiser Wilhelm II urged his troops to behave like the Huns of old in order to instill fear into the enemy.

Jump off - To begin an attack. The jumping off point was the start line of the attack in the front line trench.

Kamerad - Friend, comrade. From German.

K.I.A./k.i.a. – Killed in action. This term was given to men supposedly killed outright on the battlefield. Some men may have experienced instant deaths. However, many died alone after being wounded..

K.O.S.B. – King's Own Scottish Borderers.

L/ - Lance as in corporal and sergeant.

Lewis gun - comprised an early light machine-gun widely adopted by British and Empire forces from 1915 onwards. Weighing 26.5 lbs the air-cooled 1914 model Lewis Gun featured a 47 round circular magazine. With its adjustable sights and bipod support the Lewis Gun proved effective to some 650 yards. By 1917 each battalion deployed 46 Lewis Guns.

Loophole - Gap in the parapet of a fire trench enabling shooting to take place whilst providing head cover. May be constructed from sandbags, steel plates or other materials.

Glossary and Acronyms

Lt. – Lieutenant.

M.C. – Military cross (officers & warrant officers).

M.M. – Military Medal (other ranks).

M.O. – Medical Officer/Orderly.

Moaning minnie – Trench Mortar shell fired from a German Minenwerfer. Name comes from the sound made when in flight, given by the British Tommies to the weapon.

Mufti - Civilian clothes. From Arabic mufti, free.

N.C.O. – Non Commissioned Officer.

N.Z. – New Zealand.

Old sweat - An experienced soldier.

O.R. – Other Rank. Soldier below the rank of Warrant Officer or Officer

O.T.C. – Officer Training Corps.

Over the top - Make an attack, to go over the top of the trench parapet.

Pill box - Reinforced concrete gun emplacement, usually German and armed with machine guns. So called, because of its cylindrical shape.

PLT/PLT'N – Platoon. Approximately 30 men when at full strength.

P.O.W. – Prisoner of war.

Pte. – Private soldier

R.A.M.C. – Royal Army Medical Corps.

R.E. – Royal Engineers.

Revetment – French revêtment. The retaining lining of a trench. To protect sides of a trench and provide support.

R.F.A. – Royal Field Artillery.

R.N. – Royal Navy.

Glossary and Acronyms

Rough house - A fight or disturbance. So-called from the type of public house where this type of behavior could arise after drinking.

R.S.M. – Regimental Sergeant Major.

T.M.B. – Trench Mortar Battaery

S.A.A. – Small arms amuunition

S.A.L. – South African Light Horse.

Sap - A listening post in no man's land, connected at ninety degrees to the fire trench joined by a narrow communication trench. During an advance, saps were often joined together to make the new front line trench.

Section – Approximately 15 men when at full strength.

Sgt. – Sergeant.

Shrapnel - Shell for anti-personnel use designed to burst in the air and eject many half inch diameter lead balls contained therein. Pieces of fragmented shell case were also known as shrapnel.

Star shell - Artillery projectile consisting of a magnesium flare and a parachute, intended to illuminate the battlefield during night operations. Coloured star shells, not always incorporating the parachute, were used for signaling purposes.

Tommy - British Army soldier. From Tommy Atkins, a name sometimes used on specimen forms to represent a typical British army private soldier. Said to be derived from a British soldier who distinguished himself at the battle of Waterloo.

Up the line - Proceed to the front line, into the trenches.

Whizz-Bang - High-velocity shell. Given the name due to the noise it made during its rapid flight and subsequent explosion. Usually applied to the German 77mm gun.

Wind up, to have the - to be scared.

Wriggly tin – Flat or curved sheets of corogated steel used for construction of dug-outs - British

Acknowledgements

This work would not have been possible had it not been for the input and assistance of a great many people and organisations.

But first I feel I should thank my wife Susan for her patience and support over the many years of my involvement with my passion from the many trips to France and Belgium, my time spent away with many people and for listening to the results of my written attempts of putting it all on paper.

Next will be my father, Roy Marks for the many years of his interest, understanding, support and encouragement. Really, without him I feel I would not have achieved what I have.

Then a group of people that took me in and answered my questions and provided all they could in my cause. Most are the family members; daughters, sons and wives of some of the original battalion members. Others are people that have shared a common interest. Among them and in no particular order; Andy Stevens of Pastimes, Bristol, Patricia Bozworth, John Cheston, Dolcie Brown, John Fowles, Gerry Hedges, Olive Green, Anthony Keyes, Peter Cope, Alan King, Peter John, John Bright, Vera Tovey, Eileen Shanks, Roz Donelly, Lucy Kemp-Welch, Phillis Milton, Esme Archer-Shee, Elizabeth Edwards, Mary Carter, Heather James, Jean Moles, Marjorie Davis, Angus Evans, Patrica Upton, Tom Coombs, Ron Notton, Mike Denning, Rosemary Marshall, Gerry Hedges, George Bradley, Don Gullifer, Peter Littlewood, Mrs. Cross, Mr. E. Seaman, Mrs. K. Pope, Mrs. Hodgson, Mrs. Wilkins, Mrs. P. Caws, Mrs. Thorpe. Capt. Christopher Rawlins, Maj. Gen. Robin Grist.

Regimental Headquarters and Museum - The Gloucestershire Regiment, Soldiers of Gloucestershire Museum, The National Archives, The Bristol Records Office, The Imperial War Museum, The Imperial War Museum photographic collection: Q4245 – p.139, Q3964 – p.146, Q4545 – p.147, Q1312 – p.154, Q4289 - p.154, Q1633 – p.161, Q11,504 – p.197.

I have also received constant encouragement from a small number of friends that constantly, over the years reminded me of the tasks that I needed to perform and the book I should write. Albert Fairchild, a true friend and gentleman for his unstinting interest, his persuasion and his reminders. Nick Fear for his being there and lending a hand when ever it was asked for and Chris Ryland for finally getting me moving toward completion and publication.

Finally I am indebted to the old soldiers. The original battalion members. The men that enlisted into 'Bristol's Own' during 1914 and 1915, the men that opened up to me and told me things they had been keeping at the back of their minds all their lives. They provided me with priceless memories, anecdotes and written records from themselves and past OCA members. They were: William Ayres – 'D' Company signaller, Harold Hayward M. C. – 'B' Company, Ewart Hale – 'C' Company, Stan Streets – 'B' Company, Lester Trott – 'D' Company, William James – 'A' Company, William Smallcombe – 'B' Company, and later members William Pain – 'C' Company and Bert Hickory – 'A' Company. These men provided me with the feel of the character of the battalion which led me to write the book the way I have. Meeting them was a pleasure and a privilege and I am in their eternal debt for that experience.